JOHN CHRYSOSTOM AND HIS TIME

JOHN CHRYSOSTOM

AND HIS TIME

BY

DOM CHRYSOSTOMUS BAUR, O.S.B.

VOL. II

CONSTANTINOPLE

Translated by Sr. M. Gonzaga, R.S.M.,
St. Joseph Mercy Hospital,
Ann Arbor, Mich.

SANDS & Co. (Publishers) LTD
LONDON   GLASGOW

Nihil obstat: JOANNES M. T. BARTON, S.T.D., L.S.S.
CENSOR DEPUTATUS

Imprimatur: ✝ GEORGIUS L. CRAVEN,
EPŪS SEBASTOPOLIS
VIC. GEN.

Westmonasterii, die 16ª Oct, 1958

MADE AND PRINTED IN GREAT BRITAIN
BY NORTHUMBERLAND PRESS LIMITED
GATESHEAD ON TYNE

TABLE OF CONTENTS

vi   *Contents*

CHAPTER I

CHRYSOSTOM BECOMES BISHOP OF CONSTANTINOPLE

O N the 26th of September, 397, the word went from mouth to mouth in Constantinople: Nectarius, the eleventh Bishop and first "Patriarch" of Constantinople, was dead.[1] For sixteen years he had been the spiritual overlord of the capital city. The rolling wave of a storm-tossed time had elevated him suddenly and unexpectedly to the first and most important episcopal see of the Eastern Empire, after a saint, Gregory of Nazianzus, had had to yield to unfavorable circumstances; the time was not ripe for Gregory's fiery zeal. In his place had been chosen the yet un-baptized state official, the Praetor Nectarius. His irreproachable private life and his bland and peace-loving character had commended him at that moment to public attention.[2] His deeds corresponded to his life. He had not accomplished great things. He was not especially noted either as an author, or as an orator, or as a clerical statesman and leader. As a Bishop he remained what he had always been: a correct official, who took anxious care not to clash with any party. With his pre-dominantly passive temperament, he had witnessed the course of affairs rather than influenced it. Yet he had had the extra-ordinary good fortune to be Bishop of the capital city just in the reign of the great Emperor Theodosius. This Emperor was so much the active principle both in religious and ecclesi-astical affairs, that Nectarius, without too much trouble, was content to let affairs and the Emperor go their way, and to assume at least with dignity his place as the executive voice in the existing situation.

So that was what he did. And even that was made easy for him without his co-operation. For the same Fathers of the Council who had made him Bishop in 381, had freed him from practically every control through their agreement, of course

not sanctioned by Rome, that Constantinople should henceforth take second place among episcopal sees; for Constantinople was New Rome.

So Nectarius was favored by fortune during the whole
period of his incumbency. Neither political wrangles nor
ecclesiastical disputes, nor any other complications or problems disturbed the calm of his spirit, nor in the two years
just past, under Arcadius and his ministers Rufinus and
Eutropius, had he in any way influenced the course of
events. He lived in peace and quiet, and in peace and quiet
he died.

Scarcely had Nectarius closed his eyes, when there began
behind the scenes a vital struggle for the vacant episcopal see
of the capital city. One must admit that it presented a strong
temptation for ambitious spirits. The Bishop of Constantinople, especially if he was a man of ability, naturally surpassed
all the Bishops and Patriarchs of the Empire in actual influence. He was in constant communication with the Emperor,
the whole court and the highest officials; he was the man to
whom each Bishop turned when he wished anything at all
from the Emperor; he had at his disposal abundant ways and
means to help when he wished to do so, and to offer his protection to the oppressed. The Patriarch was invited to all
the court ceremonies; he blessed the marriage of the Emperor,
he baptized his children. He could be second to the Emperor
in influence and respect in the Empire, as he was henceforth
the first among all the Bishops of the world after the Pope, the
Bishop of Rome.

So whoever had a feeling for splendor and honor, could only
with difficulty withstand the temptation.

Unfortunately all too many people showed that they
possessed this feeling, but not sufficient virtue, to leave the
determination of a successor to Providence, and to the free
decision of those who were entitled to vote. The idea that the
episcopal see of Constantinople could be a dangerous gift, that
one moved in the Court on a very slippery floor, on which one
might easily fall, and above all, that an enormous moral
responsibility was bound up with these dignities, none of this
was able to turn the eyes of many priests and bishops away
from the dazzling splendor of the exterior dignities of the posi-

tion. Influential court officials at that time saw clergy entering their doors to recommend themselves to their protection.[3]
There were even some among them who were not ashamed
to advance their requests by gold and gifts, while a third class
of candidates flattered the people and made obeisance to
them.[4] There may even have been candidates from the ranks
of the laity or the official class, who hoped to make their
fortune, as Nectarius had done earlier.

The fourth century was accustomed to much in this respect.
There were to be seen duly installed married men, like
Gregory of Nazianzus, the father of St. Gregory, and Paulinus
of Nola, mounting the episcopal throne all unprepared. State
officials, like Nectarius and Ambrosius, who but yesterday
were still pagans or catechumens, today were chosen as
spiritual leaders and shepherds of the Christian people. Sons
of rich and prominent families, like Hilary of Poitiers, Maxi-
minus of Trier, Basil of Caesarea, and others, as well as simple
artisans and weavers, like Zeno of Majuma, Severus of
Ravenna, and the shepherd Spyridon of Trimithus in Cyprus,
and monks from the simplest and poorest social strata, entered
into the ranks of the Bishops at that time. Occasionally even
their success in the care of souls stood in inverse ratio to the
extent of their education and their theological knowledge.
The Emperor Constantius in the year 356 appointed out of
hand one of his Guards officers named Eleusius to be Bishop
of Cyzicus—the shepherd's staff was held fast in the soldier's
strong fist—and a sergeant named Marathon, the paymaster of
the pretorians, was appointed offhandedly by Valens to be
Bishop of Nicomedia.

That was a new and practical method of rendering harmless
any suspicious officials or generals, or possible aspirants to the
throne, without being inhuman. When about the year 439
the people of Constantinople applauded their prefect Cyrus
at the racecourse louder than the Emperor, the unfortunate
man was quickly relieved of his office and deprived of all his
property, and dared only regard it as a favor, that he was
appointed Bishop of Smyrna by force. Of course this was not
a special mark of favor, for his four direct predecessors in the
shepherd's seat at Smyrna had been murdered one after
another by their own mangy sheep.[5]

The fact that Constantinople was less dangerous to life, only increased the number of candidates. "Only see," Chrysostom had written about twelve years earlier, "what happens on the great feast days, when according to the old custom the choice of church officials takes place. Then all who have the right to put in a word for the bestowal of a position, are split into many parties, and the clergy are neither united among themselves nor at one with him who is chosen Bishop. Each one goes his own way, each one gives his voice to someone different. The result is, that no one pays attention to that to which all should pay attention, namely, the virtue of the soul. So other considerations are allowed to prevail, which should have nothing to do with such dignities. For instance: Choose this one, because he comes from a good and distinguished family; or that one, because he is a convert and comes to us from the adversaries. And one wants a bishop with whom he stands well, another wants one who is a relative, and a third wants to give the preference to one who understands nothing except how to flatter. But no one looks at the one who is really suitable, whose virtue has stood the test."[6]

So it went in the smaller and more insignificant episcopal cities. So one can imagine what strong passions were aroused when the first episcopal see of the Empire was to be conferred, at a time in which the people, the priests and the provincial bishops were all entitled to vote, but in which the Emperor and the court, more than once, asked or unasked, gave the decision. So this temptation was especially imminent in Constantinople, naturally.

Matters came to a crisis in the year 397. Foreign competitors were interfering again in the choice of a bishop. The Patriarchs of Alexandria knew only too well what influence could be at the disposal of the bishop of Constantinople under certain circumstances, and that Alexandria, on which the undisputed spiritual leadership of the Eastern Church had devolved until that time, might lose very much through an ambitious rival in Constantinople, or at least might be placed definitely in the background.

On that account the Patriarch Peter, seventeen years before, had attempted to place the Alexandrian Maximus on the episcopal throne of the residential city (Constantinople). For the same reason, the Patriarch Theophilus, who was very sensible of the advantages of power, exerted himself to win influence for the new enrichment of the see of Constantinople. Theophilus wished to make Isidore, an Alexandrian priest devoted to him, bishop of the chief city, although he was more than seventy years old.[7] Perhaps he wished to have him as a place-holder for his nephew, who was yet too young. Isidore had lived earlier as a monk in the Nitrian desert, and then became a priest and the steward of the almsgiving and of the guests' hospice in Alexandria.[8] Theophilus believed that in any case he would have nothing to fear from him, but would always find in him a ready friend and advocate at court for himself and his interests. Malicious tongues reported that Theophilus had sent this Isidore several years before to Rome, when Maximus was carrying on a war against the Emperor Theodosius. At that time he had given Isidore, besides gifts, two letters of congratulation, one to Theodosius, in case he should win, and the other to Maximus, if the fortunes of war should be favorable to him.[9] Even if that story is not true, it shows at least how Theophilus could be relied on. Palladius, who otherwise grants Theophilus nothing at all, does not know anything of this affair.

With what matter-of-factness, what publicity, what dissension and hatred, the pursuit of the episcopal throne in the East was carried on, was portrayed thirty years later by no less a man than the Emperor Theodosius II. When the ambassador of the Council of Ephesus, the Archimandrite Dalmatius, on order of the Council, requested the Emperor to confirm the deposition of Nestorius, the Emperor reminded him of the affairs which had preceded the appointment of Nestorius. "Shall I recall to you the officiousness, the running about, the promises, and count the oaths of those who haggled over the episcopal dignities? . . . The candidates were numerous and not of the best. Each party exalted its candidates to heaven, and blackened the others. You could not agree on a common name. The monks were not at one with the priests; the priests were not united among themselves. The bishops were divided, the people the same. . . . At last you left the choice to me, and I thought it would be best not to choose anyone from here, so that he would not have the jealousy and hate of the others against him from the start. For you all hated, each one hated the others. Therefore I chose a stranger . . . who was distinguished for his oratorical gifts and his merits."[10]

That had been only a repetition, true to life, of what played itself out in the imperial city in the autumn of 397. The strife between good and bad candidates for the episcopal throne in Constantinople upset at last the well-disposed people so that they went to the Emperor and begged him urgently to interfere and appoint a capable man to be bishop.[11] In this case of course the Emperor was not of much consequence.[12] The issue was decided by Eutropius. He had given an Empress to the Empire three years before; why should he not now give the capital city a bishop? The courtier saw through the designs of Theophilus, and probably entertained little sympathy for the domineering man. The activities of the remaining candidates probably roused in him a feeling of cold contempt. As a cunning diplomat, he had led everyone to believe that his candidacy was the best prospect. He himself had his own candidate, of whom at that time no one in the Empire had thought, least of all the chosen one himself.

Appointment and Consecration of Chrysostom

One day, perhaps about the middle of October, 397, Chrysostom received from Asterius, the Count of the East, or imperial governor of Antioch,[13] the invitation to meet him at the Martyrium which lay before the Romanesian Gate. He came, all unsuspecting; the governor invited him to seat himself in his chariot, and at once they started posthaste for Pagrae, the first post-station between Antioch and Tarsus.[13a] Meanwhile the governor imparted the news to the disconcerted priest that imperial messengers were waiting for him in Pagrae, a palace eunuch and the military adjutant of the Magister Sacri Palatii; these had the order to bring him to Constantinople, for he had been chosen Bishop of the imperial city.[14] In consideration of the approach of winter, and the height of the Taurus mountains, Eutropius must have made haste to bring Chrysostom to Constantinople.

History does not tell us of the thoughts and feelings with which Chrysostom received this unexpected message.

Whether he was glad or sorry, no one asked him at that time. He had simply been caught by authority, and like a state prisoner of the better class, was brought to Constantinople. Bishop Flavian, the clerics, and the people of the city of Antioch, first learned after the accomplished fact: the one, that he had lost his most zealous priest, and the others, that they had lost their best preacher.

The affair had been so suddenly and secretly managed so that tumult might be avoided; for it was known that the people, in their dependence on and love for Chrysostom, would not voluntarily have let him go. After the deed had been done, nothing could be changed, and the honor intended for their parish priest mitigated their sorrow for his loss.

Just what had moved Eutropius to make this choice? The wish to prevent the influence of the Alexandrian from becoming too great in Constantinople? Or the idea of giving the clergy of the capital city a somewhat stricter, more upright shepherd, whom they surely needed? Palladius says that Eutropius had become personally acquainted with Chrysostom, and learned of his character and accomplishments, when he once sojourned in Antioch on some business of State.[15] It might also be possible that Caesarius had noticed him—the same Caesarius who in the year 386 had come to Antioch as commissioner after the Riot of the Pillars, and who just then, in 397, was invested with the highest dignity of the consulate.[16] Perhaps Eutropius also wished simply to increase the brilliance of the capital city, through a bishop whose fame as a preacher was known far and wide, whose writings were read and praised throughout the Empire, and, at the same time, whose ascetic character gave promise that he would never willingly mix in political affairs.

The journey to Constantinople must have lasted ten to fourteen days. It was certainly not very pleasant, in the midst of early winter. The way led, for the most part, over the same great imperial road over which the Apostle of the Gentiles, St. Paul, had traveled more than three hundred years before, to conquer paganism, and over which, thirty-five years before, the Emperor Julian had come to Antioch and meditated on how he might abolish Christianity.

What mighty changes had taken place in that time in the Empire and the world! The travelers had plenty of leisure to think of these things. They had about 800 Roman miles (about 1100 kilometers) to cover. The great imperial road[17] led out from Antioch in a northerly direction to Alexandretta, which lay on the Gulf of Issus, then turned in a sharp curve around the gulf toward the west, where the travelers reached Issus and Mopsuestia.

Here Chrysostom surely did not miss the opportunity of seeing the friend of his youth, Theodore, and of sharing some happy hours of memories of their youth. From there the way went on straight to Tarsus.

That was the easiest and most pleasant part of the journey. What feelings must have stormed the heart of the inspired lover of St. Paul, here in Tarsus, when for the first time in his life he entered the birthplace of the great Apostle whose fame and honor he had so often trumpeted with glowing words from the pulpit! Here also his honored teacher and fatherly friend, Bishop Diodorus, to whom he owed so much, was buried. And not far from there stood solitary and forsaken the burial place of the bones of the last persecutor of the Christians, the Emperor Julian, before whom he, in his early youth, had trembled, along with the rest of Christendom. Truly there were plenty of emotional reactions and great memories.

From Tarsus on, the journey was more difficult. It was necessary to cross the great Taurus range of mountains, which separated Syria and Asia Minor. That was a toilsome affair even in the best time of the year, but especially difficult in winter, when deep snow lay in the mountains; and Chrysostom, since his early years as a hermit, was especially sensitive to cold. On the other side of the mountain range, the way wound in a northerly direction, past Faustinopolis, to Tyana in Cappadocia. This place was the origin of the pagan "wonder-worker" Apollonius, who understood how to unite the arts of an Indian fakir with the name of a neo-Pythagorean philosopher, and who was later considered by old and new pagans as a pagan antithesis of Christ.[18] Chrysostom himself had called him from the pulpit a charlatan and a deceiver, who would make himself spoken of for a short time, and then would be forgotten, while Christ would be worshipped all over the world.[19]

Meanwhile how often must the traveler have thought of his dear Antioch, of his pulpit and his congregation, of Bishop Flavian and of all his friends! He had not been able to say farewell to any of them. Meanwhile they had long since discovered why they could no more see or find him, and their prayers and ardent wishes doubtless accompanied him on his journey.

So the pitiless journey went on, further and further north, over Colonia and Aspona, toward Ancyra in Galatia, which in a later time became the capital city (Angora) of the new Turkish Empire.

The greater half of the journey was by then accomplished. The nearer they approached to Constantinople, the more the thoughts of the travelers hastened on before the chariot and the horses, and the stronger the feelings of expectation and tension.

From Ancyra onwards, the road led directly westward, past Juliopolis, to Cerata (Gordium?), where they crossed the border between Galatia and Bithynia, and reached the province on the northwest border of which Constantinople lay. Already the travelers were in Nicaea (the modern Isnik). That was the memorable place where, seventy-five years before, 318 Catholic bishops had held the first Church Council in the presence of the first Christian Emperor; by this council the heresy of Arius was rejected. Chrysostom had had to preach against the Arians often enough. The same Council had also decreed that the Christians might not celebrate their Easter at the same time with the Jews, and that young women consecrated to God might not dwell in the same house with clerics or lay people; these were public affairs which had also occupied him often enough.

Soon the travelers came through Nicomedia (the modern Ismid), whose splendid imperial palace recalled the time when this city, before the founding of Constantinople, had been temporarily the residence of the Roman Emperors. From here the Emperor Diocletian in 303 had issued the edicts which unloosed the last and bloodiest of all the Christian persecutions, which bore his name, but which was actually launched by his co-ruler, that fanatical man of blood, Galerius.

Next they arrived at the Propontis. The last stretch of road led straight along the ocean. Shortly before Chalcedon was reached, they came upon a great and splendid church, which stood between a gorgeous palace and an unassuming little cloister; it was the Church of the Apostles St. Peter and St. Paul, which had been built by the minister Rufinus; he had been murdered three years before. The place was called, after him, " Rufinianai," but was more commonly known under the name Epi Dryn, "at the Oak," and to-day is called Djadi Bostan.[20] From here could be seen the outline of the walls and towers of Constantinople; here also was the station for the last change of horses before reaching the metropolis.

No doubt Chrysostom utilized this short delay to send up to heaven a silent prayer to beg the blessing of God and the intercession of both the Apostles for his future apostolic labors in the capital city.[21]

How little he could know that only six years later, in this very same place, the destiny of most of the Apostles would have its beginning for him too: the road to martyrdom.

Finally they reached Chalcedon, and there lay, on the opposite coast, visible, almost within reach, the goal of the long journey, the scene of his future activity; Constantinople, the queen of two oceans, the capital city of the Empire, the imperial residence, as distinguished by its incomparably beautiful natural situation as by the splendor of its buildings and its political significance. His heart may well have beat faster, as for the first time the splendid panorama opened before him from the heights of the last mountain chain, and as with one comprehensive glance he saw the whole city lying before him, as well as the Bosphorus and the Sea of Marmora, on which small and large ships from every part of the world billowed out their sails. So then this was to be the stage of his activities for the last part of his life—he was to be placed as shepherd over this great city, with its brilliant throng of people, and its imperial palace!

Chrysostom himself knew that his burden would not be light. He had indeed learned from his companions on the road, that his appointment would mean a disillusionment for many, and the grave of many ardently cherished aspirations for many more, who did not at all suspect that their new arch-bishop was already so near.

Since Eutropius had used the same method in the choice of a new Bishop as he had in the choice of a new Empress three years before, Constantinople did not know until the last moment who the chosen one was.[22] Invitations to the conse-cration and enthronement had been issued long since to a large number of bishops. Theophilus, the Patriarch of Alexandria, had even been invited to come and bestow the episcopal blessing on the chosen one; and he came. His conduct until shortly before the consecration day showed that he did not know, either, anything certain until the last moment. For when he finally learned who the chosen one was, he showed himself so utterly astounded and disappointed, and obviously felt so openly that he had been outwitted, that in his first wrath he emphatically refused to go through with the consecration of the priest from Antioch.[23] Perhaps his disgust at the rejection of his candi-date was increased by the special circumstance that the new Bishop came from Antioch, and was the most renowned repre-sentative of that school which, in the last decade, had put its Alexandrian rival definitely in the shade. There was a certain long-standing jealousy between Antioch and Alex-andria. Added to this, was a still stronger jealousy against the aspiring Constantinople, which for sixteen years now had attained to the same honorable pre-eminence as Alexandria. Theophilus would be very glad to have that undone, as was proved by his later conduct at the Synod of the Oak. To think that a priest from Antioch should attain the See of Constanti-nople! One must admit that the disappointment was a grievous one for Theophilus. The fact is that he did not make any attempt to conceal his disgust, or at least he was not able to overcome it.

How the first greeting went between the newly named Bishop and the Patriarch of Alexandria, no chronicle has told us. It was certainly not hearty. Palladius, who of course was a declared opponent of Theophilus, says that the real cause for his opposition was his ambition for power. Theo-philus did not want a man of upright character in Constanti-nople. He had already read in Chrysostom's countenance that he could not bend him to his will. Palladius may be right so far. But then he added this malicious remark: Theophilus had only appointed useful and capable men to bishoprics in Egypt when, by way of exception, he had been deceived in their character. The imperious man would have none but insignificant, submissive creatures about him, and would rather rule over stupid people than listen to wise and intelligent ones. But this time, fortunately, Providence frustrated his plans.[24]

Naturally, Theophilus could not admit the actual reasons for his disgust and opposition. Outwardly he acted as though only the person of the newly chosen Bishop was not acceptable to him. Socrates says that Theophilus attempted to "smear" John's good name as much as he could.[25]

However, Theophilus might oppose as much as he would. Eutropius, like a good politician, always had another arrow in his quiver. Now he brought it out. It must have been unpleasant for him as well as for the Emperor, if the Patriarch, through his refusal of the court's choice, had expressed open disapprobation. The all-powerful Eutropius wished above all things to prevent that, and at the same time to show Theophilus who was master.

Among the assembled Bishops—at least in Alexandrian circles—many complaints against Theophilus were being voiced. Naturally this became known to Eutropius. He had the accusations submitted in writing, laid them before Theophilus, and gave him the choice of taking part in the consecration of Chrysostom, or of answering the accusations and defending himself before a synodal court. Theophilus chose what seemed to be the lesser evil.[26]

So Chrysostom became Bishop of Constantinople, the twelfth in the line of historically known Bishops of Byzantium.[27]

That Theophilus at first openly refused to participate in the consecration, certainly had another reason. If he agreed to consecrate Chrysostom, it was equivalent to an indirect and unspoken recognition of the precedence of Constantinople over Alexandria. According to an earlier law, it was the affair of the Metropolitan of Heraclea to consecrate the Bishop of Constantinople. But since the Council of 381, it obviously

devolved upon the Patriarch of Alexandria, as the next in
rank, to perform the consecration. Outwardly, Theophilus
could not make use of this consideration, for he could not
openly combat the decision of the great council, since he
himself had been involved at one time, when the See of
Alexandria had been vacant. He could not argue the matter
now on account of the court. But he finally consented unwillingly enough. He took his resentment over his defeat
back to Alexandria.

Unfortunately Palladius gives no further account of the day
on which the consecration took place. Socrates writes concerning it: "So after John had received the episcopal consecration, he was enthroned on the 26th of February" of the
year in which Honorius in Rome and Eutychius in Constantinople were consuls. That was the year 398.

With the solemn enthronement was united the official
delivery of Church property to the new Bishop.[28]

Here the Greek Synaxarium of Constantinople offers perhaps the correct clue. It sets the consecration of St. Chrysostom on the 15th of December, 397.[29] From whence the Synaxarium took this exact date, and from what time it originated, unfortunately cannot be ascertained. At any rate the
report is credible in itself, and fits well into the frame of other
known events.

What legal significance was attached to the "enthronement" at that time, and why, in this case, it took place two
and a half months after the consecration, are questions to
which unfortunately history does not give us a satisfactory
answer.[30] One can only suspect that it had something to do
with the surrender of the episcopal "throne," the bishop's
palace and the church property belonging to it. Something
similar took place at the Emperor's accession. Here also the
naming or proclamation, and the enthronement, were legally
and practically separated.

The elevation of the preacher of Antioch had begun with
the humiliation and defeat of the Patriarch Theophilus. This
proud imperious character did not forget his defeat. It was
the first dark cloud in the clear and fair sky of joy and jubilee
which gleamed over Constantinople on the day of the consecration and the enthronement of Chrysostom. This cloud was

later to enlarge and darken, until all unexpectedly it sent down a deadly stroke of lightning.

But the joy which the people themselves showed for their new shepherd was sincere and inspired. They came in crowds to see and hear him in the Cathedral. " I have spoken to you now for the first time," he began a sermon on Arianism, which in Constantinople was always strongly defended, " and I have already become as fond of you as if I had grown up among you from my earliest youth; and I feel so strongly bound to you by the bonds of affection as though I had for many years had the pleasure of being with you. Not because *I* am so worthy of affection, but because *you* abound in goodness and kindness. Who would not admire and wonder at your fiery enthusiasm, your sincere love, your kind feelings for your teachers, your mutual harmony? Therefore we love you as we love the members of that other church (Antioch) among whom we were born, grew up and were educated. This church here is the sister of the other, and you have indeed shown spiritual relationship with it. But if the church of Antioch is older, this one (Constantinople) is warmer in its faith. There the congregation is larger, the theatre more famous, but here the endurance is greater and shows more firmness. From all sides the wolves (the Arians and other sects) surround the sheep, but the shepherds stand fast. Storm and tempest and boiling seas rage around this sacred ship (the Church) and still its crew does not fail. It is threatened roundabout with the firebrands of heresy; but those who sit at the hearth, refresh themselves with spiritual dew. To see this Church still living in the midst of this city is as wonderful as if one should see in a furnace a blooming olive tree, adorned with its foliage and laden richly with its fruit."[31]

FOOTNOTES

1. Socrates 6, 2 (67, 661).

2. Besides, Nectarius had a brother named Arsacius, who was a priest, and who, after the deposition of Chrysostom, became his successor. Cf. Ch. 27. But the Hist. Laus. 38 (ed. Butler 117) says (about 20 years after Nectarius' death) that he was a skilful speaker in the battle against the heretics.

3. Palladius 5 (47, 19): πραιτωριοκτυποῦντες.

4. *Ibid.* τοὺς δήμους γονοπετοῦντες.

5. Chronicon Paschale 92, 809. See Millingen, Byzantine Constantinople 49.

6. De Sacerdotio 3, 15 (48, 652). Occasionally it came even to bloody blows and fights between the individual parties. Cf. J. Grafton Milne, A history of Egypt under the Roman rule (London 1898) 98 and 100. Gregor Naz., Or. 43, 37 (36, 546).

7. Socrates 6, 2, and Palladius 6 (22).

8. Sozomenus 8, 2 (67, 1517).

9. Socrates 6, 2 and Sozomenus 8, 2.

10. Nestorius, Le livre d'Heraclide de Damas, ed. F. Nau, 243-44.

11. Palladius 5 (19).

12. Theodoret HE 5, 27 (82, 1256 ed. Parmentier 328) ascribes the appointment of Chrysostom to the Emperor, and sees therein a proof of his zeal for the things of God. The remark is only a proof of the political anxiety of Theodoret.

13. So according to Sozomen 8, 2 (67, 1517B), while Palladius 5 inaccurately gives him the title " Count of Antioch." Claudian had been Count of the Orient since 395: see Rauschen, Jahrbücher 449. How long Claudian remained in office is not stated there. The very unreliable Theodore of Trimithus, Ch. 4 (MG 47, P. LVII) says that the city prefect of the East was named Victor, and he gives the contents of a letter which Arcadius allegedly wrote to Victor: "Arcadius, the gloriously reigning Emperor, writes the following to Victor the patrician, commander-in-chief of the East: Since some fools, who in their folly fear neither shame nor contempt, are striving for the episcopal dignity, therefore we wish, guided by the fear of God, to frustrate their aims. So I command you, through this our all-highest letter, to send the priest John quietly here to us, without anyone in the city finding out about it. By the fortunate execution of this command, you will merit the highest praise from us." This letter, in form and content resembling various letters from the imperial chancellery, is, like all others from Theodore, a literary product of this author.

13a. Pagrae was also a fortress, which dominated the approaches to Antioch. (Pauly-Wissowa, Real-encyclop. 18, 2 (1942) 2315.)

14. Palladius 5 (19); Sozomen 8, 2 (1517). The choice of these two ambassadors shows that Eutropius considered the matter very definitely an affair of State. Obviously, no member of the clergy was in the delegation. Perhaps also there was an idea of keeping the secret in Antioch as well as in Constantinople. Sozomen is

doubtless quite wrong if he writes, out of sympathy for the church, that the sending of the messengers was the result of the unanimous choice of John by the people and the clergy, and that the Emperor only confirmed this choice (HE 8, 2). That nothing could be said of unanimity among people and clergy has been sufficiently proved. Also Sozomen ineptly contradicts his own account when he says that Theophilus first began to make difficulties *after* the entrance of John into Constantinople. Had he known before who was to be made Bishop, he would either not have come, or would have gone away before John arrived.

The " Romanesian Gate," which had previously been called the Seleucian Gate, lay by the riverside, where there still exists a bridge on four levels, surviving from Roman times, crossing the Orontes. The gate stood in the form in which it had probably stood since the time of Justinian, until about 1867. See Förster, *Antiochia am Orontes, loc. cit.* 115 (Fig. 4).

15. Palladius 5 (19).

16 Caesarius was religiously inclined, for he founded in Constantinople the church and cloister of St. Thyrsos: see Sozomen 9, 2 (67, 1597 f.).

17. The travel route described here is verified by the exact accounts of (a) *the pilgrims of Bordeaux*, who in May 333 made the journey from Constantinople to Antioch; see Itinerarium Burdigalense = Itineraria Hierosolimitana, IV-VIII centuries, ed. P. Geyer = Corpus Scriptor. Eccles. Lat. vol. 39. Vienna 1898, p. 13-17. (b) the Spanish pilgrim Aetheria (Egeria), who, about 400, traveled the same way from Antioch to Constantinople; see S. Silviae, quae fertur, peregrinatio ad loca sancta. Ed. R. Geyer *loc. cit.*, m. 69-70; ed. Pomialowsky 37-38. Cf. Bardenhewer, GAL 3, 416-20. The Emperor Julian also used this same road on his march from Constantinople to Antioch.

18. J. H. Newman, Historical Sketches 1 (London 1882), 301 ff.

19. Hom. 4 de laudibus S. Pauli (50, 490); cf. Hom. 5, 3 adv. Judaeos (48, 886).

20. Cf. Synod of the Oak Ch. 20. Rufinianai was three miles southeast of Chalcedon, near the sea.

21. When Nestorius in 428 came to Constantinople in the retinue of the imperial commander Dionysius, he followed the road over Nicomedia, then along the sea to the monastery of St. Hypatius, where there was a " Statio " with a change of horses, which indicates an imperial road; then past Rufiniana (Djadi Bostan) to Skutari (Chrysopolis) and from there, over the Bosporus. See Vita St. Hypatii of Callinicus (ed Leipzig 1895) p.

113; and Acta SS. Juni III 308-349 (3. ed. Junii IV 247-82). Meliopulos, Πον ἔκειντο αἱ Ρουφινιαναὶ =Syllogos 29 (1907), 278.

22. That Eutropius actually acted thus, can be deduced from the state of affairs as well as from his own character, and it also results from the conduct of Theophilus.

23. Palladius 5 (47, 19-20); Sozomen 8, 2 (67, 1517-20).

24. Palladius 5 (19-20).

25. HE 6, 2 (67, 664).

26. That Theophilus actually performed the consecration is proved by the fact that Chrysostom, in a letter to him, refers to himself as the spiritual son and brother of Theophilus (Palladius 7 = 47, 25).

27. So according to the list given by Mommsen = Mon. Germ. Auct. Ant. XIII, 560.

28. According to Grotefend, Zeitrechnung 1, 88 (Tabellen) the 26th of February, 398, was a Friday.

29. Ed. H. Delehaye = Acta SS. Nov. Propylaeum (1902) 312-13. M. Gedeon, Byzantin. Heortologion, 191, erroneously assumes that Socrates spoke only of the consecration, and considers therefore the 15th of December as the day of the appointment.

30. Eudoxius was already Patriarch of Antioch, when, in the year 360, he was named (or chosen) Bishop of Constantinople, and was then enthroned, on the 27th of January, 361, in the presence of 72 bishops. Philostorgius, HE 7, 31 (ed. Bidez 224-25) and Chronicon Paschale a. 360 p. 543, 16. Cf. F. X. Funk, Die Bischofswahl im christlichen Altertum und im Anfänge des Mittelalters = Kirchengesch. Abhandlungen und Untersuchungen 1, 29-32.

31. Hom. XI, I contra Arianos (48, 796 f.).

CHAPTER II

CHRYSOSTOM AND THE RECONCILIATION BETWEEN FLAVIAN AND ROME

O N E may well assume that at the beginning, no one told the newly chosen Bishop of the opposition of the Patriarch, in order not to spoil the joy and sincerity of his welcome. But did Chrysostom himself notice anything of Theophilus' interior disgust and disappointment? At any rate, at first he showed the Patriarch perfect impartiality, even trust.

The first thing which Chrysostom had at heart as a newly consecrated bishop, arose from a feeling of kindly gratitude for his former chief shepherd, the Patriarch Flavian of Antioch. That his relations with the first bishop of the Church, at Rome, had not been made entirely clear, was obviously perceived by Chrysostom to be an abnormal and disturbing state of things. Now the moment seemed to have come, when the old line of separation should be abolished. It was the custom for the Patriarchs and Metropolitans to announce their consecration and assumption of office to one another, and above all to the Bishop of Rome, and at the same time to send him their confession of faith. Thereby the others would recognize their orthodoxy, and on the ground of the same, would enter into ecclesiastical fellowship with them.

The newly-chosen Patriarchs of Alexandria, after announcing their choice to the Bishop of Rome, would then receive from him the "letter of fellowship" (κοινωνικὰ γράμματα).[1] A request for ratification was not necessarily bound up with such a notification. So if the Bishops of Constantinople sent the Pope such a notification of their election and consecration, therein lay the evidence that they no longer considered themselves mere Bishops, but as those who stood in the ranks of the great Metropolitans, or even Patriarchs.

Chrysostom sent such a document to Rome.[2] For this purpose a special ambassador had to go there, and Chrysostom wished to use this opportunity to accomplish a long-cherished wish of his heart, to reconcile the Patriarch Flavian and his paternal city of Antioch with Rome. He had communicated his purpose to the Patriarch of Alexandria, who, as consecrating bishop, had to sign the document. They agreed that Acacius, Bishop of Beroea, should be entrusted with this duty. His gray hair and venerable aspect made him appear especially suited for it. As an escort, and at the same time as a special representative of the Patriarch of Alexandria, the priest Isidore was appointed, the same whom Theophilus had wanted to make Bishop of Constantinople.[3]

As to the success of the embassy, Sozomen says it went according to their wishes.[4] Acacius returned home through Egypt to Syria, and brought letters of fellowship from the Western and Egyptian bishops to Antioch for Flavian. So the Antiochene schism was finally ended in its principal particulars; and Evagrius, the successor of Paulinus, soon died, and he himself had no successor.[5] Only a part of the so-called Eustathians, although without a bishop, carried on with their special Divine Liturgy for a long time. Socrates attributes the ending of the Antiochene schism to this embassy, although he states erroneously that it took place under Pope Damasus.[6] Cavallera also states that this combined embassy of Chrysostom and Theophilus accomplished a "full success;" only he states that Acacius was chosen by Flavian, and that several clergy were sent to Rome together. He does not quote any document in support of his statement.[7] But that Chrysostom acted in agreement with Flavian may well be assumed, even though, on account of his sudden departure from Antioch, a previous arrangement had not been possible. Perhaps Flavian had sent Acacius as his representative to the episcopal consecration and enthronement in Constantinople, and sent these instructions with him. The credit of Chrysostom is not diminished thereby.

It is quite incomprehensible how Photius could have taken out of the air the statement that Rome had not acknowledged the new Bishop of Constantinople at first, "because he . . . would not have ventured to go away from Antioch to go as Bishop to Constantinople."[8]

As has been noted before, the conduct of Chrysostom in the affair of the Patriarch Flavian, for itself alone, apart from his literary expressions, must be considered unhesitatingly as a proof that the unity of the Church was considered by him to be an extremely important factor, the preservation of which must be the first and highest duty of a bishop. One thing may therefore be said with absolute certainty: the unfortunate actions of a Photius and a Michael Cerularius, his successors in the See of Constantinople, never would have had the approbation of Chrysostom; but on the contrary, he would have sought to end them again as soon as possible.

Also, how resentful the Paulinians (Eustathians) had become in their uniquely separated position, is shown by the fact that they did not now wish to know anything of Flavian, although he was the only Bishop of Antioch and therefore formally recognized by Rome. The Patriarch Alexander (413) was first able to effect a reconciliation with some of them, while the really obstinate ones persisted in their schism until almost the end of the fifth century.

FOOTNOTES

1. Batiffol, Le Siège Apostolique 268.
2. Palladius 4 (18). Nestorius also in 428 sent a similar consecration notice and letter of fellowship to Rome; see Celestin Pp. epist. ad Nestorium = Mansi 4, 1025 CD.
3. Palladius 6 (22).
4. HE 8, 3 (67, 1520).
5. Evagrius died about 393.
6. HE 5, 15 (67, 604).
7. Le schisme d'Antioche 289.
8. Respons. 2 (104, 1221). It is also an error, as stated by Compernass, Two Treatises of Arethas of Caesarea concerning changing of episcopal sees, in: Studi bizant. e neo-hellen. 4 (1935) 89; Chrysostom was made an exception to this prohibition. This concerned only the transfer of *bishops* from one see to another, not the call of a *priest* to be bishop in another diocese.

CHAPTER III

CONSTANTINOPLE, THE CITY AND THE PEOPLE

ONSTANTINOPLE, in the few decades since its new foundation by Constantine the Great, had grown so much in greatness and splendor that it was not far behind Antioch. In the incomparable beauty of its geographical situation it far surpassed the "Queen of the East." It must have been a pleasure for the new Bishop, if in the first weeks and months of his life in Constantinople, he was able to enjoy the splendid view out over the ocean and the city from the terraces of his cathedral, or from the height of the Church of the Apostles, or if he encountered in his walks through the streets, new architectural glories and works of art, which aroused the admiration of every beholder.

By imperial command, the most beautiful statues of gods and goddesses from Rome, Sicily, Antioch, Athens and Asia Minor had had to emigrate to the new metropolis in the course of the years, in order to adorn the center and symbol of the greatness and unity of the Roman-Greek double empire. Old trophies of Roman military exploits, statues of renowned generals of the armies, politicians and artists of the past—all these had to go, in order to establish, at least in effigy, the union of the new metropolis with the empire, the historical past with the newly formed present. Not unreasonably had St. Jerome complained: Constantinople is built with the ruins of almost all the other cities![1] It was at the same time a metropolis and a living museum of the empire. It offered the beholder a flexible compendium, hewn in stone, of the history of the empire, and a considerable part of the history of the world.

Rare creations and relics of ancient splendor, works which originated in part from the third and fourth centuries before Christ,[2] can be seen today in the Museum, which the Turkish

Government has arranged in the ancient Church of St. Irene, over which one may well write the words: Sic transit gloria mundi!

A description of the old city, which was founded only about twenty years after the death of St. Chrysostom (about 430) counts among the most outstanding sights of the city: a Capitol (University), a circus, two theaters, eight public and 153 private baths, 52 porticoes, five granaries, eight aqueducts and reservoirs, four great Basilicas for senate and court sessions, fourteen churches (or martyr's shrines), fourteen great palaces, and 4380 dwellings which were distinguished from ordinary dwellings by their size and beauty.[3]

The principal street of Constantinople, the so-called " Mese," led from the main gate of the imperial palace and of Hagia Sophia to the Augusteion, or Imperial Square, and on to the Forum of Constantine and that of Theodosius. From thence one street branched off to the right, past the Church of the Apostles, to the Porta Polyandrii, while the left branch led, as a Via Triumphalis, through the Forum of Arcadius to the "Golden Gate," through which the Emperor and the victorious generals made their entrances.[4] On the left and right, these streets were bordered by flat-roofed porticoes, for pedestrians.

The imperial palace itself, even in the time of Theodosius and Arcadius, must have been very large. The oldest part had been built by the Emperor Constantine[5] and was not far south of the Hagia Sophia (Magnaura).[6] There is no doubt that it sheltered everything that the wealth and luxury of the time could offer. The East had always had more regard for external splendor than the Western countries. The court ordinarily attended the Divine Liturgy in the palace chapel. But on high festival days, the rulers also appeared in the Cathedral or in other churches. The fact that the court ladies, and especially Eudoxia, showed themselves on such occasions adorned with the richest splendor, and that many ladies of distinguished society tried to do the same whenever possible, had more than once evoked the silent disapprobation, and once the open disgust, of Chrysostom.

The Empress Eudoxia, moreover, lived in a special palace, which the Emperor Theodosius the Great had originally built for his daughter, Galla Placidia. In a later time, this palace was the residence of the Apocrisiarius, or Papal Nuncio. Gregory the Great lived there as Nuncio, as well as Pope Vigilius, during his thorny sojourn in Constantinople.[7]

But it appears that the Emperor Arcadius had built still another palace for Eudoxia in the eleventh region of the city. Perhaps this is connected with the story of the confiscated vineyard, which later gave rise to a source of conflict between her and the new Bishop.[8]

The imperial palace was a long, rectangular building, 536 by 154 feet, enclosed by porticoes. In the midst of the square was the heroic statue of Theodosius the Great, who had built the Augusteion, and named it in honor of his mother Helena. Here also took place the ceremony of the taking up of arms by the new Emperor.[9]

The most beautiful public square in all Constantinople was the Forum of the Emperor Constantine. It had the form of a great ellipse, and was surrounded by colonnades. Almost exactly in the middle stood the great porphyry pillar; upon it stood the bronze statue of the Emperor. An old statue of Jupiter had been given the features of the first Christian Emperor; and within this column of porphyry Constantine had concealed a particle of the new-found true Cross, with the inscription: In this sign conquer. The pillar stands, with its dumb voice, in the ancient square, until this day.[10] On each of the long sides of the ellipse stood a great portico with triumphal arches. One of these united the portico with the neighboring Forum of Theodosius I. Here the image of the great Emperor looked down in greeting from a high pillar. In the year 1204 the Venetians, after the conquest of the city, hurled the captive Greek Emperor Alexius V from the top of this pillar. The image of Theodosius had long ago yielded to the changes of time. But the pillar itself still stands, as an accusing witness of the bygone power of the Christian Emperors.[11]

Among other splendors of the city, the Senate House is distinguished above all; it was adorned with valuable statues by Greek artists.[12] It was separated from Hagia Sophia by only one street. The senators numbered about a thousand. They were all named by the Emperor, and therefore constituted merely an innocuous remnant from ancient democratic times. They constituted a great burden on the treasury, since each senator received a special income from the state. They do not seem to have had much to do. Of course at any rate they had nothing at all to say; for the " Basileus " ruled absolutely, without benefit of the senate or house of representatives. He alone made the laws and regulated the taxes. Only a very few of the senators had descended from the old senatorial families of Rome, such as Olympius, Verus, Severus, Urbicius, Callistratus, Florentius, Eubulus, Studius, Zoticus. The rest were noisy upstarts of a later time.[13]

There was also a great library in Constantinople, in which, since the time of Valens, eight officials were occupied with the copying and correcting of Greek and Latin manuscripts, while the " High School " (about 425) was staffed by ten Latin and ten Greek grammarians, as well as three Latin and five Greek sophists or philosophers, and two teachers of law, all of whom lectured.[14] Unfortunately, the ancient library was burnt down in the year 476. In the time of Chrysostom, Ammonius of Alexandria, Helladius and Syrian taught here.

As an ancient city, Constantinople naturally made use of its great Thermae, which in plan and arrangement were similar to the Roman baths. The greatest and most luxurious of all ancient baths was that of Zeuxippos, which the Emperor Severus had built for old Byzantium. It was on the principal street, not far from the imperial palace.

Though Chrysostom could find joy and pleasure in all these buildings and monuments, he certainly found none in the great Circus (Hippodrome), which lay critically near the Cathedral, and was of the size of the Circus Maximus in Rome —indeed it surpassed any other circus in the world.[15] This Hippodrome was the special heart of Constantinople, where not only bets were made on the horse races, but all sorts of political and actual battles were fought out there; the passion of those fights sometimes brought the dynasty and the Empire into danger. In the fifth century, perhaps already in the fourth, there were in Constantinople two chief circus parties, the *Blues*, that is, the nobles, the wealthy people and the patriots, who were naturally conservative minded, and the *Greens*, who were the liberals, the reformers and agitators, who, under the protection of the masses, sometimes said very disagreeable things in the Circus, even to the Emperor.

Under Justinian I. there occurred a riot in which three thousand people were killed in the Circus. The last historically demonstrable horse race took place here in the year 1203. During the conquest of the city by the Venetians in 1204, the Circus was destroyed by fire. Only the obelisk which the Emperor Theodosius had brought from Alexandria in the year 390 defied the storms of 1500 years, and still keeps its ancient place.[15a]

Was Chrysostom ever able to make up his mind to enter the Circus? Probably no more than he would enter the theaters, of which the oldest, to his sorrow, was also near the Cathedral.[15b] These two places were the special centres of the city, where all the splendid buildings stood together—the imperial palace, the senate, the cathedral, the bishop's palace, the theaters, the circus and the baths.

Outside the Golden Gate the street led to the so-called Hebdomon,[16] the modern Makrikeui (Turkish Bakirköi),[16a] a port which lay on the sea-coast seven miles from Constantinople. Here the Emperor had a country house, the ruins of which are still visible. Here also the Gothic troops had their garrison. It was the Versailles of the Byzantine administration. In the palace of Hebdomon the new Emperors were first proclaimed, and clothed with the purple. From here also the triumphal processions of victorious emperors or field generals started; they went through the Golden Gate to Hagia Sophia, and then to the imperial palace. The Emperor Constantine built a church in Hebdomon to St. John the Apostle. Theodosius the Great built a larger circular church in honor of St. John the Baptist, whose head was buried there. Probably it was in this church that Chrysostom gave his famous sermon on the Feast of the Baptist; it was destined later to play a great role in his life.[17]

The people of Constantinople did not differ essentially from those of Antioch. But while Antioch was a rendezvous and arena for travelers and merchants from the east and west, Constantinople was not only the most important center of commerce between east and west, but also, since Theodosius, it was the social and political focus of the Empire. Here, since the new foundation of the city, had come together in a brilliant medley, the various elements from all the provinces of the Empire. Here political aspirants and ambitious opportunists sought to outrank one another, to surpass one another in malice and cunning; here place-hunters and benefice-beggars knocked on any hopeful doors; here one met court lackeys, state officials and officers of all ranks, honorable and upright characters, but also evil and hypocritical ones, who measured the dose of their courtesy and dignity by the rank and influence of those with whom they had to deal.

Would Chrysostom be able to differentiate the one kind from the other? Here the wealth and luxury of the nobles and the successful merchants contrasted strongly with the poverty and misery of the slaves and the wage earners, for whom no social legislation existed, whose only help was the public help and the alms of the Church. The great mass of the people consisted of small merchants and artisans, free workers and slaves—just as in Antioch. The population of the city at that time was probably about the same as that of Antioch.[18] And as for love of amusement and of satire, the people of Constantinople were certainly equal to those of Antioch.

The variable climate of Constantinople must have had an unfavorable effect on the weak health of the Bishop. There are few places in which the whims of a fickle climate are displayed as they are in this city. The temperature often changes suddenly and violently, and with a great difference in degree, after the north or the south wind blows.

Even more than Antioch, Constantinople was in constant terror of earthquakes. The earthquake statistics, as collected by O. Weismantel for eastern Asia Minor, show for Constantinople the second greatest number among all the cities listed. From 500 B.C. until 1850 A.D., there were 154 earthquake years, with 501 earthquake days historically demonstrable. Taking the years 1850-1885 as average, this gives for Constantinople, over a period of not quite 2,500 years, the count of 1,992 years, with 8,830 days, in which there were light or severe earthquakes, with an entire count of over 12,000 shocks.[19]

So whoever had the good fortune to live in Constantinople and at the same time to live in court circles, stood in two respects upon a volcano which at any moment might bring ruin.

With all this, there were, besides, the abundant conflagrations, which were often of such immensity that the city had to be rebuilt almost from the ground up, on an average of every five years. It is a matter of wonder that the architectural marvel of Justinian's Hagia Sophia has fortunately withstood all these dangers, even to the present day.[20]

FOOTNOTES

1. Chronicon (ML 27, 677).
2. P. A. Dethier and A. D. Mordtmann, Epigraphik von Byzantion und Constantinopolis . . . = Denkschriften der kaiserl. Akademie der Wissenschaften. Phil. Hist. Kl. 13 vol. (Vienna 1864). Tables I-IV.
3. Salzenburg, Altchristl. Baudenkmäler 1-2.
4. Strzygowsky, Drei Miszellen 294-95, has re-discovered the ancient inscription of Theodosius.
5. Cf. Ebersolt, Le grand Palais 1-15.
6. Antoniades, 1, 45.
7. Du Cange, Constantinopolis Christiana 2, 112-13.
8. Cf. Ch. 16.
9. Antoniades 1, 54-56.
10. Grosvenor 1, 375.
11. *Ibid.* 1, 387.
12. Sozomen 6, 18 (67, 721).
13. Cf. Allard, Julien 1, 195; Th. Reinach, Commentaire archéologique *loc. cit.* 86-87.
14. Schemmel, Hochschule von Constantinopel 3 ff.; Heisenberg in the Byz. Zeitschrift 21 (1912) 630-31.
15. Grosvenor 1, 321 gives a fine reconstruction; see also Antoniades 1, 43 f.
15a. E. Weigand, in Byz. Ztschr. 37 (1937) 454.
15b. A. Vogt, Le Théatre à Byzance . . . in Revue des Quest. hist. 115 (1931) 259.
16. Thibaut, J. B., L'Hebdomon de Constantinople = Echos d'Orient 21 1922 (31-44).
16a. See Orient. chr. Per. 12 (1946) 394.
17. 59, 485-490; cf. Socrates 6, 18 (67, 717) and Sozomen 8, 20 (1568). R. Janin, Les Eglises Byzantines au précurseur de Constantinople, in: Echos d'Orient 37 (1938) 312-351.

18. Chrysostom (Hom. 11, 3 in Act. Ap.=60, 97) of course estimates the number of Christians (Catholics) in Constantinople at about a hundred thousand, which would lead us to conclude that the total population was about a hundred and fifty thousand; but Schultze, Geschichte des Untergangs des röm. greich. Heidentums 2, 290, considers this figure too low.

19. Weismantel 7. Grosvenor 1, 11-12. According to Marcellinus Comes (Chronicon = ML 51, 922) a "dreadful earthquake" took place in the year 402.

20. Concerning the religious situation in the capital city, see Chapter 6.

CHAPTER IV

CHRYSOSTOM AND THE COURT

ONSTANTINOPLE had become, since the time of
Theodosius, the special center of the great Eastern
Empire. But the midpoint of Constantinople, about
which everything else in the metropolis turned, was the court
of the Emperor, and his person. From here streamed out all
power and all influence; around the court revolved all earthly
life, and often also the life of the Church. Just at that time,
of course, the court of the Emperor was more significant than
his person. Arcadius had ascended his father's throne two
years before the elevation of Chrysostom. As an independent
personality he hardly counted for anything at all. It had been
the greatest misfortune for Theodosius and for the Roman
Empire that he had had to leave behind him these two sons,
who in so many ways were the violent opposites of their great
father.[1] The mother of both of them, a Spanish woman, had
been sickly, and died early. Theodosius, rightly estimating
the situation, had been careful to see to it that the most
capable men obtainable, Rufinus and Stilicho, had been
appointed as ministers and advisers to his sons. But the
avarice, mutual jealousy, and vindictiveness of those two
brought all his good purposes to nothing.

Arcadius, at the age of six (in 383) had been named
Augustus and co-regent by his father. As a youth of scarcely
eighteen, he succeeded him, in 395, as ruler of the entire
Eastern Empire. Now he was to rule an empire which was
almost as large as the later Turkish Empire at the time of its
greatest extent; the whole of the Balkans, bounded on the
north by the Danube, on the west by the Drina and the Sava;
this included all of modern Rumania, Serbia, Bulgaria, Macedonia, Greece, then Asia Minor with the Crimean peninsula,
Syria, Palestine, Egypt, lower Libya and Pentapolis,[2] all this
depended, with body and life, and property, of nobles, citizens,

and slaves, upon the intelligence and will of a youth who, if he lived in our day, would scarcely have finished high school.

He was absolute ruler of an area of about 50,000 square miles.   It is true that the Western Empire was still greater, richer and more productive; it encompassed an area of 70,000 square miles, and had an eleven-year old boy as ruler.   Nevertheless the Eastern Empire was the more important half of the Roman Empire.   From thence threatened the warlike Parthians (Persians); from thence the Germans and Huns, in ever greater multitudes, thronged over the Danube and menaced the existence of the Empire.   The Eastern Empire was a great compact body of land, whose line of communication was formed by the Mediterranean Sea.   Its average situation between the 25th and 45th degrees of north latitude meant that, apart from a few districts, it scarcely knew winter.   Far more important was the cultural similarity of the higher strata of its people, who for the most part were Greek, or had been hellenized since the time of Alexander the Great.   But most of all it was important that Theodosius had so far established religious unity in the Empire, that paganism and Arianism henceforth had no political importance.

What might or could one expect from such an administration, in which all experience in the judgment and the handling of men was lacking?   It was one of those cases of an absolutely monarchical system of government in which children, or almost children, were forced on the people as leaders and rulers of the state.   But youth was not the most critical attribute of the new monarch, for this is a lack which time will remedy.   Philip of Macedon, too, left his kingdom at his death to an eighteen-year-old son.   But unfortunately that is the only parallel between Arcadius and the genius Alexander. The new ruler was not a genius; he had not even a talent. Of the two poor-spirited sons of Theodosius, he was the poorer. His gifts were below the normal measure.   Gibbon allows himself the lese-majestical remark: "The keen satirist, who expressed his discontent by a partisan and passionate criticism of the Christian Emperor, injures more the dignity than the truth of history, if he compares the son of Theodosius to one of those harmless, silly animals, who scarcely notice that they are the property of their shepherd."[3]   Zosimus says that Arcadius was "very limited in his capacities," and George Cedrenus declares that his only good quality was his beautiful handwriting.[4]

The Byzantine court chronicler Malalas, more from prudence than from love of truth, praises the Emperor by saying that he was "clear-sighted and skilful in negotiation."[5] Philostorgius, who had very probably seen Arcadius himself, describes him as follows: "He was small and slender in figure, without strength, and of a dark complexion. His languid spirit showed itself in his speech and also in his eyes, whose lids were droopy and sleepy-looking."[6] He never became a ruler. He let himself be ruled by those who were successful in pushing him about or winning his confidence.

The entire "reign" of Arcadius was a standard example of the weakness and danger inherent in the system of absolute rule, when all power is gathered into the hands of one single person, who incidentally possesses neither power nor strength of will, and so is compelled to play the role of a puppet on the throne. And yet it must be confessed that for that time, and for Byzantine conditions, absolutism was relatively the best means of holding together the heterogeneous elements and provinces of the Eastern Empire; and, notwithstanding all the court intrigues and palace revolutions, it qualified the Empire to stand steadfast for a thousand years against all the inroads of barbarians and later of Islam, and to serve as a protecting bulwark for the cultural development of the Roman-Germanic West.

This was the man who had been wearing the crown for two years when Chrysostom, at the end of 397 or the beginning of 398, was made Bishop. What would not Chrysostom have been able to accomplish, had Theodosius only lived longer! They would have shone in the sky of the Empire like two stars of the first magnitude. But it was not to be. Arcadius, on account of his weak and vacillating nature, brought no good to the Empire, and misfortune to Chrysostom. In all this, the Emperor meant well. He was even considered unusually pious. He showed great zeal for the purity and unity of the Catholic faith, and continued the religious policy of his father, as far as he understood it. He issued new laws against schisms and their adherents, confirmed the privileges of the churches,

abolished the pagan festival days as legal holidays, and again
forbade sacrifices and visits to the temples.[7]   To what extent
the Emperor here followed his own impulse or the leading
of others, cannot be decided.

To the new Archbishop the young Emperor accorded all the
impersonal benevolence of which he was capable.   Chrysostom
must soon have felt that one might expect from him only so
much as his current entourage permitted.

Of himself, Arcadius would never have permitted any interference with the rights and the mission of the Church.   The
feeling for the special rights of the Church and its independ-
ence of the State was still vigorous in Catholic circles at that
time.   *State and Church* under the Catholic Emperors Constantine the Great and Theodosius the Great, were *united
but not one.*   Only the Arians Constantius and Valens had
shown Caesaropapistical tendencies.   Constantine the Great
had shown himself only as ἐπίσκοπος τῶν ἐκτος[8] and had not
once proclaimed himself as authorized (οὐ θεμιτὸν) to judge
priests or bishops.[9]   He, as well as Theodosius, held, above all
in questions of faith, to the decisions of the Bishops in synods
or councils.[10]   A law imposed by Honorius in his name and
that of Arcadius, lays down as a principle that "Whenever an
affair is a question of religion, it is for the Bishops to decide."[11]

Unfortunately Arcadius, in his dependence, allowed himself
to be led into actions which were in direct opposition to the
laws of the Empire.   In non-political, ecclesiastical and charitable affairs, the greatest influence was possessed by the young

Empress Eudoxia.

By nature Eudoxia was the direct opposite to the languid
indolence of the young Emperor.   She possessed a vivacious,
sanguine temperament.   Philostorgius even says that she
possessed "the unruly vigor of the barbarians."[12]   At any rate,
the life of the heart and the feelings was predominant in her.
This might explain the remark of Zosimus, who said that she
was influenced in the highest degree by her court ladies, even
ruled by them.[13]   Her father had been a Frank named Bauto,
one of the numerous Germans who had entered the Roman
Army, and had made his fortune there. He became a general,
and in the year 385 was raised to the highest dignity in the

Empire, the consulship, together with the eight-year-old
Arcadius, who a few years later was to raise Bauto's daughter
to the imperial throne. The official festival eulogy was given
in Milan, in the presence of Bauto and the Emperor Valentinian, by the young Augustine, the official teacher of rhetoric
in Milan, who later became the world-renowned church
teacher and bishop of Hippo.

Whether Bauto became a Christian is not known. Under
Valentinian he was the most influential man at the Roman
court. Zosimus praises especially his military ability, and,
what at that time was very significant, his integrity.[14]

It was not permitted to him to live to see the good fortune
of his daughter. He died about 388. His daughter, Eudoxia,
found a second mother in Marsa, a Goth, the widow of the
dead general Promotus.[15] For her elevation to the throne she
had to thank the cunning Eutropius. Rufinus, who had been
the real leader of the Empire in the early days of Arcadius,
would have been glad to marry his own daughter to the
Emperor. His position and his influence at Court would
thereby have been greatly strengthened, and would have been
almost impregnable. That was what his secret antagonists
feared. By a real court coup Eutropius was able to bring
their projects to nothing. He dexterously turned the attention of the young Emperor to the young and handsome
Eudoxia. The latter cannot have been an unknown personality at court. The sons of the general Promotus, in whose
family she had lived for seven years, had been the youthful
playmates of Arcadius, and so the two must have seen each
other often. The fact is, that Eutropius had his marriage
project all settled, while Rufinus still believed that his own
daughter would be the next to wear the diadem of an Augusta.

In order to let his adversaries feel the deepest smart of
defeat, Eutropius united to the disillusionment of Rufinus the
malediction of ridicule. When everything was settled, a
rumor was circulated in Constantinople that the Emperor was
thinking of being married. Actually, one day a brilliant company of court officials and court ladies came out of the gate of
the palace. They carried in public procession a splendid
purple bridal garment, a diadem and other gifts. Everyone
believed that the delegation would make its way to the palace

of Rufinus. But it went to the palace of Promotus: the chosen bride was Eudoxia, the daughter of the dead Frankish general.

Rufinus swallowed his wrath. Eutropius, on account of his success, naturally was under the protection of the new Empress. The all-powerful minister was powerless against the resourceful eunuch. On the 27th of April, 395, the marriage of Eudoxia and the Emperor was celebrated, and a few months later, on the 27th of November, Rufinus was murdered by soldiers of the Gothic leader Gainas, before the Emperor's eyes. It was said that it was the revenge of Stilicho, the highest minister and the army leader of Honorius, and it was also whispered that Eutropius had had a hand in it. At any rate, Eutropius became heir to the power and influence of Rufinus.

Eudoxia was not without good qualities. At the side of an upright man, she might have become a distinguished empress. But natural strength of character was lacking in her, and as far as guiding the Emperor was concerned, she was as yet too young, too inexperienced and, above all, too feminine. Her credulity, and her hasty passionate disposition were soon made the most of, by all sorts of tale-bearing and insinuations. Moreover the Empress was religiously inclined.

To the new Archbishop she brought sincere kind feelings and frank veneration. She was ready to assist, as far as she could, his efforts on behalf of religion. She showed this in connection with the night processions, for which she supplied the silver candlesticks; and she also allowed her chamberlain, the eunuch Brison, to supervise the practice and the conducting of the choir.[16] Neither did she shrink from personal participation in the religious celebrations. It happened one day that the relics of the holy martyr Phocas were transferred from Pontus to Constantinople. The Imperial Majesties appeared at the solemn reception of the relics, and Chrysostom preached the festival sermon.[17] The day must have been a Saturday, because on the next day the Divine Liturgy was again celebrated, with a sermon, in which the preacher mentioned the events of the previous day with praise.[18] The transfer of the martyr's relics took the form of a solemn procession to the Martyrium of the Apostle Thomas, which was nine miles from the city, in the suburb of Drypia. The relics had first been laid in the Cathedral. From thence they were borne in a night procession, with torchlights, to the Martyrium of St. Thomas.

What was new and extraordinary on that occasion was, that the Empress Eudoxia herself appeared, in the Cathedral, and bore the relics in her own hands through the city and accompanied them to Drypia, in the midst of an immense procession of courtiers and state officials, of monks, priests and virgins, men and women of the people, rich and poor, old and young, people of the city, and strangers. Everyone wished to be present at the unusual spectacle, in which hymns were heard sung in various languages.[19]

Chrysostom himself, at the head of his clergy, led the procession, and then, as day came on, gave the festival sermon, in the Martyrium or in front of it; the sermon, with almost Oriental exaggeration, began: "What shall I say, of what shall I speak? I am soaring, I am out of myself . . . I am flying and dancing, and I feel myself lifted on high, and am drunk with spiritual joy. Indeed, what shall I say, of what shall I speak? Of the power of the martyrs, the participation of the city, the zeal of the Empress . . . of the multitude of monks, the choir of virgins, the crowds of priests, of people of the world, of slaves and free men. . . . Even women, more delicate than wax, have rivaled the strongest men, and have traveled this long way on foot. And even she who wears the diadem and the purple, did not wish to abandon the relics along the road, but served the holy things like a handmaid, and carried the shrine and the veil which covered it. . . . Therefore the Christ-loving Empress has followed the relics, and has touched them again and again, in order to receive the blessing for herself, and also has taught all others to partake of this splendid spiritual wealth, and to draw from the fountain which flows forever and never dries up. For as the water flows from a fountain . . . so flows out the grace of God, which is bound up in the relics, and dwells within the saint, for those who, believing, long after it. It flows from the soul to the body, from the body to the garments, from the garments to the shoes, from the shoes to the shadow.[20]

"Therefore I am dancing and flying for joy, because for you today the solitude has become a city, and the city a solitude,

and it is allowed for us to behold the entire riches of the
Church.   It seems like a sea of fire, when one sees the number-
less burning torches which are approaching this Martyrium.
And for this purpose the fiery torches of love and inspiration
have burned in your souls.   The moon and the stars are
shining over us, but down below here are shining the stars of
faith, and the Empress shines brighter than the moon!

"What shall we most admire in her? Her ardent faith, or
her modesty and humility?   She has indeed laid aside all the
evidences of her imperial dignity, the diadem, the purple
garments, and every pomp, and has so mingled with the people
that one can scarcely notice the difference.   She has followed
the relics all the way, without wearying, without falling
behind.   Therefore we praise her, and not only we, but all
coming generations.   For the whole world will learn what has
happened today.

"The Emperor has been kept at home today, through the
prudence of the Empress, lest his household and bodyguard
encroach upon the procession and the celebration.   But he
will come tomorrow, when the Divine Liturgy will be celebrated again.   So the feast will last another day.   And as we
today, with the whole City, have seen the Empress, so tomorrow we will see the Emperor with his host.   And we will
beseech for them from the holy Martyrs: long life, a happy
old age, children and children's children, but, before all, that
they may reign and rule some day in Eternity with the only
begotten Son of God! "

If one had never heard any other expressions but these from
Chrysostom, one might believe that he had before him a standard example of late Byzantine rhetoric and flattery.   And yet
it was only the echo of a soul, which through the sight of a
nocturnal procession, and of the Empress, had been uplifted
by honest and glowing enthusiasm.

But the prayer which he had invited the people to offer for
the Imperial Majesties was unfortunately not granted fulfilment.   Everything turned out very differently from what these
first honeymoon months led him to expect.

The next day the Emperor really came, with his whole
garrison.   Again Chrysostom gave the feast-day sermon.
However, this time he did not find the opportunity for such

a eulogy as he had given the day before, for the military piety distinguished itself on that occasion only by its brevity: the Emperor and his guard departed before the beginning of the sermon and of the Divine Liturgy.[21] Therefore Chrysostom spoke on the Fall of Man, Cain's murder of Abel, and the resurrection of the dead.

But it would be a great error to assume, from these songs of praise, that Chrysostom was a Byzantine courtier and flatterer. This sort of praise was the simplest and most moderate which was bestowed on rulers in public speeches at that time. One might compare with it the high-flown eulogies of a Libanius, a Themistius or other contemporaries, on their imperial lords. On the other hand, Chrysostom pleaded for the personal position of the Emperor, for the relation of the principles of worldly authority to religious authority, and his sermons left nothing to be desired in clarity and strength. "The Emperor," he once said to the people of Antioch, who were trembling before the judgment of Theodosius, "the Emperor is a man as we are, with the same feelings that we have, and he has the same soul. And because he is a man, he first gives way to anger and then afterwards he atones for his sins.[22] Indeed, the Emperor is our fellow-servant before God."[23]

Still more, he compares the dignity and position of a Bishop with that of an Emperor, and says: "The Bishop is also a ruler, and indeed more worthy of honor than an Emperor. *For the holy laws of the spiritual authority of the Bishop render the person of the Emperor subject to him.*"[24]

In another sermon he expressed himself as follows: "If you wish to understand the difference between a king and a priest, think of the difference in the power which is entrusted to each, and you will realize that the priest stands much higher than the king. If the throne of the king instils respect in us on account of the diamonds and the gold with which it is adorned, nevertheless the king has received power only over *earthly* things, and further than that his arm does not reach. But on the other hand, the throne of the priesthood is erected in heaven, and to him is entrusted the things that are of heaven. And what the priest judges on earth, is confirmed by God in heaven. *Therefore has God subjugated even the person of the king to the power of the priest*, in order to teach us this power is greater than that. For that which is less, receives the blessing from that which stands higher."

" It is the duty of a king to rule in earthly things; however, the authority of the priesthood comes from heaven (see Matthew 18, 18). To the king is entrusted what is of this world below; but to me, the priest, those of heaven. *Bodies* are entrusted to the king, *souls* to the priest. The king absolves from taxes; the priest absolves from sins. The king uses force, the priest only admonishes. The one operates through power, the other through persuasion. The king has material weapons, the priest spiritual. The former fights against barbarians, the latter against demons. Therefore the empire (power) of the priest stands higher."[25]

That was clearly and distinctly spoken. The ancient world had never heard such a speech from the mouth of its pagan priests. They made their current ruler the Pontifex Maximus, the chief priest, and after his death he was placed among the gods, even though in life he had been an object of horror. Now Christendom came in, and brought a different language. It announced the equality of all men, before a common higher power, before God, the King of kings, and gave to men, in the spiritual authority of church leaders, a treasury of freedom for their consciences. The " imperial gods " vanished, and their earthly power at least was forced out of the sphere of religious consciences. With this, not the separation but the diversity of both spheres of influence was established, and at the same time it was emphasized, that even the person of the Emperor was not exempt from the authority of the Church, in religious affairs.

Now Chrysostom was a man who not merely recognized principles, but followed them. After he himself had been made bishop, and in the imperial city at that, he had the opportunity to give practical proof of the principles which he had announced as a priest, and which were also the principles of the Church. And he did so. He expanded his pastoral solicitude to include the court and the powerful ones of the earth; he admonished and warned, in the interest of souls. The victory was not to his side, but the greatness of his character was not thereby lessened.

FOOTNOTES

1. Gibbon, Decline and Fall of the Roman Empire (ed. Bury, London 1897). 3, 216.

2. Güldenpenning, Geschichte des oströmischen Reiches 3.

3. Decline and fall . . . 3, 369 (ed. Bury).

4. Zosimus, Historia 5, 12 and 24 (ed. Mendelssohn 229 and 245); George Cedrenus, Histor. Comp. (121, 624).

5. Chronographia 13 (97, 520).

6. Historia Ecclesiastica 11, 3 (65, 597).

7. Cf. Rauschen, Jahrbücher 454 f. Cod. Theod. VI, 226, 1, 10; 7; 11; XVI, 5, 34, 35. (ed. Mommsen-Meyer I, 866-67).

8. Eusebius, Vita Constantini 4, 24 (20, 1172).

9. Sozomen 1, 17 (67, 913 A).

10. Eusebius, Vita Constantini 3, 17 (20, 1073); Socrates 1, 9 (67, 89); Sozomen 7, 9 (67, 1437A); Cod. Theodos. Constit. Sirm. ed. Mommsen 910.

11. Codex Theodos. 16, 11, 1 (ed. Mommsen 905).

12. HE 11, 6 (65, 600).

13. Hist. 5, 24 (ed. Mendelssohn 245).

14. Hist. 4, 33 (ed. Mendelssohn 187).

15. The presumption that Marsa herself was a Goth is almost made a certainty by the fact that Promotus gave one of his estates to the Gothic monks for a monastery. But while the foundress was one of the most bitter enemies of the Archbishop, still these brave Germans held with the firmest fidelity to Chrysostom, even after his banishment. See Chrysostom, Letter 207 (52, 726).

16. Socrates 6, 8 (67, 689).

17. 50, 699-706.

18. The Homily, if genuine, can only have been issued in the early days of Chrysostom's bishopric, and not as Montfaucon says, at the end of 403 or the beginning of 404. The persecution which the speaker mentions was not instigated by the Emperor and Empress, but by the heretics (Arians).

19. Also after the introduction to the sermon, which Chrysostom preached in the Martyrium of St. Thomas (63, 468 and 472).

20. An allusion to the healing of the sick by the mere touch of the clothing, shoes, or even the shadows of Jesus and the Apostles. See Acts 19, 12 and 5, 15; cf. 3 Kings 19, 19, and Daniel 3, 94; 4 Kings 13, 21.

21. Hom. 3 Title (63, 473). Codex 211 of the National Library at Athens contains, with the above-mentioned sermon, a miniature which represents the Emperor, sketched before the pictures of the

three martyrs whose relics had been translated the day before. See A. N. Grebar, Miniatures grecques-orientales II: Un manuscrit des homélies de St. Jean Chrysostome . . . (Prague 1932) 259-97, n. 13, pl. XXI, 2. (a. An. Boll. 51 (1933) 148.

22. Hom. 4, 2 ad pop. Antiochenum (49, 62).

23. Hom. 7, 2 ad pop. Ant. (col. 93).

24. Hom. 3, 2 ad pop. Ant. (49, 50).

25. Hom. 4, 4-5 in: Vidi Dominum (56, 126). Here Chrysostom took this from the Old Testament priesthood; but he made the application to the new. Cf. Hom. 2, 4 de Anna (54, 648) and Hom. 8, 3 in Act. Ap. (60, 74). In a similar sense Hosius of Cordova had also written to the Emperor Constantine: " Do not mix in church affairs, and do not make any regulations for us about them. Rather obey us in these affairs. God has given you the kingship, and has entrusted the Church to us." (St. Athanasius, Hist. Arianorum 44 (25, 745 D).

CHAPTER V

CHRYSOSTOM AND EUTROPIUS

THE minister and chamberlain Eutropius was no doubt a very difficult problem. He had made Chrysostom bishop, and according to his feelings and expectations, the new chief shepherd should show him some gratitude. This would surely not have been difficult for him, if Eutropius himself had not made it so by his handling of affairs; he made things very difficult for Chrysostom. The possession of the greatest power in the Empire had gone to the head of the formerly despised eunuch, and made him dizzy. He was not the man of character whom the memory of his earlier low state might have made modest and unassuming, and the knowledge and experience of suffering and misfortune in a subordinate position, and among simple people, might have made just and sympathetic toward those who had not had the good fortune or the opportunity to rise to such splendor.

Eutropius was not that man. The intelligent, but cunning and avaricious courtier possessed neither the far-seeing eye of the great statesman nor the noble and selfless character of a great man; he was and remained basically only a successful diplomatic actor, one of those numerous political adventurers with whom every means is good which, regardless of any crime committed, enables them to attain their end—to get a political opponent or rival out of the way; and they are not able to accomplish any great work, because they are only intriguers and not natural leaders. The man actually had a life destiny behind him, which somewhat explains his shady side, and gives him a claim to extenuating circumstances in judgment.

Eutropius came originally from the eastern region of the Empire, perhaps from Armenia. At any rate, a very difficult youth and young manhood were his lot, which he must have found very hard to bear because of his unusual intellectual gifts. In his earliest years he was sold as a slave, and emascu-

lated, possibly as a victim to the disturbances of war. He was
passed from hand to hand like a piece of merchandise. At last
he managed to attain freedom. For a long time he earned his
living in the business of matchmaking. Perhaps this noble
calling brought him into contact with the court circles. It is
a fact that in the time of Theodosius he appeared settled at
the court, although no one could say how or through whom he
had come there. There one day the general Abundantius
became aware of this capable man, and Eutropius had him to
thank for being elevated to the rank and dignity of imperial
chamberlain, in return for certain excellent services. At that
time he was already well on in years. He astonished people
by his large bald head and his wrinkled, shriveled countenance. After he had had to labor as a slave in the lowest walks
of life, the sun of good fortune began shining out of the dark
clouds of the past, and then, after a short period of brilliance,
sank again suddenly and forever.

Eutropius had soon learned how to draw the attention of
Theodosius to himself by his intellectual superiority, and to
gain his trust by his readiness for any court service. When
Theodosius had to go to war against the rebellious Eugenius,
he sent the chamberlain to Egypt, to ask the hermit John,
who was rumored to have prophetic powers, what the outcome
of the war was to be. However, Theodosius was too much of
a soldier and field general, and favored generals and officers
too exclusively, for Eutropius to have been able to gain very
much influence over him. Moreover, the not less distinguished Rufinus stood in his way, a noble by birth, superior
to Eutropius in education and in mental ability. Rufinus had
been placed by Theodosius the Great at the side of his son
Arcadius as a sort of imperial chancellor. But Rufinus' attention was directed too much toward Stilicho for him to have
the time to look very closely at the crafty Eutropius. He had
to discover too late, and to his sorrow, that the sly chamberlain was next in line for his position of power. Only the
grateful favor of the new Empress prevented him from taking
bitter vengeance on the destroyer of his life's most daring
dream. Eutropius, as a reward for his work, was made high
chamberlain or chief steward of the court.

He now knew well that there was only one thing for him:

either to destroy Rufinus or be destroyed by him. It is therefore not incredible that he had long ago initiated a plan for murder, which was carried out when the soldiers of Gainas, on the orders of Stilicho, struck down the unfortunate Rufinus in the year 395 before the eyes of the Emperor. At any rate, for Eutropius, the moment had now come, when he had reached the apex of his life, his influence and his power. He was, says Philostorgius, like a father to the Emperor, since he had no children of his own.[1]

Unfortunately he did not understand how to use his power well. From the beginning he showed the attributes of an upstart, which had made Rufinus so much hated. Avarice and love of power took possession of him, and soon undermined his position.

As chief chamberlain of the court, patrician and first counselor, one might almost say guardian,[2] of the Emperor and therefore of the Empire, Eutropius ruled a brilliant court for himself. He gave great feasts and banquets for his friends; he arranged great spectacles at the circus, and plays at the theater, for the people.[3] Besides, he kept at his own expense a multitude of spies and base underlings, who were ready to do any deed of shame at his nod. For all this he needed money, very much money. For at that time money also meant power.

To find the necessary money, Eutropius was not at all fastidious as to the means. Even at the beginning he had the goods and immense possessions of his predecessor Rufinus seized by imperial edict, and then brought the greater part of them into his own possession. He sold his protection and the highest offices for money,[4] or brought into influential positions only those who would yield to him absolutely. On the other hand, if he found or suspected a rival, or an antagonist, Eutropius had no consideration for him. The military party was especially disliked by this upstart. His first benefactor, the man who had first obtained a position for him at court, and who perhaps unwillingly endured his present overlordship, Abundantius, who had been "earlier crowned by fame as a general and consul,"[5] he exiled to Sidon in the year 396, and from there sent him to Pityus in Colchis, where he ended his days in solitude.[6] In the same year Eutropius accomplished the fall of another highly placed general, who had previously been Consul and Magister militum, Timasius. Under Theodosius this valiant man had held the high command over the infantry in the war against Maximus. Unfortunately he was not only bold in fighting but also in drinking.[7] It is quite possible that his tongue became loose while drinking, and that he made remarks about the court and the government, which at that time was much more dangerous than it is today. The change of affairs since the time of the great Theodosius cannot have been pleasing to an old soldier like Timasius. Eutropius had him accused of high treason by a certain Bargo, who was Timasius' own servant. He himself sat in the court which condemned Timasius. The latter was sent into exile, to the punishment colony in the great oasis of Egypt. He was never heard of again.[8] Sozomen says he perished on the way to the desert.[9]

A specially odious touch in the picture of Eutropius is his persecution of Pentadia, the wife of the unfortunate Timasius. The anguished woman, who was in fear of her life, fled to the altar of a church, where the right of asylum protected her by law. This right of asylum was especially recognized and confirmed by Theodosius in a law of the 18th of October, 392.[10] Only state criminals were excluded from it. But in order to close this way of escape to his future victims, Eutropius requested Arcadius to pass a law by which those guilty of high treason and other criminals were to be excluded from the right of asylum.[11] In this way, every one of his political opponents was left defenseless. Pentadia spent her last days as a deaconess of the episcopal cathedral, at the side of Olympias and Procla, and belonged, together with these, to the number of Chrysostom's truest adherents.[12]

In order to protect himself from possible attacks, Eutropius in the year 397 had the law against lese-majeste, with its death penalty, extended to all those who were accessory to a murder, or to a plot against an imperial adviser, senator or servant. Even their sons were to be disinherited and dishonored.[13] This brought on such a flood of denunciations that in the same year, on the 8th of November, it had to be followed by a restriction, in which slaves were excluded from the right of denunciation.[14] Moreover, Eutropius gladly utilized such talebearing for the sake of a welcome opportunity for the extortion of money. He himself had a whole network of spies at work for him.[15] In spite of all these precautions of a bad conscience, Eutropius could not escape his fate.

So that was the man whom Eudoxia had to thank for her dignity as Empress, and Chrysostom for his elevation to the most influential episcopal see in the Empire, and who so often, in his character of chief chamberlain, had led him in to the Emperor, the first time and each time thereafter, when he came to audience. Should and could the Bishop be silent on the subject of the activities of the minister? No! Chrysostom was too manly a character for that. He had not asked to be made Archbishop and Patriarch. But since he had been, he would do his duty. So he went to the minister and made a remonstrance.

"Why do you accumulate such riches?" he asked. "Wealth is like an unfaithful slave. What is the use of spending such immense sums of money on the circus and the theater? The beneficiaries of it are but insecure friends. Why do you restrict the rights of the Church? You are only hurling yourself into the abyss!"[16] Eutropius received these admonitions very ungraciously, and defended himself in a way that was very damaging to the Bishop. Chrysostom did not allow himself to be frightened. He made the same representations to him repeatedly. He said to him, "I will prove a better friend to you than all your flatterers and admirers. Better the wounds of a friend than the kisses of an enemy."[17] Eutropius paid no attention to him.

When St. Gregory of Nazianzus departed from Constantinople, he said bitterly: "They only want an orator, not a priest!"[18]

FOOTNOTES

1. Historia Ecclesiastica 11, 4 (65, 597).
2. Zosimus, Historia 5, 12 (ed. Mendelssohn 229) says that he led the Emperor around like a sheep. Cf. Palladius 5 (47, 19).
3. Chrysostom, Hom. in Eutropium 1 (51, 391-396).
4. Güldenpenning 72 ff.
5. Zosimus 5, 10 (ed. Mendelssohn 228).

6. Cf. Rauschen, Jahrbücher 390; Güldenpenning 75 f.

7. Zosimus 4, 49 (ed. c. 206).

8. St. Jerome, letter 60, 10 of the year 396 (ML 22, 606); Asterius, Hom. 4 in festum Kalend (40, 224); Zosimus 5, 9 (ed. M. 226-27).

9. Sozomen 8, 7 (67, 1533).

10. Codex Theodos. 9, 44, 1 (ed. Mommsen 518).

11. Cod. Theod. 9, 45, 3 (ed. Mommsen 519) and 45, 1 (*ibid*). Socrates 6, 5 (67, 673) and Sozomen 8, 7 (*ibid.* 1533) surely go too far when they claim that the Church's right of asylum was denied to him. Such an encroachment on the rights of the Church would surely have aroused a much stronger echo. Cf. Isidore of Pelusium, Epist. I, 174 (78, 296 f.). Concerning the origin of the right of sanctuary, see E. Hermann, S.J., Zum Asylrecht in byzant. Reich, in: Or. Chr. Per. 1 (1935) 214-38. NB: Eutropius only limited this right: he did not abolish it.

12. Palladius 10 (47, 35). Chrysostom wrote him several letters from exile; Nos. 104 and 185 (52, 663 and 716).

13. Cod. Theodos. 9, 14, 3 (ed. Mommsen 458).

14. Cod. Theod. 9, 6, 3 (*ibid.* 444-45).

15. Zosimus 5, 10 (ed. M. 228); cf. Güldenpenning 74.

16. Hom. in Eutropium 1 (51, 392).

17. *Ibid.* 1.

18. Oratio 42, 24 (36, 488B).

CHAPTER VI

CONSTANTINOPLE: CHURCHES AND MARTYRIA

So the three most distinguished sheep of the flock were not those who caused the least care and worry to the new shepherd. But also the remainder of the flock imposed upon the new bishop a great and unusually difficult burden, as much by their numbers as by their composition. Constantinople, toward the end of the fourth century, numbered about half a million inhabitants; the population was about the same as that of Antioch.

The overwhelming majority of the people of the city were Christians and Catholics, though of course they had not been so for very long. Arianism had been supreme there for forty years, from 339 to 379. In all this time the Catholics did not possess a single church. When they chose a bishop of their own in 370, Valens had him expelled from the city at once. "No church, no bishop, no Divine Liturgy"[1] was always the Catholics' complaint. When after the death of Valens the Emperor Gratian called Gregory of Nazianzus to be the provisional episcopal steward of Constantinople, the Catholics had as a chapel only a room in a private house. The capital city had first to be reconquered for the Catholic faith.

But Gregory possessed both the courage and the confidence of a conqueror, and an Apostle. He purposely gave his chapel the name of Anastasia; for the Catholic Church was now to celebrate its Easter, that is, its resurrection. And so it came about. Gregory began his splendid sermons, and soon the chapel was too small. He implanted more Catholic spirit and Catholic memories in the hearts of the people. The Arians were very angry over the ever greater success of the Catholic Bishop, and did their best to counteract his influence; indeed, they would have had him expelled from the city if it could possibly be accomplished. When scorn and derision had no effect, they had recourse to force. They made several attempts to murder Gregory, which fortunately failed. Once, when he was conducting divine service in the middle of the night, they fell upon the assembly, wounded many of those present, and hurled the Host and the chalice to the floor.

That happened eighteen years before the entrance of Chrysostom into Constantinople. In the meantime, under the Emperor Theodosius, Arianism of course lost not only its political power but most of its adherents. To the mass of the people, the metaphysical controversies of their clergy and bishops remained only a mystery, and they adjusted themselves to the new conditions without difficulty. However, a moderately small group still held obstinately to their Arianism. Their bishop, whose name was Dorotheus, was almost a hundred years old, and came, like Chrysostom, from Antioch.[2] They were no more allowed to have churches, at least within the circuit of the city walls, as was the case with other heretics. They endured the change of fortune only with suppressed wrath. When in the year 388, ten years earlier, a report had spread in Constantinople that the Emperor Theodosius had been struck down by the pretender to the throne, Maximus, they had collected in a mob and had set the palace of Bishop Nectarius on fire.[3] When Chrysostom came to Constantinople, the new building was not yet completed.

Besides, Chrysostom found in his diocese another bishop, Sisinnius, the spiritual head of the Novatians. They were the only ones whom Theodosius had continued to tolerate, because they had admitted the Nicaean "Homoousios." They said that they differed from the Catholics only in a stricter way of life. Of course it was a source of scandal that Sisinnius, in spite of his alleged asceticism, visited the baths twice a day. When he was asked why he took a warm bath twice a day, he promptly answered "because to go three times a day was not good for him."[4]

The number of pagans seems to have been significant. Especially the Germanic peoples, who entered into the service of the Empire, had brought numerous pagan elements into the army and the city. This meant that very much troublesome work must be accomplished before all these separate elements could be bound together into a religious unity,

before a shepherd and a flock could exist in this great
metropolis.[4a]

For other reasons also, the care of souls in the then aspiring
Constantinople presented many difficulties. The people were
overwhelmingly Greek in nationality and language. At the
same time, there also existed members of other nationalities
of the Roman Empire and neighboring lands. The largest
fraction of foreign colonials at the end of the fourth century
seems to have been formed by the Germanic peoples, and
among them especially the Goths, who just at that time, at the
beginning of the folk migrations, had been driven from their
settlements by the Huns. Some of them had established themselves by force within the jurisdiction of the Eastern Roman
Empire, and some of them had managed to establish themselves there in a friendly way, as settlers and colonists.

Besides these, the Latin Romans also began to appear in
larger numbers from the Western Empire. Above all, the
important commercial routes of the Bosphorus and the Dardanelles had brought merchants and sailors from all nations and
countries into this great center of trade, in which merchants
from Marseilles, Cordova and Rome met with those of Greece,
Egypt and Syria, Armenia and Persia. A brilliant medley of
nationalities and costumes could be observed in the streets;
the language and idioms of all Europe and half the Eastern
lands could be heard there. Quite naturally, Constantinople
presented at that time the picture of a modern residential and
mercantile metropolis, with all its aspects of light and shade.

Much wealth and comfort flowed into the city through the
narrow seas; but also luxury, prodigality, profits, avarice, and
hard-heartedness were universal, as well as deep poverty,
hunger, and the misery of a great city. Frivolous fops, and
gold-bedecked women in silken garments, went through the
streets riding or lying in their litters, never noticing the poor
woman who brought her last obol to market to buy bread or
vegetables; never noticing the ragged children in their dirty
tatters, playing in filthy alleys. There could be seen great
marble palaces, adorned with costly furnishings and precious
works of art, attended and guarded by an army of servants and
slaves, and surrounded by luxuriant green parklands; but also
there were wretched huts, and four or five-story tenements,

which gathered in themselves whatever a great metropolis
could offer of want and poverty and misery, of sorrowful
patience and bestial degradation.   There could be found great
public baths, open to everyone for a small fee; great market
halls, warehouses and bazaars, where everything was to be had,
and taverns and dens which were the gathering places of those
whose lives avoid the light.

Whosoever sought his legal rights, might go into the basilicas, adorned with pillars; for the pious and the orthodox,
splendid churches and houses of God stood open.   Many
schools, from those which taught simply the alphabet, to the
" University," taught all the knowledge and skill which the
world of the fourth century valued, to the youth who longed
to learn it.

Such was Constantinople at the end of the fourth century,
scarcely seventy years after its founding by the first Christian
Emperor.   Over this cosmopolitan city the priest of Antioch
was placed as bishop and shepherd of souls.   How would he be
able to find his way in the midst of this chaos, by the purity
of his ideals, his rectitude of character, his sincere nature?
How accomplish with success his task for the best good of souls
and for the Christian religion?   He, who was so earnest about
the practical proof of moral precepts, he who had been so
accustomed to reproving openly the crimes and errors of the
great and the mighty, the rich and the comfortable, as well as
those of the poor; he who in the hour of danger intervened for
the downtrodden and violated rights, and for persecuted innocence, who never bowed himself before the golden calf, and
who was not downcast before the dark looks of potentates
wounded in their dignity and their omnipotence.   Chrysostom was a soul which must pursue a straight way.   Falseness,
hypocrisy, dissimulation, were things which would have been
impossible to him.   To be silent and inactive, when duty
called for speech and action, was not his nature.   He was not
an episcopal courtier and would never become one.   However,
there was nothing defiant, nothing haughty, in his manner or
appearance.   He knew how to combine strength of character
and sincerity with discreet tact and prudence, and had more
than once given proof of it.   He sought no quarrels; but
neither could he stand aside at the price of his conscience.

Certainly many well-intentioned people asked themselves how the new bishop would be able to steer the bark of the Church through the ever stormy waters of the human sea of the great city, and how he could come through the reefs and shoals of the various interests, of politics and of the court. Chrysostom must also have asked himself these questions, most earnestly.

To conclude from the number of churches, Constantinople must have had a pious population. The so-called "Great Church," dedicated to Hagia Sophia, the Holy Wisdom of Christ,[5] surpassed all the others in size and splendor, and the Church of the Apostles was next. The latter had been built, or at least begun, by the Emperor Constantine, and was considered first of all an imperial mausoleum. But the oldest church in Byzantium had been in existence before Emperor Constantine. It must have been scarcely larger than a bedchamber or a chapel. After the proclamation of religious peace, Constantine enlarged this little church into a splendid basilica,[6] and consecrated it as the "Eirene", so that as the "church of peace" it might keep alive the memory of his deeds and all his victories. For about thirty years this "church of peace" was at the same time the Bishop's church of Constantinople. In the year 381, the second ecumenical council of Constantinople was held in it.[7] A sermon which Chrysostom preached in this old church still survives.[8] In the Victory riots of 532 the church was burned down; and in the form in which Justinian rebuilt it, it now awaits, as a Turkish Army museum in the first court of the Seraglio,[9] a future which it is to be hoped will be more fortunate.

On account of the rapid development of Constantinople, the Church of Peace soon became too small. So the Emperor Constantius built near the old church his new "Great Church," which was consecrated on the 15th of February, 360. So Constantinople, like Antioch, had an "old" and a so-called "great" church. The latter, the Hagia Sophia, lay, like the later Hagia Sophia, on the southwestern slope of the highest summit of the city, in a northwest-southeast line.[10] The customary atrium and narthex stood before the entrance to the church, while on the northeast side was a forecourt bordered by columns, and containing the fountain or great basin. This church was also built in the basilican style, and covered by a wooden roof.[11] The baptistery and sacristy (Σκευοφυλάκιον) were also attached to the church. Above the altar hung "an eternal light."

This "Megale" was the special episcopal cathedral of Constantinople. Chrysostom was consecrated Bishop in it, he preached most of his sermons in it,[12] and the Divine Liturgy was held there.

Directly beside the Cathedral, probably toward the south, stood the episcopal palace, from which Chrysostom could come to the church without having to go outdoors.[13] It was separated by only one street from the splendid Senate building.[14] At some distance from this great church, in the eleventh region of the city, was situated the great Church of the Apostles, which far surpassed the Cathedral, not in size, but in splendor and magnificence. It stood the fourth and highest of the seven elevations of the city. The Emperor had had this "Martyrium" erected to the Apostles, with the as yet unspoken design of finding his own eternal rest beside the tombs of the holy Apostles.[15]

Eusebius, in his Life of Constantine, gives a short description of this building. The unusual height of the church is astonishing. The walls, from top to bottom, were covered by a shimmering layer of marble slabs. The ceiling, divided into ornamental sections, was entirely overlaid with glittering gold, and the roof was covered with tiles of gilded bronze; these glittered from afar in the sunlight and formed a lattice-work pattern. Around the church lay a great court, open to the sky. Porticoes ran around this broad court to form a square, in the middle of which the church stood. Buildings with colonnades, fountains and promenades extended around the porticoes, together with numerous other buildings, arranged as shelters for the convenience of the guardians of the square.[16]

At any rate, this original Church of the Apostles was a basilica, as were all of Constantine's buildings. The churches of Constantinople possessed at that time their own clergy, and performed the Divine Liturgy regularly.[17] Constantine the Great had expressly stipulated that a permanent altar should be placed in the Church of the Apostles.[18] The Emperor Constantius completed the church, and probably also enlarged it. In the year 360 its solemn consecration was celebrated, on which occasion the relics of the Apostles St. Andrew, St. Luke and St. Timothy were deposited there.[19] The Emperor Constantius, and later Theodosius the Great, found their last resting places there. On the anniversary of the death of Theodosius, Chrysostom gave a short sermon there, after two bishops had spoken before him.[20]

The little Anastasia-church, which originally was only a small chapel, was enlarged later. Chrysostom preached several times there.[21] It served for the Divine Liturgy until the year 1204, when it was half destroyed in the conquest of Constantinople by the Venetians. In the year 1571 the Turks built on its ruins the Mosque of Mehmet Sokoli Djami.[22]

Eusebius writes, in his Life of Constantius, that the Emperor had built several places of prayer, and great, splendid Martyria, in Constantinople, such as those of St. Mokion, St. Acacius, St. Agathonicus, St. Michael the Archangel, and the Apostle St. John.[23] It is certain that in the time of Chrysostom a Church of St. Paul was already in existence; this church the new Archbishop granted to the Catholic Goths for divine worship.[24]

Chrysostom also once preached in the Martyrium which stood ἐν τῇ παλαιᾷ πέτρᾳ.[25]

Under the Emperor Constantius, and especially Theodosius the Great, there was great activity in church building in Constantinople. The famous pilgrim Aetheria was able to visit " the individual churches " and " very many Martyria " in the city in the year 400.[26] According to the Auctor descriptionis Urbis, who probably lived under the Emperor Honorius, there were about fourteen churches and martyria in the city toward the end of the fourth century.[27]

The Imperial court possessed a special palace chapel with its own priests. This place was occupied in Chrysostom's time by a certain Helladius, who proved to be a true and loyal friend to his bishop in time of need, and preferred to give up his distinguished place rather than forsake and betray the cause of Chrysostom.[28]

FOOTNOTES

1. Hefele KG 2, 1.
2. Socrates 7, 6 (67, 748); Sozomen 7, 14 (1452).
3. Socrates 5, 13 (600); Sozomen 7, 14 (1452); St. Ambrose, epist. 40, 13 (ML 16, 1106).
4. Socrates 6, 22 (728); Sozomen 8, 1 (1512 B); see Zellinger, Bad und Bäder 17.

4a. More than 100 years later, under Justinian, the Metropolitan John of Ephesus alone converted 80,000 pagans in the four provinces; Asia, Caria, Phrygia, and Lydia. See Gelzer, Pergamon unter Byzantinern und Osmanen, in: Phil. Hist. Abhandl. d. K. preuss. Ak. d. W. 1903, Abhandl. 2.

5. There was probably no St. Sophia. A.M. Schneider, Die vorjustinianische Sophienkirche, in: Byz. Ztschr. 36 (1936) 77.

6. Ebersolt and Thiers, Les églises de Constantinople, 64; Millingen, Byzantine Churches 84 ff.

7. Vita S. Stephani jun. (100, 1144 CD).
8. MG 63, 485.
9. Grosvenor 2, 474. Ebersolt and Thiers, Les Églises de Constantinople, p. 55-72.

10. So according to Antoniades 1, 4, 69 and 73 ff.; Lethaby gives the contrary opinion on pages 9 to 18.

11. Antoniades gives a reconstructed ground plan and elevation of this basilica, 1, 7 and 8-9.

12. This is expressly noted by some. The present Hagia Sophia, dating from the time of Justinian, covers a far greater area than the old "Great Church" under Chrysostom; see Antoniades 1, 33-34.

13. Cf. Palladius 10 (47, 35). The episcopal palace in which Chrysostom lived, and in which he probably did the greatest part of his work, was burned down, apparently not with the church in 404, but at the time of the so-called Victory riots in 532 (Antoniades 3, 184); cf. Ch. 42.

14. Antoniades, 1, 64.

15. It appears from Eusebius, Vita Constantini 4, 60 (20, 1209) that Constantius' plan to have himself buried here did not become known until his death; so he could not have had a mausoleum built there, separate from the Martyrium, because if he did, his project would have been known about from the beginning.

16. Eusebius, Vita Constantini 4, 58-60 (20, 1209-12) and Heisenberg, Grabeskirche und Apostelkirche 2, 98-99. O. Wulff, Die sieben Wunder von Byzanz *loc. cit.* 328; R. Egger, Die Be-

gräbnisstätte des Kaisers Konstantin *loc. cit.* 212 ff.; Heisenberg, Grabeskirche und Apostelkirche 2,100 f.; Th. Reinach, Commentaire *loc. cit.* 91-94.

17. So a certain Paulus appears as "Deacon at the Anastasia Church" (Palladius 20 = 47, 72); Philippus was military chaplain (*ibid.*); Helladius is court chaplain, that is, priest of the imperial palace (*ibid.*). The same is shown by Palladius, Dial. 2 (ed. Norton, p. 9, 28-29).

18. Cf. Millingen 24.

19. Concerning the fate of the Church of the Apostles, see Ch. 38.

20. MG 63, 491. Obviously, Hom. 10 (63, 515) was also given in the Church of the Apostles. Homily 11 may have been given long before in Antioch.

21. MG 63, 477 and 493. The pastor of this church, Paul, was a faithful adherent of Chrysostom, and lived later in exile in Jerusalem. (Pall. Dial. 20; ed. Norton 128, 9).

22. Grosvenor 2, 417, errs, when he called the Anastasia Church the national church of the Goths; according to Chrysostom Hom. 8 (63, 499) this was the Church of St. Paul.

23. Book 3, 48 (20, 1108); cf. Πάτρια (ed. Preger) 140, 10 and 214, 2; Heisenberg, Grabeskirche und Apostelkirche 2, 10. Concerning the martyrs Sts. Mokion and Acacius, see An. Boll. 31 (1912) 163-176 and 228-29.

24. 63, 499. Cf. P. Batiffol, De quelques hom. de S. Jean Chrys. et de la version gothique des Ecritures, in: Revue bibl. 8 (1899) 566-72.

25. 63, 461.

26. No. 24 (ed. Pomialowsky 38; ed. Geyer 70).

27. Du Cange, Constantinop. christ. 3, 2; from K. Lübeck, Zur ältesten Verehrung des heiligen Michael in Constantinopel = Hist. Jahrb. 26 (1905) 773. Concerning the church (Martyrium) of Sts. Marcian and Martyrius, begun under Chrysostom, completed under Sisinnius, see Pio Franchi dei Cavalieri, in: An. Boll. 64 (1946) 154. No. 1. Cf. the Synaxarium of Constantinople for the 25th of October, in: ASS. Nov. Prop. 162.

28. Palladius 20 (72; ed. Norton 128, 10).

CHAPTER VII

CHRYSOSTOM'S FIRST REFORMS

Howevere difficult the field of labor might appear, Chrysostom entered it with all the fiery enthusiasm which inspired him always for every good cause; and with the trusting optimism which never forsook him he began the difficult business.

The clergy, upon whose willing co-operation he had counted above all, offered, in their composition, a true picture of the whole people; there the various elements of all parts of the Empire were mixed together—Egyptians, Syrians, men of Asia Minor, and Armenians, were among them. It is difficult to estimate the number of clergy in Constantinople at that time; the sources differ. By way of comparison, the patriarchal church alone, about 135 years later, under Justinian, had not less than ninety priests, about one hundred deacons, ninety sub-deacons, one hundred and ten lectors, twenty-five psalm singers and one hundred doorkeepers; altogether about five hundred and fifteen persons.[1] In the following centuries their number rose to eight hundred.[2] The number of clergy in the metropolis could not have been small even at that time. The splendor and riches, and possibility of success in the great city, had their powers of attraction even in the fourth century. Whoever trusted to his abilities, especially to oratorical talent, for him the province would easily be too narrow. If the provincial bishops themselves had not been able to withstand the temptation to linger in the vicinity of the court longer than their business required, they were able to exercise a certain influence there which in some circumstances might become disagreeable to the Patriarch himself.

It was a more serious matter that, during the years-long Arian conflicts, not a few intrusive and entirely unworthy elements had been able to obtain an entrance to the ranks of the clergy. It is quite unbelievable, what degradation and chaos of all moral ideas had found place in these decades under the Arian clergy. One deed of these clergy in Constantinople under Valens might be called to mind, when the Arians (only twenty or twenty-five years before Chrysostom's elevation) had loaded into a ship all the Catholic priests whom they could get their hands on, and had set the ship on fire in the open ocean.[3]

Still earlier, under Constantius, Bishop Paul of Constantinople, another predecessor of Chrysostom, was sent into exile in Cucusus and murdered there.[4] They tried more than once to take the life of St. Athanasius, and the scandalous stories of the Arian clergy offered at that time the richest material to those who found a malicious joy in such tales. It might easily be thought that the mild and ineffectual régime of Nectarius, in the sixteen years of his ecclesiastical rule, was hardly able to establish order in the ranks of his own clergy, and to elevate significantly the general spiritual and moral level. At any rate, many Arian clergy were able to find ways and means to come to terms with the changed circumstances, and as " converts " to make their future secure. At all events, it is a fact that, under Nectarius, two members of the clergy remained in office, one of whom had committed a murder and the other was guilty of adultery. The infuriating cause of the abolition of the penitentiaries in Constantinople in the year 391 was still too fresh in peoples' minds to be forgotten. Actually, the evil opportunities and temptations of a great city, whose life was half European and half Oriental, placed especially high demands on maturity and stability of character. If one counts the naturally emotional nature of the Orientals, all together one has the principal points which adduce mitigating circumstances.

The necessity of a sure reform therefore could not be denied. But Chrysostom showed insight and character enough to go ahead with a good example and begin the reform in his own house. The new bishop's palace of Nectarius must have been extremely large and roomy.[5] If it had been necessary, it could have offered shelter, not only to the Patriarch, his immediate clerical entourage and their servants, but also to the often numerous provincial bishops with their attendants, who came to Constantinople on ecclesiastical business. The old palace had been burned down just ten years before (about 388),[6] and Nectarius had built the new one with considerable splendor and luxury. He had not lived to see its completion. Costly marble pillars and similar sumptuous items lay ready for the further building and decoration of the almost finished building. But Chrysostom wished rather to dwell in apostolic simplicity. He had the marble sold, and used the money for social and charitable purposes. Also he appears to have used for this purpose a part of the church treasure. At the Synod of the Oak, he was accused of this, and of the sale of the marble, because this had been supposedly set aside for the Church of the Resurrection.[7]

So then Chrysostom, to the considerable fear of the personnel, called in the stewards of the episcopal and ecclesiastical properties, and inquired about the current expenditures. Whenever he found something superfluous or purposeless, he struck it out.[8] The greatest slash was made in the kitchen budget. Great inefficiency was uncovered there. The steward, or stewards, and the purchaser, had entered items in the budget which they had never purchased, and such things as they had purchased were entered ten times over.[9] Chrysostom interpreted that as stealing the property of the poor. For he made all his savings for them, not for himself. He himself, as far as food was concerned, lived just as simply as when he had been a simple priest at Antioch. The great banquets which had been so numerous under Nectarius, and which had caused so much expense, were abolished. He considered it a "robbing of the temple" to use the property of the Church for such things.[10]

Of course this displeased many, including the clergy, who had enjoyed such hospitality before. They began to consider the new Archbishop's innovations with critical eyes. But it also caused remark, that Chrysostom not only did not invite guests, but even usually dined alone. The chief reason for this was that during his life as a hermit monk, his excessive austerity of life had given him a disease of the stomach. He had to observe a strict diet; and it had been occasionally noticed that he left well-prepared food untouched, and asked for something else which agreed better with him.[11] Added to this, he would drink no wine, because it gave him a rush of blood to the head. But wine drinking and toasting at that

time, even more than today, belonged to the essential cere-
monial of banquets. Finally, he became so busy with work,
studies and prayer, that often evening came on before he
remembered to eat.[12] Palladius asks, not without malice,
what priests under these circumstances would have waited
until they could eat with the Archbishop.[13] To sit at a richly
set table, in the midst of noisy guests, enjoying their food, was
so unsuitable to the person and the character of the Archbishop, that one can understand that this sort of thing must
have been for him the greatest kind of penance. Therefore
he gave no banquets and accepted no invitations.[14] Not once,
if he had bishops as guests, did he partake of the common
table, nor did he invite other members of the clergy, as Nectarius had been accustomed to do.

Many were very much offended at this, especially those who
liked to receive invitations.[15] Constantinople was well known
as a city in which hospitality was well thought of, and social
life was in its fullest bloom. There it was frankly expected
of the bishop, who actually, after the Emperor, was, or could
be, the most prominent man, that he should come forward
publicly, as a prince of the Church, and a great lord, just as
was the case later in the age of humanism. The so-called
" better " society had little understanding of the manner of life
of a " monk on a bishop's throne." For the same reason, St.
Gregory of Nazianzus, as Bishop of Constantinople, had been
despised because of the modesty of his table, his simple
clothing and his unassuming life.[16] Even St. Basil had
offended in his provincial city because of his modest manner
of life.[17] So much the more must Chrysostom have offended,
as a successor of Nectarius. But a very important reason for
his conduct was certainly the purpose of opposing the great
lordliness of the clergy, which had been disagreeably strengthened by the favor of the Emperor and the influx of riches into
the Church; and another aim was to give his fellow bishops
and the clergy an example of the simple apostolic life. That
was really necessary.

People were scandalized at that time on account of the conduct of various bishops. Some had acquired their offices
through simony, others had shown themselves far too greedy
for money and riches. Some bishops enriched their relatives

c

with church property, or wasted it in other ways; some interfered in other dioceses and were consecrated there; some who
had no place, took dioceses by force; some ambitious priests
accused their bishops of heresy or other failing, in the hope
of succeeding them.[17a] This was possible in a time in which
the Church's right had not yet been established, and the Arian
heresy had thrown all ecclesiastical relations into confusion.
Some were afflicted by the building mania, and wanted to per-
petuate their memory in edifices of stone; others again used
much money and wasted much time in banquets,[18] instead of
caring for the poor and the sick. There were certainly enough
poor people in Constantinople. For them, Chrysostom wished
to save, and it is surely to his great honor that his eyes were
not dazzled or deceived by the brilliance of the court, but saw
always and before everything the social needs of the common
people. The money which he managed to save by his econo-
mies he used for the erection of hospitals for the sick, and
hospices for strangers, which were very badly needed. He not
only provided those which already existed with a richer
income, but built new ones, and at the head of each he placed
two suitable priests, who provided doctors, cooks and nurses
for the sick.[19] That showed a social sense which was, unfortunately, not prominent in the East. The poor people were
more in favor of this than of great and brilliant banquets, of
which they were only able to see the lighted windows. The
people also possessed a fine and grateful perception of these
practical activities of Christian love of neighbor, and preserved to the last an unchangeable loyalty and devotion to
their chief shepherd.

Chrysostom was probably moved to this work by the splendid example of St. Basil the Great, who, in spite of the wicked
times in which he lived, had founded hospitals in almost all
the cities of his extensive diocese. The hospital in Caesarea
was so large and so well equipped that the somewhat less
charitably disposed governor of the city ridiculed it.[20]

Chrysostom, on his part, seems to have served as a model
and example for others. About the year 400, two years after
him, a certain Florentius (or Florus) built a hospice in Constantinople.[21] Later arose a whole series of other hospitals
and hospices for strangers.[22]

It is perhaps to be regretted to a certain extent, that Chrysostom, whether from inclination or necessity, imposed such absolute withdrawal. The metropolitan society in Constantinople, especially in the "higher" circles, was sociable and happy, and known everywhere for its great hospitality.[23] So the Archbishop, by eating alone, must have given double offense, all the more since his predecessor Nectarius had met the companionable spirit of the time so well just on this point. Actually, the withdrawal of Chrysostom had aroused, in high society and among the clergy, so much remark that not only Palladius, but also Socrates[24] and Sozomen[25] and the later biographers, spoke of it in detail, as if it had been a weighty affair of state.

But his opponents later made use of the state of affairs in order to circulate among the people the report that the Archbishop ate alone only that he might gorge and carouse undisturbed "like a Cyclop."[26]

After the renovation of things in the episcopal palace, came a series of reforms among the clergy themselves. First of all, Chrysostom decreed that the two deacons who were guilty, one of a murder and the other of adultery, should be expelled from the ranks of the clergy.[27] Theophilus of Alexandria, later, did not shrink from allowing these two ornaments to the priesthood to appear at the Synod of the Oak, as the chief accusers of their Archbishop. Socrates says that Chrysostom expelled "many" others from the ranks of the clergy for various reasons.[28] Sozomen says only, that by censure and punishment he sought to improve the life of one, but had expelled "others" from the service of the Church.[29] That the two before-mentioned deacons were not the only ones who had to pay up on their accounts is very credible, according to earlier sayings, and considering the number of clergy in the city, which was surely not small.

A priest named Porphyrius and another named Venerius came into conflict with the secular court. The first was banished by Eutropius;[30] whether justly or unjustly, is not clear. Considering the character of Eutropius, one may assume that it was the latter. On another occasion three deacons stole the Archbishop's mantle. In short, there must have been among the clergy of that time in Constantinople elements which make it credible and clear that Chrysostom once in a moment of indignation spoke of that sort of clerics as "dishonorable, wicked men" who were capable of anything.[31]

However it is quite probable that Socrates, who was not inclined to be friendly to Chrysostom, in using the word "many" permitted himself an exaggeration. That Chrysostom, even in the beginning, should have acted in this blindly furious manner, does not seem probable in view of his known character. But to punish when it was deserved, and to do away with actual scandals, he would not shrink, not for a moment. Frankly, those who were struck with surprise at the greater strictness of the new Archbishop did not keep this in kind remembrance, but valiantly co-operated in making new enemies for him.

To these belonged still others, who indeed had committed no crime, but who still yielded to passions which were equally unsuitable for the clergy. There were some who manifested scandalous avarice. Others again ran far too willingly after the "fragrance of a roast", and were constantly to be seen at parties and banquets.[32] And Chrysostom stepped in against these "cut-purses, parasites and gluttons"[33] and demanded that the clergy live a simple, temperate life, and be satisfied with their own tables. So therefore he himself gave them a good example. Certainly he did not wish to issue an absolute prohibition, but only to check excess, which would harm the vocation of the clergy. But even that was enough to make his efforts hated, and to make his person the target of the wicked speech and calumny of the evil-minded.

Finally, even in Constantinople, the problem of *Syneisaktai,* or housekeepers* for the clergy, or "parish cooks," had not been satisfactorily solved. Concubinage, the dwelling together of clergy and young women consecrated to God, must here be considered as a separate problem. This much we may rightly assume from the statement of Palladius,[34] even though he has erred in his statement concerning the time of authorship of the two treatises on the "*Syneisaktai*". It is clear, without further argument, that Chrysostom could not endure as bishop what he had written against as a monk, or in

* Tr. Note. The so-called *Syneisaktai* were priests' housekeepers, who sometimes became concubines.

the beginning of his clerical career. Now, indeed, he possessed "the authority to make a valid decision,"[35] which in former times had been lacking to him. Furthermore, it was not necessary for him to make new or special decrees. It was quite sufficient to enforce the exact or more exact observance of the third canon of the first general Church Council of Nicaea (325), which stated that no bishop, priest, or any other cleric was allowed to keep a "*syneisakta*" in his house, unless it was his mother, sister or aunt, or other such person, whose presence could prevent suspicion.

The battle against this scandal, in so far as it concerned young women "consecrated to God," or at the same time monks living alone, or "hermits," who lived in the cities, must have reacted indirectly on the monastic life and on the situation of the young woman. If concubinage would or could not be permitted, and at the same time reasons for this impropriety were advanced, then nothing was left but to compel the monks to join monks and the virgins to join virgins, in a common cenobitic life in the cloister. To this end the efforts of St. Pachomius and St. Basil had been directed; for this purpose they had written their "rules." Marin has allowed himself a very uncritical exaggeration when he states that at the death of Constantine the Great (337) there already existed fifteen monasteries of his founding.[36] But it is a fact that monasticism was already known in Constantinople when Chrysostom came there. The bishop and later heretic Macedonius of Constantinople had especially applied himself to the furthering of monasticism, probably through the urging of his friend Eustathius of Sebaste.[37] But it appears that these "Macedonian" or Eustathian monks, after the condemnation of their chief and founder in Constantinople, were no longer able to maintain themselves, and fell into complete dissolution. In the year 390 the Emperor Theodosius even forbade the monks to live in the city; although two years later he repealed this law.[38]

When Chrysostom became Bishop of Constantinople, there was at least one monastery there. Its abbot at that time was named Isaac.[39] As a cenobitic convent of women, one may consider that of Olympias. Besides these, there were many monks and virgins who did not live in cloisters, but lived alone, either with their own families or in private dwellings. Such monks and virgins enlivened the picture of the city streets, often in far too large numbers, and without visible reason, or frequented private houses with the object of obtaining spiritual influence, without really promoting the edification of the public thereby, especially since many of them were not priests, but lay monks and hermits, and did not have any spiritual or other duties to fulfil. But many professional beggars and tramps often dressed as monks in order to get better results.

Chrysostom could not allow this unfortunate situation to go on without action. He had been a monk himself, and had always kept his high ideals of monasticism; so everything that cast a shadow on the respect and honor of this "life of the angels" touched him deeply. According to Sozomen, he spoke in highest praise of those who lived a secluded life in their cloisters and cells, and carefully saw to it that they had everything necessary, and that they did not suffer injustice from anyone. On the other hand, he required that idle and unemployed monks should stay off the streets, and that none of them should allow himself to be seen outside his cloister or cell without reason. For such things brought reproach upon monasticism.[40]

All this caused much uproar among the monks. While some of them decided to stand beside their new Bishop, many others complained that it was no longer allowed them to go to the people and families who showed them respect and confidence, and they went to their spiritual father, the Abbot Isaac, and complained to him about the Bishop, who must certainly be an enemy of the monks.

This Isaac, father of the monks, was one of the most remarkable figures of Constantinople at that time. He came from Syria, and so was a countryman of Chrysostom; still his native language was Syrian, not Greek. He had never enjoyed the benefits of higher education, and he became a priest late in life.[41] On the other hand, he showed a great inclination toward a strict, ascetical life. He became a hermit in the Syrian desert; and here his disposition and character seem to have taken that direction and quality which one calls idealism, as long as it is accompanied by insight and discretion, but is called fanaticism when it has lost insight, discretion and true love of neighbor. Isaac possessed that kind of zeal and inspiration for what he considered right and good which easily mistakes individual ideas and inclinations for the will and the purposes of God, and then will endure no opposition.

One day, in the midst of the Arian disturbances under the Emperor Valens, he believed he heard the voice of God commanding him to go to Constantinople, and there to give testimony to the true faith. He went, and found a favorable opportunity of making himself noticed. The Emperor was on the point of starting out at the head of his army to engage in a war against the Goths. Isaac rushed up to him, took hold of his horse's bridle, and exclaimed: Give the Catholics back their churches, or you will not come back alive from this war! The Emperor, irritated at this kind of an audience, as well as the demand and the prophecy of the ascetic, had him jailed. Theodosius I freed him again. After this involuntary sojourn in the solitude of a prison, Isaac felt an intense longing for the Syrian desert, which it would have been better for him not to have left. But two officers of the Emperor, Saturninus and Victor, who had interested themselves in him, persuaded him to remain, and to occupy a cell which they had built for him in the district of Psammathia just outside the city. Soon curious people began to come, then pupils, and in a short time a whole colony of hermits had gathered about the Syrian monk, who was their focus and spiritual father. Many people came, even from the court, to beg a blessing for themselves from the pious Isaac. Even the Emperor Theodosius, whose courtesy was everywhere known, visited him several times. At that time he was the first example of his kind in direct proximity to the city.

So henceforth Isaac lived as spiritual father or abbot of the monks assembled around him. It is not absolutely certain whether they lived as colonies of hermits like our Carthusians or Camaldolese, or in a common house under a common rule. Probably their union was rather loose, at least at first, so that Isaac exercised more of a moral than a judicial authority over them.

His pupil and successor Dalmatius created a more vigorous organisation. However, he felt himself to be here in his own jurisdiction, over which he had hitherto exercised an authority questioned or restricted by no one. Therefore, when Isaac heard the strict demands and admonitions of the Archbishop, whether personally or from his monks, he felt not a little aggrieved.[42] It is possible that he considered the admonitions of the Archbishop as an unwarranted intrusion into his own presumed sphere of action, although the idea of "exempt" monks was at that time unknown. At any rate, Nectarius had never spoken to him thus, and his long habit of commanding and of being respected everywhere had very much diminished his inclination to obey.

But it is also possible that Isaac was too much concerned with visits and invitations in the city. This malicious rumor found remarkable corroboration in a biographical sketch which a grateful monk later dedicated to his spiritual father. This states expressly that Isaac, on account of his great holiness, was *invited out on all sides*. Indeed, on one occasion when he was returning late at night from such a visit, outside the city, and had found the city gates already closed, they had miraculously opened to him of themselves, at his prayer![43]

So at any rate it seems that Isaac considered himself the first to be affected by the new Archbishop's reforms, and felt his freedom threatened. That aroused violent ill-humor in him. But at first this remarkable saint kept his anger in his heart. Later, at the Synod of the Oak, he came out as an open opponent of his ecclesiastical superior. For this, Palladius calls him a "mountebank and a leader of bad monks", and says that he always had the habit of speaking evil of the bishops.[44] On the other hand, it sounds like a timid answer and defence, as the second obituary expressly certifies that Isaac had always spoken well of all men and evil of none.[44a] He might, of course, have honorably deserved the halo which the Greeks placed upon his head. But if so, he must have gained it in the last years of his life.

Chrysostom's attempts at reform were of no long duration. Nestorius came out much more radically thirty years later, against the monks who liked to appear in private houses, where they had nothing to seek, and in the streets, where they had nothing to lose. He excommunicated them summarily.[45] Perhaps it was not merely for dogmatic reasons that the abbot

Dalmatius, the successor of Isaac, was to be found shortly thereafter among the decided opponents of his patriarch. At any rate, the Draconic measures of Nestorius had not been of benefit. The idleness and leisure of their solitude had, all through the centuries, enticed the monks out on to the highways. The Council of Chalcedon (451) complained that often strange clerics and monks came to Constantinople without permission of their bishops, and caused disorder. The Defensor of the Church was supposed to order them out in case of necessity.[45a] The Patriarch Athanasius (1289-1293), who himself had lived earlier as a strict ascetic and hermit, who always slept on the floor, and never washed his feet, gave toward the end of the thirteenth century the command that monks should only be seen on the streets of the city in case of strict necessity, and on order of their religious superiors; and then not on horseback, but on foot, since he himself also went on foot. "That," added the historian, "would also be observed by all—as long as Athanasius was Patriarch."[46]

There was still a third class of people who were not approved of by their spiritual shepherds: the *widows*, who lived in the world, but not in the way which might be expected of such women. Whether the so-called "ecclesiastical" widows were among them, that is, those who had vowed not to remarry, but to consecrate their lives thenceforth to the service of God, the Church, and the practice of charity to their neighbors, cannot be certainly determined.[47] In any case, Chrysostom had such women in mind, who played the role of "merry" widows, who decked themselves out to appear more youthful than they were, who wore fine rich clothing, and allowed themselves to be seen even in the public baths. Chrysostom informed himself exactly on the manner of life of each individual, then had them called, and told them either to refrain from the things which were unfitting for their state of life, or else to enter into another marriage as soon as possible, that the command of the Lord should not become a mockery.[48] He said to them, "Why do you wish to appear young in your advancing age? Why do you wear curls on your foreheads like demimondaines, and bring respectable people into disrepute? Why do you deceive those whom you meet? And all this, even though you are widows!"[49]

In this benevolent but blunt manner did Chrysostom impart his admonitions, both privately and in the pulpit. Not everyone took them as they were meant. Not all understood his language. One of these widows, Eugraphia, who was probably related to the Empress, or possessed influence at court, felt herself monstrously disgusted and offended by this uncomplimentary speech, and above all by the insinuation that she was already an old woman. She treasured thenceforth for the inconsiderate preacher of virtue an enmity which bordered on hatred, and sought for revenge. Her palace was later the focal point of plots against him.[50]

So Chrysostom worked in the beginning of his episcopate, so he spoke in public. Above all he sought to elevate, to improve the clergy and the people. One may ask if he handled these things prudently, if he proceeded with that measure of tact and discretion which is the only guarantee of the success of all reforms. The question is an old one. Palladius quotes a deacon as saying: Chrysostom obviously does not understand his time; that one should not disturb what had become natural and customary. Palladius gives his answer: "Then neither did Moses, Elias, Micheas, Daniel, John the Baptist, Isaias, Peter and Paul understand their times, nor did Job. They all sharply rebuked the vicious people of their times. John the Baptist lost his life, because he rebuked Herod. And had not St. Paul called the Cretans liars and lazy belly-worshippers, had he not called the Galatians fools and the Corinthians arrogant men? Chrysostom spoke with the same courageous frankness." He praised virtue and rebuked vice.[51] And at any rate he was far removed from the reckless, fanatically brutal frankness by which his later successor and countryman, Nestorius, who was so unlike him, had lost the sympathy of his flock.[52] Socrates says only of Chrysostom, that he was very strict about duty with his clergy, whose lives needed reformation. His Archdeacon Serapion had been a great offender in this regard—he was an Egyptian, who had often been the cause of the Archbishop's taking very sharp measures.[53]

It is obvious that Chrysostom gave no joy to those who were affected by his reforms, and made no friends for himself among them. But they formed a small minority who did not dare show their discontent openly.

The great mass of the people stood entirely on the side of the Archbishop; for his practical understanding of their social problems won their hearts, and his sermons, which everyone understood, and in which he told the truth to everyone, including the rich and the distinguished, filled them with enthusiasm.

FOOTNOTES

1. Justinian, Novella 14, 1 from the year 535 (ed. C. E. Zachariae von Lingenthal, Leipzig 1881, 1, 71).
2. Chr. Bondelmontius, Lib. Insularum Archipelagi. Leipzig-Berlin 1824. P. 122.
3. Theodoret, HE 4, 21 (82, 1181).
4. S. Athanasius, De fuga 3 (25, 648); Theodoret 2, 4 (997).
5. Socrates 6, 14 (67, 705) speaks of ἐπισκοπικοῖς οἴκοις.
6. S. Ambrosius, Epist. 40, 13 (ML 16, 1106), written at the end of 388. Cf. Rauschen, Jahrbücher 534.
7. Photius, Bibliotheca 59 (103, 108).
8. Palladius 5 (47, 20).
9. Palladius 12 (39).
10. *Loc cit.*
11. Palladius 12 (39).
12. *Loc. cit.*
13. Dial. 13 (45).
14. Sozomen 8, 9 (67, 1541).
15. Palladius 13 (45).
16. Oratio 42, 24 (36, 488).
17. Allard, Julien 1, 130.
17a. Conc. Cstpl. Can 6 (MCC 3, 560); Conc. Afric. 120 (*ibid.* 819) and others.
18. Palladius 12 (46-47) and 16 (55). Cf. Chrysostom, Hom. 6, 4; 10, 3 and 11, 2 ff. in Ephes. (62, 48, 78, 81 ff.).
19. Palladius 5 (20); cf. Sudhoff, Aus der Geschichte des Krankenhauswesens *loc. cit.* 3-6.
20. S. Basilius, epist. 94 (32, 488).
21. Anonymus, Antiquitates (122, 1265 C); George Codinus, De aedificiis Constantinop. (157, 585 B and 600 B); cf. Pargoire, Les débuts *loc. cit.* 92.
22. That of St. Samson was especially famous (sixth century); Millingen, Byzantine Churches 88-89; Antioniades 1, 43.
23. Palladius 12 (41); "Constantinople, where everyone practices hospitality."

24. HE 6, 4 (672).
25. HE 8, 9 (1541).
26. Point 25 of the list of accusations at the Synod of the Oak (103, 108).
27. Palladius 8 (27).
28. HE 6, 4 (672).
29. HE 8, 3 (1520).
30. Photius, Bibliotheca 59, Points 21 and 22 (103, 108 C).
31. *Loc. cit.* Point 5.
32. Palladius 5 (20).
33. *Loc. cit.*
34. Dial. 5 (20).
35. Adversus Syneisact. 1, 1 (47, 496).
36. Les moines de Constantinople 8.
37. Sozomen 3, 14 (1080) and 8, 27 (1589); Socr. 2, 39 (333 C).
38. Codex Theodos. 16, 3, 1 and 2 (ed. Mommsen 853).
39. According to the Vita S. Hypatii, n. 8, by Callinicus (ed. Soc. phil. Bonn. Leipzig 1895, p. 23), written between 447 and 450, there was in the year 394, when Hypatius came to Constantinople, only one monastery, that of Isaac.   Not until 406, under Atticus, were other monasteries founded, over which Isaac and his successor exercised a sort of spiritual fatherhood.   There is no doubt in my mind that this Isaac is identical with the Isaac who was Chrysostom's enemy.   See Pargoire, Date de la mort de St. Isaac = Echos d'Orient 2 (1898-99) 138-145.
40. Sozomen 8, 9 (1540).
41. The "Hesychast Isaac" in Palladius 8 (23) is at any rate identical with the "Isaac Syriscus, father of the monks" in Palladius Ch. 6 (21).   Concerning Isaac see Acta SS. Mai VII 246 ff.
42. Sozomen 8, 9 (1540); cf. Palladius 6 (21); Sozomen traces the quarrel between bishop and abbot back to these demands of Chrysostom.   Strange that the otherwise so considerate J. Pargoire should attribute this whole quarrel to Chrysostom's jealousy of Isaac! (Pargoire, Les débuts *loc. cit.* 122: "Chrysostome est par contre infiniment jaloux de son autorité.")
43. Vita S. Isaaci n. 15 Acta SS. Mai VII 257.
44. Ἰσαακίῳ Συρίσκῳ, περιτρίμματι, ἀφηγητῇ ψευδομοναζόντων, ἐν κακολογίαις κατατριβέντι πάντοτε κατὰ ἐπισκόπων, thus runs the verdict of Palladius, Dial. Ch. 6 (47, 21).   This Isaac is not to be confused with the two Egyptian Isaacs, abbots and priests, one of whom had 150 monks under him, and the other 210, and both of whom were later banished by Patriarch Theophilus.   Pargoire, in the Revue d'histoire et de Litt. rel. 3 (1898) 465 believes that Isaac was the teacher of St. Hypatius, and calls him "le vrai pére

de la vie monastique à Constantinople." On the other hand, the community of St. Hypatius held St. Chrysostom in great honor.

44a. Alia Vita n. 7, *loc. cit.* 260.

45. Nau, Nestorius, Le livre d'Héraclide, P. VI.

45a. Canon 23 = Mansi 7, 379-80; Hefele KG 2, 525.

46. Nicephorus Gregoras, Byzantine Histor. 6, 5 (148, 337 AB).

47. Palladius 5 (20) calls them all in general: τὸ τῶν χηρῶν τάγμα.

48. *Loc. cit.*

49. *Palladius* 8 (27).

50. *Loc. cit.*

51. Dialog. 18 (65-67); cf. Theodoret 5, 28 (82, 1256-57).

52. Cf. M. Brière, La legende syriaque de Nestorius = Revue de l'Orient chrétien 15 (1910) 19.

53. HE 6, 4 (67, 612). Cf. Ch. 10, p. 97-98.

CHAPTER VIII

THE LITURGY AND DIVINE SERVICE

CHRYSOSTOM, as an outspoken religious man, was not satisfied with merely removing the weeds from his new garden of God. A positive renewal and re-animation of the people lay nearest his heart. From the beginning, he gave the greatest care to the encouragement of attendance at the Divine Liturgy, and above all, to arranging the celebration of the Liturgy so that it might be possible for the people to attend it. The Liturgy probably did not claim as much time as had been the case heretofore. At least a document issued under the name of the Patriarch Proclus of Constantinople, "Concerning the tradition of the Divine Liturgy," states: "The people have begun to stay away from divine service because the Liturgy lasts too long. Therefore St. Basil shortened the Liturgy. Then Chrysostom shortened it still more. He cut off a great deal, and allowed the service to be shortened so that the people would not stay away altogether."[1]

It cannot be definitely ascertained in just what particulars the liturgical reforms of Chrysostom consisted.[2] But they seem to have been significant, otherwise it could scarcely be explained why the Greek Liturgy took its name from him. Probably the Antiochene liturgy had been a model for the reform. It was probably time for a renovation in Constantinople, since during the Arian disturbances the Catholic Church itself had been without a bishop, almost without priests, indeed almost without believers. Therefore the traditions of every Catholic place had probably more or less died out, and Nectarius, who had been elevated to the Bishopric from his position as a member of the laity, and who had scarcely any theological education, had been satisfied to continue things as he had found them, in this important matter. Still it is possible that St. Gregory Nazianzus, as a Cappadocian, had introduced the Liturgy of St. Basil, which Chrysostom had then shortened.[3]

At any rate, one ancient church custom was again resumed by the Catholics in Constantinople; this was the so-called *Stations*, or night services, on the vigils of Sundays and great feast-days. The people had formerly been accustomed to gather in a specified place, and go in solemn procession, with singing, to a church in which the Divine Liturgy was held. The Arians had taken over this custom from Catholic times. They also continued to keep their churches within the walls of the city, even after it was forbidden. Indeed they even used these Stations purposely for demonstrations, and sang hymns there, whose contents provoked and offended the Catholics. So they became the direct occasion of Chrysostom's re-introduction of the Stations for the Catholics.

Socrates portrays the course of events very clearly: "The Arians held their Divine Liturgy outside the city. Every week, on Saturday and Sunday, on which days they assembled in the church, they came inside the city walls, under the porticoes, and sang Arian choir hymns. This continued the greater part of the night." The people who lived nearby probably did not enjoy this nocturnal singing very much. "Early in the morning, after the city gates had been opened, they went through the city chanting their hymns, and went out by another gate to their churches. By all this they did not cease to provoke the Catholics; they sang by preference a hymn whose chorus went thus: Where are they who say that the *Three* are only *one* power?[4] Bishop John was afraid that simple people might be led away from the church by such songs. Therefore he ordered that his people should also hold processions, in order that by their nocturnal hymn-singing they might outstrip the Arians and strengthen their own people in the faith. His purpose in this was good. However, it led to dangerous unrest."[5] So much for Socrates.

So the Catholics sought, with their nocturnal hymn-singing, to surpass the Arians. Chrysostom himself, perhaps in imitation of an Antiochene custom, had conceived the idea of having the procession bear silver crosses, in which the burning lights were placed. The Empress Eudoxia had offered to pay the expense of this, and had also lent her chamberlain Brison, who was skilled in music, to take charge of practising, and leading the singing. Then the Arians became furiously jealous and sought to bring about a conflict for the sake of revenge. They could not endure the final loss of their earlier power and their unique prominence. Intentionally or not, the two processions met one night and a real brawl began, in which the poor chamberlain Brison was struck on the head by a stone.[6] But he was not the only victim of this warlike piety. There were not merely wounded people on both sides, but some were even killed. As a result of this incident, the Emperor forbade the Arians to continue further their nocturnal processions.

But the less zealous portion of the clergy were not edified by this re-introduction of the celebration of the Stations. They were accustomed "to sleep all night, through it all."[7] Many grumbled about these liturgical disturbances of the night, and about the new Bishop.

Moreover, only the men took part in these processions. The women attended the Divine Liturgy in the daytime.[8] This custom seems to have been observed for quite a long time. Even the specially zealous members of the devout sex did not allow themselves to take part, at least in the nocturnal hymn-singing. Thirty years later Nestorius considered himself obliged to forbid it to them.[9]

The Patriarch also sought to introduce another custom into Constantinople, which had been practiced at Antioch. It often happened that people, whether from necessity or custom, felt obliged to expectorate soon after receiving Holy Communion. For fear that the Holy Sacrament might be desecrated in this way, Chrysostom recommended to the faithful to do as he himself did, namely, to take a sip of water as soon as possible after receiving Holy Communion, as the priest does today in the Latin liturgy, when he takes the ablution after the Communion. But because this is not very well possible in the church, he recommended that they swallow a morsel of bread. To this custom may be traced back the present practice among the Greeks, in which the so-called "Eulogia", which the priest distributes after the Liturgy, are eaten in the church itself.

However, in Constantinople, this custom, although quite

harmless in itself and intended for a good purpose, was new, and later, when everyone had to suffer as much as possible, this point was brought up as No. 28 among the accusations at the Synod of the Oak.[10]

As to how far Chrysostom had introduced reforms in the essential Liturgy, the Holy Sacrifice of the Mass, cannot be determined with any certainty. Only from Palladius it appears that in Constantinople, the Bishop came into the church with with his fellow-bishops, and there offered the greeting of peace to the assembled people.[11] Then the Bishop seated himself, with the other Bishops, and readings from Holy Scripture followed. After this, came the essential Sacrifice, and at the very end, the dismissal of the people. Fortunately, as has been pointed out before, these rudimentary outlines can be filled in from the writings of Chrysostom himself, since he often explained and pointed out to the people the actions and special prayers of the Mass. Only in regard to this it is difficult to say with certainty which customs were of Antioch and which of Constantinople, or which were first introduced into the capital city by Chrysostom.

Besides, Chrysostom made every effort, through ecclesiastical solemnities, to lift the hearts of the people to participate in religious activities. To this end belonged above all the honoring of the holy martyrs. When, in the fourth century, came the longed-for external peace of the Church, zealous Christians turned their thoughts gladly and admiringly to their co-religionists, who in times of persecution had offered their blood and their lives for Christ. The possession of a martyr's grave was therefore the pride and joy of every Christian congregation. But the young Constantinople, founded after the time of the persecutions, had no martyrs' graves. So they were compelled to have martyrs come from some place in which there were enough of them, or from where they could most easily be obtained.

So in the fourth century, there began, especially in Constantinople, a real battle to obtain relics of martyrs. And since almost every " Martyrium " was gradually enlarged into a church, on account of the rapid growth of Christian congregations, so another custom arose of itself, namely, that every new church must have its relics of martyrs or its grave of a

martyr. So already in the year 325, by order of the Emperor
Constantius, the bones of St. Timotheus were brought to Constantinople; in the following year, the bones of the Apostle
St. Andrew and the Evangelist St. Luke; and later, those of
St. Euphemia. The Emperor Theodosius I had a martyrium
or a church built outside the city, in Hebdomon, for the head
of St. John the Baptist. Under the Emperor Arcadius, some
bones were brought to Constantinople from Judea, which
were said to be those of the prophet Samuel.[12]

It is therefore not to be wondered at, that Chrysostom also
endeavored to satisfy the piety of the faithful, by acquiring
new relics of martyrs for his rapidly growing congregation.
So, as has been noted before, the relics of St. Phocas were
brought to Constantinople, and were carried in solemn procession, with lights, all through the city, with the imperial
court at the head of the procession.[13] Relics of martyrs were
also brought out of Egypt; the names of the martyrs were not
mentioned.[14] In a more general sermon, all the martyrs were
mentioned, granting the supposition that a "feast of all
martyrs" existed.[15]

The two sermons which were given in the Church of St.
Thomas on the occasion of the translation of the relics, and
one of which the Empress attended, has been mentioned
before.[16] It is also of interest that, at that time in Antioch
and perhaps also in Constantinople, many men and women
wore particles of the true cross set in gold, as an ornament
and protection around their necks.[17]

According to the testimony of Sozomen, Chrysostom also
had a martyrium erected outside the city for two other
martyrs, the sub-deacon Martyrius and the lector Marcian,
who had been murdered by the Arians. This martyrium was
probably erected over their graves, and it had a portico for
the devout who wished to pray there. The building was completed under Patriarch Sisinnius (426-27).[18]

The demand for martyrs' relics in aspiring Constantinople
seems to have been known about, all over the Empire. A
certain Jacobus, "an apostolic man," seems to have applied
to the Bishop of Trent, St. Vigilius, to obtain relics of the
youngest and last martyrs, perhaps for a church which had
been built by him personally. Vigilius turned over to him

the relics of the holy martyrs Sisinnius, Alexander, and Martyrius, who had lived in Anagni. They had gathered there one day for the "Hymnus matutinus," when suddenly some pagans fell upon them. Sisinnius, the deacon, was felled by an axe; the lector Martyrius was pierced by spears, and Alexander was dragged to death through the streets of the city. Bishop Vigilius also gave Jacobus a document describing the sufferings of the martyrs, which he delivered to "St. John," together with the relics.[19]

The apostolic zeal of the new Bishop extended itself to everything which could serve for the advancement of the Catholic faith. Among the Goths who lived in Constantinople, there were quite a number of Catholics. Chrysostom assigned to them the Church of St. Paul, where they could celebrate the Divine Liturgy in their own language. He even attended their Liturgy once himself, and the sight of Christ being honored also by the barbarians inspired him so much that in Eastertime of 399, after the sermon of the Gothic priest, he mounted the pulpit himself, and gave a splendid sermon on the vocation of the pagans and barbarians to Christianity. An interpreter had to translate the sermon for the Goths. So Chrysostom became the founder of a "German" national church in Constantinople, the oldest known to history.[20]

"I wish," said Chrysostom, "that the pagan philosophers were here, that they might recognize the power of Christianity. For where now are Plato, Pythagoras, and the other philosophers of Athens? Forgotten! The teaching of the fisherman and the tentmaker, however, shines not merely in Judea, but also in the language of the barbarians. For the Scythians, the Thracians, the Sarmatians, the Hindus, the Moors, and the dwellers in the extreme ends of the earth, know the Gospel, which has been translated into their languages. . . . The Jews should blush, who read the letter of the Scriptures, but do not understand its meaning. What a wonderful and unexpected sight! The new-born son of God was first praised by the barbarians (Magi) in Judea, where the prophets and patriarchs, the just, the law, the Ark of the Covenant, the Temple, sacrifice and prayer, were at home. But the Jews did not let themselves be converted by the barbarians, and these became

the teachers of Christendom, although they had never heard
of these things before. So let no one think that it is a shame
for us, if I call upon the barbarians in the midst of the church
to rise and speak. That is, on the contrary, an ornament and
a distinction for the Church, and a proof of the strength which
lies in our faith. For today you see the rudest among the barbarians become as the lambs of Christ, in the common sheep-
fold of the Church, partaking of the Table as all the others
do."[21]

The introduction of the Christmas feast into Constantinople, as a special liturgical service, may well be ascribed to
Chrysostom. While Usener[22] says that Constantinople had
taken over the Roman Christmas before Antioch, Baumstark
cites evidence from Jacobus of Edessa, who lived in the seventh
century and died in 708.[23] Jacobus says in one of his letters
that the Christmas feast was introduced into Constantinople
under Arcadius and Chrysostom. Baumstark considers this
evidence to be unquestionable proof. At any rate, it is, until
now, the oldest and the first positive proof on this question.
K. Lübeck has opposed him, but on the ground of purely
negative arguments.[24] Furthermore, the Synaxarium of Constantinople expressly says that Chrysostom introduced the feast
of Christmas into that city.[25]

An individual note also distinguishes the feast of the Ascen-
sion. Socrates says that this feast, "in conformity with
custom," was celebrated in the suburb of Elaia, which lay in
front of the city.[26] Unfortunately, Socrates does not give any
reason for this unusual custom. Perhaps there was a special
church there, dedicated to the Resurrection of Christ.

In regard to confession, it seems that in the time of Chrysostom in Constantinople the same practice prevailed as at
Antioch. Before that time, there had been certain "peniten-
tiary priests" who accepted the public confession of sins. As
a consequence of a great scandal under Nectarius, the priest
Eudaimon had advised the Patriarch to abolish all the peni-
tentiary priests and "*to permit each one to partake of the
Eucharist according to his own conscience*."[27] How long
things remained thus is uncertain.

Concerning other special points in the Liturgy from the
time of Chrysostom, we have no further information.[28]

On the other hand, his explanation of the Acts of the Apostles, which he preached in Constantinople, speaks in one place of how near to the heart of the zealous chief shepherd were the people of the cities, and also the country people. "There are many rich Christians, who possess whole villages and great estates; but for the souls and the religion of their peasants they cared nothing. Whether these country people are Christians is a matter of indifference to them. Many build market places and baths, but none build churches; everything else comes before that. Therefore I admonish you and beg you most earnestly, indeed I make it a law, that no one shall possess estates without a church. Do not tell me that there is a church near by; or that the expense for this is great and the income small. No! If you have alms to give, set aside some for this. Maintain a priest and a deacon and whatever else belongs to the upkeep of a church. If you wish to marry, or give your daughter a dowry, instead of this, give a contribution for the building of a church. There you will be prayed for always; hymns will be sung, and the Divine Liturgy held, and every Sunday the Holy Sacrifice will be offered. . . . And is that something insignificant, that your name will be mentioned each time in the Holy Sacrifice, and that every day prayers will be offered for your welfare? So I beg you, prepare yourselves for the work."[29]

How many Christian land barons entered into this imitation marriage is not known.

FOOTNOTES

1. 65, 849-52. It is not absolutely authentic. Cf. Synaxar. Cstpl. 23 Oct. (ASS. Nov. Prop. 155 ff.).

2. Pl. de Meester, Les origines et les développements du texte grec de la liturgie de St. Jean Chrysostome = Chrysostomica (Rome 1908) 245 ff.; A. Baumstark, Zur Urgeschichte der Chrysostomos-Liturgie, *loc. cit.* 299.

3. Liturgia S. J. Chrysostomi (63, 901-22); Greek-French edition with introduction and notes by Pl. de Meester O.S.B.: La divine Liturgie de . . . S. Jean Chrysostome. Third edition. Rome-Paris 1925. In its present form, the liturgy of St. Chrysostom is the result of the development of centuries. The oldest text of the

present Chrysostom liturgy is shown in the Cod. Barberini III 55 of the Vatican Library; it was in use " apparently between the years 788 and 797." Also, among the Armenians, the monophysite Syrians and the Abyssinians, an entirely different eucharistic formulary bears the name of the Chrysostom liturgy; see A. Baumstark, Zur Urgeschichte der Chrysostomusliturgie = Theologie und Glaube 5 (1913) 199-300.

4. «Ποῦ εἴσιν οἱ λεγόντες τά τρια μίαν δύναμιν»; Soc. 6, 8 (689 A B).

5. HE 6, 7-8 (67, 688 ff.). According to Socrates, the Divine Liturgy at night was already in use before the time of Chrysostom; he introduced only the night processions. According to Palladius, who was better informed, the vigils had gone out of use, and their re-introduction had angered some of the clergy.

6. Brison, or Brisson, was at that time a common name. St. Basil's letter 3,302 (32, 1050) is addressed to a certain Brison. The Bishop of Philippopolis at that time was named Brison; he went over to the side of Chrysostom's enemies (Soc. 6, 18). Finally, the brother of Palladius was named Brison; he was a Bishop and a resolute partisan of Chrysostom (Pall. 20 = 47, 71).

7. Palladius 5 (20).

8. *Loc. cit.*

9. Nau, Nestorius p. VI.

10. Palladius 8 (27). Cf. Photius, Bibliotheca 59 (103, 109).

11. Dialog 14 (48).

12. H. Delehaye S.J., Les origines . . . 2nd ed., p. 56.

13. Hom. in S. Phocam Mart. (50, 699-706).

14. Encomium in Martyres Aegyptiacos (50, 693-698). Whether this sermon was given in Antioch or in Constantinople is not certain. The speaker indeed emphasizes that the Egyptian martyrs' relics had been scattered " all through the world " (col. 693, p. 5 and 16); this does not except Egypt, which was united with Antioch in various ways; on the other hand, the fact that the official ecclesiastical business between Antioch and Constantinople had been resumed again in the year 398 speaks for Constantinople. That the sermon actually originated with Chrysostom, there appears to be no doubt.

15. 50, 705-712.

16. Ch. 4, p. 35.

17. Contra Judaeos et Gentiles 10 (48, 826). Sulzberger, Le symbole de la Croix. in: Byzantion 2 (1925) 436, even claims from Chrysostom that the veneration of the Cross had become " actual worship " by the end of the seventh century. There is no doubt that an all too credulous piety was taken advantage of, at that

time, by unscrupulous deceivers. Cf. ASS June 7, 401; Riant Les dépouilles relig. 92. Some even made the pilgrimage to Arabia to see Job's dunghill. (Hom. 5, 1 ad pop. Ant=49, 69). Already in the year 386 Theodosius passed a law against the dealers in false relics (Cod. Theod. IX, tit. XVII, no. 7).

18. HE 4, 3 (67, 1116).

19. ML 13, 552-58. That this was St. John Chrysostom is indeed only a guess, but it is very probably right. Also Bardenhewer, GAL 3, 548 takes it for granted that it was Chrysostom.

20. It is certainly not credible that this story treated of only one isolated incident in this Gothic liturgy, at a time when the Goths were settled in Constantinople in large numbers. Furthermore, Gothic hymns were sung in the night processions to Drypia. Concerning the settlements of the Goths in the Byzantine Empire, and their Christianizing, see J. Zeiller, Le premier établissement des Goths, p. 3 ff.; Al. Vasiliev, The Goths in the Crimea. Cambridge, Mass., p. 32-38; Jos. Sauer, Die christl. Denkmäler in Gotengebiet der Krim, in: Oriens Christ: 29 (1932), 188-202. Unfortunately the Church of St. Paul was sacrificed in the Gothic uprising under Gainas, on July 12, 400. (A. M. Schneider, Brände in Konstantinopel, in: Byz. Ztschr. 41 (1941) 382.

21. 63, 499-510. Theodoret 5, 30 (82, 1257) says of this incident, though he is mistaken, that it concerned the Arian Goths.

22. Das Weihnachtsfest 240.

23. Die Zeit der Einführung des Weihnachtsfestes in Konstantinopel = Oriens Christ. 2 (1902) 441-46.

24. Die Einführung des Weihnachtsfestes in Konstantinopel = Histor. Jahrbuch 28 (1907) 109-18.

25. Acta SS. Nov. Propyl. 313: ἐν ᾗ ᾗ καὶ ἡ ἑορτὴ τῶν Χριστοῦ γεννῶν ἀπῆρξατο ὑπ' αὐτοῦ τελεῖσθαι.

26. HE 7, 26 (67, 799).

27. Socrates 5, 19 (67, 613-20). Cf. Ed. Schwartz, Bussstufen 55 ff. The meaning of Socrates can only be that never more would either public or private confession be binding. And Chrysostom gives no signs at all that he made any difference between the discipline of the confessional in Constantinople and that in Antioch.

28. Except what is noted already in Ch. 19 of the first volume: Chrysostom as Liturgist. The Lenten customs apparently did not assume their final form in Constantinople until later. Cf. A. Rahlfs, Die alttest. Lektionen der griech. Kirche 92 ff.

29. Hom. 18, 4-5 in Act. Ap. (60, 147-48).

CHAPTER IX

CHRYSOSTOM AS PREACHER AND AUTHOR IN CONSTANTINOPLE

THE efforts of the Bishop toward the spiritual and moral elevation of the clergy could only succeed if he himself showed a good example. This he did in the pulpit.

Chrysostom, in his earlier years as Bishop, preached almost every Sunday and feast day. That was expected of him, and indeed it had been the principal reason why he was called to Constantinople. That he preached pretty often, he himself testifies in his explanation of the Acts of the Apostles, composed in Constantinople: "If it is too much for you when I call you together one day in the week, how would it be if I did this more often?" Also: "We have not preached day and night, but only every third or every seventh day."[1]

On the whole, Constantinople offered the same social and moral conditions as Antioch did. However, the people there presented a more variegated picture than those in Antioch. They did not have the history and tradition, and as for money and pleasure, although they were, if possible, more devoted to it than the people of Antioch, still they did not have the spirit and wit of the latter. So it happened that Chrysostom had to battle with the same religious errors and moral improprieties in Constantinople as in his native city. In the mere choice of his sermon material, one can hardly decide whether a sermon or a commentary originated in the metropolis of Syria or in that of the Empire.

Only the difference between rich and poor, between poverty and luxury, between high and low, are more noticeable here in the vicinity of the imperial palace than in Antioch. By preference, then, Chrysostom preached to the rich, urging them not only to help the poor, but above all not to bear themselves in a haughty or condescending manner toward them.[2] That certainly revealed no ordinary understanding of the psychology of the simple people. The rich man, said he, is at bottom like a city without walls, given up defenselessly to all the attacks of the malicious enemy. The rich are also much harder to teach and to discipline than the poor. For the soul of the rich man is full of vices and follies, of ambition, of numberless desires and curiosities, of wrath and ill-humor, of avarice, of unrighteousness and of whatever other vices there are.[3] Therefore the rich are an easy prey of the devil.[4]

And of what benefit to the rich are their luxurious banquets, their silver and gold dinner services, the heavy tables, the soft beds and carpets, the great golden pitchers and goblets, the army of young, beautiful and richly clad servants, the many musicians with their devilish songs, and the shameless dancers? The poor are actually better off. The poor man lives modestly and remains healthy, has no worries about his guests, since he has none, and thanks God for the little which has been given to him. So he has a healthy sleep, and will one day eat at the table of God, while the rich man will hear these words: Thou wicked and idle servant![5]

One can understand that these and similar admonitions were not received as compliments by the rich and great gentlemen and ladies prominent in society, and gave them little pleasure.

But Chrysostom ventured to give a forceful message to the rich. It was not only urgently needed, but he had also given a good example in his own house, and had done what he could for the poor. Moreover, as far as sensitiveness was concerned, Constantinople was a much more ticklish ground than Antioch, for there the rich were, for the most part, the same ones who possessed the power and influence at the Emperor's court. And in this respect, the weak and devout sex showed itself far more critical and sensitive than the strong and rude. It was just those women who, clothed in silk and adorned with gold, went about like arrogant peacocks, to let themselves be seen in church in such pageantry, who were not at all to the taste of the new shepherd of souls. "Why must you adorn yourselves with costly garments and ornaments of gold? That is more dishonorable and shameful than if you wore nothing! Such pageantry is suitable for the stage, for spectacles, for buffoons, dancers, and beast fighters. God has given other garments to a Christian woman. All of you who have been baptized in the name of Christ, have put on Christ."[6]

Such rhetorical sallies are naturally only to be considered as a reaction against the extravagance and unsocial conduct of the rich. But they, and similar admonitions, were taken very much amiss by the gold-bedecked ladies of luxury. They pleased the simple people just as much. The latter soon showed themselves inspired by the new chief shepherd, who spoke to them so freely from his heart. He spoke from the pulpit just what they themselves had thought a hundred times, and discussed among themselves. The fact that, above all, their Bishop dared to rebuke publicly the luxury and ostentation of the hard-hearted rich, and to tell them fearlessly what he thought, in a city in which there was so much poverty and misery to be alleviated, took their hearts by storm. And when they saw how simply the new Bishop lived, and that he neither gave nor attended banquets, and that he used whatever he could spare for the poor and the sick, and above all for the hospitals, the people knew that he was no court-bishop, but at last a people's bishop, whose heart and hand belonged first of all to the poor and needy, the little people and the downtrodden. And so he was.

Therefore the people attended his sermons gladly and zealously. Sozomen certainly did not exaggerate when he wrote: "The people depended so much on him, and were so insatiable to hear his sermons, that they brought him into danger by their pushing and shoving; everyone wished to come nearer to him, in order to hear him better. During the sermon he sat, not on the episcopal throne, as was customary, but at the lector's ambo, in order to be in the midst of the people."[7]

When Chrysostom on a certain Sunday turned over the pulpit to his guest, a bishop (Leontius?) of Galatia, when the people had expected him to speak, the people, like the children of nature that they were, expressed their disappointment very loudly and openly, and left the church in droves.[8] "Now," he said in his next sermon, "the last time, I reprimanded you sternly and rebuked you about the theater and the circus. But you are like young swallows in the nest, you hang so on my lips. You are like children who have been whipped. In spite of the whipping, the child will not leave its mother; it follows her weeping; goes beside her, clinging to her skirts; and continues to follow her, sobbing and crying with woe. I am glad of such dependence, and am happy to preach to such listeners."[9]

In Constantinople, too, the new Bishop was very often applauded in the midst of his sermons. He took these expressions of love with very mixed feelings. "Believe me," he once said in a sermon, with an almost childlike frankness, "if one of my sermons is applauded, I feel for a moment a very human pleasure. Why should I not tell the truth? I rejoice over it, and am glad. But then when I go back home and remind myself that those who applauded me have received no benefit at all from the sermon, and have even flung away the little good they might have gained, just by their noisy applause and praise, then I feel pain, I sigh and weep, and feel that I have spoken entirely in vain. Then I say to myself: Of what benefit is all my trouble, when my listeners will derive no profit from my sermons? And I have often thought of forbidding these manifestations of applause altogether, and of demanding that you listen in silence and with a suitable quiet.

"Therefore, if you agree, I hereby make the rule that no listener be allowed to applaud during the sermon. If anyone wishes to admire the sermon, let him admire it in silence; no one will hinder you from doing that. On the other hand, your whole thought and aspiration will be directed toward benefiting from what has been said. Now why did you *applaud again?* I have just issued a prohibition against that very thing, and you will not obey it! And yet that will only have good results, and will promote piety. The worldly philosophers often speak without being applauded by anybody; the Apostles also preached, and we do not read of them that their listeners interrupted the speaker with applause in the middle of the sermon. It would be very profitable for us to do the same ourselves. So from henceforth this rule will hold: that we will listen to the speaker in quiet and silence. . . . Christ also preached on the mountain, and no one interrupted Him, until the sermon was ended. So I do no injury to those who wish applause. On the contrary, I will see that they have still more admiration. For if one listens in silence, then afterward applauds by thinking of the sermon, at home and on the street, that is much better than if he applauds noisily and then forgets everything and goes home empty, and cannot remember why he applauded in the first place.

"And does not the listener make himself ridiculous, and must it not be considered flattery or contempt, if he can only say, 'The preacher spoke beautifully today'—and at the same time he has no knowledge of what he really said? Only flatterers do thus. . . . Nothing is so becoming to the Church as quiet and order. Noise and tumult are for the theater, the baths, processions and market places. But where such exalted teachers are preaching, there quiet and silence and holy recollection should rule, as in a windless harbor.

"Therefore I beg you earnestly, everyone of you, to pay attention to this. I am thinking of how I may benefit your souls by any possible means. One way seems to be this, which may be of benefit both to you and to us. . . . Go into the workshop of a painter and you will see what great quiet reigns there. So also it should be here. Here also we paint with the colors of royal virtue, not ordinary pictures. But what is this? *You are applauding again!* It seems very difficult to break one's self away from it. . . . But again I beg you. We now make it a law, that in all things we may conduct ourselves according to God's pleasure, and become worthy of His love."[10]

But there was no great joy in Constantinople over that. Here again he found, to his sorrow, the two old enemies with which he had carried on a continuous battle in Antioch: the theater and the circus. Gregory of Nazianzus, on his part, had already tried to put a stop to the mad passion with which the people followed horse racing, theaters, circuses and wild beast shows.[11] Since then, however, the situation had not improved one iota. Indeed, the people were sincerely devoted to their new bishop, and attached to him, from their hearts. But they were no more ready to renounce their horse-racing and theater-going than were their countrymen of Antioch, to the inexpressible sorrow of their preacher and bishop.

Even on Good Friday, many people preferred to go to the horse races and the circus, than to go to church. This pained the Bishop deeply. And when on Sunday, the 3rd of July,

399,[12] the church again stood half empty, while the whole city was at the circus, from which loud yells sounded, he could contain himself no longer. "Is this to be endured, is it to be tolerated?" he cried. "Now I have preached so often and instructed you for so long, and still there are those who simply leave us here alone, and run off to the circus and the charioteers and the horse races! So far have they yielded to their passions, that they fill the whole city with their cries and unrestrained yelling, at which one would have to laugh if it were not so sad. When I heard the storm of noise from my house, it was more discouraging to my spirit than being tossed to and fro upon the ocean in a storm-wind. . . . When that immense noise struck my ear, I threw myself on the floor and hid my face. But what can I say, or what excuse can I give, if a stranger in the city should say: Is this the city of the Apostle?[13]   Is this the city which received the prophet Samuel?[14] Is this the people who love Christ? . . . Not once have you paid any attention to the holiness of the day on which the mystery of the redemption of our race was accomplished! On Good Friday, the day on which our Lord was crucified for the whole world, and offered such a great sacrifice, when Paradise was opened and the thief returned to his ancient fatherland, when the curse was taken away and sins were blotted out, when the long-continued war came to an end, and God was reconciled with men, when all things were changed: on this day . . . you stayed away from the Church, and the holy sacrificial meal, and the fellowship of brethren, and the holy fasts, and let yourselves be led by the devil, like captives, to that spectacle. Yes, is that endurable or tolerable? . . . How will we reconcile ourselves with God in the future, how appease His anger? Three days ago, when violent torrents of rain submerged everything, and, as it were, took the bread out of the mouths of the peasants . . . then you prayed and wept, went in crowds to the graves of the Apostles, and begged the help of St. Peter and the blessed Andrew. . . . And then, only a day later, you are jumping with joy, and making an uproar, and watching your soul, like a prisoner of war, being dragged away by your own passions!

"If you wish to see unreasoning animals run, why do you not couple together the animal passions in yourselves, the

anger and the fleshly lust, and throw over them the yoke of
piety, and give them your own conscience for a charioteer, and
drive them to the goal of your own supernatural vocation, in
which you do not run from the outrages of the circus to those
of the theater, but from earth to heaven? That kind of
chariot racing is not merely entertaining, it is also very advantageous!

"But you run from the smoke into the fire . . . and then
you ask: What is bad about it? That is just what pains me,
that you are sick without knowing that you can at least call
a doctor. Your hearts are filled with thoughts of adultery, and
you ask: What is wrong about it? Is your body perhaps made
of stone, or of iron? It is made of flesh, of human flesh, and
it is set on fire by the spark of passion more easily than dry
hay!

"And what have I long said about the theater? You often
get off balance even when you meet a woman on the street.
Then if you see a shameless woman in the theater, who treads
the stage with uncovered head and bold attitudes, dressed in
garments adorned with gold, flaunting her soft sensuality, singing immoral songs, throwing her limbs about in the dance,
and making shameless speeches . . . do you still dare to say
that nothing human happens to you then? Long after the
theater is closed and everyone is gone away, those images still
float before your soul, their words, their conduct, their glances,
their walk, their positions, their excitation, their unchaste
limbs—and as for you, you go home covered with a thousand
wounds! But not alone—the whore goes with you—although
not openly and visibly . . . but in your heart, and in your conscience, and there within you she kindles the Babylonian
furnace . . . in which the peace of your home, the purity of
your heart, the happiness of your marriage, will be burnt up!

"Therefore I make it known and announce in a loud voice:
If anyone, after this sermon and admonition, runs to the sinful
outrages of the theater, him will I not allow to pass the
threshold of this church, him will I not allow to partake of the
holy mysteries; let him no more approach the Holy Table. I
will do as the shepherds do, who separate the mangy sheep
from the flock, lest they contaminate the others.

"It is now a year since I came to your city, and again and

again I have warned and admonished you. So if some will still persevere in their moral corruption, they will finally be separated and cut off. . . . They will be excluded from the congregation. If you shudder with horror at this judgment, then let the guilty ones simply show repentance, and the judgment will be lifted. For we have the power to bind, and we also have the power to loose . . . and we will not excommunicate our brethren, except to save the Church from disgrace. So he who perseveres in this impurity, let him enter the Church no more, but let him avoid it, as though he were a common enemy.[15] Therefore do not receive such into your houses, do not invite them to your tables, keep far away from them, even on the street! In that way we will win them back more easily and more quickly. May the guilty ones return quickly, through the intercession of the saints! I will do everything in my power; and if I have had to grieve you, if I have had to be disagreeable and troublesome to you, it is in order that some day I may be able to answer without fault or reproach before the dreadful judgment seat of God."[16]

What Chrysostom meant by these last words, the people of Constantinople were soon to learn. Scarcely two months after this classical lecture, in August, 399, the Emperor Arcadius issued a law which stipulated with laconic brevity: "In no city will theatrical plays or horse races or any other spectacles take place on the Lord's Day (Sunday). . . . Only on the Emperor's birthday can such celebrations be held on Sundays."[17]

Chrysostom surely must have had something to do with this law. Anyhow, it was only a renewal and extension of a law of Theodosius I, who had forbidden spectacles on Sunday as far back as 392.[18] Ten years later (409) the exception in favor of the Emperor's birthday was done away with.[19]

The spectacles of the circus and the theater naturally remained. Only now they had to be confined to weekdays, which was not very pleasing to business people and workers.

A tragic accident which happened in Constantinople one day proved moreover that the circus was not merely a danger to the soul but to the life of the body as well. A young charioteer, who was soon to be married, unfortunately had his chariot overturned in a race, and his head and legs were

broken by the wheels of the other chariots.[20]   This event
naturally strengthened Chrysostom's opposition to the passionate circus spectacles.

One must perhaps feel tempted to consider it a pity that
Chrysostom waged such a continuous battle against the circus
and the theater, a battle which was hopeless in the face of the
Eastern nature and the customs of centuries.   However,
Chrysostom sought more to remove the malignant growths in
the life of the circus, and in this he partly attained his end.
It must have been much more difficult to bring about a palpable change and improvement in the prevailing scandalous
conduct in the theater.   Basically, the Christians had to create
a completely new theatrical literature with a new spirit and
new motives, and for this, up until the end of the fourth
century, there had been really no time.

On the other hand, to employ Christian ideas and material
for the stage was felt to be a sacrilege, and it could not have
been otherwise in the half pagan world of spectators of the
fourth century.   It would be centuries yet before the religious
mystery plays of the entirely Catholic Middle Ages appeared,
and even these were not always protected from degeneration
in their relation to the stage.[21]

*   *   *

Chrysostom thenceforward felt very bitterly that, in spite of
all his preaching, so little visible improvement could be
noticed.   "See, every day I cry myself hoarse, 'Stay away from
the theater!'; and many laugh at me.   A thousand times have
I warned you: 'Stop your cursing and your dishonest dealings!'; and no one listens to me!"[22]   Indeed, whether it was
illness or longing for his beloved Antioch, or whether Constantinople was actually so low in regard to Christian religion
and morals, Chrysostom occasionally had moods in which the
most hopeless pessimism attacked him.   In one Homily on the
Acts of the Apostles, he said: "How many, do you think, will
be saved, out of this our city? You will perhaps take it amiss,
when I say this, but nevertheless I must say it: Among so
many thousands one can scarcely find a hundred who will
work out their salvation; and even of these I doubt!   For:

How much evil is in our youth? How much light-minded-
ness in our own people? There are scarcely any who act in
a becoming way to their own children.

"No young person considers taking an old man for a model.
Do not tell me: There are so many of us! People who speak
thus look only on external things. You may indeed speak
thus before men; but before God, who does not need us, that
is not worth anything. Therefore, in regard to the Church,
no one should wonder at the great number of its members;
the chief thing is that we should take the trouble to make
them useful and good. There is for example the common
prayer in the church; but young and old remain cold: they
are more outcasts than youth, for they joke, laugh out loud
and amuse themselves, and carry on mischievously with one
another even while they are on their knees. You, whether
young or old, if you are standing nearby and see this, reproach
them, reprimand them vigorously; do not endure such things;
call the deacon, threaten them, do whatever you can, come to
me and tell me about it—I cannot see everything myself. I
know of others, who, while they are standing during the
prayers, chatter among themselves; and others, who talk not
merely during prayer, but even while the priest is saying the
Canon! What impudence! How long must we go on cen-
suring these people? How long reprimand them? Would it
not be better to exclude them from the church, as people
who only mislead and corrupt others? Or is the church then
a theater? But I believe that it is just the theater which is
to blame for these things, for it makes most of them unrestrained and unruly. What we build up here is torn down
there. Therefore I tell you what should be salutary for you:
God's judgment will come upon you, if you see people who
are disturbing order by amusing themselves, especially at
that time, and do not at once warn and reprimand them."[23]

One can understand how that sort of bad manners on the
part of the youth of a great city, in regard to church affairs,
should displease the sensitive bishop so much. Unfortunately
these were not the only matters which he had to denounce.
Among families even, there were still many unseasonable
reminders of the scarcely conquered paganism.

"Just see what the devil has contrived again: because the

D

natural inclination of women restrains them from the theater
and its immodesty, so the devil has brought the theater into
the women's chambers; I mean this, unchaste men and dissolute women. Our wedding customs demand such smut . . .
or rather, our absurdity demands it. Man, you know not
what you do. You bring a wife into your home for the sake
of chastity and of children. Then why do you have dealings
with dissolute women? For the sake of increasing your
pleasure? But in this way you shame your bride and the
women who have been invited. . . . For it is very shameful
and humiliating to bring immoral men and dancers and all
their devil's pomp into your house. You can beautify your
wedding with other things; with costly banquets and beautiful
clothing; that I will not forbid. But what is the purpose of
these masks and made-up faces? Repeat what they have said
—it would shame you to say it. You disgrace yourself, but do
you compel others to do it? Where only chastity and modesty
should reign, they jump about like camels and donkeys! I
approve of maidens and wives being present; the former to
give away the bride, the latter to receive her. The bride
stands in the midst: she is neither maiden nor wife, she is no
more the former and not yet the latter.

"So what have the dissolute women to do there? At a wedding one should hide and bury them, and still we bring them
there! On any other occasion you would not even speak to
such women, and here you bring them in yourself! Does your
bride wish to dance? But these people should not even show
themselves at a bridal banquet. Or is the wedding then a
theater? It is a Sacrament, a mystery, and a model of the
Church of Christ, and still you invite dissolute women to it!
But who will dance there, if neither the bridesmaids nor the
newly married? No one! But why is there any need of
dancing at all? They dance at pagan ceremonies; but at ours,
silence and decorum should prevail, respect and modesty.
Here a great mystery is accomplished; away with the dissolute
women, away with the profane! "[24]

Furthermore, the Synod of Laodicea had decreed the same
long before.[25] Still, the dancers had not been frightened away
by the canons.

If the Christians of Constantinople were just as slow as the people of Antioch in observing the admonitions of the sermons, so also they showed themselves just as quick in criticism: "I know that many ridicule me and say that I always speak on the same subject; so much so that it becomes wearisome. But we are not to blame for this, but the listeners themselves. For whosoever leads a righteous life is glad as often as he hears the same, as though he had been praised personally. But he who does not lead a good life, for him one time is too much; and if he hears it a second time, he says the same, that he has heard it too often."[26]

Literary Activity

With the unaccustomed and multiform burdens of the episcopal office, and besides, his numerous sermons, Chrysostom must have felt it a pleasure to be able to spend at least the evening and the early hours of the night in his beloved literary activity. This must have been for him a necessity and a refreshment, otherwise it could scarcely be understood how he could have found time for writing, besides all the duties of his episcopal office. Regard for his health could not have been the only reason why he restricted all time-consuming business transactions to the most necessary; above all he did not wish to lose his time by long sitting at the table, and therefore neither gave nor accepted invitations, indeed did not partake of the common table with his episcopal guests. To him, time was too valuable for such things.

Only to this circumstance, and to his iron industry, is due the fact that Chrysostom, as Bishop of the metropolis and the imperial city, was still in a position to explain the Acts of the Apostles, and also the Epistles of St. Paul, in continuous homilies.

Without doubt, the twelve homilies on the Epistle to the Colossians were published in Constantinople.[27] Bonsdorff has brought out all the reasons for this assumption, and has given the autumn of 399 as the exact point of time.[28] Likewise the sixteen collected homilies on the first and second Epistles to the Thessalonians certainly originate from this episcopal period. Their exact date, however, is not known.[29]

The greatest and most important Commentary, which certainly originated in Constantinople, is composed of the fifty-

five homilies on the Acts of the Apostles.[30]   Chrysostom himself said in one Homily that it had been three years already
(or the third year $= \tau\rho\iota\epsilon\tau\iota\alpha\nu$ $\check{\epsilon}\chi\omicron\mu\epsilon\nu$) that he had preached in Constantinople.   So the Homilies in all probability fall in the
year 400.[31]   Likewise the three Homilies on the letter to
Philemon belong to Constantinople, as Bonsdorff has shown
to be positively probable.[32]

After all this, there remains only the Epistle to the
Hebrews.[33]   The 34 Homilies which are attributed to him
were first issued after Chrysostom's death, as the work of the
Antiochene priest Constantine (or Constantius) and indeed
$\dot{\alpha}\pi\grave{o}$ $\sigma\eta\mu\epsilon\iota\omega\nu$, which Bonsdorff translates as "Stenogram." This
led naturally to the supposition that Chrysostom had actually
given all these sermons in Constantinople, and indeed at a
time when the storm of the first banishment had already
broken over his head.[34]   In and for itself, that would be
possible.   Only neither these nor the earlier mentioned series
of Homilies give the impression of being actually stenographic
copies.   The indications of concrete actuality are too markedly
missing there.   Furthermore, it is not understandable why
one should have had to fetch a priest from Antioch for the
publication of a stenographic transcript already prepared in
Constantinople, especially at a time when a state of war existed
between the successor of Chrysostom and the "Johnites."

Among the $\sigma\eta\mu\epsilon\iota\alpha$ may well have been the first project for
these sermons, the "Concept," originating from Chrysostom
himself.   This project can hardly have originated in Antioch
and then have been suddenly left behind at Chrysostom's
unexpected departure.   For later on, he had, doubtless, had
his most important personal effects sent after him.   Thus it
would not be understandable, why in this case Constantine
should have waited more than ten years before he actually
released these Homilies.   But if the manuscript of Chrysostom
actually originated in Constantinople, how did it get into the
hands of the priest who surely lived in Antioch?   So one must
assume that one is dealing here either with a Constantine not
otherwise known, or that the Homilies originated during the
enforced hours of leisure while he was in exile.   Chrysostom
actually had some brief relations with the priest Constantine
during his banishment,[35] and this priest visited him in his

exile at Cucusus.[36]   At any rate, this Constantine kept himself hidden in Cyprus for a long time on account of his loyal adherence to Chrysostom.[37]

A reliable answer to this question does not appear possible from the materials hitherto available.

FOOTNOTES

1. In regard to his remark in Hom. 5, 4 on the 2nd Epistle to the Thessalonians (62, 498): "They can listen to me once or twice a month, or not even that," Bonsdorff rightly remarks (Die Predigttätigkeit, p. 106) that Chrysostom does not mean that he only preached once or twice a month, but that the people came to the sermon only once or twice or even less often. Cf. Hom. 30, 3 in Act. Ap. (60, 217).

2. Palladius, Dial. 5 (47, 20).

3. Hom. 13, 4 in Act. Ap. (60, 110-11).

4. Hom. 51, 5 in Act. Ap. (60, 358).

5. Hom. 1, 4 in Col. (62, 304 ff.).   Likewise in Hom. 7, 3 (346).

6. Hom. 10, 5 in Col. (62, 372-73).

7. HE 8, 5 (67, 1528).

8. Hom. in: Pater meus usque modo operatur 1 (63, 511): καταβοῶντες ἀνεχορεῖτε, δεινοπαθοῦντες.

9. *Ibid.* (512).

10. Hom. 20, 4 in Act. Ap. (60, 226-28).

11. Oratio 36, XI de Seipso (36, 280).

12. J. Pargoire, Echos d'Orient 3 (1899-1900) 151-162.

13. Obviously because of their famous Church of the Apostles and the valuable relics of the Apostles.

14. Cf. p. 76 of this volume.

15. Cf. 2 Thess. 3, 14.

16. Hom. contra ludos et theatra 1 ff. (56, 263-270).   Concerning the art of the rope-dancers and the buffoons in the fourth century, cf. also Hom. 19, 4 ad pop. Antioch. (49, 195-96).

17. Cod. Theod. 2, 8, 23 (ed. Mommsen p. 89).

18. *Ibid.* 2, 8, 20 (Mommsen p. 88).

19. *Ibid.* 2, 8, 25.

20. Hom. 9, 1 in Jo. 5, 17 (63, 512).

21. R. Heinzel, Beschreibung des geistlichen Schauspiels im deutschen Mittelalter.   Hamburg and Leipzig 1898, p. 213-215. E. K. Chambers, The medieval stage.   Oxford 1903.   Vol. 2, 68 ff.

22. Hom. 44, 3 in Act. Ap. (60, 312).   Cf. Hom. 8, 2-3 in Act. Ap. (60, 73-76) against swearing.

23. Hom. 24, 4 in Act. Ap. (60, 189-192).   Cf. Hom. 42, 4 in Act. Ap. (60, 301).

24. Hom. 12, 4 in Coloss. (62, 386-87).   Cf. Hom. in: Propter fornicationes n. 2 (51, 211).

25. Between 340 and 341, Can. 53 and 54 = Mansi 2, 590; Hefele KG 1, 773.

26. Hom. 44, 3 in Act. Ap. (60, 312).

27. 62, 299-392.

28. Zur Predigttätigkeit . . . p. 82-85.

29. Bonsdorff gives it as 402.   Still, the effort of getting a continuous and uninterrupted chronology for the writings of Chrysostom may have influenced the fixation of this period more than the text itself gives one to understand.

30. 59, 13-384.   According to the Berlin. philol. Wochenschrift 37 (1917) 1140, E. Preuschen, in his Erklarung zur Apostelgeschichte (Tübingen 1912) showed that the Greek text of Chrysostom's commentary on the Acts of the Apostles first became comprehensible through the Armenian Catena, and: "What we now read in Greek is only a mutilated abridgment of which the source can perhaps clarify research into the Greek tradition."   I do not think this very probable.   The quotation from Preuschen I did not find.

31. That Chrysostom in H. 37, 3 (60, 267) spoke of the expulsion of the Goths (Bonsdorff p. 94), is a misunderstanding; he spoke of the expulsion of moral enemies (vices), which dwell side by side with the citizens (virtues) in the city of the soul.

32. Bonsdorff 108.

33. 63, 9-236.

34. According to Bonsdorff, the commentary "falls in the second half of 402 and the first half of 403."

35. Cf. Letters 221 and 225 (52, 732 and 735).

36. Chrysostom, Letters 13 and 114 (52, 611 and 670).   Cf. Palladius 11 (c. 37).

37. Palladius 16 (54).

CHAPTER X

THE FRIENDS OF THE NEW BISHOP

FROM the beginning, Chrysostom was put in the most difficult position by his own clergy. In the first place, his
arrival had meant a cruel disappointment for more than
one hopeful aspirant. Then, he was considered by the inhabitants of the city more or less as a "foreigner," who had never
even seen Constantinople before. Finally, and this was what
decided the issue, the new Archbishop was renowned, not
merely as a great orator, but also as a strict ascetic, who himself practised in all things what he preached to others. But
asceticism and strictness of life were plants which did not
thrive very well or luxuriantly in the soil of Constantinople.

However, it would be false to believe that there were none
among the clergy who did not warmly welcome the reforms of
their chief shepherd. Indeed one of them, at least, found the
new Bishop much too mild. At the head of the strict reform
party stood Serapion, the Archdeacon and steward of the
episcopal palace and hospice. He was, in a certain sense, the
most important man after the Patriarch, and his right hand in
all things. He came from Egypt, the land of radicalism, and
he showed decidedly belligerent tendencies. The irreligious
behavior of so many members of the clergy filled him with
displeasure and contempt, and once in a Consistory he is said
to have made the significant remark: "Bishop, you can never
rule over these people unless you chastise them all with a
single whip."[1] This remark flew quickly from mouth to
mouth, and from that hour, Serapion was a hated man among
all the less pious group of the clergy. If Socrates attributes
to him at the same time arrogance and haughty, lordly ways,
which were quite unendurable, he is essentially only the
echo of the people who were associated with the priest and
later Patriarch, Atticus.[2]

On the other hand, Serapion was perfectly faithful to his

Archbishop, in body and soul. Chrysostom, on his part, also gave him his fullest confidence; he knew that he could rely on him absolutely. The result was frankly this, that the aversion to the Archdeacon was transferred to a certain extent to the Archbishop, as is noted expressly by Socrates. Some other clergy, who were also known as specially faithful adherents of Chrysostom, were the priest Tigrius and the lector Paulus;[3] another was the cantor Eutropius, the priest and court chaplain Helladius, the deacon Eusebius and others, whom we shall encounter in the course of events.

Many pious women also followed the Archbishop zealously. Chief of these was the superior of the ecclesiastical deaconesses, the famous Olympias, with whom he was joined in a bond of true spiritual and sympathetic relationship.[4] This lady came from the Roman-Greek high nobility of Constantinople. Her grandfather Ablavius had held the position of Praefectus Praetorii (Minister of War) under Constantine the Great. Her aunt, Olympias, had been betrothed to the Emperor Constans, and married King Arsaces of Armenia. Olympias herself had lost her parents at a tender age.[5] A relative, the pious Theodosia, sister of Bishop Amphilochius of Iconium, and related to St. Basil and St. Gregory Nazianzus,[5a] thereupon undertook her further education. Gregory of Nazianzus had visited in their house during his term of office as Bishop of Constantinople; so he was acquainted with the youthful Olympias. She herself appeared certain of a brilliant future. She had all the necessary conditions for it: nobility, immense riches, also beauty and spirit. But all these were outshone and ennobled by a deep inclination to piety and benevolence.

When she reached the age of eighteen, and was in the full splendor of her youthful beauty, she married, in the year 385, Nebridius, who, in spite of his youth, was already city prefect of Constantinople. A number of Bishops were invited to the wedding. Gregory of Nazianzus would gladly have come, had he not been prevented by illness. So he sent at least to the wedding a beautiful poem, to celebrate the occasion—it is the oldest Christian " Mirror for Women " which we possess.[6]

But their married happiness was of short duration. Nebridius died shortly after the wedding, and Olympias decided to remain a widow, as the young Anthusa, the mother of Chrysostom, had done before her.[7]   She remained true to her purpose, when the Emperor Theodosius, with the best intentions, sought to give her in marriage to a relative of his, named Elpidius.[8]

When she was about twenty-five years old, she received from the Patriarch Nectarius, in spite of her youth, the consecration as deaconess in the Cathedral in Constantinople.[9]

In commemoration of this day, she sent to Bishop Nectarius,[10] for the church of Constantinople, ten thousand pounds of gold, twenty thousand pounds of silver, and furthermore all her possessions in Thrace, Galatia, Cappadocia, and Bithynia, as well as three palaces in Constantinople.   Lastly she had a cloister built on the south side of the Cathedral for the deaconesses and young women consecrated to God, where they led a common life of " contemplation and praise of God." In all, there were about 250 young women there.   Olympias was their first abbess.   The cloister also had the right, on certain occasions, to place four of its members in the class of deaconesses.   No secular person, either man or woman, could enter the cloister, except only the Patriarch, John, who gave them regular lectures.[11]

Olympias stood by the Patriarch Nectarius with her influence and her abilities, as far as she was able.   Palladius even says that in ecclesiastical affairs she had a great influence over him.[12]   The truth of this statement is not certain.   At any rate, her influence can have been only a good and wholesome one.   As a deaconess she lived with great asceticism.   She never ate meat, and used the bath only in case of illness, which for Romans and Greeks of that time was a very great privation. She suffered much from stomach trouble.

When Chrysostom became Bishop, their spiritual relationship must soon have taken on the character of a sincere mutual trust and noble esteem.   In any case, Olympias depended on him with the entire devotion and admiration of a sensitive and noble soul.   She never suffered such pain in all her life as when she was forced to see the holy Archbishop gradually becoming a victim to intrigue and passions which she could not have imagined in such a position.   Chrysostom remained to her a true friend and consoler until death.

However, Chrysostom was no weak leader.

Olympias inherited great possessions from her parents, but she had given up all these possessions for benevolent purposes. One might call her the Greek counterpart of the Roman Melania the Younger. She also devoted all her wealth and her entire income to the poor, and to the Church. In regard to this, her conduct was quite indiscriminate. Whoever came, received what he wished.[13] Naturally many people took advantage of this blind generosity, when they were not in real need of it. Not only unfortunate and needy people came to her, but also young women consecrated to God, monks, clergy and bishops, such as Amphilochius of Iconium, Optimus of Antioch in Pisidia, Gregory of Nazianzus, Peter of Sebaste, Epiphanius of Cyprus, and others. For all, she undertook the role of a beneficent Providence.[14]

Even the rich and powerful Patriarch Theophilus of Alexandria never forgot, when he was in Constantinople, to knock at Olympias' door and ask her for money, first for his building, and again for other purposes. It is also related that the Patriarch had on such occasions even thrown himself at the feet of the hesitating Olympias, and kissed her knees, in order to get money; but she became so ashamed over such humility and self-abasement that she cast herself on the floor in tears before the Patriarch.[15]

Also the Bishops Antiochus, Severian, and Acacius of Beroea were among those upon whom not only the spiritual riches of the pious deaconess exerted an attraction.[16]

So when Chrysostom heard that Olympias was dispensing her wealth all too carelessly, and giving to everyone who asked her, he said to her one day: " I praise your good will. Only you must give alms in the right way. If you give to them who already have enough, it is just as though you poured your wealth into the sea. Now you know well, that you have dedicated your possessions to the poor for a special motive, for God's sake; so you are only the steward of these possessions, and must give an accounting of them. So if you will listen to me, in future limit your gifts according to the need of the suppliant. So you will be able to help a greater number of poor and will be rewarded by God for your merciful assistance."[17]

Probably this sensible advice displeased those who had hitherto been the chief beneficiaries of the carefree liberality of Olympias.

For himself, Chrysostom had accepted the service of Olympias only on one special point. He, like Olympias herself, was a great sufferer from stomach trouble, and could eat only bland food. So the deaconess begged the favor of being allowed to prepare his food.[18] Since he ate only a little, and often not until evening, that could not have been much trouble.

Other deaconesses of distinguished family were Pentadia, Procla and Silvina.[19] The last was the daughter of the Numidian leader Gildo, also wife of Nebridius and mother of two children. St. Jerome had persuaded her to remain a widow after the death of her husband.[20] She must have become a deaconess soon after this (about 400), and this through the persuasion of Chrysostom. At any rate, she also remained true to the Bishop through good and bad days.

As to the fate of Pentadia, the wife of the former General and Consul Timasius, that has been related before.[21]

Of Procla, nothing is known but her name.

Another young woman named Nicarete, from Nicomedia, was among the most loyal adherents of Chrysostom until the end.[22] Out of modesty she had never wished to become a deaconess or a superior of young women, but led in quietness a life of extraordinary and universal benevolence.

But the new Bishop found friends not merely among the devout sex. Even in the court there were those who greeted his endeavors warmly, indeed even personally supported him. There was Brison the eunuch, and the chamberlain of the Empress Eudoxia. He was skilled in music, and helped Chrysostom in the creation of good choirs.[23]

The later Consul Anthemius, who under Theodosius the Younger guided the destiny of the Empire for a long time, seems to have belonged to the group of the Patriarch's friends. At least Chrysostom wrote to him from his exile a very courteous letter, full of high praises.[24]

Still many other personalities from among the clergy, court and official world belonged to the circle of Chrysostom's friends, without finding an opportunity to play a historical role in his life. But many others doubtless belonged to that species of friend of whom it is said "a friend in need is a friend indeed."

The great mass of the people depended on him with a sincere love, and that not alone in the first years of his good fortune, but also in time of need and affliction. Socrates, who otherwise was no special friend of Bishop John, says of him: "The people bestowed great applause on him on account of his sermons in the church, and depended on him with love."[25] Sozomen confirmed this testimony, and said: " John governed the Church of Constantinople for the best, and brought many pagans and heretics back to it. The people flocked to him from all sides, some because they wished to hear his sermons, others only to see how he was. He won them all, and moved them to embrace the same religion."[26] Even Zosimus, the pagan, must needs pay him due recognition, even if he put it in this maliciously wicked form: "The man possessed the power to win the silly crowd."[27]

That Chrysostom furthermore especially espoused the cause of the poor, in regard to social charity, has been mentioned before, and was surely not the last reason for the people's affection.

FOOTNOTES

1. Socrates 6, 4 (67, 672 A).
2. Palladius, Dial 11 (47, 37).
3. Socrates 6, 15 (709 C).
4. The name of her father has been given in different versions. According to Palladius, Hist. Laus. 56 (Butler 2, 150) and the Fragmentum histor. II (85, 1812 B) he was named Seleucus. The less credible Menologium of Canisius calls him Anysius Secundus.
5. The sources for the Life of Olympias are: 1. Palladius, Dial. 10, 16 and 17; Hist. Laus. cp. 56; 2, and 61. 2. The seventeen letters of Chrysostom to Olympias (52, 549 ff.). 3. Sozomen HE 8, 9 and 24 (67, 1537 and 1578). 4. The anonymous Vita S. Olympiadis Diacon. from the fifth century=Analecta Boll. 15 (1896) 409-423; translated into French by Bousquet in the Revue de l'Orient chrét. 11 (1906) 225-250. 5. The Narratio Sergiae de translatione S. Olympiadis (seventh century)=Anal. Boll. 16 (1897) 44-51; French by Bousquet=Revue de l'Orient chrét. 12 (1907) 258-268. 6. Gregory Naz. Carmen 2, 6 (37, 1542-50). Cf.

Bohringer, Chrysostomus und Olympias. 2. A. Stuttgart 1876; Meurisse, Histoire d'Olympias diaconesse de Constantinople. Metz 1640.

5a. S. Gregory Nazianzus, Carmen 11, 2, Verse 97 ff. (37, 1549).

6. 37, 1542-50.

7. According to Palladius, Hist. Laus. 56, the marriage lasted only "a few days." With Ch. 56 of the Hist. Laus. cf. Butler, the Laus. History 2, XLVI.

8. Another Nebridius was the husband of Salvina, to whom Letter 79 of St. Jerome (22, 724-732) is addressed.

9. Cf. the law of Valentinian-Theodosius of the 21st of June, 390 concerning the deaconesses = Cod. Theodos. 16, 2, 27 (ed. Mommsen 843). According to the old Byzantine formulary of consecration, a deaconess was consecrated in the same way as a deacon; by the laying on of hands, the prayer of consecration by the Bishop, the clothing with the *stola*, and the offering of the chalice. Cf. A. Kalsbach, Die altkirchliche Einrichtung der Diakonissin, p. 69-71. The deaconesses had to help with the baptism of women; they took part in the choir prayer of the clergy, and performed many services of the modern lay apostolate in the world of women.

10. The name "Ioannes" in the Vita Olympiadis cp. 7 is an error here. (An. Boll. 15 (1896) 415.)

11. So the Vita Olympiadis cp. 6-8. *loc. cit.* 414-15.

12. Dial. 17 (47, 61).

13. Palladius, Dial. 17 (61).

14. *Ibid.*

15. Pall. Dial. 16 (56).

16. *Ibid.* 17 (61).

17. Sozomen 8, 9 (1540).

18. Pall. Dial. 16 (61) and Vita Olympiadis cp. 8 (*loc. cit.* 415).

19. Called Salvina by the Latins; St. Jerome, Epist. 79 and 123 (ML 22, 724 and 1059). Pall. Dial. 10 (35).

20. Epist. 79 and 123, 18 (ML 22, 724-732 and 1059). Cf. Cavallera, S. Jérôme 1, 184.

21. Cf. Güldenpenning 77 and 89.

22. Sozomen 8, 23 (67, 1576 B).

23. Socrates 6, 8 (689 C); Soz. 8, 18 (1564 A).

24. Letter 147 = 52, 699. Cf. Socrates, HE 6, 20 (67, 725 and 740).

25. HE 6, 4 (67, 672); cf. *ibid.* 6, 7 (688) and 6, 10 (696).

26. HE 8, 5 (1528).

27. Hist. 5, 23 (ed. Mendelssohn 244).

CHAPTER XI

POLITICAL STORMS: THE REVOLT OF THE GOTHS: DISGRACE AND END OF EUTROPIUS

ALMOST a year and a half had gone by, during which Chrysostom had preached, written, and ruled in his episcopal office in outward peace and with holy zeal. Then clouds began to gather in the political sky, and to threaten trouble for Constantinople.

The imperial minister and master of the court, Eutropius, had, since the death of Rufinus (395) continued to build up his powerful position at court and in the Empire.[1] He had so far attained his object with the Emperor Arcadius, that he had attained equal rank with the chief military prefect, the war minister of that time. He had had himself named assessor, and later, chairman of that imperial commission which dealt with important affairs of justice, especially those dealing with high treason. It represented also a sort of high court of justice. Finally, the eunuch even decided to celebrate a triumph, in military uniform, for victories which others had won over various barbarian hordes.[1a] This naturally angered the generals, especially the one who had long regarded his powerful position with envy and jealousy, namely Gainas, leader of the Goths.

At last something happened which had never happened before, in the Roman Empire: Eutropius was named Consul of the Empire for the year 399.[2] The entire Roman and Greek world felt it an outrage that a member of the despised tribe of eunuchs, a former slave, of whose origin no one knew anything for certain, had been elevated to the highest and most honorable position in the Empire. It is true that the eccentric Emperor Caligula had once appointed a horse as Consul; but he was a fool whom no one took seriously. The Emperor Arcadius, although he was not a real man, was not a fool. He was not to be figured out.

Psychologically, the ambitious struggle for power on the part of the eunuch Eutropius may be considered as a passionate protest against the unjust contempt in which eunuchs were held at that time—the pitiable sacrificial victims, but not criminal evidences, of an evil barbarian custom.

It is true that Eutropius, in his choice of means for his end, showed himself an unfeeling man. He kept a whole army of spies, who reported everything to him, and of accomplices of the lowest sort, such as Bargos, who betrayed his best benefactor Timasius, and the crafty and flattering Osius, a former kitchen slave, who in 395 attained to the office of imperial treasurer and master of the imperial chancellery; and also Suburmachius, a depraved Colchian from a lordly race, who yielded to Eutropius and to wine in equal measure,[3] and became commander of the Imperial bodyguard.

The means of satisfying these people, and his own necessities, were procured by Eutropius, in part, through arbitrary, unjust extortions, confiscations and banishments.[4]

In order to get his hands on his opponents and those he wished to sacrifice, he even dared to violate the ecclesiastical right of sanctuary, which at least in certain cases, such as high treason and the like, he wished to make ineffectual. Also, he must have allowed many encroachments and acts of despotism in the ecclesiastical sphere. At any rate, Chrysostom, on account of this, was put into a very painful position from the beginning. He knew, and the whole world knew, that it was chiefly through Eutropius that he had been made Bishop. Could he allow it to come to a break with the all-powerful man, just at the beginning? It gave brilliant proof of Chrysostom's greatness of character that he did not hesitate a moment to do his duty, without any consideration of his own person.[5]

Eutropius certainly knew his Orientals, and the people of the metropolis. He gave entertainments in honor of his consulate, the like of which Chrysostom had seldom seen: circus spectacles, free theatrical shows, festal banquets, distributions of money; everything had to serve to celebrate the "Consul," and—to allow the "eunuch" to be forgotten.

As always, the momentary success was on his side. Whether it was fear of his power, or hope of profit, all bowed them-

selves before this upstart. Senators, officers, and people contended with one another to offer homage and good wishes to
the eunuch who had been decorated with the insignia of the
Consulate.   More than one even fell at his feet, sought to
grasp his hand, and gave him flattering titles such as " Pro-
tector of the Laws," " Father of Rulers," the " Third Founder
of the City."   Statues were even erected to him by the city
and by private citizens, and even the Senate did not consider
it beneath its dignity to place busts of the minister in the
Curia.   Eutropius stood at the very summit of his success
and of his power.

But in the same year came a sudden fall into the abyss.

Revolt of the Goths

Considering the currency and the means of communication
of those days, it must have been very difficult to rule the
Empire and to keep it peaceful, since it embraced an area of
120,000 square miles, and was inhabited by many millions of
people; of these, there were perhaps twenty various nationalities and races, who spoke many languages.   There were
Etruscans and Romans, Latins and Greeks, Celts and
Germans, Egyptians and Syrians, Sarmatians, Persians and
Armenians, Macedonians and Illyrians, and many other races,
who were continually on the move throughout the Roman
Empire.   But outside, across the frontiers, there were on all
sides wild barbarian hordes, with whom neither a just war
could be fought nor a defensible peace be concluded; today
they might be pushed back, and tomorrow there would be
new invasions and predatory excursions.   The most feared
frontier neighbors, for the Western Empire, were the
Germans; for the Eastern, the Persians or Parthians, and the
migratory Goths, Huns and other splinter races from the
human chaos, which in the middle of the fourth century
were in movement like breaking ice, and were drifting down
in the stream of folk migrations, towards the south and west
of Europe.

In the interior of the Empire, two outstanding cultural
groups stood opposite each other; the Roman conquerors in
the West, whose focal point was always Rome; the political
overlordship was theirs; but the leadership in the intellectual

and cultural spheres lay with the Greeks, whose chief power was in the Eastern Empire. They possessed three focal points: old Alexandria, the gathering point for Africa, then Antioch, the bulwark and sally port against the Asiatic East, and finally the youngest, although most significant politically, namely Constantinople. Its geographical position made it a natural point of union between the East and the West.

In ever greater numbers, poor and homeless Germans, especially Franks and Goths, offered themselves as mercenary soldiers, to serve in the Roman armies, during the course of the third and fourth centuries. They formed the first "foreign legion" of the Roman Empire.[6] Soon whole bodies of troops, under their own leaders, entered the Roman service, as the Swiss regiments later served in the courts of foreign princes and in foreign armies. Moreover, Goths and other Germans were often seen serving as slaves, workers or servants, in almost all positions and families: it was a peaceful invasion of the Roman Empire, which preceded, indeed smoothed the way for, the folk migrations and the break-up of at least the western part of the Roman Empire.

But the Germanic pride and self-consciousness grew also, along with the numbers and the influence. The powerful indigenous figures, who wore their own national costumes, and were never willing to be separated from their own weapons, often looked at the enervated Romans with pride and contempt, and despised the Greeks, polished and over-refined by a centuries-old culture. Soon they began to look upon themselves no more as mercenary soldiers of the Romans, but as protectors of the Empire, who might very well be or become its overlords.

These Germanic peoples, especially the Gothic auxiliary troops and leaders of the army, had slowly become a power with which the Emperor would have to reckon, and under certain circumstances would have to fear. The Germans knew that very well, and began to feel themselves a power in the Empire.

Already in the West, the Frank Arbogast, under Theodosius, had made a disguised attempt to seat himself upon the

imperial throne of the West.   In the East, in the Balkans, the
Gothic leader Alaric had placed himself in power in the far
Roman-Greek provinces, and had to be confirmed there by
Arcadius.   Soon he was to march out again, to show the
frightened Romans that the proud queen of the world, un-
conquerable Rome, had lost the glory and fame of invinci-
bility.   Empresses of Germanic blood sat upon thrones in
Rome and Constantinople at the same time; in Rome the
daughter of the Goth Stilicho, in Constantinople the daughter
of the Frank Bauto; both of them at the side of weakling
rulers, born to rule but not able to do so.   The army itself
consisted in large part of Germanic troops, whose leaders
were not merely placed beside the Roman generals, but also
strove for equal influence at court.

It is clear that under these circumstances it must have
come to friction and rivalry here and there between the
"foreigners" and the Romans.   Everything separated the two
parties: nationality, language, clothing, sympathies and aims.
But the difference in religion formed the deepest chasm.   In
this the Greeks themselves were to blame.   The Goths, like
other Germanic races, had adopted Christianity from the
East Romans, just at the time when Arianism had been in
the ascendant.   While between the Greeks and the Romans
the heresy died out again, the sluggish Goths always remained
Arians.[7]

Among these Goths, a certain man had for a long time lain
in wait for an opportunity to overthrow the powerful Eutropius; one whose own heart was full of the most ambitious
plans and aims: Gainas, the supreme commander of the
Gothic legions.   This man, for his part, came to the Romans
as a deserter.   On account of his ability, he had risen, during
a period of years, from a simple soldier to the position of
general.   As leader of the Gothic auxiliary troops, he had
taken part in the year 394 in the campaign of the Emperor
Theodosius against the pretenders to the throne, Eugenius
and Arbogast.   Gainas must have been an energetic and keen
officer.   At that time, he had had to make the first attack in
the victorious decisive battle, in which the Goths fought with
such bravery that ten thousand of them lay at evening on the
bloody battlefield.   A year later Gainas led to Constantinople

the troops which Stilicho had had to send to the East, at the command of Arcadius (or Rufinus), and had Rufinus killed, at a military parade, before the eyes of the Emperor.[8]

One can easily understand that a brave soldier of such native strength and impetuosity could regard only with contempt and fury the management of the imperial court by eunuchs and women. So thoughts arose in him which were to be fatal to Eutropius, and which did not stop before the Emperor himself.

Gainas went about his plan with the calculated cunning of a barbarian. Among the Gothic troop leaders he had a trusted friend named Tribigild.[9] This man commanded the Gothic garrisons in Phrygia and had his command post in Nakolea. Now Theodosius had settled a large number of Gothic immigrants in just this province, and in the neighboring districts, in the year 386. So a levy of the Goths would promise special success in just this part of the Empire, and this would be the best place from which to set in motion a military attempt against the Empire. The events of the following time also showed clearly that Gainas and Tribigild had a secret understanding; this is testified by Zosimus,[10] Socrates,[11] Sozomen,[12] and Theodoret.[13]

Actually in the year 399 the metropolis was frightened by the news that the Goths in Phrygia had revolted, under the military leadership of Tribigild.[14] He succeeded, in the shortest possible time, in seizing the Asia Minor provinces of Galatia, Pisidia, Paphlagonia and Bithynia, and in isolating the chief city from the Eastern provinces.

A multitude of German slaves and rabble, anxious for plunder, very shortly joined together to form a small army. Tribigild conducted the war altogether in accordance with barbarian customs. He burned and plundered cities and villages; he killed the inhabitants, men and women. Everyone who was able fled to the ocean or to the islands.

At the court in Constantinople, everyone was busy with preparations for moving to the summer residence in Galatia, when the first news of the revolt came in. So they had to unpack their trunks. The way to summer coolness was blocked. Eutropius, the Lord High Steward and Consul, did not immediately recognize the danger in all its magnitude.

Then, when ever more alarming reports began to come in, he decided, not perhaps to collect an army, but—to open the purse, on whose almighty power he had hitherto seldom depended in vain. He attempted to bring Tribigild to submission by offering him a great sum of money.[15]

Tribigild or Gainas obviously reckoned on being able soon, themselves, to obtain this and very much more. So nothing was left but to try the fortunes of war. Certainly, the choice of a field-general was difficult. He did not wish, under the circumstances, to entrust the war against the Goths to a Goth, such as perhaps Gainas or Fravitta. But among the Greeks and Romans he could find no one at the moment who had a special military name, and at the same time possessed the confidence of Eutropius. So the calculating chamber diplomat did the most imprudent thing that he could have done: he chose an officer named Leo,[16] who was very devoted to him, but entirely incapable of great military undertakings, to be commander of the army against Tribigild. Even Gainas with his troops was put under him. Leo was to drive Tribigild to the lower end of Asia Minor, and Gainas in the Thracian Chersonesus was to protect the shore of the Dardanelles and the Empire from the rear. All that was wisely thought out by Eutropius.

The two Goths were separated, the Roman army under Leo stood between them, and in the metropolis the eunuch and consul Eutropius meanwhile reigned without a rival. But things did not go as they should. The former woolworker and now field-general Leo was, according to Claudian's statement, "rich in flesh and poor in spirit,"[17] while the rabid Eunapius says that Leo always had more dissolute women about him than soldiers, and that he drank more than all the rest of mankind together![18]

Certainly no battles would be won with these. Leo did not dare come to grips with Tribigild, and the latter, at any rate, preferred to plunder unprotected cities and villages. Of course the inhabitants set themselves against the Goths, with their own weapons for protection, and it seems that things did not always go so well with the Goths. Once, at Selge in Pisidia, Tribigild was able to rescue only himself and 300 men from the danger of complete annihilation.

It remains a mystery why Leo did not take advantage of the opportunity to render the rebellious Goths completely harmless. It is a fact that, at the right time, a great part of the Gothic army, under Gainas, went over to Tribigild, while the remaining ones fell on Leo's troops and partly annihilated them, partly threw them into disorder. The field-general Leo himself found there an insignificant end.

Now Gainas had the hilt in his hand. But now he showed himself true to the Emperor, apparently. He sent messengers to the court, and gave the most urgent recommendations to settle with the invincible Tribigild; but the latter demanded the deposition and surrender of Eutropius.[19]

The purpose and aim of both the Goths must now have revealed itself, though slowly. There could not be the slightest doubt that Gainas was the real originator of this challenge against Eutropius. He might very well have expected that after the death of Rufinus he would take the latter's place, and play the role in Constantinople which Stilicho played at the court of Rome. But the cunning chief chamberlain was a more artful player than the uncouth German. Now his brutal power was to attain what had not been possible to his prudence. If Eutropius were once overthrown, then Gainas would automatically be promoted to the position of supreme and most influential adviser to the Emperor. To this end he quite openly aspired.

Moreover, Eutropius himself had made things easier for him. His avarice, his violence and depredations, his boundless conceit and ambition, had in four years made him so much hated that the people only awaited an opportunity to get revenge on the all-powerful eunuch. More than anyone else, the officers and generals of the metropolitan garrison were furious against the courtier, who had brought shame and defeat on the army.

But the Emperor Arcadius was so much under the influence of his minister that he could not make up his mind to let him be disgraced. However, the Empress Eudoxia gave the final blow. The arrogance and violence of Eutropius had apparently begun to displease her, and she could not hide her dislike of him, or did not wish to feel that he was the author of her good fortune. Indeed, he had once even threatened her, saying that, as he had brought her into the imperial palace, so also he could get her out again.[20]

That must have stifled every feeling of gratitude in the heart of the proud German woman, to give place only to a feeling of insulted honor. Now the opportunity had come to make an end of a situation which had become painful. She went to the Emperor, with her two children in her arms, and told him, weeping, of the deeds of Eutropius, the misery of the Empire, the endangered future of his children; and entreated him not to place all at stake for the sake of such a man.[21]

Arcadius yielded. It seems that the Emperor himself, at the last, had not been very respectfully treated by Eutropius. This was in August 399.[22]

When Eutropius noticed the change in the situation, and felt that the days of his good fortune were numbered, and foresaw what might await him, despair seized him. When he realized that arrest was imminent, he fled in anguish and terror into the cathedral nearby, and sought, at its altar, protection from the soldiers who not far from there were knocking at the gates of the palace to seize him. Now his own deeds took revenge on him. He had hindered and obstructed by law these last refuges of the persecuted, as sacrifices to his avarice and violence. Now he lay there himself, trembling in the anguish of death, begging for grace, awaiting his fate.

The news of what had happened spread like lightning. The people streamed into the church, which was filled in an instant, to view the rare spectacle of greatness so suddenly fallen. Curiosity, malicious joy, hate, desire for revenge, sympathy—all these the anguished Eutropius could read in the faces of those who stared at him there, and who, through reverence for the sanctuary and the altar, dared not lay hands on him. Even the soldiers themselves were held back by religious awe. They did not venture to use force in the church.

Meanwhile, officers and soldiers had gathered outside before the Emperor's palace, and stormily demanded the death of Eutropius. They blamed him for the defeat and death of their comrades. The Emperor had much trouble in appeasing them. He did not wish to violate the holiness of the ecclesiastical sanctuary.[23]

Nothing is more difficult than to hold back, either for a long time or completely, the instinct of a multitude thirsty for revenge and blood. The scene was repeated the next day. Eutropius had not forsaken his protecting sanctuary. The people filled the church, and they were not sure what moment the soldiers might come and tear Eutropius forcibly away from the altar. Suddenly a deathly silence came over the multitude. The Archbishop was seen to appear and go into the pulpit.

"O vanity of vanities," began Chrysostom, in the most famous of his special orations, "all is vanity! One may say that at any time, but most of all here today. Where is now the brilliant splendor of the Consulate? Where are the bright lights, where the joyful applause and the singing of choirs, where the festal banquets and eulogies? Where are the garlands and the costly tapestries, where the noisy acclamations of the city, where the homage of the circus and the flattery of the spectators? All that has vanished away.

"A furious storm has blown the leaves off the trees, and convulsed them to the very roots. Where are now the pretended friends, where the drinking parties and feasting, where the swarm of parasites, where the unmixed wine, that flowed in rivers every day? Where are the arts of the kitchen, where are those who did and said whatever one wished, until their power lay in the dust? All that was a dream in the night, the day has dawned now, and all has disappeared. It was a flower of spring, that vanished with the spring; a shadow that passed away; like smoke, it has blown away; like soap bubbles, it has burst; like a spider's web, it has been torn in pieces. Therefore I repeat again the word of the Spirit: O vanity of vanities, and all is vanity!

"Have I not always said to you, that riches know no loyalty? But you have never listened to me. Have I not told you that you cannot rely on the gratitude of your hangers-on? But you would not believe it. And now—now is shown to you the actual proof that wealth is not only unreliable and ungrateful, but even a murderer. It is wealth that is to blame for your trembling and quaking here. Have I not told you, when you were often displeased because I spoke the truth, that I dealt better with you than all your flatterers? That I benefited you more with my reproaches than those who told you pleasant things? Have I not added that the wounds dealt by a friend are more wholesome than the voluntary kiss of an enemy? Had you endured my wounds, the kisses of your enemies would not have killed you.

"Where are now the cup-bearers, where are those who showed themselves so zealous to serve you in the streets, and who praised you in so many keys? They have run off to your enemies, they have denied your friendship, and they hope to save themselves by your death. But we do not deal thus: we did not bow before your displeasure, and now, when you have fallen, we will support and protect you. The Church, indeed, which you have wronged, has opened its doors to you and taken you in. But the theater, for which you have done so much, and for whose sake you have so often been angry with me, has forsaken and betrayed you. And still we have always told you: Why do you do that? You fight against the Church, and hurl yourself into the abyss! But you have thrown all my words to the winds. The circus and the horse races have eaten up all your wealth, and sharpened the sword for you; but the Church, which had to bear your undeserved anger, hastens to you and wishes to set you free.

"I say this now, not in order to shame the fallen, but to exhort to prudence those who are still upright; not in order to push a shipwrecked person into the deep, but to warn the others before they are also shipwrecked. If this man had kept the vicissitudes of human affairs before his eyes, and had feared them, he would not have had to undergo this. But because he did not improve himself, either by his own efforts or through outside advice, therefore you may learn at least, that you boast of your riches out of his misfortune. Nothing is more fickle than human happiness. One may call it smoke, or grass, a dream, or a spring flower, or anything else, but still one cannot reach the truth; it is so perishable, and less than nothing.

"Who stood higher than this man? Did he not surpass the whole world in wealth? Had he not attained the highest honors and dignities? Did not everyone fear him and tremble before him?   And see, now he is poorer than a prisoner, more miserable than a slave, more pitiable than a beggar, who wastes away from hunger; every day he has before his eyes sharp swords, ruin, the executioner, and death.   Indeed I cannot express in words what he has now to suffer, since every hour he awaits death.

"But of what need are our words?   He shows it you him-self, clearly enough.   Yesterday, when he was arrested by soldiers in the imperial palace, and fled to the sanctuary, his face was as pale as that of the dead; it is the same today; his teeth chattered, he trembled and shook all over his body, his voice forsook him, and his tongue was dumb; it seemed as though his soul had been turned to stone.

"I do not say this to deride him, nor to make merry over his misfortune, but to awake your hearts and to stir them to sympathy, in order to bring home to you that you must bear patiently with the punishment you have suffered until now. Many make it a reproach to me that I granted him the pro-tection of the altar; I should like to soften their hardness of heart; that is why I speak so often of his misfortune.

"For you it does not seem right that he was able to flee to the Church, whose rights he always denied.   However, we must praise God just on this account, because He let him come here in this time of need, which first showed him the power and the love of the Church . . . for now the Church holds her shield before him, who fought against her, and takes him under her protecting wings, offers him perfect security, thinks no more of what is past, but opens to him her arms with great love.   That is more beautiful than any triumph, that is a splendid victory . . . that she saves her enemy, taken prisoner in war; and while everyone despises him in his for-saken condition, she, with the love of a mother, hides him behind the curtains of the altar, and stands opposed to the displeasure of the Emperor, the fury and hatred of the people. That is the most beautiful ornament of the altar.   A fine ornament, you say, when such a criminal, thief and robber clings fast to the altar!   But did not the sinful, impure and dissolute woman embrace the feet of Christ?   And that did not conduce to the reproach of Jesus, but to admiration and great praise.

"So do not think of the evil which he has done. We are servants of the Crucified, who has said: Forgive them, for they know not what they do. (Luke 23, 34.)

"But, you will say, he himself has made escape to the altar impossible through his exemptions and different laws! But see, he has now experienced in his own body what he has done; he is now the first who upheld the law through his flight into the Church. So he has become a spectacle to the whole world, and he preaches silently to everyone and says: Do not do what I have done, that you may not suffer what I have suffered.

"Now the wealthy should come and learn a lesson for themselves. Whoever sees this man now, before whom the world trembled, as he has been hurled down from such a height, as he cowers there, as frightened as a hare or a frog, fettered without chains to this pillar, chained by anguish; as he fears and trembles and has lost all his arrogance, has been deprived of all his conceit, he has learned to see human glory in its true light; he will find realized here the word of Scripture: All flesh is as grass, and all human glory like a flower; the grass dries up, and the flower withers. (Is. 40, 6-7.)

"And when the poor come here and see this spectacle, then they do not feel so miserable, and do not complain so much about their poverty. Rather they will be glad that it serves them as a sure sanctuary, as a quiet haven and a strong wall of protection.

"So you see how his terror has become like a sermon for both rich and poor, for the lowly and the ambitious, for slaves and free.

"Have I raised your spirits now and appeased your wrath? Have I conquered your pitilessness, and aroused your sympathy? I think so. Your faces and your tears reveal it to me. Now we will fall at the feet of the Emperor, or rather, supplicate the dear God, that He may appease the displeasure of the Emperor and rouse his heart to hear our requests graciously."

Of course the Emperor was easier to appease than the military. Arcadius had already, on the previous day, interceded for Eutropius with the angry soldiers and officers, and had pointed out that the fallen man had not only done wickedness, but also good.   Indeed, he had requested, with tears, that they at least respect the holiness of the altar and the church sanctuary.

"So," continued Chrysostom, "if the Emperor forgets a wrong which has been done to himself, why will you, to whom nothing has happened, still persist in your wrath? Now is not the time to judge but to practise mercy.   So let us save the fugitive, that we may please the Emperor, and find grace and mercy from God ourselves.[24]   Amen."

Many had given a bad interpretation to this sermon. Instead of sympathy for the fallen man, Chrysostom has been accused of reproaching him.   Socrates[25] and Sozomen[26] even say that he alienated many hearts on account of it.   As a matter of fact, his almost naïve frankness in this sermon moved them in a peculiar manner.   However, one cannot judge such a sermon, originating in the excitement of a great moment, by the verdict of unconcerned readers, and still less by the feelings of a woman's soul, which feels only sympathy for fallen greatness.   If Chrysostom wished to appease the angry people and the soldiers, he surely would not have spoken a eulogy over Eutropius; he had to recognize the just displeasure of the people, and bring it to expression, before he could begin to work on their sympathies.

Moreover, Chrysostom was too much of a moralist and preacher of ethics to let pass an opportunity of making the most of such an impressive moral example.   Since he wished to save Eutropius for the future, one could not know to what extent such a truly deserved exhortation might yet benefit him.   Actually, one might rightly call this speech a masterpiece of psychology and rhetoric, and not for nothing was it read more often than all of Chrysostom's other sermons, even in the higher schools, insofar as they are not confined to the narrow limits of the textbooks of the state schools.

As a matter of fact, Chrysostom saved the life of Eutropius, and so attained the object of his oration under the most difficult circumstances.   That is the essential thing.   Of course the enemies of Eutropius took advantage of the state of affairs as well as they could.   Shortly after this event appeared an imperial decree, which is preserved to this day in the law of the Byzantine Empire, the Codex Theodosianus, and which is

so unusually significant for the value of its favor to the people
in general, as well as for the cultural conditions of the court
in Constantinople at that time, that it seems well worth
quoting here in its essential points.

"To Aurelius, the prefect of the Praetorium. The entire
possessions of Eutropius, the former imperial lord high
steward (praepositus sacri cubiculi) have been sequestrated for
the use of our imperial treasury. His dignities shall be taken
from him, and the consulate shall be freed from the shame of
the mention of his name. All his decrees shall be annulled,
history shall be silent concerning him, no one shall be
reminded of the shame of our century by the inclusion of his
name (in the consular list), and those who, by their bravery
and their wounds, enlarged the borders of the Roman Empire
or guarded them, shall not grieve over the fact that a foul
monster has defiled the highest dignities of the Consulate by
his connection with it. Also he shall be deprived of patrician
rank, and of all the lesser orders which he has defiled by his
wild passions. All his statues, whether of metal, marble, or any
other material whatever, shall be removed from all cities,
markets, or private and public places. He himself shall be
taken to the island of Cyprus, under sure guard, and there
kept in strict custody, so that he may never dare to make
trouble by his absurd schemes.

"Given at Constantinople, on the 17th of January 399 (?),
in the consulate of Theodore."[27]

This document shows, better than any others, how the
Emperor Arcadius was estimated by his companions and his
officials. He seems not to have noticed at all what witness
he had brought against himself in the ratification of this document; for it had been he who had appointed Eutropius to
the Consulate. And the same man, whom the imperial hand
had recently raised so high, whom the Emperor had consulted
in all things and had allowed to rule, was now in the imperial
edict designated as the "shame of our century." So quickly
could one rise and fall in the court of Constantinople! Chrysostom was right: O vanity of vanities, and all is vanity!

Claudian, on receiving the news of the fall, wrote his second
abusive poem on Eutropius.

The enemies of Eutropius did not take calmly this issue

of the affair. They did not rest as long as they knew that the
one who had been so much feared was still alive. A new
turn of fortune might come again. For this reason they
insisted to the Emperor that Eutropius should be executed.
But some one had assured Eutropius under oath, in the name
of the Emperor, that his life should be spared. But that held
good only in and for the metropolis. Arcadius yielded.

The fallen minister had scarcely arrived at Cyprus, when
he was put on board another ship and taken to Chalcedon,
brought before a court of justice presided over by Aurelian,
condemned for high treason, and promptly executed. Such
was the fortune and the end of Eutropius.[28]

Betrayal and Death of the Gothic Leader Gainas

Avenging justice did not stop halfway. It felled a row of
heads of the imprudent, who, dazzled by the brilliance of
power, came too near the throne.

Scarcely was Eutropius out of the way, when Gainas made
common cause with Tribigild, or at least let it be known that
the latter had until now only been his tool. The Emperor
felt himself too weak against Gainas. Discussions were proposed at court. Gainas took part in them. However, he
demanded that the discussions should not take place in Constantinople. He did not feel secure enough in the great
metropolis. So the Emperor had to decide to come out to
Gainas.

At the chapel of St. Euphemia near Chalcedon, only two
stadia from the Bosporus, the Emperor met Gainas early in
the year 400.[29] Gainas claimed that he and Tribigild should
have the right to come to Constantinople, that is, Europe.
Gainas was to remain, or to be, the commander of the entire
imperial army. For security, three hostages were handed
over to him: Aurelian, military prefect and newly-appointed
consul; Saturninus, an eminent man, and the prefect, Count
John, who was a special favorite of the Empress. All sorts
of malicious rumors went about among the people concerning this. From the eleventh accusation against Chrysostom
at the Synod of the Oak[30] one might draw the conclusion
that the Count had sought refuge in the Cathedral or in the
Bishop's palace.

The choice of these personalities shows that Gainas was determined to be rid of all possible rivals for the highest place in the Empire. As dangerous and humiliating as these demands were, Arcadius was too weak, in character as well as in the means of helping himself: he granted everything.

Great was the terror, the confusion, and the shame of the Greeks, when they learned of the "terms of freedom" of the Gothic leader of the mercenaries. Everyone feared for the fate of the three hostages, of whom Aurelian was considered the head of the "Roman" patriotic party. Aurelian was also of a distinguished family. His father Taurus had been pre-torian prefect, and he himself had held the same high position in the year 396.[31] In the year 400, after the fall of Eutropius, he was even consul. He was a "prudent man, of strong character, respected even by his enemies, and who, in spite of his high rank . . . led a quiet, retired life, and besides his more serious work, devoted his life to acquiring knowledge and the art of poetry. He was the very image of a real Roman of the olden time."[32]

Meanwhile, most people had lost their spirit and courage, and no one was found who would dare to go as intercessor to the victorious Goths. In this time of need they turned to the Archbishop. Chrysostom made up his mind, without hesitation, to go personally into the camp of Gainas and negotiate for the lives of the hostages.[33] Through his entreaties, representations and admonitions, he persuaded Gainas to release the three state and court officials. He demanded, however, that the three would at least depart from the metropolis and go into exile.[34]

With this half success, Chrysostom returned to the city. He had done what his intrepid heart and his love of his people had commanded him to do. But at least John and Saturninus took it ill of the Archbishop that he had not obtained complete success. Castricia, the wife of Saturninus, belonged thenceforth to the number of those ladies of the court among whom Chrysostom was held in low estimation, and John, the imperial treasurer, brought it about, either by his actions or by his silence, that Chrysostom was accused, at the Synod of the Oak, of treachery to him.

Soon the two victors, Gainas and Tribigild, with their

whole army of about 30,000 men, made their entry into Constantinople. In the first days only Goths were seen on the streets. The city seemed to have become the capital of the barbarians, and the Greeks their prisoners.[35] The real ruler of the empire in those days was of course Gainas. Only the imperial guard and some garrison troops were still under the orders of the Emperor. But Gainas sought to remove these also. He slowly moved one garrison after the other among the Greek troops to other headquarters, and soon the city was possessed by the Goths alone. Now one more clever *coup d'état* and Gainas could call himself Emperor.[36] But the crafty Goth was not yet *the* strong man.

Whether it was a want of resolution at the last moment, or whether his power was not yet great enough, Gainas missed the most favorable moment, got lost in non-essentials, and allowed the Roman-Greek party time to collect itself and to make a counter-attack.

One of these questions which was non-essential at the moment concerned a special church for his Arian Goths inside the walls of the city. Gainas was also an Arian, and the heads of his sect[37] did not wish to lose the opportunity of abolishing the hated law of Theodosius, who had forbidden to the Arians all churches and all divine service within the city walls. So he represented to the Emperor that it was derogatory to his dignity, as commander of the army, not to be able to attend divine service at a church of his sect within the city. He wished to have one of the Catholic churches in the city turned over to him and his men.

That was imprudent of Gainas, to say the least. He certainly touched the overwhelmingly Catholic population of Constantinople, and the whole Empire, in their most sensitive part, and aggravated exceedingly the religious opposition between the Goths and the Greeks. The eternal strife between the Arians and the Catholics was still in such evil memory that no one could have wished it renewed again. Arcadius saw himself caught up again, with his advisers, in the utmost embarrassment. Then Archbishop John came forward for an audience. Chrysostom had hardly heard the demands of Gainas when he began to try to prevent what, in his eyes, appeared to be a disgrace to the nation and a wrong

against God. Soon he made these representations to the
Emperor, saying that he could not endure that the holy things
should be thrown to the dogs. He, as Bishop, found it impossible to agree that those who announced and praised the
true Word of God should be expelled from their churches,
and that those who disgraced and slandered it should take
possession in their places.

The Emperor would have liked to postpone the issue, and
look into it, since he was perplexed, and perhaps pointed out
the possibility that Gainas might use force. The undaunted
Archbishop retorted: "Emperor, do not fear these barbarians; but summon both of us, me and him. You may rest
assured, that I will bring him to this, that he will be more
moderate, and will not make any demands that will be really
unjust."[38] Who was happier than Arcadius, when suddenly
the possibility was opened to him of appeasing a demand
against which his own conscience objected, and that without
having the anger of Gainas directed against himself? So he
accepted the Archbishop's proposal with joy.

On the appointed day, Chrysostom appeared in the
imperial palace, with several bishops, who were present in
Constantinople at the time, and soon he stood beside Gainas
in the presence of the Emperor.

It must have been an unusual picture: the physically and
spiritually weak, nominal ruler, and before him the actual
ruler of the moment, the keen and ambitious Gothic leader;
and as the third party, Chrysostom, small of figure, but the
greatest of the three in spiritual and moral power.

Chrysostom emerged victorious from the battle. With
astonishing frankness he reproached Gainas with having
entered the country as a poor fugitive Goth, and of having
sworn fidelity to Theodosius, the present Emperor's father,
and to his children, and of having solemnly sworn to obey
the laws of the Romans. Now he is beginning to break those
laws. Then he placed the text of the law before him:
"Here," he said, "Theodosius has forbidden people of other
faiths to hold divine service within the walls of the city."[39]
Then he turned from the disconcerted Gainas to the
Emperor, and begged him to uphold the law against the sects,
for it would be better to lose his sovereign authority than to

sin by surrendering the house of God. In this frank and manly fashion, Chrysostom secured himself against any robbery of the churches under his authority. In this he had only done his plain duty.[40]

The Emperor, supported by the determination of the Archbishop, held firm, and Gainas felt that for the moment it was not advisable to obtain his will by force. So Chrysostom remained the victor; he had kept the Catholic churches, and had saved the capital from a revival of Arianism.[41]

But the peace between the Greeks and the Goths in Constantinople was not to be of long duration. In the beginning of summer, rumors were spread through the city that the Gothic leader intended to plunder the banks of the city to pay his troops and to get money for further projects. A comet which appeared in the night sky at this time seemed to the superstitious to predict warlike and bloody events. It was said that Gainas had twice attempted to burn down the imperial palace; soldiers whom he had sent out had twice been terrified by the appearance of numerous soldiers of immense size; indeed the Gothic leader himself had been eventually a personal witness of these supernatural appearances.[42]

The truth of the matter may have been that Gainas was not trusted at court, that the palace guard had been strengthened, and perhaps even troops from the garrisoned cities had been ordered there. It was clear that affairs were mounting to a crisis; there was much tension, and it had to find a release. Gainas had obviously noticed the danger. He did not wish to await the appearance of a Roman army in a city inimical to him, and therefore decided to move his troops out of Constantinople. He wished to do this as inconspicuously as possible, in order that his divisions, which had to march separately, might avoid the danger of a surprise attack.

With excuse of wishing to visit the Church of St. John the Baptist,[43] which had been built by Theodosius outside the city, he left the city on the 12th of July, 400,[44] in company with a part of his forces. Only about ten thousand men remained behind. Weapons and shields, hidden by the soldiers in wagons, were taken out after them. When the Roman guards at the city gates noticed this, they tried to prevent the removal of the weapons, and it came to a fight, in which the guard was killed by the Goths. That was the signal for a general rally against the Goths. The city gates were closed; the Roman garrison, the palace guard, and a great part of the citizenry seized weapons, and fell upon the Goths who had remained behind, wherever they could find them. A general slaughter followed; thousands of Goths were slain. A great number of them were able to find refuge in the " Church of the Goths;" the Church was set on fire and the Goths burned with it.

Gainas himself was outlawed as an enemy of the Empire. When he learned what had happened in the city, he turned with the rest of his troops toward Thrace, in order to reach the Chersonese peninsula along the coast of the Sea of Marmora, and from there to cross over the Hellespont (the Bosporus) to Asia Minor. However, the Goths did not have any ships, or not enough, for the journey over.

Meanwhile the Emperor had appointed Fravitta commander of his Roman battle forces, and sent him to follow and fight Gainas. But Fravitta was also a Goth, and not even a Christian, but a pagan. Theodosius had taken him into his service at one time, as he did so many other German mercenary leaders, and made him leader of a Gothic corps. But in contrast with so many German adventurers, who were enticed into the Roman ranks only by hope of pay and plunder, and who were always ready for riot and insubordination, Fravitta proved himself a real model of the ancient, genuine Germanic loyalty. He had been so when he once killed the Gothic leader Eriulph because the latter would no longer keep his sworn loyalty to the Emperor.[45] The Roman officers may not have been too happy over this choice. Still it was doubtless an adroit move, for he alone could prevent the Goths who still remained loyal from going over to Gainas.

At this moment everything depended on the loyalty of Fravitta, and he remained loyal.

The new field commander immediately had his troops seize the Asia Minor coast of the Dardanelles, and kept a fleet in readiness. The Goths, for want of ships, began to cross the narrow straits in hastily made rafts. But these weak ferries could not stand up under the wind and the currents; some of them were lost, and others, with horses and men aboard, were run down by the Roman ships. Whoever was able to reach the other side fell under the swords of the soldiers. So, at the end of December in the year 400, ended the lives of thousands of Gothic Germans in the cold ocean floods, at the same place where, 700 years earlier, even the fury of a Xerxes was unable to subdue; and which, 334 B.C., Alexander the Great crossed for the conquest of Persia and India, and in 1356 the Turks crossed it when they broke into Europe.

Gainas made a stand on the further bank, when disaster broke over his forces. Dumb and despairing, he had to watch the destruction of his army, without being able to help them. Now was the time to think of his own rescue. With a little band of still loyal followers, he turned toward Thrace (the modern Bulgaria). There he rushed into a division of Huns,[46] was engaged by them, and killed with all his followers. On the 3rd of January, 401, his head was brought to Constantinople as a trophy.

Fravitta, who had saved the kingdom and the throne, and freed the nation from calamity, was honored as a victor and named consul for the following year.[46a] Aurelian, Saturninus and John were at last recalled from exile.

Eusebius the scholastic, the pupil of Troilus, composed four books in heroic verse on the adventurer Gainas, which he called Gaineas. The ungrateful world allowed this heroic poem to be lost.[47]

Arcadius, who was not at all responsible for the victory, erected in 403 a triumphal pillar, which, on the model of Trajan's pillar in Rome, perpetuated the great warlike deeds of his reign in the form of reliefs. These included scenes from the Gothic war, which showed among other things the drowning of the Goths in the straits of the Dardanelles. From the height of this pillar the victorious Arcadius looked out over three hundred years of his city's history, until in the year 740 it fell down. The pillar itself outlived him by another thousand years. An earthquake damaged it in 1719 to such a degree that the Sultan had it carried away. Today the pedestal stands, to the stony fame of Arcadius, in the

women's bazaar in Constantinople, with the shaft of the pillar
and some figures in low relief.[48]

The political tumults of the revolt of the Goths had convulsed the Empire and the capital to the depths. Without
his assistance, and without his having wished it, Chrysostom
had played therein a role which had made him appear the
first man in the Empire. His esteem and importance
mounted to unusual heights. But it was just this which
awakened envy and aversion in those who would gladly have
played such a role, but who had not had the opportunity or
the courage in the midst of the confusion. Palladius notes,
unfortunately without mentioning names, that Chrysostom
had had some enemies among the court officials, but only two
or three, who in the party of Theophilus (at Easter 404) supported the military.[49]   One of these court officials appears to
have been the court treasurer John, otherwise accusation no.
11 at the Synod of the Oak could not be well understood.
Why he disliked the Archbishop, no one knows. Perhaps at
that time Chrysostom, when he (John) sought some protection for himself, had taken advantage of the opportunity of
pointing out some of his sins, as he had done with Eutropius.

FOOTNOTES

1. Zosimus 5, 8 ff. (Mendels. 225 f.); Eunapius, Fragm. 71
(Müller, Fragm. hist. gr. 4, 45).

1a. Claudian, In Eutropium 1, 230-286 and 297 (MGH Auct.
ant. 10 (1892) 83).

2. Marcellinus Comes, Chronicon, AD 399 (Pl 51, 921) says of
Eutropius: "This Eutropius was the first and last eunuch ever
to become Consul. The Consul-eunuch put all monsters in the
shade."

3. Eunapius, Fragm. 77 (Müller *loc. cit.* 48-49).

4. Zosimus 6, 10 (ed. Mendelssohn 228); Claudian 1, 190 ff.

5. Cf. ch. 5, p. 45.

6. According to Grosse, Rom. Militargesch. 257-58, since the
reign of Julian at least half of the higher military positions had
been held by Germans. Among the troops themselves the per-
centage was higher. Soldier and barbarian were identical con-
cepts. The total strength of the Roman army in its best time

(that of Diocletian) was about 300,000 men. In the fifth century it was significantly less. Theodosius took many "barbarians" into the Roman army, which resulted in many quarrels and much rivalry between "Roman" and "barbarian" soldiers and officers.

7. J. Mansion, Les origines du Christianisme chez les Gots = An. Boll. 33 (1914) 5-30.

8. Zosimus 6, 7 (Mendels. 225).

9. Socrates 6, 6 (67, 676) calls him συγγενὴς of Gainas, which may mean no blood relation but related by race.

10. 5, 13 ff. (*loc. cit.* 230).

11. 6, 6 (676).

12. 8, 4 (1521).

13. 5, 32 (ed. Parmentier 333).

14. Philostorgius 11, 8 (ed. Bidez 138).

15. Claudian 2, 317-324 (*loc. cit.* 108). Cf. Ludwig, Der heilige Joh. Chrys. in seinem Verhältniss etc. P. 27-42.

16. Zosimus 5, 14 (Mendels. 230); Claudian II, 376 ff. (*loc. cit.* 110); Eunapius, Fragm. 76 (ed. Müller 4, 48).

17. In Eutropium 2, 380-81. Güldenpenning p. 82.

18. Fragm. 76; ed. C. Müller, Fragm. 4, 48.

19. Socrates, Sozomen and Philostorgius do not connect the fall of the minister with Gainas; they trace it back to the disfavor of the Empress, who was offended and demanded punishment.

20. Philostorgius 11, 6 (ed. Bidez 136).

21. Chrysostom, In Eutropium 4 (52, 395).

22. Codex Theod. 9, 40, 17 (ed. Mommsen 505).

23. Chrysostom, In Eutropium 4 (52, 395).

24. 52, 391-396.

25. 6, 5 (67, 673 B).

26. 8, 7 (c. 1536 A).

27. Cod. Theodos. 9, 40, 17 (ed. Mommsen 505). The date, January 17, 399, cannot be right.

28. Zosimus 5, 18 (Mendels. 236). Philostorgius 11, 6 (Bidez 136). Palladius passed over the history of Eutropius, as he did all purely political events.

29. Socrates 6, 6. Sozomen 8, 4; ASS, Sept. 5, 279 f.

30. Photius, Bibl. 59 (103, 108).

31. So according to Rauschen p. 370 with a quotation of Mommsen's dating of the Cod. Theod. IV. 2, 1 (*loc. cit.* 167). Güldenpenning says he attained this dignity in 399.

32. Güldenpenning 97.

33. Theodoret HE 5, 33, (82, 1261; ed. Parmentier 333). Socrates and Sozomen are completely silent about the embassy of Chrysos-

tom. Yet this is proved through his own Homily and through Theodoret.

34. Homilia cum Saturninus et Aurelianus acti essent in exilium (52, 413-420).

35. Socrates 6, 6 (c. 677).

36. Socrates 6, 6 and Sozomen 8, 4 state expressly that Gainas had struggled for the mastery.

37. Sozomen 8, 4 (1524).

38. Theodoret 5, 32 (*loc. cit.* 332). The wording of the speech is naturally Theodoret's.

39. Cod. Theod. XVI, 5, 15; *ib.* 13 (ed. Mommsen 860-61). One may well believe that Chrysostom's speech did not sound like sweet music in Gainas' ears. But that he " insulted " the commander-in-chief may have been an exaggeration arising from prejudice on the part of Socrates. The first eulogy of Theodoret, who alluded to this incident, is unfortunately lost. Cf. Photii Bibl. 273 (103, 48).

40. Socr. 6, 5 and 6; Soz. 8, 4. Theodoret 5, 35 (*loc. cit.* 333).

41. St. Nilus carried on a correspondence with Gainas (Epist. 1, 70, 79, 114, 116, 205, 206, 286 = MG 79, 112 ff.). The authenticity of these letters must first be proved, and this may be very difficult. Gainas was not a man who would have any special interest in monks or saints.

42. Socr. 6, 6 (c. 680) and Soz. 8, 4 (c. 1524-25).

43. According to Socrates 6, 6 (c. 680) the church was dedicated to the Apostle St. John.

44. So according to the *Chronicon Paschale* 400 (92, 780). Cf. Güldenpenning, 125.

45. Zosimus 4, 56 (ed. Mendels. 212); Eunapius, Fragm. 60 (ed. Müller 4, 41).

46. According to Socrates 6, 6, they were Romans.

46a. A certain " Fravitta," perhaps a descendant of the Consul Fravitta, was Patriarch of Constantinople in 489-90; but he reigned only four months.

47. Socrates 6, 6 (c. 682).

48. Th. Reinach, Commentaire archéologique *loc. cit.* 78-82. Gurlitt, p. 1 ff. O. Wulff, Die sieben Wunder = Byz. Zeitschrift 7 (1898) 318. J. Kollwitz, Die Arkadius-Säule, in: Bericht des 6. Archäolog. Kongresses. Berlin 1940. p. 594-96.

49. Dialogus 4 (16).

CHAPTER XII

CONSTANTINOPLE AS A
PATRIARCHATE

CONSTANTINOPLE had always been of little significance, as far as church affairs were concerned, until
the day when it became, first temporarily, then per-
manently, the residence of the Emperor and capital of the
Empire. The old Byzantium did not even have its own
Bishop until the third century. The first Bishop mentioned
in history, named Metrophanes, came upon the scene at the
beginning of the fourth century, in the year 306. He was
suffragan bishop of the Metropolitan of Heraclea, the modern
Eregli.[1] In regard to this, Philostorgius also emphasizes the
fact, in his Ecclesiastical History, that the Metropolitan of
Heraclea possessed the right to take part in the consecration
of the chosen Bishops of Constantinople.[2]

But after the Council of Constantinople, in the year 381,
granted to the Bishop of the capital city a rank directly after
that of the Bishop of Rome, the Byzantine clergy gradually
perceived the necessity of tracing out somewhat further the
genealogical tree of the new "Patriarchate." They chose as
alleged founders and ancestors of the Church of Constantinople, first St. Andrew, who indeed had been first among
all the Apostles, whom the Lord had called to the Apostolate.[3]
This genealogical tree had nothing to do with history.

Actually, as has been said, the Council of Constantinople,
in the year 381, first elevated the suffragan See of Constantinople above its previous rank. In the East this principle
had hitherto prevailed, that the ecclesiastical rank of a city
corresponded to its secular rank. The Synod of Antioch in
the year 341 had laid down this principle as a law, and later
the general Council of Chalcedon, in 451, had renewed and
confirmed it.[4] When, for example, the Emperor Valens
wished to annoy St. Basil the Great by weakening his hier-

archical standing, he simply divided Cappadocia into two
political provinces, and forthwith announced himself the
Bishop of the new " Metropolis" of Tyana, with the claim of
possessing henceforth the rights of a Metropolitan, and of
being independent of Caesarea.   He succeeded in his claim,
in spite of the opposition of St. Basil.

Naturally such ecclesiastical changes did not take place
automatically.   A corresponding degree of regular ecclesiastical authority, usually a synod, constituted the legal source
of such a promotion.   But now, at that time, Constantinople
had developed from the small town of Byzantium to the real
capital of the East.   The Emperor Constantine the Great, who
recognized the military and political significance of the place,
had set his residence here, and had moved the splendor of the
court, the power and the sphere of influence of the highest
political power hither.   On account of this, the esteem and
the importance of the Bishop of the new capital had to grow
of itself, and soon it surpassed that of a provincial bishop.

Indeed it could not be otherwise than that the Emperor,
who had become Christian, came into close contact with the
Bishop of the city in which he lived, and that, in return, the
influence of the Bishop upon the court must increase to
the degree in which he knew how to make his personal
relations with the Emperor pleasant.   How quickly the new
state of things became understood and appreciated in the
whole Empire is proved by the circumstance that, already in
339, the Metropolitan Eusebius of Nicomedia, and in 360
even the Arian Patriarch Eudoxius of Antioch, solicited the
episcopal office of Constantinople for themselves.[5]   Philostorgius even says that Eudoxius, when Bishop of Constantinople, had appointed Bishops, as for instance Eunomius of
Cyzicus; this was done, naturally, at the wish of the Emperor.[6]
All these incidents had occurred at the time of the Arian
disturbances, in which the Canons had a diminished value;
but the position of the Bishops of Constantinople, as a result
of the new relations, became more and more elevated over all
the other Bishops and Metropolitans, even the Patriarchs of
Antioch and Alexandria.

The latter, especially, observed with jealous eyes this dis-
location of the moral powers, and sought to win as much

influence as possible in the choice of the Bishop of Constantinople. In this matter they were not always fortunate in
their choice of means. The dishonorable way in which
Patriarch Peter of Alexandria sought to make the philosopher
Maximus the Bishop of Constantinople, in the year 380,
formed finally the ostensible occasion for speaking the deciding word in this rivalry between the two most important
bishoprics of the East. The Council assembled in Constantinople in 381 defined in its third Canon: "The Bishop of
Constantinople shall have first rank after the Bishop of Rome,
because Constantinople is New Rome."[7]

Of course Hefele states that the Synod of Constantinople
wished to grant to the Bishop of the capital not merely the
first place over all the other bishops, except Rome, but also
to transfer the metropolitan power of Heraclea in Thrace,
whose suffragan Constantinople was, to the latter itself.[8] But
of this the Council said nothing. On the contrary, in Canon 2
it expressly emphasizes: "The Bishops of Thrace shall govern
only Thrace," and of course, in the sense of the hitherto
existing tradition. Still in the year 431 the Metropolitan of
Heraclea had the right to name the Bishops of *his* metropolitan jurisdiction.[9]

As far as strict legality was concerned, Constantinople was
not elevated to a "Patriarchate," for the Council only conferred upon it expressly the first rank before the other Patriarchs and Bishops, not an elevation in rank or an extension
of jurisdiction in relation to its former legal position. However, this Canon was only the natural bridge to a final development, which had already begun before it. The settlement
with "New Rome" indeed provided the real motive for the
change: it was not the "ecclesiastical" but the political Rome
that was meant. The Bishop, who resided in the second
greatest seat of political power in the Empire, and therefore
possessed the second greatest significance for the Church, had
to meet externally the splendor and brilliance of the court
with splendor and brilliance of his own,[10] and take the second
highest place in the Church.

The decisions of the Council, it is true, were not sent to
Rome for confirmation, and therefore not sanctioned by it.
Nevertheless it would be an error to believe that the expres-

sion " New Rome " signified already a point opposite to Rome.
If the decisions of the Council had a point, this was most of
all directed against Alexandria.   It struck the hour of Constantinople's accession to the position of chief city of the
Empire: its hierarchical elevation corresponded to a general
rule in the East and to the actual state of affairs.

It is true that the Canon to a certain extent was significant
also for the spirit of the East.   The imperial court had certainly long since become not only the central point for
political affairs, but very much so far ecclesiastical affairs
also.   On the other hand, the primacy of Rome and the extent
of its authority had in many ways not yet become very clear
in the consciousness of the Eastern Bishops.   The summoning
of synods was extremely detailed and expensive, and the
clerical authority of the Patriarch or Metropolitan did not
always suffice in these primitive relationships, especially if
the Patriarchs or the Metropolitans themselves were deficient.

Then the Christian Emperor was the final authority; if
not the only one, at least the simplest and most convenient
authority for bringing about efficacious order.   So they were
not unwilling to summon this authority, in the East as well as
in the West, without thinking that the secular authority was
superior to the spiritual, or that the authority of Rome had
been disavowed.

When, for example, in the year 335, St. Athanasius wished
to disband the Arian Synod of Tyre, the patriarch appealed
first of all, not to Rome, but to the Emperor.[11]   The Synod of
Antioch, which was inimical to Athanasius, had in the year
341, indeed forbidden appeals to the Emperor.   But the prohibition was followed least of all by those who had instituted
it.[12]

It cannot be denied that such appeals concealed within
themselves the great danger of developing open Caesaropapism among the Emperors, and not merely when they were
asked to help, but also when not asked, it brought on all sorts
of pernicious interference in ecclesiastical and religious affairs;
and as a matter of fact this developed soon enough.   So much
the greater was the influence of the Bishops of Constantinople,
to whom the Emperors turned over a multitude of all sorts of
things for their opinion, or to be settled by them.

Theodosius the Great had done the same. On the other side, the Eastern Bishops also sought, even in the most difficult matters, to obtain the co-operation and favor of the Bishops of the capital, in order that through them they might obtain entrée to the imperial court, or to accomplish things which had hitherto been impossible. So, in the year 383, St. Gregory Nazianzus requested his successor Nectarius to settle a matter in dispute for a bishop in Cappadocia. St. Ambrose of Milan turned to the same Nectarius with the request that he depose Bishop Gerontius of Nicomedia, a runaway deacon of Milan, who had various matters against him. It is therefore not so much the effect of the paragraphs of the Council's law of 341 and 381, but rather more the power of actual circumstances, that the honorary primacy of Constantinople had become under Nectarius a *de facto* primacy.

The learned P. Batiffol therefore rightly says: "The sixteen years of the lusterless episcopate of Nectarius were the years in which the primacy of the bishopric of Constantinople changed from an honorary primacy (in 381) to an actual primacy. Did the purpose of Nectarius contribute much to this change? We do not know, and the question is not important: the authority of the imperial city must have of itself bestowed a hegemony upon the Bishop, whether he wished it or not."[13]

Actually Nectarius had already appointed candidates for foreign episcopal sees, and presided over synods in which no delegate from the Pope was present.

Atticus, the successor of Chrysostom, later nominated Sylvanus as Bishop of Philippopolis, and transferred him later to Troas, the canon law remaining the same. Sisinnius, the successor of Atticus, made Proclus Bishop of Cyzicus in the year 426 or 427, and on this occasion Socrates speaks of a (synodal or customary?) "law which forbids a Bishop's consecration to be undertaken against the will of the Bishop of Constantinople."[14] Proclus himself, as Bishop of Constantinople, nominated Thalassius as Metropolitan of Caesarea, and Basilius as Metropolitan of Ephesus. At the Council of Chalcedon in 431, a great number of Bishops declared that they had been consecrated and installed by the Bishop of Constantinople.[15]

Then what legal title and what position came to Chrysostom when suddenly, in 397, he was promoted to the Bishopric of Constantinople? There, where Canon 3 of the Council of 381 was recognized, as it was in the entire East, he doubtless enjoyed honorary precedence before all other Bishops and Patriarchs. On the other hand, the title and rights of a "Patriarch" did not belong to him by law; although in fact the title was given before 451 to his successors, who were in the same legal position as he was.

Still less did he possess, legally speaking, the title and rights of Metropolitan or Archbishop. Palladius always speaks of him simply as "the Bishop", while the Vita of the holy Olympias speaks of him three times as Archbishop and four times as Patriarch.[16] But actually it was a matter of indifference to Chrysostom, and if it does not entirely agree with the strictness of ecclesiastical law, it is not a historical error if one gives him all three titles at the same time.[17]

Actually, during his comparatively short episcopate, there came to Chrysostom calls for help, not only from Asia Minor and Ephesus, but even from Egypt, Phoenicia and Cyprus. And those were the only ones whose history has accidentally survived.[18]

At the Synod of the Oak, Chrysostom was reproached with having consecrated four bishops at the same time.[19] So he actually exercised metropolitan power. Still it is significant that they did not reproach him with having consecrated them at all, but that he consecrated four of them at the same time. So he had thereby, in the eyes of the Synod, not committed an oecumenical offence, but only a ritual one. So he had only extended further an already existent customary right.

With the "legality" of the installation and deposition of bishops, and similar exercises of their office, the Bishops of Constantinople, between 381 and 451, might have stood in just about the same position as with the legality of the exercise of power of a government, whose right stands predominantly in the fact of its existence. As long as the government is "strong," its decrees are legal; as soon as it falls and is overthrown, they become "illegal," and may be legally suspect.

As long as the individual Bishops of Constantinople possessed favor and influence at the court, it did not occur to anyone to find anything illegal in their metropolitan or even in their patriarchal rights. If this influence at court disappeared, their actions could be considered illegal, and they could be made the foundation for legal accusations. The obscure state of the laws in those days was therefore a double-edged sword, which under certain circumstances could be directed against the law itself.

The only ones who observed and resented the development of events, and who could not conceal their resentment, were the Patriarchs of Alexandria. Their jealousy and irritation increased in the same measure as the influence of Constantinople increased. Chrysostom must have felt this deeply, still more since his successor, Flavian, who was so abused by the angry Alexandrian clergy and monks in the so-called "Robber Synod of Ephesus" (449) that he died as a result.

The Council of Chalcedon, in 451, gave the answer to this last scandal. At the instigation of Bishop Anatolius of Constantinople, it laid down its 28th Canon: "that the Metropolitans of the provinces of Pontus, Asia and Thrace . . . shall be consecrated by the Archbishop of Constantinople, after their election has been peacefully accomplished in the customary way, and the Bishop of Constantinople has been informed of it."[20]

Thereby the effectual patriarchal power was legally sanctioned for Constantinople, at least for the sphere of the East.

FOOTNOTES

1. Vailhé, Les Patriarches grecs = Echos d'Orient 10 (1907) 210-21; 287-95.
2. HE 9, 10 (65, 576).
3. Cf. Pseudo-Dorotheus (= Procopius?) (circa 525)=92, 1073. V. Benesevic, Die Byzantinischen Ranglisten = Byzantinisch-neugriech. Jahrbücher 5 (1926) 101. Vailhé, Constantinople, Eglise, in: Dict: de Théol. Cath. 3, 2 (1923) 1308.
4. Hefele 1, 516 and 2, 529.
5. Cf. Lübeck, Reichseinteilung p. 194. Janin, Formation du Patriarcat de C., *loc. cit.* 136.
6. HE 5, 3 (ed. Bidez 68-69).
7. Mansi 3, 560; Hefele 2, 17-18.

8. Konz. Gesch. 2, 18; with a quotation from Socrates 5, 8 (67, 580), which says: " Nectarius had the capital city and the province of Thrace assigned to him."

9. Lübeck, Reichseinteilung 211.

10. So the Council of Chalcedon also confirmed it (451) in Canon 28 (Hefele 2, 527 ff.).

11. Apologia contra Arianos 86 (25, 401).   Cf. S. Vailhé, Le droit d'appel, *loc. cit.* 129 ff.; Hefele KG 1, 469.

12. Canon 12 (Mansi 2, 1313; Hefele 1, 517).

13. La Siège Apostolique 282.   E. Gerland, Die Vorgeschichte des Patriarchates von Konstantinopel, in: Byzant. Neugriech. Jahrbücher 9 (1932) 226-28, exaggerates when he represents Nectarius as the creator of the " Patriarchate " of Constantinople; and K. Müller, Canon 2 and 6 of Constantinople 381 and 382, in: Festgabe f. Ad. Jülicher, Tübingen 1927, p. 190-202, misrepresents the facts, when he marks Chrysostom for it on the ground of his journey to Ephesus.   Also Ed. Schwartz, Palladiana, p. 177 ff., has represented the affair one-sidedly.

14. HE 7, 28 (67, 801).

15. Janin = Echos d'Orient 13 (1910) 138.

16. Anal. Boll. 15 (1896) 412-419.

17. At any rate it is a complete lack of appreciation of the actual state of affairs, when S. Vailhé, Le droit d'appel *loc. cit.* 143 ff., calls the Metropolitan of Heraclea "le supérieur légitime" of Chrysostom in the year 403.   Furthermore, Chrysostom could not have named and consecrated his priest Serapion as Metropolitan of Heraclea in the same year.

18. Cf. ch. 18 and Letter 221 (52, 732-33).

19. Photius, Bibl. 59 n. 14 and 24 (103, 108).

20. Mansi 7, 369; Hefele 2, 528.

CHAPTER XIII

CHRYSOSTOM'S JOURNEY TO EPHESUS

EARLY in the year of the thirteenth indiction[1] (that is, September 399 to September 400), and so in the year 400, several bishops came from the provinces of "Asia,"[2] having business in Constantinople, where they took up their dwelling in the episcopal palace. Their business concerned certain colleagues of theirs, the old man Theotimus, Bishop of Tomi, Ammonius the Egyptian, Bishop of Thrace, and Arabianus, Bishop of Galatia, all aged Metropolitans. In all there were 22 Bishops, enough to make a small synod, who casually appeared in the capital at Chrysostom's episcopal palace. As they all sat together on a Sunday morning[3] before divine service, Bishop Eusebius of Valentinopolis[4] entered, all unexpectedly, before the assembly, and demanded to be allowed to present a writ of accusation against his Metropolitan, Antoninus of Ephesus, who was one of those present at the gathering. Chrysostom was as disagreeably surprised over this peculiar beginning of Sunday as was the Metropolitan of Ephesus. All quarrelling between Bishops was offensive to him, and the ambition to sit over Bishops in judgment was entirely absent from his character. He therefore attempted to quiet the excited Eusebius, and to allow an opportunity for settling the dispute in a friendly way.

"Bishop Eusebius," said he, "sometimes accusations are made in anger which are afterwards hard to prove. Therefore hear my request, and refrain from making the written accusation against Bishop Antoninus; we ourselves will take care that the cause of your anger will be looked into."[5]

This discreet and well-meant offer was made to the wrong man. Eusebius went into a rage, began to insult Antoninus and inveigh against him in his presence, with violent expressions, and stood by his accusation. Then Chrysostom besought Bishop Paul of Heraclea, who passed as a friend of Antoninus, to adjust matters between them, and reconcile them. Then he rose up and went with the other bishops to the church; for it was time for the Divine Liturgy. He offered the people the accustomed greeting of peace, and then took his place with the bishops. But they could not rejoice themselves with devotion very long. Suddenly Eusebius appeared in the Presbyterium.

Without any regard to the holiness of the place, or the presence of the people, who filled the church, and ignoring the Divine Liturgy, which was about to begin, he went directly to the Archbishop, uttering loud cries and dreadful oaths " by the welfare of the Emperor;" he tried to give Chrysostom the written accusation against Antoninus, and so force him to begin the process against the latter. The frightened people in the nave of the church believed that the man, who was unknown to them, wished to beg for his life from the Emperor through the favor of the Archbishop.

Chrysostom was very painfully surprised during this violent scene, and was brought out of his spiritual calm. What should he do? It was impossible, here in the church, to enter into a discussion with the passionate Eusebius, who could not be reached by reasonable arguments. To put him out by force would also not be good. In order to make an end of the scandal, at least for the moment, so that the disorder and confusion among the people might not be increased, he accepted the written accusation quickly without a word being said. Probably he had intended to preach after the Gospel. It was no longer possible for him. As soon as he had read the document, he asked Pansophius, Bishop of Pisidia, to finish the Holy Sacrifice. He felt that he himself was no longer in a spiritual condition to do it. He departed, and the other bishops followed him.

When the Divine Liturgy was over, Chrysostom called all the bishops present to a conference in the baptistery of the Cathedral. To this conference Eusebius was also invited. The Archbishop opened the conference by saying: " I repeat to you what I have already said, that it often happens that one says or writes many things in displeasure or anger, which one afterward cannot prove. So if you can prove the accusations that you wish to bring here, we will not reject you, if you are specific. So choose the right, before the writ of accusation is read aloud. As soon as it is read aloud to all present and has come to protocol, you are no more free as bishops to reverse the process."

It is impossible not to recognize here the extraordinary self-discipline, discretion, love of peace and aversion to all strife which Chrysostom showed, as well as his complete lack of every desire to take part in foreign matters for the enlargement of his own power. But nevertheless it was proved by his own words that not merely he himself, but also the other episcopal participants in the conference, did not have the slightest doubt that Eusebius had a right to bring his written accusation to their forum, and that they themselves had a right to take up the accusation, and decide on its validity. Indeed, there must have been, for such canonical processes, an exactly regulated procedure, copied after secular law.

As was to be foreseen, Eusebius declared, after this second attempt at kindness, that he stood by his accusation. So then Chrysostom gave order that the written accusation be read aloud. It contained seven points and read thus:

" 1. Antoninus has had church moneys melted down and diverted the gold to the use of his son.

2. He has taken away the marble slabs from the entrance to the baptismal chapel, and had them placed in his own bath.

3. He has had pillars, which belonged to a church, and which had been there for several years, placed in his own dining room.

4. He allowed a servant to remain peacefully in his service, although he had committed a murder.

5. He sold estates which were bequeathed to the Church (of Ephesus) by Basilina, the mother of the Emperor Julian the Apostate, and used the profit for himself.

6. He had taken back his own wife, from whom he had separated before his episcopal consecration, and had children by her.

7. It is a regular practice with him to give episcopal consecration to the highest bidder. The buyer of the consecration and the receiver of the money are here present; also for them I have the proof at hand."

Of course that was a serious list of faults for a bishop and Metropolitan occupying the seat of the one-time beloved youth and disciple, St. John. All eyes were turned to the accused, in the attempt to read guilt or innocence in the expression of his countenance.

Chrysostom, as chairman, opened the discussion. One of the oldest Metropolitans made the motion: "If each individual accusation concerns a sacrilege forbidden by the sacred canons, then we should begin the discussion with the worst and gravest one, in order not to lose the whole time with the more insignificant ones. If that point is proved to be true, then we cannot doubt the others. For one who dares to sell the gift of the Holy Spirit for money will not stop at dealing with holy vessels or pillars or ecclesiastical properties."

Then Chrysostom began the examination thus: "What do you say to these accusations, Brother Antoninus?" Brother Antoninus did not at the moment find the courage to acknowledge himself guilty before all the bishops. Shameful deposition would be his lot if he did. So Antoninus lied.

The others were asked if their consecration had been bought with money. They followed the example of their Metropolitan, and lied also.

What to do? The conference went on until two in the afternoon. When evidence was asked for, so that the offer and acceptance of money for episcopal consecration could be proved, none was forthcoming. Nothing could be done without evidence. To have witnesses come from Ephesus was difficult; that would take time and money. The affair seemed to have reached a dead end. But the case, from the standpoint of ecclesiastical discipline, was too important to give up the process already begun, apart from the fact that Eusebius himself had not been satisfied with it. But if they wished to wait until witnesses came from Ephesus, on the one hand lay the danger of the disappearance of the witnesses, and on the other, the bishops against whom Eusebius had brought his accusations would be held in Constantinople for an indefinite time. The bishops present were not in a mind for either of these things.

In these circumstances it is easily understandable that Chrysostom proposed the only solution still open, and offered to go to Ephesus himself in the interest of the Church, in order to save the witnesses the journey, and to be able to undertake the affair on the spot. Thereupon all those present agreed to this. Antoninus and his accused suffragans raised no objection. Actually a great fear went through him when he heard Chrysostom's proposal. Under the compulsion of his bad conscience, he determined to do everything he could to prevent the Patriarch from making the journey. The continuation of the process in Constantinople would not have bothered him much, but he did not wish Chrysostom to come in person to Ephesus. There obviously more would be said of him than he liked. A fortunate circumstance was helpful to him in his design.

Antoninus had at court a very highly placed and influential friend or acquaintance[6] who possessed great properties in the neighborhood of Ephesus. Perhaps some of the Church properties which Antoninus had illegally sold were among these. This man's striking interest in the Process of Antoninus can thus best be understood. Indeed, because he could not very well manage his properties while in Constantinople himself, he had entrusted the management of them to the Metropolitan of Ephesus, whose skill in business affairs must have been known to him. This man was also bound to Antoninus by ties of gratitude.

To this man, then, went the harried sinner. He besought him urgently to prevent Chrysostom's journey to Ephesus at all costs; he would himself bring the witnesses to Constantinople. What sort of witnesses these were, is not difficult to guess.

The friend agreed to aid his friend.

Shortly after this, Chrysostom received an order from the court, as follows: They had heard that Chrysostom intended to journey into Asia. That was a dangerous and unseasonable undertaking at this time. For, first, he was their Bishop and spiritual shepherd, and they could not and would not do without him; and second, following the Gothic uprising under Gainas, great unrest was to be expected in the capital; and finally, it would be easy to let the witnesses come themselves.[7]

Chrysostom may perhaps have been touched by so much love and solicitude. Certainly, in his guilelessness, he did not see the connection. He actually allowed himself to be persuaded by these representations to remain in Constantinople, especially as the writer promised that he would make it his personal business to see that the process and the calling of witnesses were attended to. Apparently some of the bishops, who knew Antoninus and some of his connections very well, were somewhat less guileless. They called Chrysostom's attention to the suspicious interest on the part of the court official, and to how easy it would now be for Antoninus to render the witnesses harmless through money or other influence. The Archbishop understood that these ideas were not unfounded. He called the bishops to another conference, and it was decided at this session that Chrysostom should indeed remain in Constantinople, and instead, in his place, three other bishops from the assembly were to be chosen at once, and should travel to the province of Asia to confer with the witnesses and give judgment. The three chosen were: Syncletius, the Metropolitan of Trajanopolis (in Thrace); he was to be the leader and head of the group; then Hesychius, Bishop of Parium (a seacoast town on the Hellespont), a personal friend of Antoninus; and finally Palladius, Bishop of Helenopolis.

Hypaipoi was chosen as the place for the discussions, because this city belonged to the ecclesiastical province of Asia, and was the easiest and most convenient place for the accused, as well as the accusers and judges, to reach. It was situated at the south end of the pass which led over the Tmolos range of mountains, 2,050 meters high, between Sardis and Ephesus.[8]

The Synod gave full powers to the three bishops, with the admonition: "Whoever does not appear within two months, and attend these proceedings, will be excluded from the fellowship of the Church."

The first, who did not appear, and escaped the duty imposed by the Synod, was Hesychius, the friend of Antoninus. When the embassy was ready to set out on its journey, he took to his bed and sent out a report that he was sick. That was a bad beginning. After this, Syncletius and Palladius set out alone. They left for Smyrna by boat early in June, 400, announced their arrival by letter at once to those concerned, and summoned them to Hypaipoi.

Meanwhile Antoninus had not been idle. His notorious business sense had not made him a rich man for nothing. His money had to help him now in his need, if it ever did. Bribery and corruption had long been the cancer of the Roman Empire, and from the beginning had been the universal panacea in the East. So it helped this time. By the time the two ambassadors from Constantinople had arrived, he had brought his opponents, his accusers and his witnesses over to his side with gold, and the swearing of oaths.

The comedy went on with true oriental cunning. Accusers and accused agreed precisely in Hypaipoi. The only ones who did not appear were those without whom no judgment could be passed: the *witnesses*. But they were all ostensibly traveling on various affairs to all the points of the compass. The judges pressed Eusebius, the accuser: "How many days will it take to bring the witnesses here? Then we will wait." The middle of summer was coming on, with its unendurable heat. So Eusebius hoped that if he set as late a final date as possible, that the ambassadors, for fear of the heat, would go away again. He promised that within forty days he would either bring in the witnesses or submit himself to ecclesiastical censure. The ambassadors took up the offer, in spite of the heat. They had the promise made in writing, and Eusebius departed, to bring the witnesses. But, instead of going to Ephesus, he went to Constantinople, where he kept himself hidden, under the protection of the powerful friend of Antoninus.

The two ambassadors waited patiently in the little town of Hypaipoi for forty days, busied with that worst of all labors, inactive waiting. The forty days were finally over, but they saw neither Eusebius nor the witnesses. As had been agreed, the ambassadors sent a document to all the bishops of the province of Asia, announcing that Eusebius, either on account of his flight or of his slander, was excluded from the fellowship of Holy Church. Good or bad friends encouraged them, saying that the witnesses would perhaps still come; that they had probably been delayed for this or that reason. The ambassadors, for whom it must have been painful to return to Constantinople after being cheated in that way, persuaded themselves to wait still another full month on the spot.

Finally they gave up all hopes, and returned to the capital. Fortunately the height of summer was over. Thus ended the first stage of this disedifying episode, so fateful in its consequences.

Eusebius could not remain in hiding forever. One day he returned again to the light of day in Constantinople. When Syncletius and Palladius met him, they reproached him severely for his conduct. Eusebius said he had been sick, and consequently had not been able to search for the witnesses; but now he would surely bring them! More time passed. Autumn came on, and still no witnesses. Meanwhile an incident occurred which gave a new aspect to the affair. Antoninus, the Metropolitan of Ephesus, did the best thing he could have done under the circumstances: he died. With this, the chief obstacle in the way was removed.

It had not been long since Chrysostom had received letters and documents from the bishops of the ecclesiastical province of Asia, as well as from the clergy of Ephesus itself, begging him most urgently, with the strongest expressions,[9] to come to Ephesus himself and to set things in order there. "In the past years, the Church laws have been badly administered, and we ourselves have been ruled badly. We beg you therefore to come and set in order the Church of Ephesus, so that it will answer to the laws of God. For years our churches have been sunk in evil; part of the blame belongs to the Arians, but part also to those who, although having the name of Catholics, have at the same time devoted themselves to avarice and lust for power. There are even many who, like ravening wolves, strive to purchase the episcopal dignity for themselves with money."

What was Chrysostom to do? Could he let the urgent entreaties of the Bishop and clergy on behalf of the Church simply to go disregarded, and allow the disorder to increase? He was sickly himself at the time. Winter was coming on. The trip by sea was dangerous, on account of the many winter storms. Personal difficulties and dangers did not frighten him off, if it was necessary to make a sacrifice for the restoration of ecclesiastical order and discipline.

Obviously no one had raised any question of Church law here. As well as he was able to judge on the basis of an already existing customary right in Constantinople, over an affair which happened in Ephesus, he could just as well, or better, bring to an end in Ephesus itself, this process which had already been made dependent on him.[10] Added to this, the fact that not merely the bishops of his "house-synod," but the leading personalities of the Church of Ephesus had besought him, most urgently and repeatedly, to make this journey. Finally, the Council of Constantinople had decreed in the year 381 that no Bishop should undertake any official Church business in a foreign diocese without being asked to do so;[11] if he was asked, it was approved. This was actually the case in this instance.[12]

So finally Chrysostom, in spite of many considerations, decided to accept the repeated invitations, in order to settle the trouble in the province of Asia. Meanwhile he placed the episcopal palace under the supervision of his faithful deacon Serapion; the office of preaching he placed under the care of Bishop Severian of Gabala; and the Archpriest was to care for the Divine Liturgy.

After Christmas and the Epiphany were past, the Archbishop took ship. It was in the latter half of January 401.[13] The first stop was Apamea. There the Bishops Paul of Heraclea, Cyrinus (of Chalcedon?), and Palladius of Helenopolis would await him, to accompany him on the remainder of the journey.

The journey was very difficult. A strong north wind had made the sea very rough. The captain feared that his ship would be cast up on the coast of the Proconnesus, and therefore he sailed around the headland of the Triton. There he let down the anchor and wished to wait for a south wind to come up, in order to reach Apamea. They lay there two days, tossed by the waves. Seasickness prevented them from taking food. Finally, on the third day, the ship was able to reach Apamea. The three companions were punctually on the spot, and so they came to land ($= \tau \hat{\eta} \ \pi \epsilon \zeta \iota \kappa \hat{\eta} \ \pi o \rho \epsilon \iota a$) at Ephesus, the city of St. John, the beloved disciple.

Ephesus! St. Paul had established the first Christian congregation there, and St. Timothy had been its first Bishop. St. John the Apostle himself had had his residence there, and there he had been buried. Also Mary, the mother of

God, is said to have died and been buried in Ephesus. While
the beginnings of Christianity in Ephesus were bound up with
the most tender and at the same time the greatest memories of
Christian piety, unfortunately, in the course of the fourth
century, a great moral decay had entered into ecclesiastical
life in Ephesus. The Metropolitan Menophantes ruled it,
with many Arians among his followers. In the wake of
Arianism came a far-reaching bargaining in Church positions
and offices, which, as a result of the rich endowments established in the fourth century, had become very desirable posts
of responsibility. So, for example, the Arian pseudo-Patriarch
George of Alexandria (355 ff.) had sold the vacant episcopal
see of his Patriarchate for money, to one of his most evil
creatures.[14] St. Basil had to warn his suffragan Bishops against
simoniacal conferring of consecration,[15] and Chrysostom,
while still at Antioch, had, in his little book on virginity, made
the complaint that there were many who had obtained their
priesthood for money.[16]

In the light of these facts, the following will be more comprehensible.

The Bishops of Lydia, Asia and Caria had meanwhile
assembled together for the selection of a new Metropolitan.
Some from Phrygia came uninvited, because they wished to
become acquainted with Chrysostom, and hear him speak.
In all, there were about seventy, so they all together formed
an important provincial synod.

In this same meeting appeared Eusebius, the accuser of the
dead Antoninus, with six other bishops, who were all accused
of simony. He begged that he might be admitted to the
synod. Several bishops opposed him. Eusebius besought:
"Since this Process has already been prolonged for two years,
and the inquiry for the most part settled and only adjourned
for lack of witnesses, so I beg the reverend bishops that it may
be allowed me to bring forward the witnesses. Antoninus,
who conferred consecration for money, is indeed dead, but
others are still living who bought their consecrations for
money."

Then the majority of the bishops decided that the affair
should be investigated. The earlier proceedings of the previous Process were brought in and read. Then the witnesses

appeared, and also the six accused bishops. They lied this time as they had done before. Among the witnesses were both priests and laity, and also some women. They related in detail, to the terror of the accused, what kind of gifts Antoninus had received; where, when, and how many of them had given gifts to him. That helped their memory by degrees, and at last they recalled, though somewhat unwillingly, that they had actually rendered themselves guilty of simony. So they confessed: "Yes, we received the consecration in return for money and gifts. But we do not see anything illegal in that; we only wished to escape from the curial service.[17] Now we beg, if the canons allow it, that we may either keep our ecclesiastical offices, or that we may have our money back; for some of our wives have used it to buy household furniture."

This confession, of course, threw a very sinister light over the existing circumstances in the ecclesiastical province of Ephesus. The simoniacal bishops, to all appearances, had reverted to the customs of the laity, and some of them had even married. In order to free themselves from the troublesome curial service, they had wished to become bishops, and had given money to obtain bishoprics. How much those people understood of theology and ecclesiastical law can more easily be imagined than proved.

Still, Chrysostom's concern was not to punish individuals, but to abolish wrong conditions. Therefore his judgment was given with extraordinary mildness. He said: " I will free you from the curial service, with the help of God, through intercession with the Emperor. But you may depend on it that you can get your money back from the heirs of Antoninus." The Synod agreed to this proposition. They decided that the guilty parties should get back the money they had spent, from the heirs of Antoninus; they were allowed to partake of the Divine Liturgy inside the Presbyterium, but on the other hand they were deprived of their episcopal and priestly offices, lest, through toleration of such abuses, the Jewish or Egyptian immorality of buying and selling the priesthood for money should become prevalent.

Palladius adds here in explanation: "It is said that the detestable and false Patriarch of the Jews is changed every

year, and also the leader of the Synagogue, that money may
come in; the same is the case with the Patriarch of the
Egyptian Jews."[18]

The six simoniacal bishops declared themselves satisfied
with this judgment. One of them later became a lawyer; of
the others nothing is known. In their places, new bishops
were consecrated, who had distinguished themselves by
education and purity of morals, and who had never been
married.[19]

The depositions of these bishops later gave the Patriarch
Theophilus an important point of accusation against Chrysostom. He had laid down the law in a foreign diocese; the
whole affair was put through in a single day, and sixteen
bishops had been expelled from their sees! Three statements and three untruths. Chrysostom had not forced himself in, but had been repeatedly and urgently besought and
implored by different parties to come and restore order. So
it is also only another unjustified phrase to state, as Gelzer[20]
does, that Chrysostom, on his "visitation journey," had
forced Asia, with pitiless power, to bow under the lordship
of the . . . prelates of New Rome, and that indeed he stamped
himself on this occasion as the founder of the patriarchal
power of Constantinople. R. Janin also unfoundedly designates this action of Chrysostom in Asia as an "encroachment
on the law."[21]

As for the second point, the entire Process against the
simoniacal bishops was not completed in one day, but went
well into two years. Finally, on this occasion, not sixteen
bishops were deposed, as Theophilus stated, but six, and
these for a reason for which the ecclesiastical canons always
and everywhere demanded the penalty of deposition. And
lastly, this penalty was inflicted, not by Chrysostom alone,
but by a provincial synod of seventeen bishops, and accepted
by the guilty parties. The acts of this Process were seen by
Palladius, the author of the Dialog.[22]

The whole affair moreover formed for the Synod a not at
all foreseen interlude. The special purpose for which they
came together was the filling of the vacancy in the metropolitan See of Ephesus with a worthy successor to Antoninus.
This was found in the person of Heraclidus, deacon of the

Church of Constantinople. It is uncertain whether he was placed in nomination by Chrysostom, or by one of the Asiatic bishops, who often stayed in the capital. Heraclidus came from Cyprus, and had previously been a monk in the desert of Scete, as a pupil of Evagrius; he had distinguished himself by many-sided knowledge, especially in the field of Holy Scripture. He had been a deacon for three years.[23]

Sozomen also brings the deposition of Bishop Gerontius of Nicomedia into connection with the Synod of Ephesus. This Gerontius had originally come from Milan, where he had been made deacon by St. Ambrose. He united extraordinary facility in speaking with a somewhat frivolous character and a lively imagination. One day he related that the Onoskelis, or Empusa, a nocturnal phantom, had appeared to him; he said he seized it, struck off its head, and threw it into the grinding-mill. Worse things than these stupid jokes were attributed to him, such as that he practised medicine, which was forbidden by canon law to the clergy. According to Sozomen, he understood something of the healing art.

However it may have been, St. Ambrose found himself one day obliged to administer a punishment to this deacon. He had to observe house arrest and do penance. That was not to the taste of Gerontius. He escaped out of that, and went to Constantinople. The world was bigger and broader there, and the possibilities for getting on were many, especially since Nectarius was no Ambrose. His skill in speaking enabled him in a short time to secure the favor of influential people at court, and soon it was heard in Milan that the disciplined and much regretted Gerontius had become Bishop of Nicomedia. In vain Ambrose wrote to Bishop Nectarius, to depose this charlatan, and not to tolerate having the canons brought into contempt through him. The people of Nicomedia did not wish him removed, since he understood so well how to handle their spiritual and bodily needs, and showed himself worthy of respect from both rich and poor. Chrysostom succeeded in replacing him by Pansophius, who had been a teacher of the Empress Eudoxia.[24]

Of course Chrysostom was concerned with the deposition of Gerontius; but this must have happened earlier. Socrates knows nothing of the whole story, and Palladius assures us three times that only six bishops were deposed at the Synod of Ephesus. The promotion of Eudoxia's teacher to a bishopric would be more suitably assigned to the earlier time when his relations with Eudoxia were still sincere and friendly.

The fame of Chrysostom's doings in Asia Minor has grown almost boundlessly through history. The eulogy ascribed to St. Proclus credits him with performing an extensive work of cleansing, although not merely during his stay in Asia. "Every place," says the speaker, "he has freed from error. In Ephesus he robbed Artemis,[25] in Phrygia he took away the sons of the so-called Mother of the Gods; in Caesarea he repressed the dishonorable houses of joy; in Syria he removed the synagogues which had been battling against God; in Persia he spread the Word of the Faith, and everywhere he laid the foundations of orthodox belief."[26] Unfortunately, this rhetorical flourish cannot be taken for truth.

George Alexandrinus[27] and his successors may well have drawn from Proclus. They had Chrysostom caring for all of Thrace, Asia, Pontus, Phoenicia, as well as the Celts, nomads and Scythians (Goths).

According to Socrates, finally, Chrysostom had, on the occasion of his stay in Asia and Lydia (?), closed or abolished many churches of the Novatians and Quartodecimans, who always celebrated Easter on the 14th Nisan.[28] The other sources know nothing of this. Chrysostom could not have abolished any churches of the Novatians for that reason, because it was recognized by law. And the leader of the Quartodecimans says, on the contrary, that Chrysostom won them by goodness and by meeting them halfway.[29]

If we exclude all the later editions, Chrysostom, in the three months of his stay in Ephesus, gave a new Metropolitan to the See of St. John, and placed six other bishops in the sees of the simoniacal ones. In the interest of ecclesiastical discipline, this was surely to be welcomed.

The carrying through of the process, with all that depended on it, had indeed delayed him longer than he could have foreseen. Easter (the 14th of April, 401) was already over before he could finally begin his return journey, after having been away from his episcopal see for a little over three months. The people in Constantinople received their beloved Bishop with great and sincere joy. A few days afterward, he preached his sermon of greeting. " Moses," he said, " was away from his people for only forty days, and even during that time they left him, to go after idols. I was away more than one hundred days, and you have remained true to your faith and your bishop. That does not mean that I am greater than Moses, but that you are better than the Jews. In this I feel an unutterable joy. The old Jacob rejoiced when he saw his only son Joseph again; I have found a whole people again. This is more than the happiness of Paradise. I would have a heart of stone if the sight of your joy at my return had not touched me; the whole city seems turned into a church. True, we could not celebrate the Easter feast together, and many have received the Easter baptism in my absence. But do we not celebrate Easter each time we celebrate the Holy Mysteries, and was not Christ present, instead of me, at the baptism? I was always with you in spirit, and so your prayers and your love have accompanied me to Asia and back. Wherever I stayed or went, I always prayed: Lord, protect the Church, which Thou has entrusted to me! The Lord has protected you, the flock rejoices, and no wolf has shown himself. While I was in Asia, to correct improprieties in the churches, you have kept your love for me, and this love is my wealth. Your prayers may help me further to be your teacher in Christ, to whom be honor, praise and power for all eternity. Amen."[30]

Such was the pleasant conclusion of the journey to Ephesus. It was probably the last day of joy which Chrysostom ever was to experience in Constantinople.

FOOTNOTES

1. Pall. 13 (47, 47). Palladius was an eyewitness of the Process from beginning to end. So here he is a first-class witness. With special minuteness of detail he pictures the entire course of the proceedings, because this formed a principal point of accusation against Chrysostom, not merely at the Synod of the Oak, but also in the letter which Theophilus sent to Rome for his own defense,

and in which he stated direct untruths. This whole chapter therefore rests, in its essentials, on Palladius.

2. "Asia" as an ecclesiastical province embraced the ancient kingdom of the Attalids. It was the "Province of the five hundred cities" (Mommsen, Röm. Gesch. 5, 299 f. and 327); cf. V. Chapot, La Province Romaine proconsulaire d'Asie p. 86-87.

3. Τῇ μιᾷ Σαββάτου (Pall. 13; col. 47).

4. This lay in the Tmolos mountain range, near the Kelba plain of the Caÿster valley, in Asia Minor. Ramsay, The historical geography 106, 114 and 122.

5. Palladius 14 (c. 48).

6. ῞Ενα τῶν κρατούντων, says Palladius 14 (49).

7. Palladius 14 (49).

8. Ramsay 167.

9. Palladius 14 (50).

10. Socrates 6, 11 (67, 697) takes it as a matter of course that Chrysostom consecrated the new Bishop of Ephesus.

11. Canon 2 = Mansi 3, 560; Hefele 2, 15-16 and 533.

12. Hergenröther, Photius I, 39 ff. A. Thierry, Chrys.-Eudoxie 75, has obviously read Palladius only casually, since he says that Chrysostom had interfered in the Ephesian affair "sans y être appelé."

13. This date proves that Chrysostom returned to Constantinople soon after Easter (401). Easter fell on the 14th of April that year. So his absence lasted somewhat more than a hundred days (= Oratio post reditum 52, 421). This agrees with the statement of Palladius (Ch. 15; col. 51), that the opponents of Chrysostom, after his banishment, hence toward the end of 404, had restored to office the bishops whom he had deposed *four* years before.

14. Hefele 1, 664. This George was formerly a pig dealer and an Army contractor.

15. Epist. II, 53, 1 (29, 397).

16. De Virginitate 24 (48, 550); cf. Hom. 6, 4 in Ephes. = 62, 48. Bonsdorff, Zur Predigttätigkeit p. 90 ff. even sees in the Commentary on the Acts of the Apostles, which originated about 400, an allusion to the simony of Antoninus.

17. Concerning the oppressive conditions of the curial service, see: Pauly-Wissowa, Real-Encyclopädie d. klass. Altertumswissenschaft (Decurio) = 8 (Stuttgart 1901) 2347-51.

18. Palladius 15 (51).

19. Palladius *loc. cit.*

20. In Krumbacher's Geschichte der Byzant. Literatur, 2 A., 2nd edition, p. 914 and 921. Likewise in his essay: Das Verhältnis

von Staat und Kirche in Byzanz (=Ausgewählte kleine Schriften II) p. 61-62.

21. "Empiétements," in: Formation du Patriarcat oecuménique de Constantinople=Echos d'Orient 13 (1910) 138. Concerning law infringement see also: Hergenröther, Photius 1, 39 ff.

22. Palladius 15 conclusion; col. 52. Concerning the number of deposed bishops, the accounts vary widely. While Theophilus, in his pamphlet against Chrysostom, gives the highest number, sixteen, Palladius asserts in three different passages (ch. 13, 15 and 20), that it was no more and no less than six, and the existing Acts, which were signed by seventy bishops, could prove it (ch. 15, col. 52). The less well-informed and later Socrates (6, 15) says very vaguely that there were "many" bishops deposed. Sozomen (8, 6) on the other hand, gives the number as thirteen, who had had their sees, some in Lycia and Phrygia, and some in the province of Asia. But at the Council of Chalcedon (451) Philip, priest of the cathedral in Constantinople, said that Chrysostom, during his stay in Asia, had deposed fifteen bishops and installed others in their places (Mansi 7, 293). On the other hand, the seventh general Council of Nicaea (787) knows of only six, in which it produces written evidence, and introduces a literal quotation from the fifteenth chapter of Palladius (Mansi 13, 467-470). The truth may be this, that Chrysostom, in union with the Ephesian synod of seventy bishops in the province of Asia, deposed six bishops, and in the course of his entire episcopal career perhaps some others, who deserved it, in case Theophilus, and after him Sozomen, did not count in the mere priests and deacons whom Chrysostom had removed in the first year of his rule.

23. Palladius 15 (52) and 20 (71); Socrates 6, 11 (697); Sozomen 8, 6 (1529). According to what is stated in the dubious, broad style of the eleventh chapter of Socrates (col. 732), it was just the installation of Heraclidus which caused the unrest in Ephesus, and for that reason Chrysostom was detained there longer; if so, then this stands in direct contradiction to the genuine Ch. 11 (col. 697), where Socrates expressly says that the installation of Heraclidus had restored peace in Ephesus. Sp. Lambros, Eine neue Fassung des 11th Kapitels des VI. Buches von Socrates' Kirchengeschichte in the Byzantine Zeitschrift 4 (1895) 481-86, has apparently perceived that the "new" composition has been long known and published.

In some manuscripts Heraclidus is even called the author of the Historia Lausiaca, even though wrongly. Cf. Preuschen, Palladius und Rufinus 234; Bardenhewer, GAL 4, 152; Butler, The Laus. History, 2, 183, and Palladiana *loc. cit.* 148-49.

24. Sozomen 8, 6 (1532).   Cf. Batiffol, Le siège apostolique 291: " Il est sûr, qu'il intervenait en Bithynie comme s'il en avait été plus que le métropolitain."   Theodoret HE 5, 28 (82, 1257) says that Chrysostom governed the three provinces of Thrace, Asia and Pontus with twenty-eight archdioceses (?).   Theophanes makes this observation in his Chronography, composed in the beginning of the ninth century, concerning the year 396: From the fact that Chrysostom kindled his spiritual light in Thrace, Asia and Pontus, " came the result that the Bishop of Constantinople possessed jurisdiction over these churches, even before the Council of Chalcedon " (108, 216; ed. Boor 1, 77).

25. This reading (instead of artem Midae) is proposed, with reason, by Prof. R. C. Kukula, in the Zeitschrift für österreiche Gymnasien (1904) p. 7.   See Brockhoff, Studien zur Geschichte der Stadt Ephesus p. 12, note 1.

26. MG 65, 832.

27. Ch. 23 (Savile 8, 189).

28. HE 6, 19 (724 B) and Ch. 6, 11 (697 C).

29. Ch. 29 = ML 53, 597.   It is true that the manner in which he won them sounds rather dubious.   On the other hand, Leontius, Bishop of Ancyra, took a church illegally from the Novatians = Socrates 6, 22 (729).

30. The sermon survives only in Latin, in MG 52, 421-24.

CHAPTER XIV

SEVERIAN OF GABALA, THE FALSE FRIEND

IF there were in the fourth century monks and abbots who found their cells too narrow, and gladly sought the cities,[1] many bishops also, whose provinces had become too small, liked to go to Constantinople. Sometimes they seemed to be so numerous that they became a great cross to the Patriarch. While many came from necessity, others came only because of ambition and place-hunting. The evil in this lay in the fact, not that they came, but that many of them did not wish to return again. Already in the year 341, the Church dedication Synod of Antioch had forbidden, under pain of deposition, bishops to come to the court and to "trouble the ears of our sacred Emperor" unless they were summoned thereto by the Metropolitan or by the Bishops of the Eparchy.[2]

Only three years later, the Synod of Sardica had to forbid any bishop to stay a long time in the city of another bishop, in order to preach there, to put the less learned bishop of the place in the shade, and in this way to possess himself of this bishop's see.[3] A law of the Emperor Justinian from the year 528 directed the "reverend bishops" not to leave their dioceses without necessity, or without written permission of their Patriarch or Metropolitan. But if they came to Constantinople, they must first report their presence to the Patriarch or the Archdeacon of their province, and then they might only be brought to court through him if it was pleasing to the Emperor. Also, no one was to remain away from his episcopal see longer than one year.[4]

Even in the twelfth century, the Emperor Manuel Comnenus was compelled to forbid the visiting bishops to remain in Constantinople longer than was absolutely necessary for the transacting of their business.[5] But that did not help either. A hundred years later, the Patriarch Athanasius of

Constantinople (1289-1293), in no fewer than ten documents, reminded the Byzantine Bishops of their duties to their residential cities, and repeatedly turned to the Emperor in order to compel the provincial Bishops, through him, to return to their dioceses.[6]   So it went on further, until Constantinople fell into the hands of the Turks.

When Chrysostom went to Ephesus, he had, as was mentioned before, directed his Archdeacon Serapion to supervise affairs temporarily.   For help in the celebration of the Liturgy, and above all, in the preaching office, he had, to all appearances, invited Bishop Severian of Gabala, in Syria, to Constantinople;[7] the latter was certainly not unknown to Chrysostom. Gabala belonged to the Patriarchate of Antioch, and was, according to the evidence of Theodoret, "a small but very pleasant town."[8]   Bishop Severian found it even too small for his personality and his talents.   Socrates says that the example of his countryman, Bishop Antiochus of Ptolemais, had led him on.   Antiochus had come to Constantinople earlier, probably with the usual designs, and had there attained the kind of success as a preacher, chiefly through his pleasant and sonorous voice,[9] which opened the hearts and purses of the rich, and provided him with ample means to return to Ptolemais.

The news of this significantly resounding success soon disturbed the spiritual calm of Bishop Severian of Gabala.   As a Syrian by birth, he was not a master of Greek, and the harsh Syrian accent was always heard in his speech.   However, he set to work, composed a series of Greek sermons, practised his pronunciation, and then, with his sermons in his traveling bag, happy and full of pleasant anticipation, he set out for the capital, where, to a good orator, especially if he were a Bishop, honors and distinctions beckoned.

Severian did not trust entirely to his rhetoric.   His chief strength lay in the flexibility of his colloquial speech, and the gentlemanly assurance of his personality.   Chrysostom received him in a very friendly manner, and Severian did his best to win his way, through attentions and readiness in service, into the confidence of his host.   In this he had complete success, since Chrysostom was so guileless.[10]   Chrysostom let him preach to his heart's content, and, what was still more important to Severian, he introduced him at court, where the cunning Syrian knew how to establish himself in the shortest possible time. Above all, he managed to win over the Empress Eudoxia.[11] With this, the provincial bishop had become a power against the Archbishop, which under certain circumstances might become very unpleasant.

He also knew how to make himself popular with the people. They liked to listen to his sermons,[12] although he was not able to gain the reputation of being a specially good preacher, either as regards language or content. His voice was rough, slightly hoarse and worn. The speech itself was hard and rough, and expressed chiefly in short, often broken-off sentences.[13] Without energy and without flexibility, Severian spoke far more in the dry tone of a learned theologian than as a preacher and shepherd of souls. Even in moral admonitions, all warmth was absent from his speech, and one can understand how it was that five or six times during one sermon he had to beg his hearers to pay attention, and to take his weak voice into consideration.[14] Many times one finds pretty thoughts and observations interspersed through the sermons, perhaps the result of his extensive reading; but one soon notices that Severian did not possess outstanding oratorical gifts, and in general, had only a mediocre talent.

Only when he preached against heretics, or when he turned upon critics of his sermons, he became somewhat lively.[15] Polemics seems to have suited his temperament and character best. At all events, his ambition went far beyond his abilities. He was not able to make a name for himself through good deeds. His immortality is not due to his literary performances, but to the role which he played in the tragedy of Chrysostom. But this gives sad evidence of his character and his virtue. But, in this regard, a characteristic irony of fate has willed it that his collected orations, as far as they have survived in Greek, have been handed down under the name of his rival, St. Chrysostom, and apparently owe their survival only to this circumstance.[16] So Chrysostom, after his death, was the unconscious benefactor of the man from whom in life he received only ingratitude.

What was the direct cause of Severian's ingratitude is hard to say. One may assume that, at that time, a resentful atti-

tude against the Archbishop prevailed among the circle of
court ladies, since he showed no understanding of luxury in
dress, questions of fashion, and other feminine weaknesses,
even among the highest court ladies. They certainly did not
conceal their disgust from Severian, who frequented the
Court a great deal, and probably sought to influence the
Empress herself against Chrysostom. Severian, vain and
envious, was characterless enough to join his voice with the
choir of these Furies, and to betray his host and fellow-
bishop.[16a]

The new fellowship served for mutual encouragement.
Severian found opportunities of getting into the confidence
of Bishops Acacius of Beroea and Antiochus of Ptolemais, who
in any case had to come to Constantinople about this time;
and soon there was formed a group of court ladies and of
bishops, in whose midst Chrysostom was criticized and
ridiculed.

Severian was audacious. It is not at all unlikely that some
cunning characters, male or female, even awakened in him
the ambitious hope of becoming himself one day the Archbishop of Constantinople. From the sermons which he
preached in the absence of Chrysostom, one always notes that
he wished to obtain the sympathy of the people for himself.
Also, ambiguous utterances appear therein, which might be
directed against Chrysostom. Indeed, it must even have
come to open disagreement and quarreling. In any case,
Serapion, the deacon and episcopal steward, considered it
necessary to send a report to his master, and to say that
Severian's conduct had already caused complications.[17]

Severian and the other episcopal guests appear to have conducted themselves as though they were the lords of the house.
Soon there was an undercover rivalry between Severian and
Serapion, the house steward. The hostile tension came to an
open break one day when Severian went over to speak to the
Archdeacon, and the latter did not rise from his seat, as was
the custom before Bishops. Serapion merely had not noticed
him. But Severian in his irritation did not think or ask
about explanations or excuses. Full of anger over the supposed insult, he is said to have exclaimed: "If Serapion dies
a Christian death, then Christ did not become man."[18]

After the events related at length in this chapter (by an account which, however, did not originate with Socrates),[19] Severian not only deposed Serapion from the deaconship, but even excluded him from the fellowship of the Church. Severian surely could not have forgotten himself so far. He probably only threatened that he would demand Serapion's deposition, and excommunication, as soon as Chrysostom returned, which is what he actually did.

When Chrysostom finally returned from Ephesus and heard of the incident, he summoned the bishops in residence to a conference. Serapion was invited, and declared under oath that he had not stood up before Severian merely because he had not seen him; he had witnesses who could verify this. Thereupon the bishops present declared that Serapion was not to blame, and besought Severian to accept his excuse. The latter rejected all offers of reconciliation. In vain Chrysostom offered to relieve Serapion of his office for at least a week. Severian demanded unrelentingly that he should be deposed and excommunicated. This Chrysostom was not willing to do. He stood up and declared that he would no longer function as judge; the bishops should decide the quarrel without him; and he left the conference. The bishops, on their part, also got up and left the hall, after reproaching Severian with his implacability.[20]

After this rupture of cordial relations, further continuation of peace in the episcopal palace was not to be thought of. Chrysostom himself had good reason to consider himself offended by the passionate rejection of his efforts at reconciliation on the part of his guest. He saw no other way out than to have Severian told by a third person that he had better return to his diocese after so long an absence.[21] No other choice remained to Severian but to follow the unwished-for suggestion, at least for the moment. Actually he scarcely thought of leaving the place in which he had already made conquests full of promise. He prepared for departure, however, and actually crossed the Bosporus. But in Chalcedon he stopped at the home of Bishop Cyrinus, whom he perhaps influenced against Chrysostom on this occasion. At least we find Cyrinus, soon after this, among the opponents of the saint.

Meanwhile Severian had sent a messenger to the palace, to tell the Empress and some of the court ladies that he had had to leave the capital without having had time to say farewell to his patronesses and benefactors.[21a]   Also, he misrepresented Chrysostom's motives in such a way that Eudoxia was angered at the injustice done to her protégé, and considered herself insulted.[22]   The easily irritated Empress then sent without delay to the Archbishop, told him of her dissatisfaction over what had happened, and demanded that Chrysostom take Severian back without delay.

That was a painful surprise for the Archbishop.   He had scarcely been able to foresee that the Empress would ally herself with Severian in this way.   At any rate, one could see in this a proof that he no more possessed the absolute trust of Eudoxia, and that Severian must have undermined his influence at the Court also.   What was to be done?   Should he persevere in his decision?   Should he, for the sake of a purely personal quarrel, insult the Empress directly and ignore her express wish—the Empress, who was now the most outstanding personality in the Empire, upon whose good will so much depended?   Severian now possessed the imperial favor, and Eudoxia had openly taken sides with him.   Common sense and prudence demanded that Chrysostom should yield.   He yielded.

Severian returned promptly and took up his residence in the episcopal palace anew.[23]

The news of the quarrel had already penetrated to the people, and roused the greatest sensation.   People took sides for and against Severian, and it came to quarrels and dissensions.[24]   The reconciliation also must have become publicly known.   That happened, after the Greek manner, through public sermons at the Divine Liturgy.   The adherents of the Archbishop were so angry that the chief shepherd had to appeal earnestly to their obedience, that they might keep the peace with Severian and not hinder him from preaching.

"It has already become unpleasant enough in the Church," he said to them, "but I do not praise schism, and I will not have disturbances.   Let us stop it now!   Cease and desist, and keep quiet, conquer your disgust and curb your anger.

It is enough, what the Church has already suffered; now let us have an end of it, let the disturbance cease. Such is the will of God and our pious Emperor. So receive our brother Bishop Severian with full hearts and open arms! "

The listeners applauded; Chrysostom praised and thanked them. "Let us pray," he concluded his sermon, "that God will give peace to His Church, and indeed a firm and enduring peace."

Several days afterward Severian went to the pulpit and preached a sermon of reconciliation.[25]

One may believe Socrates[26] that this resolution was not easy for Chrysostom. After all that had happened, and it must have been very much, he had reason enough to expect little good of Severian's return. If an external reconciliation came to pass, who would guarantee that Severian henceforth would abstain from his activities? However, it is altogether unbelievable, that, as Socrates says,[27] Chrysostom had originally refused to hold any fellowship with him after his return. When first Eudoxia herself, with her youngest child, the heir to the throne, in her arms,[28] had thrown herself at the Archbishop's feet in the Church of the Apostles, and had wept and implored him by his head, Chrysostom had yielded, and then only with misgivings. Over this, the reconciliation had been only outward, and both bishops had kept their mutual resentment in their hearts. This state of affairs did not suit either the character of the Empress or that of Chrysostom. Such a scene, played with all publicity on account of a simple provincial bishop, is scarcely conceivable in view of the proud character of Eudoxia.

So peace was restored. But a certain dissonance between the Court and the Archbishop still remained. It was clear that relations with Severian could not improve. Of course one may believe that Chrysostom, in view of his conduct hitherto, was in earnest about the peace, and that on his part he did everything to avoid any further break. He gave a proof of his tactfulness and of his effort at co-operation in securing peace in the house by ordaining Serapion to the priesthood. With this, his position as episcopal steward was elevated, and the possibility of further friction between him and Severian was considerably lessened. In his place came a

new Archdeacon, who very soon, in opposition to his predecessor, showed himself a Judas.

That this change of circumstances must have taken place
just at this time followed from these facts, that Serapion, until
the quarrel with Severian, was designated Archdeacon and
steward of the Church's property and of the episcopal palace
and hospice,[29] that on the arrival of Theophilus, the man who
was Archdeacon at the moment betrayed his Bishop,[30] and
third, that the eighteenth point of accusation of the Deacon
John at the Synod of the Oak stated that Chrysostom had
ordained Serapion to the priesthood while he himself was
"under accusation;"[31] which could only have meant the accusation and quarrel of Severian against Serapion.

Throughout the entire incident it had at any rate become
very obvious that there were among the clergy, as well as at
court, people who were no longer in harmony with the Archbishop. That was new and unexpected, for hitherto the new
shepherd had enjoyed the greatest sympathy everywhere.
The people especially depended on him, and were ready to go
through fire for him.

But Severian soon showed how things really stood with his
wish for reconciliation.

FOOTNOTES

1. Cf. Ch. 17.
2. Canon 11 = Mansi 2, 1313; Hefele 1, 516-17.
3. Canon 11 (lat. Canon 14) = Mansi 3, 16 and 27; Hefele 1, 592.
4. Corpus Iuris Civilis 3, 39 = Novelle 6, 3.
5. 133, 788.
6. Epistola 1, 10, 13, 15, 16, 17, 31, 45, 52, 63 (142, 473 ff. and 513 ff.). Cf. Nicephorus Greg., Byz. Histor. 6, 5 (148, 335).
7. "He turned the church over to him," says Sozomen 8, 10 (1541).
8. Hist. Rel. cp. 28 (82, 1488 A).
9. Sozomen 8, 10: εὐκόλως καὶ μάλα εὐήχως ἔλεγεν. The contents
cannot have made much impression, for apparently none of his
sermons have survived. Zeitschrift f. Kath. Theologie 32 (1908)
408-410, wishes to prove a sermon under the name of Chrysostom

as having been composed of Antiochus. But Zellinger, Genesis-homilien 41, has made it probable that it belongs rather to Severian.

10. Socrates 6, 11 (67, 696-97); Sozomen 8, 10 (1541).

11. Sozomen *loc. cit.*

12. Socrates 6, 11 (67, 697). A sermon which Severian preached one Easter Day (Baptism Day) in Constantinople, survives in MG 63, 543-550. Cf. Zellinger, Studien 37-42. Another sermon made after the earthquake=63, 531-544; Zellinger, *loc. cit.* 79-84.

13. Also Zellinger, Die Genesishomilien p. 61, judges: "Severian's style is hard and rough." "There is no flow or symmetry. The diction is often wordy but shows poverty of ideas." First Gennadius of Marseille (between 461 and 469) De Viris ill. 21 (ML 58, 1075) says Severian was a "declamator admirabilis," and Ado of Vienne (875) in his Chronicon VI, 396 (ML 123, 100) quoted this from him.

14. For example, sermon 5, 5 (56, 477).

15. Cf. Sermon 1, 7; 4, 10; 5, 1 ff. (56, 437 and 470-72).

16. The six homilies of Severian on Genesis were first edited by Savile (Chrysostomi Opera Omnia 7, 587-640; Eton 1612). They are found in Migne 56, 429-500, after Montfaucon. Several other homilies which belong to Severian are also found under the name of Chrysostom. Cf. Zellinger, Genesishomilien *loc. cit.* 39 ff., and Studien p. VII f.; S. Haidacher in Zeitschrift f. kath. Theologie 32 (1908) 410-413.

16a. These frequent communications with the court ladies seem to have occasioned gossip about Severian. At any rate, he once bewailed the slander and asserted his innocence. Hom. in Mt. 21, 23 (56, 428).

17. Socrates 6, 11 (col. 697). Also the enlarged work (col. 733) allows something of the sort to peep through.

18. Socrates 6, 11 (col. 700). Also, in the Divine Liturgy, only bishops and priests were allowed to sit *in cathedra*. This was expressly forbidden to the deacons. See H. Koch, Bischofstuhl und Priesterstuhl = Ztschr. f. Kirchengesch. 44 (1925) 170-84.

19. 67, 733.

20. Socrates 6, 11 (67, 733).

21. *Loc. cit.* Socrates 6, 11 represents the affair in an entirely incredible way. Afterwards Serapion misrepresented the above-mentioned angry expression of Severian, and only said to his bishop that Severian had said Christ had not become man. Thereupon Chrysostom had expelled him from the city at once. But such hasty dealing was not Chrysostom's way. Also, as Funk, Joh. Chrys. p. 32, writes, Chrysostom did not exclude Severian from the

fellowship of the Church. That he could not have done without the judgment of a synod.

Funk considers the Herodias sermon and the statement of Socrates as absolutely authentic (p. 37) and says wrongly, that Chrysostom had been, before his second banishment, ready to "give an account" personally.

21a. Otherwise, Severian would not have needed to leave Constantinople.

22. Socrates 6, 11 (c. 700).

23. This is shown by the circumstance that it was considered an unfriendly gesture when Severian took up his residence elsewhere.

24. Chrys., De recipienda Severiano (52, 426).

25. Homilia de Pace 52, 425-428. The authenticity of this sermon appears to me to be doubtful. It is throughout the speech of furious, confusedly depressed, and grieving heretics, which is not at all suitable to our situation, for it seems that these defections attributed to Serapion scarcely apply to him. Zellinger, Studien 48-52, considers it authentic. It is edited, in a longer Greek text form, by A. Papadopulos-Kerameus, Ἀνάλεκτα Ἱεροσολυμιτικῆς Σταχυολογίας 1 (Petersburg 1891) 15-26. (This sermon might have been published much earlier, that is, in the time of the Nestorian or Eutychian controversies.)

26. HE 6, 11 (67, 700).

27. Sozomen 8, 10 (1541-43) simply copied the same from him.

28. Born on the 10th of April, 401.

29. Socrates 6, 11 (700) and Sozomen 8, 9 (1537).

30. Palladius 2 (9).

31. Photius, Bibl. 59 (103, 108).

CHAPTER XV

STRIFE WITH THE EMPRESS EUDOXIA

THE scandalous appearance of a strange provincial bishop in Constantinople could only be unpleasant for Chrysostom, but not dangerous. But now, for the first time, opposition was coming out into the light of day. The evil of this was that Severian could assert himself in Constantinople. Obviously that was only possible if there were other opposition forces which had hitherto remained hidden, but which at the first opportunity were able to unite and work together.

Unfortunately for Chrysostom, it happened that, just at the time of the quarrel with Bishop Severian, a misunderstanding with the Empress Eudoxia came up. That this misunderstanding arose after the return from Ephesus, and hence after the quarrel and reconciliation with Severian, appears to be proved by the fact that Chrysostom, at the Synod of Ephesus, had promised the deposed simoniacal bishops that he would apply to the Emperor for their release from curial service; and that in a fashion which guaranteed absolute reliance on a favorable hearing for his request.[1] When, on the other hand, soon after the trip to Asia, Bishop Porphyrius of Gaza came to Constantinople to request a favor of the Emperor through Chrysostom, the latter had to tell him that unfortunately he could not do anything for him with the Emperor, since he had fallen into disfavor with the Empress.[2] So the fateful turning point in the life of our saint came in the course of the year 401.

Eudoxia, the Frankish general's daughter, had meanwhile reached the zenith of splendor and power. After the fall of Eutropius and of Gainas, she was, on January 9, in the year 400, elevated to the highest dignity of "Augusta," by which, so to speak, every difference in rank between her and the Emperor was abolished.[3] Already this year had brought to her and to the Emperor the fulfilment of their hearts' dearest wish;

she gave, on the 10th of April, 401, to the Emperor and to the Empire, an heir to the throne, the future Theodosius II.

All this had doubtless strengthened her womanly sense of power and had also perhaps influenced her susceptibility and sociability somewhat. At any rate, the unwonted feeling of power seems to have disturbed somewhat her awareness of her rights.

Added to this was the fact that, during the three-months absence of Chrysostom, powers were at work endeavoring to turn the Empress against the Archbishop. To the first rank of these powers belonged Bishop Severian, then a group of court ladies and bishops, as well as an abbot, all of whom will appear on the stage in the next chapter; but who were now playing their roles behind the scenes. Perhaps also, since the conflict with Severian, a remnant of ill-humor and resentment remained in the heart of the Empress. From this, only a little was necessary to cause the spark to flame up into a fire.

The following event gave the external occasion for this.

One day a woman came before Chrysostom and complained of a misfortune. The Empress had taken away her property by force, because she wished it for her own purposes. So at least says the oldest and most trustworthy witness on this occasion, the Deacon Marcus, the biographer of Bishop Porphyrius of Gaza.[4]

The story of the vineyard of the widow of Theognostus is told by Theodore of Trimithus,[5] also by George Alexandrinus,[6] Anonymus,[7] and Metaphrastes.[8] The Empress had plucked a bunch of grapes in this vineyard, one day, without knowing that it was someone else's vineyard. However, an imperial law had decreed that any piece of land which had been trod by the feet of the Divine Majesty of the Emperor or of the Empress, could no more remain in profane hands, but it must revert to imperial possession, in exchange for a corresponding compensation.

Nothing is known of such a law. Also, neither Palladius nor Socrates nor Sozomen speak of such a vineyard. However, history seems to find an indirect ratification in the fact that, after the evidence of Palladius,[9] in the two documents of accusation which were directed against Chrysostom at the Synod of the Oak, he had once called the Empress a Jezebel.

When and for what cause this had happened, is not mentioned there. But now Jezebel, as is well known, for the sake of a vineyard which King Ahab wanted, had brought to ruin Naboth, its owner. For this the prophet Elias had prophesied her destruction.[10]

But this much at least is certain, that the Empress had dispossessed the owner of a certain piece of land, which probably adjoined the palace which the Emperor had built for her; that the owner, whether man or woman, had been dispossessed against his or her will, in exchange for corresponding compensation, for Eudoxia was not avaricious or common. Her royal generosity to the Bishops of Gaza and Caesarea proves that.[11] Further, it is a fact that Chrysostom took the affair upon himself, and after the example of the prophet Elias, made representations to the Empress.

On account of his lively temperament and his rhetoric, animated with biblical images and figures of speech, his utterances were possibly not clothed in the courtly style required by a "divine Majesty." It is not impossible that he not only felt the fatal similarity between this case and that of Jezebel, but that he even spoke of it. At least, not long before, St. Ambrose of Milan, during his quarrel with the Arian Empress-mother Justina, had preached a sermon in vindication of his Church, in the course of which he publicly mentioned the example of Naboth, who defended his vineyard against Ahab and Jezebel.[12]

One thing only is certain, however, that the always kindly representations of the Archbishop, and his well-meant defense of the right, were taken ill by the Empress, and she showed herself very much offended.

The above-mentioned biographers adorn the incident with childish, fantastic additions. For instance, that Eudoxia, in her anger, commanded that if the Archbishop should come again, the palace doors should be closed to him. And thereupon that Chrysostom also charged the doorkeeper of the Cathedral, that if the Empress wished to enter, that he should quickly close the door and say: "John has also commanded me."[13]

So the time of peace between "Church and State" lasted, for Chrysostom, about three years.

However, the result of this quarrel was as harmful for

Chrysostom as it was for Eudoxia. Might a reconciliation be possible? Among men, perhaps. But Eudoxia was a woman, and in the background stood a number of individuals to whom this dissension between the Archbishop and the Empress was very gratifying; for they now had powerful confederates, without whom they had been and had remained completely powerless.

FOOTNOTES

1. Palladius, Dial 15 (47, 51).

2. Marcus Diac. Vita Porphyrii cp. 37 (ed. Bonn p. 33).

3. Chronicon Paschale ad annum 400 (92, 779).

4. Vita Porphyrii cp. 37 (ed. Bonn p. 33).

5. Ch. 15 (47, p. XLIX). The story is also retained in the Vita S. Epiphanii of the alleged Polybius (Ch. 61) (41, 101-104); see Tillemont, Mémoires 11, 596-97 (Note 59).

6. Ch. 41 (Savile 8, 215-17).

7. Ch. 85 (*ibid.* 341-43).

8. Ch. 32 (*ibid.* 410-12).

9. Ch. 8 (30).

10. 1 Kings 21, 1 ff. F. Nau, in Revue d'Or chr. 27 (1929-30) 424 Anm. 1, explains the whole story of the vineyard as a fiction of Metaphrastes (961-64), which never happened. Cf. Marcus, Vita Porphyrii, No. 36 and 37.

11. Cf. Ch. 16, p. 177-178. The Panegyric on Chrysostom attributed to St. Proclus speaks of this affair of "imperialis avaritia" 65, 831). However, the Sermon is of doubtful authenticity, and, with the questionable expression, would only show the despotic violence of the Empress. What Zosimus 5, 25 tells of a later "bribery" of the Empress through Artabazes, is base and foolish gossip. Eudoxia was no longer living at the time of this alleged bribery.

12. ML 16, 1012.

13. Cf. with these legends: Chr. Baur, Zur Ambrosius-Theodosiusfrage = Theol. Quartalschrift 89 (1908) 401 ff. O. Seeck, *loc. cit.* V, 337-38, has at best given more fantasy than history when he gives as the cause of the quarrel with Eudoxia: "The effort which it cost Chrysostom's fiery southern nature, to overcome the allurements of sensuality, filled him with a hatred of women which was to become fateful in his relations with the Empress."

Concerning the credibility of the Vita Porphyrii, see: Appendix to Chapters 13-16. What here follows next is only the actual report of Marcus.

CHAPTER XVI

BISHOP PORPHYRIUS OF GAZA, AND MARCUS, HIS DEACON, IN CONSTANTINOPLE[1]

TOWARD the end of the fourth and the beginning of the fifth century, a quarrel came up between the pagans and the Christians, at Gaza in Palestine. That was nothing new there. In scarcely any other city had the pagans shown themselves so hostile and inimical to the Christians, as in Gaza. The city possessed a small high school, whose teachers were the spiritual focus of the pagan party. So it came about, that already in 395, the newly consecrated Bishop Porphyrius had only 280 Christians in the whole city. Also, the country people round about Gaza showed themselves pagan in spirit. Only in the south and south-east were St. Hilarion and some other apostolic monks able to christianize a part of the country population.[1] In Gaza itself, the pagan town council would not allow Christians to hold office; indeed it sought in every way to hinder the Christians from settling there, and getting possession of land. So the people of Gaza made life as miserable as possible for the Christians and their Bishop, Porphyrius.

The latter had been born in Saloniki, and had lived for many years as a monk, first in the desert of Scete in Egypt, then in Palestine. He was ordained priest in Jerusalem in 392, and three years later the Metropolitan of Caesarea in Palestine made him Bishop of Gaza. Porphyrius had the soul of a missionary. With the greatest zeal he dedicated himself to the conversion of the pagans. Naturally, this brought upon him the most vigorous opposition of the pagan party.[2] Then the Bishop, at the end of February 398, sent his faithful deacon Marcus to Constantinople, to obtain, through the intercession of the new Archbishop, an imperial command for the closing of the pagan temple in Gaza. That was certainly a forceful method of conversion. Nevertheless, the pagans had been the first to begin the violence. Under Julian, the Christian Church had been destroyed, and several Christians killed.[3]

Let us hear the story as told by Marcus himself, the author of the Vita Porphyrii:[4]

"Now when St. Porphyrius saw what outrages were committed every day by the servants of the gods, he decided to send me to Constantinople to beg the Emperor to have the pagan temples closed. There were several of them in Gaza, especially the so-called Marneion. So he sent a letter to the most pious and reverend John, who was Bishop in Constantinople at that time, and whose fame and praise went out into all the world. Then he escorted me to a ship, and after twenty days we arrived at the capital. There I gave my letter to the holy John, and explained the whole matter to him verbally. He listened to me attentively, and then went to the chamberlain Eutropius, who at that time was very influential with the Emperor Arcadius. He read aloud to him the letter of the holy Bishop (Porphyrius), and besought him to favor the petition. After he had obtained his promise, he came back and said to me: Have patience, my son! I hope in Christ our Lord, that He will show us His mercy, as He usually does. But I did not cease to remember the affair day by day, and he, on his part, sent to Eutropius and urged it. Then, after seven days, an order came from the Emperor that the temple of the gods in Gaza was to be closed and not re-opened. The document was delivered to a certain Hilarius, a subordinate of the Magister militum. Three days later, I left Byzantium, and after ten days reached Gaza, seven days before Hilarius. There I found the most holy Bishop Porphyrius sick. But when I gave him the answer of the holy John, Bishop of Constantinople, and he read it, the fever left him, and he became well again, through joy; he said that only the worry over the servants of the gods had made him sick.

"Seven days later, Hilarius came from Constantinople, with many officers and soldiers from Azotus and Ascalon. He had the images of the gods in the temples destroyed, and all the temples closed. Only in regard to the Marneion did

Hilarius act contrary to his instructions, that the pagans could sacrifice only in secret. They paid him gold for this."[5]

Thus far Marcus, concerning his first journey.

Soon after this came the fall of Eutropius. That gave the pagans new courage. Apparently they opened their temples again, and began once more to attack the Christians. The pagan city fathers placed all imaginable difficulties in the way of the Christians.

In order to escape the danger of new battles and new attacks of fever, Bishop Porphyrius knew of nothing else to do but to go to Caesarea, to his Metropolitan, John, to ask him for advice and help. They decided to go to Constantinople together, and lay their problem before the Emperor. Porphyrius took his deacon Marcus with him; the Archbishop Johannes took the deacon Eusebius. In spite of the wintry weather, they boarded ship, and landed ten days later on the island of Rhodes. There they visited the famous hermit Procopius, a holy man who was able to drive out devils, and to prophesy. He told them exactly how everything would go, and what they themselves should do. They should go first to the holy Bishop John, and set the case before him. However, he would not be able to intercede for them personally at court, because the Empress was angry with him. He would take them to the chamberlain Amantius, and the latter would obtain an audience for them with the Empress. In the first audience, they should merely present the case; but in the second they should say: 'If you grant our request, we hope that God will give you a son.' That will give her great joy."[6]

Thus the wise hermit.

Let us quote the Vita Porphrii further: its naïve, intuitive manner of writing, as well as its culturally and historically interesting contents, justify another short quotation from the account; so, as Marcus represents the affair, the Vita continues: "As we listened to the speech of the holy man (Procopius), we believed in his words, took his advice, and then left the same day, and went on board the ship. After ten days, we landed in Constantinople, found an inn, and set out, a few days afterward, to see the Archbishop John. Since he already knew who we were, he received us very honorably, and with great attention. He asked us what our business was.

We told him, and he remembered at once that we had already consulted him about the same affair in writing; he recognized me again, and greeted me heartily.   Next he begged us not to lose courage, but to trust in God's mercy.   Then he said to us: Unfortunately, I am not in a position to speak to the Emperor; the Empress has influenced him against me, because I reproached her on account of a piece of property which she wanted and took away by force.   However, I do not worry about that, nor do I grieve because she is angry with me; she has only injured herself, not me; and if she does my body an injury, that will be all the more advantageous to my soul; so let us leave this to the mercy of God.   But as to your affairs, I will, if God pleases, speak to the eunuch Amantius, a chamberlain of the Empress, who has great influence with her, and who also sincerely serves God.   I will turn the matter over to him, and he, with the help of God, will take care of it with zeal.   After we had received these instructions and this advice, we returned to our inn."

(Chap. 38.) "On the following day, we went to the holy Bishop again, and found the chamberlain Amantius with him; he gave attention to our business, since he had summoned him and explained the affair to him.   And when we had come in, and Amantius had heard that that we were the ones of whom Bishop John had spoken to him, he stood up and greeted us with a deep bow, and when they heard who he was they embraced and kissed him.   The holy Archbishop John now requested of us that they themselves explain their business to the chamberlain.   So the holy Porphyrius told him all he had to say concerning the pagans, how they openly and boldly committed all sorts of illegal acts, and how they oppressed the Christians.

"When Amantius heard this, he was touched to tears, and, full of holy zeal, he said to us: 'Be not discouraged, my fathers.   Christ the Lord promised to protect His religion. While you pray for this, I will speak to the Empress, and I hope to Almighty God that, as always, He will be governed by His mercy.   I will also lead you to her myself, within the next few days, and you may talk to her yourselves about the affair which concerns you; and you will find that she has already heard of it from me.'   Thereupon he took his leave, and departed. But we stayed quite a while, and had a long spiritual conversation with the most holy Archbishop John; then we also said farewell and went away."

(Chap. 39.) "The next day the chamberlain Amantius sent two deacons to us, who invited us to the palace; we hastened to get ready, and went with them. We found him already awaiting us. He took the two Bishops into the presence of the Empress Eudoxia. As soon as she saw us, she greeted us first and said: 'Give me your blessing, fathers.' And they greeted her respectfully. The Empress was sitting on a golden couch; she said, 'Excuse me, priests of Christ, on account of my bodily condition; I should have greeted your Holinesses at the door. But pray to the Lord for me, that my delivery will be happy.' The holy Bishops were surprised at her condescension, and said: 'May He Who blessed the womb of Sara, Rebecca and Elizabeth, also bless the fruit of your womb, and let it live.' They also said several other spiritual things. Then the Empress said: 'I know what is troubling you! the eunuch Amantius has told me of it. But if you wish to tell me about it yourselves, fathers, do so.'

"After this invitation, they told her everything the pagans had done; how they had boldly committed outrages, and acts of tyranny; for instance, they had not allowed any Christians to hold any offices in the city, nor even to build on their own property, on which they had paid the taxes to her Majesty.

"When the Empress heard this, she said: 'Have confidence, fathers; I hope to Christ the Lord, the Son of God, that I can bring the Emperor to take the measures necessary for our holy faith, and send you hence with honor. Return now to your inn, for you are weary, and pray that God may support my petition.' Thereupon she ordered money to be brought in; she took three handfuls and gave it to the holy Bishops with the words: 'Take this for your many expenses.'

"The Bishops took it, thanked her heartily and departed. But at their departure they gave most of the gold pieces to the grooms of the chambers, so that there was not much left.

"Then when the Emperor came to the Empress, she told him of the Bishop's situation, and besought him to have the pagan temple in Gaza destroyed. This angered the Emperor,

and he said: 'I know this city is still pagan; but it is well
disposed politically, and brings in much money in taxes. If
we suddenly put the inhabitants into a fright, they will flee
the city, and we will lose considerable income. But if it is
agreeable to you, we will at least close in on them somewhat;
we will exclude the worshippers of the gods from all city
dignities and benefices, and will command the temple to be
closed and never re-opened. If they are hemmed in thus on
all sides, they will yield to the true religion; but all too
sudden and radical measures will bear too hard on our subjects.'" Marcus does not reveal to us whether the two Bishops
were satisfied with this discreet and mild solution. Eudoxia
at least was not; she held out for the complete and literal
granting of her request. And she obtained it by true feminine
wiles. For: "When the Empress heard this, she was very
much troubled (for she was very zealous in her faith); but she
only answered the Emperor thus: 'The Lord can help His
Christian servants, whether we wish it or not. So the God-
fearing chamberlain Amantius told us.'

(Chap. 42.) "Several days afterward the Empress summoned
us. After she had greeted the holy Bishops as before, she
invited them to be seated. She spoke first at length on
religious subjects, and then said: 'I have spoken with the
Emperor, and he did not show himself especially enthusiastic;
but do not let your courage sink; if God wills, I will not give
up, until you can leave satisfied, and your purpose, pleasing
to God, can be attained. The Bishops expressed to her their
grateful respect.

"Then Bishop Porphyrius informed her of the prophecy
of the hermit Procopius, which was as follows: The Empress
will bear a son, who will come to the Throne. That rejoiced
the Empress very much, and she promised them, that if the
expected child was really a boy, she would do everything that
they wished. Specifically, she would have a church built in
Gaza, in the middle of the city. Then she commended herself again to the prayers of the Bishops, and dismissed them.
The Bishops prayed also, trusting in the prophecy of Procopius. Meanwhile we went every day to the most holy Archbishop John; we enjoyed listening to his holy speech, which
was sweeter than honey and the honeycomb. The chamber-

lain Amantius came often to us also, and told us that the
Empress hoped to meet us again at another time.

(Chap. 44.) " A few days later the Empress actually bore a
son.[7] He was named Theodosius, after his grandfather. In
Constantinople, rejoicing reigned, and the other cities sent
ambassadors, to bring messages of congratulation, together
with gifts and other proofs of loyalty. The Empress, as soon
as possible after the birth, sent Amantius to the Bishops, and
told him to say: ' I thank Christ that God sent me a son
through your prayers; pray also for him, that he may live, and
for my insignificance, that I may be able to keep my promise.
In the course of a week she summoned us, and went with us
to the door of her chamber, holding in her arms the new born
child, wrapped in purple. She held out the child to the holy
Bishops, that they might bless it, and they signed it and her
with the sign of the cross, spoke a blessing, and then sat down.
After many pious speeches the Empress said to them: ' Do
you know, fathers, what plan I have made in your affair? ' "

Eudoxia's plan was as follows: " If it is pleasing to Christ,
the child will, in a few days, receive the grace of baptism.
Therefore go and compose a petition and list all your requests
in it; then present the petition to the one who carries the
child to baptism; I will tell him beforehand what he has to
do, and I hope to God's Son that the affair will go according
to His pleasure and mercy."

No sooner said than done. Porphyrius mentioned in the
petition not only the destruction of the temple, but, wisely
taking advantage of the favorable opportunity, he also begged
for privileges for the Christians and for their church, as well
as something in the way of a foundation for its support, since
their church was poor.

Baptism of the Successor to the Throne.

So finally the longed-for day approached on which the
young Emperor was to be baptized. All Constantinople
" garlanded and adorned itself with silken and gold garments,
and every other kind of adornment, so that it is impossible
to describe in words the beauty of the city. One could see
the masses of people coming in like waves of the sea, clad in
bright clothing of every imaginable kind. I have not the

industry to describe the splendor of this lordly spectacle—
the rhetoricians can try that; I shall return to my own accu-
rate report.

"When the young Theodosius was baptized, and came out
of the church to return to the palace, one could enjoy for the
second time the splendid spectacle of the many court and
state officials, in their brilliant uniforms; they all wore white
garments, so that it looked as though snow had fallen upon
the multitude. At the head of the procession walked the
patricians, the Illustrii and all the other nobility, as well as
the ranking military officers, and they all carried wax tapers,
so that one had the impression of seeing stars come down to
earth."

Next to the child, who was carried by one of the highest
court officials, walked the Emperor, in a purple mantle, his
face shining with joy and satisfaction. The procession wound
through the baptistery and the cathedral, and into the open
air. Bishop Porphyrius, with his deacons, had established
himself in the vestibule, and he carried the petition in his
hand. As the newly baptized heir to the throne came by
them, they called out: "We have a petition for your Piety!"
This remark was not directed to the Emperor, but to the
imperial baby, for at the same time they pressed the petition
into the hand of the one who was carrying the child. He took
it, as had been agreed on, read part of it, and then laid his
hand under the baby's head, so as to make it nod, and then
called out to those standing around: "His Resplendency has
commanded that it shall be done as the petition requests."
Everyone was astonished at what had happened, but the
Emperor was charmed, and he assented. He did not know
what it was about. The Empress, however, was soon notified
that the petition was granted, for the child's sake. She
rejoiced and thanked God on her knees.

(Chap. 49.) "As the child and the Emperor came into the
palace, the Empress met them, took the child and kissed it.
Then she greeted the Emperor, called him happy, since he
had lived to see the day. Arcadius was in his best mood,
and Eudoxia quickly added: 'And now let us see what is in
the petition, so that it may be attended to at once.' The
Emperor let her read it aloud, and then said: 'That is a diffi-

cult request, but it is more difficult still, to reject the first command of our child.' Then the Empress added: 'Yes, and just at the time when he is in his baptismal dress, and has spoken for a good purpose, and brought a request of holy men.' So the Emperor yielded to the pressure. The chamberlain Amantius afterward related to Bishop Porphyrius the story of how the affair had gone at the palace."

Porphyrius was satisfied. His wish for rest from the pagans had been fulfilled, and also, he would get a new church, in the heart of the city. More the Empress could not do; she had made his cause expressly her own, out of joy and gratitude that a son had finally been born to her.

On the very next day she summoned the two Bishops to the palace, greeted them as usual, and told them herself of the favorable outcome of the petition. That everything might be quickly and surely accomplished, she had the Quaestor, the president of the imperial chancellery, summoned to appear the next day, and gave him in the presence of the Bishops the duty of having the petition drawn up in the form of an imperial edict. He dictated the "divine rescript" at once, to a scribe whom he had brought with him, and had it signed by the Emperor.

The imperial counselor Cynegius was entrusted with the carrying out of the edict; he was a trustworthy man. Eudoxia gave him, with her own hand, enough money for his expenses, with the command not to take any from the Bishops.

(Chap. 52.) "So finally came the time for departure. In the farewell audience, the Empress gave Bishop Porphyrius enough money to build the new memorial church, and a hospice for strangers. In the latter, every visiting 'brother' was to be cared for for three days, for which Eudoxia set aside a special sum. Also, the Archbishop of Caesarea received a thousand gold pieces, church furnishings, and various privileges for his church. Finally the Empress gave each a hundred gold pieces for the expenses of their trip. That was magnanimously and royally done. It is understandable that the Bishops wore themselves out in proving their gratitude, and in calling down blessings upon the Empress, the Emperor and the heir to the throne. Also the Emperor, in their farewell audience, had twenty pounds of gold given to them from the Palestinian tax income, and gave them, besides, as many pieces of gold from his private chest as both his hands could hold: it was about fifty. Three days later they left."[8]

So both the Bishops could be well satisfied with the success of their journey. Of course they had had immense luck. The birth of the heir to the throne, and the grateful joy of the imperial pair, played a decisive role in the whole affair, as is noted in the Vita. It might have happened the same way, or similarly, to many Bishops who came to the capital seeking help. One easily understands that this sort of success must lure other more or less needy provincial Bishops in greater numbers to the capital city, so that the influence of the Bishops of the capital, as well as of those of the court, in ecclesiastical affairs, would increase greatly. If the new Bishop of Constantinople were *persona grata* with the Court, then without him there would be no audiences, and—no money.

Ten days after the return of Porphyrius, Cynegius entered with troops into Gaza. In the succeeding days, all the pagan temples of Gaza were destroyed.[9] In the place of the greatest, the Marneion, Porphyrius had the new memorial church built, a very basilica, according to the plans which the Empress had sent him. In the following year, she made a gift of thirty costly pillars of marble from the island of Euboea.

She did not live to see the completion of the church.

Porphyrius called the church Eudoxiana, and solemnly consecrated it on Easter day in 406.[10] It was considered the greatest and most beautiful church in the country, and strangers came from far away to see it.

Thus far the tale of the Vita Porphyrii. In the course of the seventh century (after 639), the church became a victim to Islam.

FOOTNOTES

1. See St. Schwietz, Das morgenländ. Mönchtum 2, 103, 115 and 123; H. J. Kämmel, Der Untergang des Heidentums in Pal-ästina und Phoenicien = Zeitschrift f. hist. Theol. 13 (1843) 24 ff.
2. Marcus Diac., Vita Porph. 21-24 = ed. Bonn p. 20 ff.; cf.

Phokilides, Porphyrius Gaz.=Nea Sion 13 (1913) 79 ff. and Zeit-schrift des deutschen Palästinavereins 183. A new Greek-French edition has been published by H. Grégoire and M. A. Kugener: Marc le Diacre, Vie de Porphyre évêque de Gaza. Paris 1929 (=Collection Byzantine).

3. Sozomen 5, 9 (67, 1237 f.).
4. Vita Porphyrii 26 (p. 24-25).
5. *Loc. cit.* cp. 27.
6. Vita Porphyrii cp. 29 ff. (ed. Bonn p. 33-38).
7. Theodosius II. was born on the 10th of April, 401. More concerning this in the Appendix.
8. Marcus Diac. 47 (p. 41 f.).
9. The Englishman G. F. Hill, The Life of Porphyry, Bishop of Gaza, Oxford 1913, says of this at the conclusion of his intro-duction: "It would be absurd to judge the Bishop according to the modern point of view, as the German historian does, who complains of this violence in the persecution of the pagans." (Hist. Jahrbuch. 34 [1913] 409).
10. Marcus, Vita cp. 92 (ed. Bonn p. 73).

A CHRONOLOGICAL LABYRINTH

RÉSUMÉ OF CHAPTERS XIII TO XVI

UNTIL this hour, the Vita Porphyrii has enjoyed universal confidence. The plain, simple style of its narrative, the natural and warmly lifelike picturing of events and persons, had raised it favorably above the often artificial, unnatural and false style of most of the Greek-Byzantine lives of the saints, so that, in spite of a few demon-strable historical errors, a doubt of its authenticity could not be maintained in the long run. And yet this Vita has brought such confusion into the life of St. Chrysostom that those who know him have tried in vain for three hundred years to find a way out of the chronological labyrinth.

First of all, the Vita Porphyrii contradicts the statements of Palladius. According to " Marcus," Theodosius II was born in the winter of 400. But the oldest and most trustworthy sources are unanimous in giving the birth date as the 10th of April, 401. So Socrates 6, 6 (67, 681 B): Τῇ δεκάτῃ τοῦ Ἀπριλλίου μηνὸς. Socrates lived and wrote under Theodosius II, and every year he helped celebrate his birthday in Constantinople. So he knew the date very well. The same is true of Sozomen 8, 4 (67, 1528 A). But he gives only the year: " in the consulate of Fravitta and Vincentius," that is, in 401. Marcellinus Comes mentions only the 14th indiction, that is, 401 : "Theodosius junior natus est IV. Idus Aprilis." (= Mon. Germ. Auct. ant. XI. Chron., min. II (1894) 67). The *Fasti Vindobonenses priores* (from the sixth century) give (probably through omission of the IV) the Ides of April, in the consulate of Vincentius and Fravitta, that is, 401 (= Mon. Germ. Auct. ant. IX, 299). The Chronicon Paschale (92, 789), from the seventh century, names the 4th of the Ides of April, 401.

George Cedrenus, Compendium histor. ad. ann. 397 (121, 624 D) gives the 6th year of the reign of Arcadius, that is, 401.

So if Hydatius Lemicus, Continuatio Chronicorum Hieronymianorum (fifth century) notes the birthday of Theodosius in Olympiad 295, n. VIII, that is, 403, that is not important in view of the other sources (Mon. Germ. *loc. cit.* XI, 16), and neither is the evidence of Theophanes important, who in his Chronography (ed. Boor 1, 76; MG 108, 213) gives the seventh year of Arcadius' reign—that is, 402.

This date, the 10th of April, has also been confirmed by an inscription from Attalia in Pamphylia, which gave to the young Theodosius the title of ἐπιφανέστατος, which would only fit the time before Theodosius became Augustus, which happened on the 10th of January, 402. (S. H. Grégoire and M. A. Kugener, Quand est né l'Empereur Theodose II? Byzantion 4 [1927/28] 341-42). So, on the ground of the sources, the 10th of April, 401, must be recognized as the absolutely certain date of the birth. By this, the authority of the Vitae Porphyrii suffers considerable damage. If Marcus, the companion of Porphyrius, actually bears the only responsibility for the Vita, it is hard to understand how his memory could have suffered such a lapse, since he also must have helped to celebrate the birthday for many years on the 10th of April.

A second mistake in the Life to which Tillemont has already called attention lies in the fact that he names, as Bishop of Jerusalem at the time of Porphyrius' ordination, a man who was actually made Bishop 25 years later. No one knows of any Archbishop John of Caesarea at this time.

Furthermore, " Marcus " has St. Chrysostom staying in Constantinople just before the birth of Theodosius II, and granting a whole series of interviews to visiting Bishops, who did not even take up residence in the episcopal palace, and at a time when Chrysostom had fallen into complete disfavor with the Empress. The latter certainly happened after Easter of 401, and in the time from January to Easter, Chrysostom had been staying in " Asia," from which he did not return to Constantinople until Easter was long past.

This also decides the second question, as to who baptized the little Theodosius. Surprisingly, it is the Greek sources that are silent on this question. Marcus, as well as Socrates, Sozomen, Theodoret, Marcellinus Comes, and the Chronicon Paschale, all pass over it in silence. In the ninth century the otherwise rather unreliable Theophanes, in his Chronography[1] ascribes the baptism to Chrysostom. Probably Cosmas Vestitor[2] and George Cedrenus[3] took it from him.

Remarkably, an expressly contrary tradition of the Latins stands behind the silence and the belated statements of the Greeks. They had Theodosius baptized by Severian of Gabala. Gennadius of Marseille, in his Catalog of Authors,[4] says: " Severian died in the reign of the younger Theodosius, *his godson.*" Ado of Vienne, in his Chronicle, rightly explained this statement thus: " Severian held the young Theodosius at his baptism."[5] The word " godparents " meant nothing at that time. So both the authors wished obviously to say that Severian had baptized Theodosius II.

Actually, Tillemont[6] also shows a slight inclination to name Severian as the baptizer. Nuth[7] says the same, without reflection.

Because of Palladius, one can consider the Latins right. His silence can probably be taken to mean that it was not Chrysostom who baptized Theodosius. In the same way, the author of the Vita errs, when he says that Theodosius was

made Augustus immediately after his birth. This did not
take place until the 10th of January, 402.

Also striking is the almost word-for-word conformity in the
utterance of Chrysostom in the year 398 and that of Amantius
from the year 401 (Ch. 26): ἐλπίζω γάρ εἰς τὸν δεσπότην χριστὸν
ὅτι συνήθως ἔχει τὸ ἔλεος αὐτοῦ ποιῆσαι; Ch. 38: ἐλπίζω εἰς τὸν τῶν
ὅλων θεὸν ὅτι συνήθως ποιεῖ τὸ ἔλεος αὐτοῦ. So the speeches are composed by the author of the Vita.

Every imaginable effort has been made in past times to
bring the opposing statements of the Vita Porphyrii and of
Palladius into somewhat better harmony. For it could not be
possible that Marcus and Palladius had been eyewitnesses of
these happenings and yet had seen and stated such contrary
things. One cannot shake the authority of Palladius, and
one does not wish to shake that of Marcus.

As this book was being written, the news came from Brussels
that the "uncanny sagacity" of the learned Bollandist, P.
Peeters, S.J., brought Professor H. Grégoire indirectly on to
the right track. Professor Grégoire, in collaboration with A.
Kugener, prepared a critical new edition of the Vita Porphyrii.[8] Peeters drew his attention to a chapter of the
Historia Religiosa of Theodoret concerning Jacob of Nisibis.
Thereby Grégoire made the unexpected discovery that the
introduction to the Vita Porphyrii corresponded word for
word with the introduction to Theodoret's Historia Religiosa.
But who was the plagiarist?[9]

According to the usual dating of both authors, Theodoret's
would be the borrowed portion; and, of course, that would
be nothing new for him. In all Theodoret's writings, he is
more receptive than productive. However, an exact philological comparison of both texts brought Grégoire to the
opposite conclusion, namely, that the Vita Porphyrii is the
borrowed portion.[10] Thereupon supporting conclusions at
once present themselves for the historical reliability of the
"Marcus Diaconus." Above all, he cannot be the author of
the Vita Porphyrii in its present form. For Theodoret did
not write his Historia Religiosa before the year 444. Further,
Professor Grégoire believes that the Vita Porphyrii originated
in the seventh century.[11]

It is a satisfying thing to realize that in his first joy of discovery, Grégoire did not go so far as to throw out the baby with the bath water. He did not deny to the Vita all historical value. On the contrary, he agreed, for his part, that the form of the Vita under consideration was an actual travel record, the daily diary of Marcus Diaconus, who accompanied his bishop to Constantinople. Only the later editor, according to the taste of his time, had revised the travel record, through a miscellany of trimmings and additions, into a possibly more interesting, but not more reliable, life of a saint. Naturally it is thereby, in this particular case, difficult if not impossible to ascertain the exact boundary between truth and poetry, between the historical kernel and the legends which have gathered about it.

One can well assume that Bishop Porphyrius and his deacon, Marcus, actually made the trip to Constantinople, and indeed at the very time when Chrysostom was already in disfavor, that is, after Easter of 401, but probably soon after this terminal date, when all Constantinople was talking of the baptism of the heir to the throne, and Eudoxia was feeling the great joy over her good fortune as a mother, so that out of gratitude she had the votive church built in Gaza, a church large enough to accommodate the congregation; this had previously been impossible because of the poverty of the people and also, perhaps, because of the opposition of the pagan city councilors.

Of the year-and-a-half, or perhaps only a half-year, duration of the stay of the bishop and the deacon in Constantinople, nothing can be said. The succession of special audiences with the Emperor and Empress may well have taken place according to the diary of Marcus. According to this the stay in Constantinople may be chronicled as follows:

First day: Arrival in Constantinople.
Second day: Audience with Chrysostom.
Third day: Audience with Chrysostom, in the presence of Amantius.
Fourth day: First audience with Eudoxia.
Fifth day: Second audience with Eudoxia.
"A few days later": Birth of Theodosius.
"A week later": Third audience with Eudoxia.
"In a few days": Baptism of the child.

"A few days after": Fourth audience with Eudoxia.

"A few days after that": Fifth audience with Eudoxia. The imperial rescript.

"After winter was over and Easter had been celebrated": Farewell audience with Eudoxia and the Emperor.

Three days afterward: Departure.

All this clearly shows that the travelers were anxious to get home with the imperial decision. The total duration of the stay in Constantinople might have been about three weeks.

But Marcus cannot, in any case, pass as an absolute authority against Palladius, and to Professor Grégoire belongs the credit for having revealed the saving clue out of the chronological labyrinth.

Henceforth, there can be no doubt whether Chrysostom's journey took place in the year 401. The solution of this particular difficulty, which formerly caused doubt about this date, has simplified the chronology of Chrysostom's life very significantly. For the biographers of Chrysostom this is the great benefit arising from the new and corrected dating of the time of origin of the Vita Porphyrii. In view of all of this, the critic will scarcely find reason not to agree with Grégoire's conclusions, at least on the principal points. Thus are Hermant[12] and Nuth,[13] who placed the Ephesus journey in 402, corrected, as is Stilting also, who gave the date as 400. Tillemont's placing of Porphyrius' entry into Constantinople in January, 401,[14] is also seen to be incorrect.

While from the viewpoint of the history of civilization, one may consider it a pity that such a vivid and engaging Vita henceforth loses in authority and reliability; on the other hand, the chronology of Chrysostom's life gains in clarity and certainty. But above any consideration of this kind stands the categorical imperative of historical truth.[15]

FOOTNOTES

1. 108, 213 B; ed. Boor I, 76, 1.

2. Encomium 4, in Translationem S. Johannis Chrysostomi ed. K. I. Dyobouniotes = Epeteris 2 (1925) 72. Cf. MG 65, 829 Anm. 28.

3. Compendium hist. ad 397 (121, 624).
4. De Viris illustribus cp. 21 (ed. Bernoulli 70).
5. ML 123, 100b.
6. Mémoires 11, 164.
7. *Loc cit.* 16-17.
8. Cf. p. 178-179, Note 2.
9. Prof. Grégoire was kind enough to send me the proofs of his article: La Vie de Porphyre, évêque de Gaza, est-elle authentique? which appeared in the Revue de l'Université de Bruxelles 1929, p. 429-441. However, where Marcus is quoted as first authority, he must be taken with adequate reservations. Almost at the same time Prof. J. Zellinger (Munich) made the same discovery in regard to his new edition of the Vita Melaniae, but without verifying it more closely; this was however not important for his special purpose.
10. The deciding argument seems to me in any case to be the entirely senseless contradiction in " Marcus,": " Poets and writers of tragedies exert themselves strenuously to make people laugh," while in Theodoret the corresponding position is absolutely according to sense.
11. On the ground, of course, only of one single expression: λησμονεῖν = forget, which is first demonstrable in the seventh century.
12. La Vie de St. Jean Chrysostome 299.
13. De Marci Diaconi Vita Quaest. hist. 13-16.
14. A. SS. Sept. IV§ XLVII n. 725 ff.
15. Mémoires 11, 164 ff.

CHAPTER XVII

MORE ENEMIES IN THE BACKGROUND

CONCERNING the discord or the quiet opposition which had begun between the Empress and the Archbishop, no one rejoiced so openly as did Bishop Severian of Gabala. He sniffed the morning air. Since he was a welcome guest with the Empress and with various court ladies, Eudoxia had hardly kept their dissension secret from him, and Severian certainly did his best to promote this dissension as much as he could. In spite of an outward reconciliation, he had not forgiven Chrysostom for the fact that his first attempt to discredit the latter had turned out so badly. He also knew very well that henceforth he could stay in Constantinople only through the favor of the Empress and the court, and that a reconciliation between Eudoxia and Chrysostom would mean the end of his success in the capital. This knowledge obviously dictated his further conduct, and made him, hitherto a trusted friend, to a certain extent an ally of the Empress.

Soon Severian was joined by his personal friend and countryman, Bishop Antiochus of Ptolemais. This Antiochus, in and for himself, seems to have been no very significant person. But he had a certain facility in speaking, which had brought him from his flatterers the honorable epithet of "Chrysostom," the golden-mouthed,[1] a distinction which, however, the world took away from him later. But he showed a remarkable talent for fabricating intrigue and conspiracy. In this critical time, he stood with Severian, always in the forefront of the agitation against the Archbishop. But, according to Palladius, not only the influence of Severian, but also a certain spirit of jealous rivalry against Chrysostom had prejudiced him.[2]

It affects one painfully to learn that a man who, until then and later, had been considered a strict and almost holy ascetic, and a man zealous for the things of God, should have associated himself as a third companion with these two Bishops. This man was Bishop Acacius of Beroea, in Syria.[3] He had earlier lived as a monk or hermit in the vicinity of Antioch, under Asterius, who later was Bishop of Amasea. He gained distinguished merit for himself by preserving the Catholic faith during the constant and uninterrupted battle against the Arians, Apollinarists, and Macedonians. For this, Patriarch Meletius made him Bishop of Beroea in 378 or 379. It was he who, together with Diodorus, participated in the episcopal consecration of Flavian, the successor of Meletius; on account of which Rome would have no fellowship with him or Diodorus for almost ten years.[4] In 381 he ratified the Acts of the Council of Constantinople.[5] When Chrysostom was consecrated Bishop of Constantinople, Acacius was among the guests at the celebration. The new Patriarch gave him his full confidence. He even entrusted him with the business of bringing the news of his elevation to Rome, together with his act of submission, in order to re-unite the broken threads between Antioch and Rome or Alexandria.[6]

Theodoret says of Acacius that he was famous over land and sea, and as a bishop " had sent out brilliant rays of virtue."[7] That is not to be disputed. But at any rate, he had at least once in his life gotten a very dark stain on his virtue. The occasion for this was a very trifling and insignificant circumstance. About the year 402, Acacius must have been in Constantinople again. According to the usual custom, he was the guest of the Archbishop there. It was an unfortunate circumstance that the best room was not available; it was already occupied by some other episcopal guests. Only a small room was left free to assign to Acacius. In this the Bishop saw an intentional insult, and contempt for himself personally. He fell into such wrath that he began to abuse Chrysostom loudly, and in the presence of several clergy of the episcopal palace, he uttered this threat: " I will burn his soup for him! "[8]

Unfortunately that was no empty threat. Acacius kept, from that hour, a hatred and longing for revenge against Chrysostom, which apparently made him perfectly blind to the difference between right and wrong. Thenceforth he persecuted his victim with that sullen obstinacy and tenacious persistence which one finds only in pathological natures.

G

Perhaps one may find an extenuating circumstance in his
great age; he was more than eighty years old.[9]

The Empress and the three Bishops soon received assistance
from some of the court ladies, who were not only glad to say
what pleased Eudoxia, but who had their own reasons for
being dissatisfied with Chrysostom, the unwearied preacher
of morals. A frequent theme of the Archbishop's sermons, in
Constantinople, was women's fashions, feminine luxury and
vanity, especially if they displayed such in church, and still
more if they were older women or widows. The search for
pleasure, the frivolous lack of character, and the superficial
religion of the great city, had been bitterly bewailed twenty
years before by St. Gregory of Nazianzus. He had tried
earnestly to improve the situation, but had only made enemies
for himself. This was one of the reasons why he had resigned
from the Bishopric of Constantinople.[10] His farewell sermon,
which he gave before the Bishops of the Council and before
all the people, sounded in part like an echo of the sermons of
Chrysostom. Both had the same object, both were frustrated
because of the same problem. Even Theodosius the Great
had, in 384, attempted, through a special law, to check the
extravagant luxury and display of the rich and of high officials
—but in vain. The ineradicable human vanity found ever
more means and ways to parade its wealth before others. Men
could not oppose this impulse; women even less. The court
ladies in the company of the Empress set a bad example.
They exposed to the public the proofs of their vanity in the
form of silk and golden garments, paraded in society as well
as in church at divine service. This displeased Chrysostom.
He obviously took seriously the words of St. Paul, who admonished women that "they should not wish to shine with
plaited hair, or gold, or pearls, or costly attire, but should
behave decorously."[10a] In public, and in private conversation,
he could say: "Why do you wish, at your age, to force your
body to appear still young? Why do you put powder and
rouge on your faces like whores, and thereby bring respectable
women into contempt? Why do you wish to deceive in this
way those who associate with you, when you are already
widows?"[11]

One may well believe that this sort of blunt pastoral sermon of their zealous Bishop did not sound pleasant in the ears of the older and more coquettish court ladies. There was, for example, a certain Castricia,[12] the wife of Saturninus, whom Chrysostom had rescued out of the hands of Gainas. Instead of being grateful to the Archbishop, she showed herself an enemy and an opponent. But the enmity of Marsa was much worse and more serious. To conclude from the name, she was a Goth, and so was related to the Empress by race. Hence it happened that she or her husband, the deceased general Promotus, had given over one of their estates to Gothic monks as a residence.[13] She possessed the most influence with Eudoxia, for the Empress was to a certain extent her foster-child, since she had been taken into the family of Promotus after the death of her father, the general Bauto.

But the most furious of all was the hysterical Eugraphia, a widow by her own testimony.

She appears to have endured her widowhood very unwillingly. At least Palladius writes that, whatever might be said of her character otherwise, he wished for shame to pass over in silence.[14] Perhaps Chrysostom had spoken the above-mentioned widows' sermon against her. At any rate, Palladius says that she eventually became very furious against the Archbishop.[15] And also it was in her house that the Patriarch Theophilus led the first discussions which brought about the overthrow of the Archbishop.[16]

Other and less important opponents belonged to this choir of Furies. Palladius does not distinguish them by name. Instead, he exhibits the testimony of the three ringleaders, whose principal business had been to stir up trouble and dissension.[17] That they had surely done.

It is not difficult to imagine how fatal for Chrysostom must have been such an association, in the closest proximity to the easily influenced and already irritated Empress. They took advantage thenceforth of every opportunity and every appearance, to provoke and incite Eudoxia against the Archbishop. We will meet them several times in the future.

Thus a circle of discontent had gradually built itself up, which for various reasons felt itself hostile to Chrysostom, and showed it. It could not long remain concealed from the capital city, whose attention was always directed toward the court, that a strong wave of coolness was drifting over from the court to the episcopal palace. Of course it was still a long way between mere estrangement and dissatisfaction to a state of open warfare. However, the change of opinion and feeling began to animate criticism in higher and higher places, and also down the social ladder, especially among the clergy. The example from above acted as an incitation and stimulation. Palladius calls attention to two priests and five deacons who distinguished themselves in this connection.

Even of Isaac, the father of monks, it was heard that he made all sorts of remarks about the Archbishop among his friends and acquaintances, which remarks could not be taken in a benevolent sense, and which certainly did not remain without effect on the ascetic vocation of their author.[18]

First secretly, then ever more openly, among the bishops and the court, the dissatisfied element among the clergy came to the front, and even the monks began to imitate the example of their father Isaac. They began to find fault with Chrysostom as a fierce, proud, uncouth and hard-hearted tyrant.[19] They said the reason he always ate alone was that he wished to have Cyclopean banquets for himself.[20] The arrogance and malice of his sermons were unheard of. He had insulted Eutropius in the very presence of death; he had ridiculed Gainas in the presence of the Emperor. He would stop for no one; he had censured several of the highest officials and dignitaries.[21] Those who disseminated such criticism and calumnies were clergy who had either been removed from office for failure in their duty, or else were dissatisfied with the reforms of their chief shepherd. Now they found themselves all brothers together, and their malicious talk created much mischief among the people.[22]

However, all this dissatisfaction was not especially dangerous. But it hatched out much more in secret. The Empress Eudoxia, first of all, thought nothing of showing her displeasure with Chrysostom openly, and still less of attempting anything against him. The others were powerless without her. First of all, they were not united, and then, what was more important, they lacked a clear and positive purpose, and finally, and before all, a determined leader, who knew what he wanted, and did boldly what he could.

Just at this point the Patriarch Theophilus entered the course of events under circumstances which foreboded everything but what actually happened. The proud Patriarch of Egypt was invited to Constantinople just at this time, by imperial command, in order to justify himself before a clerical court, in which, by the wish of the Emperor, Chrysostom was to be the president. And so it came to pass.

FOOTNOTES

1. Sozomen 8, 10 (67, 1541).
2. Dialog 6 (47, 21).
3. This lies halfway between Antioch and the Euphrates. For a picture of ancient Beroea, see Fr. Cumont, Études Syriennes 13. The rank of the Bishop of Beroea was directly after that of the Patriarch of Alexandria.
4. Sozomen 7, 11 (1411); cf. Cavallera, Le Schisme d'Antioche 261.
5. C. H. Turner = Journal of Theol. Studies 15 (1914) 168.
6. Concerning Acacius' later position in the Nestorian quarrel, see G. Bardy, Acace de Berée et son rôle dans la controverse nestorienne, in: Revue des Sc. rel. 18 (1938) 20-44.
7. HE 5, 23 (82, 1249; ed. Parmentier p. 323) and Hist. Rel. 2 (82, 1313).
8. Palladius, Dial. 6 (21) and 8 (29).
9. Acacius lived thirty-six years more after that, and did not die until 432, when he was 116.
10. Gregor Naz. Or. 42, 22-26 (36, 484-492).
10a. 1 Tim. 2, 9.
11. Palladius 8 (27).
12. Palladius 4 (16).
13. *Ibid.* and Chrysostom, Letter 207 (52, 726).
14. Dial. 4 (16). That could be applied to all three.
15. *Ibid.*
16. Dial 8 (27).
17. Dial 4 (16); he called them ταραξάνδριαι καὶ ἀνασείστριαι.
18. Palladius 6 (21).
19. Sozomen 8, 9 (1541).
20. Accusation 25 at the Synod of the Oak. Cf. Ch. 22.
21. Socrates 6, 5 (673).
22. Socrates 6, 4 and 5 (669 ff.).

CHAPTER XVIII

QUARREL OF THEOPHILUS WITH THE "TALL BROTHERS."[1]
(QUARREL WITH THE ORIGENISTS)

ONE day in the year 402,[1a] Chrysostom saw a very unusual spectacle. A band of about fifty men went through the streets of the city. They aroused unusual interest by their clothing and their whole appearance. It was obvious by their dress that they were monks, and by their tired steps that they had a long journey behind them. Actually, they came from Egypt, through Palestine and Syria. Some of them were quite old. They had lean ascetic figures. Sternness and haggard care were written on the faces of all of them. At their head marched four monks of unusual height and striking features. They were called in their homeland the "four tall brothers."

This foreign band asked for the palace of the Archbishop, for they wished to speak to him and to lay before him the purpose of their journey. When they were admitted, they threw themselves on their knees before the Bishop and begged for justice and protection against Theophilus, the powerful Patriarch of Alexandria. Theophilus, they said, had mistreated them and persecuted them, although they themselves had not offended against the law of Christ or against the Patriarch.[2]

The alleged cause, they continued, was this: Isidore the priest, who was in charge of the provision for the poor at Alexandria, and who was almost eighty years old,[3] formerly a monk in the Nitrian desert, the same whom Theophilus four years before had wished to make Bishop of Constantinople, and to whom the Patriarch, according to his own statement, had always been bound by the bond of intimate friendship,[4] saw himself suddenly abandoned to the anger and displeasure of the Patriarch, for the following reason. A rich woman had given Isidore one day the unusually great sum of a thousand gold pieces, with the stipulation that it was to be used to buy clothing for the poor women of Alexandria. She added that she did not wish the Patriarch Theophilus to know of it under any circumstances, for he was very insistent on simply taking money and using it for his building. Theophilus, so Palladius says,[5] was possessed with such a Pharaonic passion for building that he even erected buildings which the Church did not need. This is confirmed by a fragment of a letter written to St. Isidore of Pelusium, in which the Patriarch is called a "money worshiper, crazy about stone."[6]

So Isidore took the money, and used it according to the wish of the donor, for widows and the poor. But Theophilus somehow found out about the affair; like all tyrants, he had his spies and tattlers everywhere. As soon as possible, he sent for Isidore. With forced calmness, he asked him if it was true that he had received money. The old man answered truly, Yes. Then Theophilus could no more control his wrath; his features were distorted, and the violent storm of the patriarchal anger broke over the unfortunate Isidore.[7]

For two months nothing happened. Then the patriarch summoned a conference of the clergy, which Isidore attended. Before the whole assembly, Theophilus—one can hardly believe it possible—produced a document in which the seventy-two-year-old priest and almoner was accused of a sodomitical sin against chastity, which he was supposed to have committed with a young sailor. "This writ of accusation, Isidore, I have already kept for eighteen years against you.[8] Because I was very busy at that time, I forgot the affair. Now I found the writ again when I was searching for some other papers. So it is now up to you to defend yourself against this accusation."

But he who had received such a shock in full assembly did not lose his calm and presence of mind. "Assuming that it is true that you held a writ of accusation against me, and forgot the affair, was not the accuser there, who could present his accusation again?"

Theophilus answered, "No, he could not; he had gone to sea." "Well," said Isidore, "if he was not there at that time, as you say, could he not have presented his accusation after the sea journey, and also in the second or the third year after it?   But at least if he is there now, order him to come here." With that, Theophilus was cornered. He postponed the affair until the next session.   Meanwhile, so Palladius says, he had a young man brought in, who consented, through promises and bribes, to make a complaint against Isidore; that is, to admit that it was with him that Isidore had sinned. The fifteen pieces of gold, which the young man received as a reward, he brought to his mother.   But she, partly through remorse, and partly through worry, for fear the affair would have a bad ending, revealed the whole design to Isidore. She also showed him the fifteen pieces of gold, which her son had received from the Patriarch's sister.

Thereupon Isidore secluded himself in his house, and sought help in prayer.   However, the young man fell into such anguish, partly because of the success of his false accusation, and partly because of Theophilus, whose revenge he felt still more, that he fled into the church in downright despair, and sought protection at the altar there. What happened to him further is not known.   The violent patriarch excluded the old priest and almoner from the fellowship of the Church, because he had fallen into such a sin, and because he had not wished to appear, in spite of all the summons from the court of the Bishops.[9]

Isidore now began to fear for his life, because of the wrath of Theophilus, and his attempts at persecution; for in case of need, said the monks, Theophilus would shrink from nothing.[10]   So he fled from there to the monks in the Nitrian mountains, where he had spent the years of his youth.   There he dedicated himself, in a solitary cell, to prayer, and to meditation on the value of human favor and man's fate. But the Patriarch had scarcely learned of his whereabouts when his wrath directed itself against the monks who had offered him hospitality.

Without delay, he wrote to the neighboring bishops in the Nitrian desert, and demanded of them, without giving any reason, that they should expel Isidore and his friends out of the Nitrian mountains, into the inner desert.   In this way the monks themselves would not be able to associate with him. They decided to go directly to the Patriarch, and ask him what induced him to proceed against them in this way.

When the Patriarch got sight of them, and the monks brought up the affair, he fell into boundless wrath. Those present afterward said that "he looked at them with blood-red eyes, like a dragon." But that was not all. Theophilus seized the aged Ammonius, who evidently was the speaker for the group, by the collar of his garment, struck him in the face, so that the blood flowed from his nose, and screamed at him: "You heretic, speak first the anathema on Origen! "

The monks were very much surprised at this, as well as at the undignified conduct of their Patriarch. For there had been no talk of Origen until then. They had believed hitherto that the only reason for the Patriarch's wrath was Isidore and the hospitality which they had accorded him. That they had now dared to demand a reckoning, as it were, from him had obviously irritated him still more. They were soon to learn the truth of that.

So while the dismissed monks returned to their cells in the desert, to take up their accustomed life again, chiefly occupied by the study of Holy Scripture, the furious Patriarch sat down and wrote to the nearest Egyptian bishop, asking to have the monks brought before a synod with all speed. Here he had the three most distinguished among them excommunicated, under the excuse that they were heretics, that is, Origenists; he did not have the monks summoned, or give them any opportunity to defend themselves. And the men to whom he had previously given more honor than to bishops, whom he had esteemed on account of their lives, their speech and their age, now he called them impostors and clowns, merely because they had had the courage to take the unjustly persecuted Isidore to themselves, and offer him protection.[11]

But still Theophilus, longing for revenge, was not satisfied with this. As a strong character, he wished to complete the work, and to return the monks' visit in his own way. He persuaded five monks from the Nitrian monasteries, who were not at all respected in their own place, and were not in the councils of the elders, to hand over a writ of accusation, which he had composed himself, and which they had only to sign. By way of reward for their acquiescence, to these people who had never been worthy of even the lowest offices in the Church, he made one a bishop of a little village, because there was no city vacant; and another he ordained priest, and the other three he made deacons. Yet, not a single one of them originated from Egypt. For one was born in Libya, another came from Alexandria, a third from Pharos and another from Paraleos.

With this writ of accusation, which he himself had handed over to the Church, and another, which he had written in his own name, he went to the so-called Augustalis, the prefect of Egypt, and demanded that the three monks mentioned therein should be expelled from Egypt by military force. The prefect agreed only unwillingly to the wish of the Patriarch. He dared not refuse him in consideration of his great influence in Constantinople. So, to give him something at least, he gave him a few soldiers.[12] But Theophilus found this military escort too weak, and he mobilized a gang from the rabble, and people who were dependents of his. First he gave them plenty to drink, and then they sallied out, with the Patriarch at their head, and in the middle of the night they entered by force into the monks' cells.

First he had the old man Dioscurus, the Bishop of the Nitrian mountains, seized by his black Ethiopian slaves, who perhaps were not even baptized yet; he declared the old man deposed, and his bishopric taken away from him, although, as at least the monks said, it had been a bishopric since the time of Christ. Then they plundered the monks' cells, and Theophilus gave them whatever trifling useful objects had belonged to the monks. The thing of most concern to him was that he should get into his power the three chief monks against whom he was most enraged. But the other monks had hidden them quickly in a well, and concealed its entrance with rush mats. In revenge for his failure, the Patriarch had their cells set afire; all their valuable books were burned, and, as eyewitnesses asserted, unfortunately a boy was burned, as well as the Holy Sacrament.

After this heroic deed, more worthy of a robber chief than of a Patriarch, Theophilus and his gang went back to Alexandria.[13] He was probably satisfied with the thought that he had given his supposed enemies a fitting punishment. This heroic deed of the Patriarch found its memorial, of course much exaggerated, in the ecclesiastical (Synaxarium) history of Constantinople. It is mentioned there on the 10th of July (No. 4): "On the same day, the memorial of number-less (μυρίων) holy fathers, who lived in caves and huts in the Nitrian desert, and whom Theophilus, Archbishop of Alex-andria, delivered up by revenge and fire, to a bitter death."[14]

The monks, on the other hand, were now of the under-standable opinion that under these circumstances they could no longer remain there. They decided to abandon the land of the new Pharaoh; they put on their mantles[15] and took to the road, to travel to neighboring Palestine, and find a new home in Jerusalem. They did not go alone. A great number of brethren decided to join their chiefs and spiritual leaders, so the collected priests and deacons of Bishop Dioscurus joined him, with not less than three hundred of the best and most respected monks: the entire "intelligence section" of the Nitrian monks' colony. It was a very eminent caravan.[15a]

The oldest and most distinguished among all these was Hierax, an old man of almost ninety years, who had known and heard St. Antony, the father of monks.[16] There was also Ammonius, who was already sixty years old.[17] Besides, Ammonius had two sisters, who lived as cloistered women, and two brothers, who were monks, and another, named Dioscurus, who had become a bishop.[17a] They were usually called only the four Tall Brothers. Under the Arian Emperor Valens, they had been condemned to chains and exile, as pillars of the Catholic Orthodox belief. In the exact know-ledge of Holy Scripture, there were few to equal them.

A second Hierax had lived for four years in the Porphyry mountains, and twenty-five years in the Nitrian desert. Two other monks were both priests, and both were named Isaac. One had been a pupil of Macarius, who himself had also known St. Antony. He had joined the monks when he was seven years old; now he was fifty, had a hundred and fifty younger ones around him, and was famous as a man who knew the whole of Scripture by heart. The second Isaac also possessed a very extensive knowledge of Holy Scripture. He had learned the monastic life under Cronius, who had also been a pupil of the great Antony. As father of 310 monks, he showed himself specially concerned over the sick brothers, and had built a special hospice for them and for strangers. A great number of his monks had been promoted to bishoprics.[18]

So these were the men who, on account of the wrath of the
Patriarch, had to leave their cells and their solitude, and go
to a strange country to seek protection.

The principal group, with the four "tall brothers," went
toward Palestine.   There in Jerusalem they hoped to find
protection and help from Bishop John, who had been a monk
himself in the Nitrian desert before, and was known as an
admirer of the writings of Origen.

It is clear that this new "departure of Israel out of Egypt"
did not remain long concealed from Patriarch Theophilus.
The fact itself, but still more the news that the fleeing monks
had found a good reception in various places roused in the
irritable man a new excitement.   Soon he wrote a circular,
which still exists in the Latin translation of St. Jerome, to the
Bishops of Palestine and Cyprus, and wherever his Egyptian
monks were staying.[19]

"In the Nitrian monasteries," so Theophilus says, "as
delegated representatives of their true masters, some false
monks, who in their delirium are capable of any crime, had,
in the beginning, sowed the heretical seed of Origen.   We
had to interpose against it, at the request (?) of the head of
the monastery.   Therefore the writings of Origen were condemned by me, at a synod.   For these contained a multitude
of errors, as the accompanying sentences will prove.   Under
the pretext of appearing for Isidore, the excommunicated
priest, these monks came to Alexandria, to raise a riot and to
spread their heresy.   A woman brought in a complaint against
this Isidore; in order to silence her (!) he entered her in the
register of widows supported by the Church.   In spite of our
repeated summons, he has not appeared for a conference.
This man is the leader of the heretical party, which has been
condemned by us, and he has been expelled from the Church.
Now, joining arrogance with foolishness, they have left Egypt,
and are wandering about in strange provinces, and seeking to
spread lies against us and against the truth.

"Therefore, brethren, watch over the flock of the Lord,
which they wish to bring into disorder, and try to bring these
people to repentance.   We have indeed done nothing to disturb them.   The only reason why they hate us is that we are

ready to defend the faith until death.   On the other hand, they have sought our lives, have tried to hinder us from entering their churches, and have bribed a common rabble with money, to bring on a blood bath.   Only through the grace of God was a greater disaster averted.   We have borne all this in humble patience (Theophilus!), and thought only of the welfare of those who have fought us with hostile intentions, for we do not wish that the precepts of the Church should be violated.   Pray to God that we may withstand the heretics, and live in peace with the defenders of the truth! "

With this slanderous composition, Theophilus moved the question at issue into an entirely different sphere, and grasped a weapon against the monks which had always proved itself most dangerous and efficient.   At least with Pope Anastasius (398-402) it had not failed in its efficiency.   The Pope, obviously informed only by Theophilus concerning the events in Egypt, called the Patriarch a "vir sanctus et honorabilis," who watched unweariedly over the salvation of souls, that they might not fall into the errors of Origen.[20]

Theophilus, in his Holy Thursday sermon, on March 29, 400, railed at the monks in insulting tones.   He called them "Satan's deacons, unfruitful babblers and seducers of souls, who are dressed in sleeveless tunics, the sign of a solitary but not a world-renouncing life . . . who make an easy impression with their robes of skins . . . in our God-protected city they have roused an extraordinary uproar.   But those who soothe the ocean storms will also silence their godless clamor! "   Then he even accused them of "denying the resurrection of Christ with their impudent mouths. . . . Where are they now, these God-deniers, these hermit-wolves . . . these false Christians . . . these most absurd of all babblers, who even deny the presence of Christ in the Holy Sacrament? "[20a]

If Theophilus could furnish proof for his accusations, the monks were lost, without any doubt.   But what did Theophilus prove?   That Origen had taught, among other things, something which was not compatible with Catholic teaching on faith.   Thereby, nothing at all was said against the monks in question, as a matter of course.   Indeed, Theophilus had never made any attempt at all to prove that his opponents shared in the errors of Origen. The only thing that all the world knew, was that the monks of the Nitrian desert read enthusiastically the works of Origen, and were full of admiration for the genius of this man.[21]

But the same was the case with many others, not merely with Rufinus and Bishop John of Jerusalem, but also with St. Jerome. St. Basil the Great and St. Gregory of Nazianzus, out of admiration for Origen, had even published an anthology of his works, called "Beauties of Origen."[22] The holy Victorinus of Pettau, Hilary of Poitiers, Bishop Ambrose of Milan, were enthusiastic readers and beneficiaries of Origen. Indeed, in Alexandria itself, under the eyes of Theophilus, the famous leader of the school of catechumens, Didymus the Blind (died 398), had taught until a few years before, and he had been an enthusiastic admirer of Origen all his life long.[23]

But above all, the Patriarch Theophilus himself was known as an enthusiastic reader of the writings of Origen.[24] Indeed, a few years before, in 396, he had sent the same Isidore, whom he now persecuted for alleged Origenism, to Jerusalem, to reconcile Jerome with Bishop John and Rufinus, who had fallen into dissension about Origen. How did it happen now, that Theophilus just now discovered Isidore's heresy, although he had lived in close association with him for years, and although Theophilus had wished to make him bishop three years before, and how did it happen that he had discovered it only when the story of the thousand gold pieces had come out? And why had Theophilus first accused old Bishop Dioscurus and the Tall Brothers, whom he had known for ten years, of Origenism, when they took Isidore in and protected him against the Patriarch's wrath?

So, one cannot avoid the harsh verdict against Theophilus, that the man, who always needed money, had acted against his better knowledge and conscience, and used the "Origenism" only as a means to an end.

Already St. Isidore of Pelusium had said that Theophilus persecuted Isidore only out of greed for money, and so he had clashed with Chrysostom.[25] That the Origenism was only an excuse for Theophilus is also the opinion of F. Cavallera, who writes: "Antiorigenism appeared to Theophilus as a suitable means of striking his enemies. He used it with an energy and unscrupulousness which appears in all his dealings."[26] Eberhard says the same.[27]

Two further facts confirm the accusation against Theophilus; these will be specially noted in the course of the narrative.[28] According to Palladius, Theophilus sent another letter to the Bishops, the contents of which were approximately thus: "You have not taken these people into your cities according to my wishes. But since you have done this out of ignorance of the state of affairs, I will pardon it. But from now on, be careful about having ecclesiastical or personal relations with these men."[29]

In order to give his letter of warning more emphasis, Theophilus sent two messengers, Priscus and Eubulus, to Palestine, to trace the fugitives, and to see to it that they were banished. St. Jerome, who saw in Theophilus' statement only the Origenism in the monks, congratulated the Patriarch on his energetic actions.

The whole world, he said, rejoiced over his victory. He had delivered Egypt and Syria, and indeed Rome and almost all of Italy, from the danger of these errors, and had pursued the heretical basilisks, by his ambassadors, to the most secret recesses of Palestine.[30] At the same time he begged that Theophilus would not anger the Bishop of Jerusalem, because he had guaranteed the reception of one of the monks (probably Bishop Dioscurus); he had done it through ignorance, and, according to his opinion, would have neither the courage nor the purpose to offend the Patriarch in any way at all.[31]

Jerome knew the state of affairs very well. The bishops who were assembled in Jerusalem on the occasion of the celebration of the consecration of the church there (on the 14th of September, 401) declared that they had never heard that anyone among them taught things such as Origen had taught, according to the statements of Theophilus. But they condemned anyone who taught such things, and would not take any one into their churches who had been excommunicated by the Patriarch, until he himself had pardoned the penitents.[32]

This letter of the bishops was perfectly correct. It condemned the real errors of Origen, without saying that the

Egyptian monks were Origenists.   But the fact that they
granted no ecclesiastical fellowship to the excommunicated
monks was in accord with the definition of the canons.   On
the other hand, the fact that Theophilus wished also to deny
civil rights to the monks was an inhumanity which would
propel his victims either into a death by hunger or a despairing recourse to arms.

Actually, the fear of this heedless man of power was so great
that people henceforth endeavored to get the monks free
again as soon as possible.   While the simple brothers, who
had not been excommunicated by Theophilus, found an
easier situation and reception in Palestinian monasteries,
their chiefs, with those who wished to remain true to them
under all circumstances, went from place to place as fugitives,
without being able to find any fixed abode.   Above all, they
felt mistrust and fear of Theophilus.

So almost a year passed away thus.

FOOTNOTES

1. Concerning this quarrel we are informed by Palladius, Dial.
6 and 7.   His report undoubtedly goes back to the Egyptian
monks themselves, for they were in Constantinople at the same
time as Palladius was (402-403).   Palladius himself had previously
lived as a monk in Egypt, and hence was very probably personally
acquainted with some of the fugitives.   Only thus can his personal
accounts of these events be explained.   As concerns his own
credibility, there doubtless appears in his story, or in the monks',
a certain bitterness against Patriarch Theophilus; one may consider this a psychological proof of truth.   For if serious and cul-
tured men, priests and bishops, who had lived sixty, eighty or
ninety years in the desert, and, like Isidore and Dioscurus, had
served the Church and the Patriarch faithfully for eighty years,
and had held positions of the highest trust, if these now come
forth suddenly with such complaints against the highest church
authorities in Egypt, and this with such publicity that it comes
to an ecclesiastical as well as a secular process, then they must
have been very sure of their cause.   As the report of Palladius
proves, the question was not one of diversity of opinions or
"misunderstandings."   The complaints of the monks against
Theophilus are so concrete, and of such a serious nature, that

the question of blame can only be answered by yes or no, while the accusations of Theophilus against the monks are only of "Origenism," of which he did not bring up a single proof, as we will see. The facts and indications for the guilt of Theophilus, on the other hand, follow from the whole course of the Process with absolute certainty. Cf. Hist. Laus. 10 (ed. Butler 29, 15-17.)

1a. As to the time of their arrival in Constantinople, see Note 15.

2. Palladius 7 (24).

3. Cf. Hist. Laus. 1 (ed. Butler 2, 15-16).

4. Theophilus, Epistola Synodica 3 (ML 22, 765).

5. Dialog. 6 (22).

6. Isidor. Pel. epist. 1, 152 (78, 284-85). Of its genuineness, naturally nothing can be decided.

7. Socrates, who did not know the Dialog of Palladius, represents in HE 6, 9 the cause of the personal enmity between Theophilus and Isidore as something else. According to him, Peter, the Archpriest of Alexandria, was blamed by Theophilus for having allowed a Manichean woman to receive the Sacraments, without demanding of her beforehand that she renounce her errors. Peter on the other hand said that the woman had renounced her errors and that the Patriarch had been informed of the fact; and that Isidore the priest could prove it. Isidore actually confirmed this, and thereby the wrath of the Patriarch against Isidore and Peter was inflamed at the same time. These representations of Socrates are more improbable and incredible than those of Palladius. An echo of the above tale is found also in Socrates 6, 7, where he relates that the four Tall Brothers had been in the service of Theophilus, but had left him again on account of his avarice; this had roused the Patriarch to a desire for revenge upon them, and he had accused them of anthropomorphism!

Sozomen, 8, 12, mentions also the affair of the money for the poor, along with the story of Peter, and also adds a third motive: That Theophilus had demanded of Peter and Isidore that they should both testify that his sister had been named as heiress of someone. But both of them had refused. But certainly so much resulted from these three reports, that the quarrel became connected with a ribald story, in which Isidore did not wish to be an accomplice; and that the reproach of Origenism was a clean means for Theophilus' purpose. A similar judgment is given also by F. Prat, Origenism=Cath. Encycl. 11 (1911) 311; also Stilting n. 896 and Valesius, Note 31 on Socrates, HE lib. VI. (67, 687), and Eberhard 52.

8. Palladius, Dial. 6 (22). At that time Isidore must have been

sixty or sixty-two years old, which does not heighten the probability of the complaint, still less the fact that Theophilus still
entrusted Isidore with ecclesiastical offices, left him in office all the
time, and had even wished to make him Bishop only three years
before.   Theophilus could not date the complaint later than that,
because it was not yet eighteen years since he had been made
Patriarch (in the year 385).

9. Theophilus, Synodica n. 3 (ML 22, 765).

10. Palladius 6 (23).

11. This Synod of Alexandria took place in the year 400.
Theophilus sent to Pope Anastasius a report on the Synod, with
an abstract of the heretical statements of Origen.   Pope Anastasius
then at any rate condemned the theses of Origen in his letters to
Simplicius and Venerius.   Probably the Synod of Cyprus took
place also in this same year, under the presidency of St. Epiphanius, to whom Theophilus at any rate sent his synodal decrees,
probably challenging him also to hold a synod in order to condemn "Origenism."   Epiphanius did not need to be told such a
thing twice.   Cf. Cavallera, S. Jérôme 257 f. and 269 f.

12. The prefect of the year 401 was perhaps still Archelaus,
who at least had the office in 397.   See Cantarelli, La serie dei
Prefetti di Egitto=Atti della R. Acad. dei Lincei=Cl. mor. V. ser.
14 (1909) 397.

13. All this according to the report of Palladius, Dial. 7 (23 f.).
The credibility of this surprising story will not be lessened by
the fact that Theophilus earlier had even established monasteries
himself (cf. P. Ladeuze, Étude sur le cénobitisme pakhômien 202).
Such inconsistencies show themselves in choleric natures like that
of Theophilus.   His change of feelings in regard to Isidore were
just as radical.   The fact that the Holy Sacrament was burnt
might have had its cause in the fact that the hermit kept the
Holy Eucharist for daily needs in the hermitage, or that a public
chapel was burned at the same time.

14. Acta SS. Novemb. Propyl. 812.

15. Μηλωτάς = Monk's mantle = Pall. 7 (24).

15a. This "flight from Egypt" can only have occurred at the
end of 399 or the beginning of 400.   It is not certain how long
the monks remained in Palestine and Jerusalem.   But their
arrival in Constantinople can scarcely have taken place before
401.   *Jerome*, Liber III, 10 advers. scripta Rufini (ML 23, 470)
writes in the year 402: Quid tibi videtur de his, qui *damnati
palatia obsident* et facto cuneo fidem Christi in uno homine
(Theophilo) persequuntur."   K. Holl, Aufsätze II, 327, on the
other hand, says that the Tall Brothers fled to Constantinople

before September of 400. Ed. Schwartz, Palladiana, p. 174.

16. Palladius 17 (58 ff.); cf. Hist. Laus. 22 (ed. Butler 69).

17. *Ibid.* 11 (p. 32). S. Ammonius ep. Epist. 35 (ed. Halkin 120).

17a. Dioscurus, like his brothers, was a pupil of the Abbot Pambo, then a priest in the Nitrian mountains, and at last a bishop. (Palladius, Hist. Laus. 10 and 12. ed. Butler, p. 29, 16 and 35, 8.) Hierax and Dioscurus were, as priests, banished to Syene by an Arian Patriarch of Alexandria. (Cf. St. Athanasius, Hist. Arianorum no. 72 (25, 780 B.)

18. Palladius 17 (c. 59-60).

19. Epist. 92 (ML 22, 759-769).

20. Epist. ad Simplicianum 1 (ML 20, 74).

20a. 77, 1028-29. That the monks denied the Resurrection and the Real Presence, or even God Himself, is of course pure slander. M. Richard, Une homélie de Théophile d'Alexandrie sur l'institution de l'Eucharistie, in: RHE 33 (1937) 45 and 46.

21. Besides, the monks in the so-called Nitrian mountains, among whom culture and education were esteemed, showed themselves zealous readers and venerators of the writings of Origen and his allegorical explanation of the Scriptures. In opposition to them, the neighboring monks of the desert of Scete repudiated the exaggerated Scripture allegory of Origen, and fell for their part into a very extreme *realism*. They even explained every passage in Scripture in which the eyes, hands, anger, etc. of God are mentioned, in an individual and real sense. Therefore they were called by their opponents Anthropomorphists, that is, people who represented God in human form. These, in return, called their accusers Origenists, which name was given to those who were suspected of any kind of heresy. (Cf. Prat in the Cath. Encycl. 11, 310-11.) The story which Socrates 6, 7 tells of the monks of Scete is hardly credible. E. Drioton, in the Revue de l'Orient chrétien 20 (1915-17) 92-100 and 113-128, has published the alleged discussion between an anthropomorphic monk and the Patriarch Theophilus. Also Severian of Gabala engaged in polemics against the heresy of Anthropomorphism, which survives " until this day." (Oratio 5, 3 = 56, 474). Cf. Cassian. Collationes 10, 2 ff. (ML 49, 820 ff.).

22. Bardenhewer, GAL 3, 132.

23. *Ibid.* 106.

24. F. Prat S.J. in the Cath. Encycl. 11, 311 even says: " Until 400 Theophilus of Alexandria was a known Origenist. Suddenly he changed his doctrine. Why, is not exactly known."

25. Epist. 1, 152 (78, 284-85).

26. St. Jérôme 257. Likewise Puech, St. J. Chrys. et les moeurs 289.

27. Epiphanius' part in the quarrel over Origen, p. 56 f.

28. Shortly after the departure of the monks from Egypt, Sulpicius Severus came to Alexandria, and heard of the "shameful quarrel" (foeda certamina) between the Patriarch and the Nitrian monks. Theophilus had indeed received him in a very friendly manner, and wished to keep the educated man in Alexandria; only Sulpicius could not persuade himself to remain, in a place where bloody fraternal quarrels prevailed, where the bishop summoned the secular power against the monks, and so persecuted them by his decrees and letters that they could no longer remain there (Sulpicius Severus, Dialogus I, 6-7) (ML 20, 187-89).

29. Dial. 7 (24). Such a letter from Theophilus has not survived. But cf. the following letter of congratulation from St. Jerome.

30. Epist. 86 (ML 22, 754 f.). In the year 402, Jerome also gave a sermon against the "Origenists;" see G. Morin O.S.B., Revue d'Hist. Eccl. 2 (1901) 810-827; 3 (1902) 30-35. Ed. Schwartz, Acta Conc. 1, 5 p. 4 f., and Palladiana, *loc. cit.* 36 (1937) 171 f.

31. The above-mentioned letter of Theophilus (in Palladius) might be the answer to this letter of St. Jerome.

32. Epist. 93 (ML 22, 769).

CHAPTER XIX

PATRIARCH THEOPHILUS' SUMMONS
TO CONSTANTINOPLE

AFTER all their many wanderings, the monks no longer knew what to do. A single star of hope still shone upon them—they knew only one bishop in the East who might possibly help and protect them, and that was the Bishop of Constantinople, John Chrysostom. He was in fact the only one who, by the circumstances of his relations with the court, might be able to effect something against the all-powerful Patriarch of Alexandria. Thus it happened that one day the monks excommunicated by Theophilus, namely, Isidore, Dioscurus, Ammonius, Eusebius, Euthymius and Hierax, with their companions, appeared before John Chrysostom, and begged the Bishop of Constantinople to help and protect them against the Patriarch of Alexandria.[1]

Now the state of affairs began to be critical for Theophilus. There was nothing he need fear from the bishops of Palestine. But if the Bishop of Constantinople took up the cause of the monks, if he was able to influence the Emperor in their favor, the results for the proud Patriarch might be incalculable. That he had many faults on his account, and determined opponents among his own clergy, Eutropius had convinced him four years before. Now, under unfavorable circumstances, if the stone began to roll again, no one would be able to say whether Theophilus would be able to escape the threatening fate a second time.

Conceivably, the unexpected news of the coming of his opponents to Constantinople made him nervous. Now he had to collect his thoughts and do his best to meet the new situation, and begin the fight again from the beginning.

Chrysostom was doubtless placed in a very painful position by the arrival of the Egyptian monks. He knew only too well that a Patriarch of Alexandria would not be easy to take on, and an opponent like Theophilus would be twice as hard. Otherwise it would of course be convenient, though hard-hearted, simply to dismiss the aged men who stood there before him seeking help and justice, and to ignore their fate. Therefore he decided, partly through sympathy, partly through settled reflection, not to drive them to extremities; for it was rumored that they had decided that, if the worst came to the worst, they intended to bring their affairs and Theophilus' before the Emperor.

Next, the monks had not entered a formal complaint against Theophilus, but only begged for his intervention and some sort of help. Chrysostom could do this better and more easily than any other bishop of the Empire.

So then he begged them first of all—and that showed again his prevailing thought, which was directed to their souls' welfare—that they would reveal to no one the reason for their coming, lest the people might be scandalized at the clergy as a result of their stories.[2] Then he would himself write to Theophilus.

Then he allowed them to take shelter in a guest hospice of the Anastasia Church. From prudence, he did not wish to have them appear as his guests. Therefore he did not allow their support to come from the funds of the patriarchal church, but asked Olympias and other distinguished women to care for them. Some of the monks also went to work to earn their living.

In all his previous and later conduct, Chrysostom showed such a measure of prudence and tact, as to offer a brilliant proof of his character and his diplomatic qualifications. It happened that some clergy from Alexandria were there at that time, whom Theophilus had sent to Constantinople to take care of the choice of officials for Alexandria and Egypt, to see that those chosen would be pleasing to the Patriarch, or had sought his protection. Chrysostom had these clergy invited to his house, and inquired of them whether they knew these monks who had arrived. The Alexandrians answered with hearty sincerity that they knew them well, and that they had been grievously mistreated. However, he could not grant them ecclesiastical fellowship, for fear of irritating Theophilus.

But for the rest, he might show himself well disposed toward them, for his position as Bishop required that.

Chrysostom accepted this advice, which was right and benevolent from a human and legal standpoint. He did not admit them to any further ecclesiastical fellowship; but next, in a personal and friendly way, he made an effort to bring about a reconciliation between them and the Patriarch. He wrote a letter to Theophilus, in which, in a discreet and courteous way, he requested: Grant to me, your spiritual son[3] and brother, this favor, and take these men back again into your clemency.

The Egyptian Patriarch was not in the least prepared to do this, especially since the rumor was going about in Alexandria that Chrysostom had taken the excommunicated monks back into the fellowship of the Church.[4]

Theophilus sent thither at once some of his most diplomatic people, some clergy, and, in a calculating way, some monks also,[5] with the order to hand over to the Archbishop the writ of accusation against the Nitrian monks. He had written it himself, as always. Therein was stated, apparently, the chief accusation, that the monks were heretical, and that besides they harbored vicious dispositions. Palladius says, in a hinting way, that the writ of accusation contained a very obvious lie, which had been dexterously brought foward, in that the accusation covered only *invisible opinions*, because he had not been able to find any *visible* errors in their lives.[6] The effect of this accusation, and still more, the effect of the speeches, and of the agitation of the ambassadors of Theophilus, were such that mistrust began to show itself every where against the monks, and soon even some people at the court began to consider the monks impostors.

The chief argument of Theophilus and his people against the monks may have been that, until that time, they had not allowed themselves to be moved to condemn Origen wholesale. Concerning individual errors in Origen, the monks stated, as Rufinus had already done, that they had been forged in the works of Origen by his opponents. So then they were glad to oppose the condemnation of Origen, merely because it had suited the Patriarch Theophilus to use him as a weapon against them, contrary to his better knowledge.

Nevertheless, the monks were openly urged in Constantinople to remove every suspicion in this regard, through an open declaration, and to bring about complete clarity, in order to snatch the weapon out of the hands of their persecutor, and also to make it easier for the Archbishop John to arrange their reconciliation.

The monks also understood that this was necessary in the existing circumstances. Therefore they gave the Archbishop the formal declaration, to the effect that they spoke an anathema on every heresy.[7]

But now, since Theophilus had refused the friendly mediation of Chrysostom, and had sent him his formal writ of accusation against the monks, and since there was no prospect whatever of a change of course by Theophilus, nothing more remained for the monks but to take up the fight, and to bring it to a good end if possible. So they, on their part, handed over their writ of accusation against Theophilus, into the hands of Archbishop John. Therein they described the whole course of the affair, and all the acts of force of which they had been the victims. Some of the points of accusation, however, were of such an extraordinary nature that Palladius himself, who does not easily pardon Theophilus, abstains from mentioning them, for fear some weak souls might waver in the faith, and for fear that those who were strong in the faith might deny that he himself was a believer.

Palladius calls this document which the monks handed in, «λιβέλλους ἐντευκτικοὺς,» a " petition," in which all the accusations of the monks against Theophilus were listed. At any rate, the latter formed its principal contents, and the chief aim of the document, as also follows from the later writings of Chrysostom to Theophilus. But perhaps it was not intentionally drawn up in the form of an accusation, but of a petition, chiefly in order to make it possible for the Archbishop of Constantinople to accept it. Otherwise, how could he have accepted a formal accusation against the Patriarch of Alexandria? Here a question must at once be raised about just competence.

At any rate, it had never happened that a Bishop of Constantinople had sat in judgment over a Patriarch of Alexandria. For this, either a general council had been required, and heretofore this had always been called by the Emperor, or else the next highest court had to be appealed to, and that was an Egyptian provincial synod.[8] Who was to bring this about? Certainly not Theophilus. And if the Emperor had commanded it, would the Egyptian bishops, Theophilus' appointees and suffragans, dare to declare their ecclesiastical superior guilty—him before whose unscrupulousness and vindictiveness everyone trembled with fear?

For Chrysostom, the state of affairs was more than critical. In any case, it meant not merely a disturbance of his personal relations with Theophilus, perhaps going over to open enmity, but it also meant a new aggravation of the old discord between Constantinople and Alexandria.

It is understandable that Chrysostom used every means of preventing a re-opening of the old quarrels, which would only be unedifying, and could raise up scandals in a day. Therefore he next attempted to persuade the complaining monks to withdraw their accusation. He sent several bishops to them for this purpose. But it was in vain. The monks probably had other enemies of Theophilus behind them—for indeed they were not the only ones who had gotten on the trail of his outrages—and they refused to back down. Neither could they be persuaded to leave Constantinople. Where would they find refuge, since the powerful hand of the terrifying Patriarch had persecuted them through all the land, and made every place of residence impossible for them?

So then at last Chrysostom wrote a second time to Theophilus: "The monks are so far gone in grief and sorrow, that they have turned in a written complaint against you. Reply to this as you see fit."[9] A copy of the accusation was obviously enclosed. But even now Theophilus was not at all ready to meet them. On the contrary, he fell into such a passion over the monks, that he at once expelled from ecclesiastical fellowship the aged Bishop Dioscurus, the brother of the three chief monks, who had spent many years in honor in the Church. Then he sat down and wrote a letter to Chrysostom, a letter which betrays by its tone the whole arrogant and belligerent character of the man: "I think," said he, "that you know the regulations of the Canons of Nicaea, which forbid a Bishop to judge a dispute outside his diocese. If those canons are unknown to you, then learn them, and keep away from complaints about me. If I am to be judged, that is the business of the Egyptian Bishops, and not yours, for you are 75 days' journey from here."

This answer at least left nothing to be desired as far as clearness was concerned. The personal irritation and sharpness in it cannot be mistaken. Out of consideration for Theophilus, Chrysostom kept the letter secret, and called the monks together again, and accusers as well as the counter-accusers sent by Theophilus. Again he begged them and admonished them to settle their differences and make peace. That was more easily said than done. He only obtained discord on both sides. One side reminded him again of the injustice they had suffered, the others declared that they could not conclude peace without their Patriarch's permission. Chrysostom perceived that nothing could be done, either legally or in a friendly manner. He handed over Theophilus' answer to the monks, and declared that he would have nothing more to do with the matter.

Meanwhile Theophilus had not ceased to busy himself as a defender of the faith and a battler against Origenism. In his Easter letter of the year 402, he ridiculed the loquacity of Origen, who had written numberless books, and even spoke of the mists and fantasies of the allegorical method of teaching, which destroyed the truth of Holy Scripture.[10] That was an official break with the whole traditional method of the Alexandrian exegetical school.

So the affair of the monks again came to a dead end, and again Chrysostom proved that neither ambition nor love of power had moved him against Theophilus. He even took his insulting answer patiently. Not so the monks, who now found themselves in an entirely different situation. They could not or would not remain forever excommunicated and banned, and refused shelter everywhere. And as for these simple monks, opposed to force and injustice, even though it came from the Patriarch of Egypt, the thought that there would be no more justice for them in this world did not enter into their minds. So they continued to insist on obtaining their rights, to return to their Nitrian cells and caves, and to be permitted to live and die there in peace.

They composed two new long and detailed writs of accusation, one against Theophilus, and the other against those
monks who had come to Constantinople as his ambassadors
and counter-accusers. The latter they accused of slander.
These writs of accusation were directed this time to none
other than their Imperial Majesties. The monks, who had
never been able to find justice, turned to the highest worldly
authority, which had long since become a settled custom in
the East. In the "Martyrium" of St. John the Baptist, they
handed their writ of accusation to the Empress, and begged
that the complaint against their monastic opponents might
be tried by the Eparchs, and that Theophilus might be compelled to appear before a court, even though against his will;
a court over which Bishop John should preside.

Under the Martyrium of St. John is said to be a church
doubtless built by Theodosius the Great, in which the head
of St. John the Baptist was venerated, and which was located
in Hebdomon, near the imperial country residence.[11] Since
the Emperor was obviously not often there, one may well
suppose that the Empress, as happened often at church festi-
vals, had come out there alone, and occasionally on the Feast
of the Baptist (June 24). So the delivery of the petition and
the writ of accusation of the monks took place in mid-summer
of the year 402, which date fits in well with the remainder of
the chronology.

Now the great question was this: Would the Empress pass
the petition on further, and, in her deciding influence on the
Emperor, allow the document to reach him? That monks
should carry on lawsuits with other monks might not specially
demand her interest. But that the Patriarch of Alexandria
was challenged, and that the Bishop of Constantinople should
be his judge, gave the affair a character of state and church
politics, and it was also not without personal interest
because of the state of affairs between the Empress and the
Bishop.

It certainly meant a sensation in wide circles both in Constantinople and in Alexandria if it came out that the Court
had actually taken up the complaint of the Nitrian monks,
and if the imperial command should go forth that Patriarch
Theophilus was to be brought *nolens volens* to Constanti-

nople by the Magister militum, in order to justify himself there before a clerical court presided over by Bishop John.

Meanwhile the Eparchs were entrusted with the lawsuit against the monks sent as ambassadors by Theophilus. The imperial rescript ordered the monks of Theophilus to prove their accusation against Isidore and the Tall Brothers, or else be punished as slanderers.[12]

Elaphius, who was later given the rank of Princeps, was entrusted with the imperial summons to Patriarch Theophilus.

With this, the die was cast. The drama entered on its climax. However, Chrysostom opposed and resisted it, when he began to suspect what would happen; nevertheless the course of events followed him like destiny, and never again let him go.

The success of the Nitrian monks speaks decidedly for this, that in the summer of 402, the plan to depose Chrysostom was not under consideration. Otherwise he would not have been placed as judge over Theophilus, and the latter would not have hesitated so long before responding to the imperial summons. One must also assume that after the first difference between the Empress and the Archbishop, concerning the confiscated property, an estrangement had begun, but not a state of war. It must not be forgotten that in the court at that time, there were two equally strong parties, one for, and the other against Chrysostom. At first, the former party had the upper hand; but the other party took advantage of the summons of Theophilus, as the latter himself did, for making a forward push.

FOOTNOTES

1. Socrates 6, 7 (67, 684).
2. Palladius 7 (25).
3. Palladius, Dial. 7 (25).
4. Sozomen 8, 13 D (67, 1549).
5. Palladius 8 (26).
6. Dial. 7 (25).
7. Palladius, Dial. 7 (25).
8. Canon 6 of a Synod of Constantinople, probably that of the

year 382, had already regulated the judicial proceedings in accusations against bishops, which then came under the Canons of the General Council of 381. After that, the provincial synod was the next court for a bishop. If this was not sufficient, then the "diocesan synod" (Patriarchal synod) convened. (See Hefele KG 2, 24-26). But for a complaint against a Patriarch, these did not suffice.

9. The last phrase is as follows in Greek: λοιπὸν τὸ δοκοῦν σοι ἀντίγραφον = Palladius 7 (25). Tillemont, Mémoires 11, 598, Note 60, does not consider this phrase authentic, because it brings Theophilus before the forum of Chrysostom. Taken alone, the phrase is certainly so general and indefinite in its aim, that for Theophilus the way of private explanation and reconciliation remained open.

10. No. 9 and 10 (ML 22, 799).

11. Cf. Vol. II, p. 25 and Millingen, Byz. Constantinople 316 ff. Theodore of Trimithus 8 says that the monks had requested of Pope Innocent the deposition of Theophilus, and that he had pronounced it. This naturally belongs to the many fictions of this Vita, but it shows what right and what authority the Greek author already recognized in the Bishop of Rome at this time. Likewise George Alexandrinus. Cf. Chr. Baur, Georgius Alexandrinus, *loc. cit.* 4 f.

12. Palladius 8 (26).

CHAPTER XX

THE FIRST COUNTERTHRUST—
EPIPHANIUS IN CONSTANTINOPLE

HISTORY is silent on the feelings with which the Patriarch of Alexandria received the imperial summons to Constantinople. But one would not go far wrong with the assumption that this was one of the worst days of his life. In fact, the haughty pride of Theophilus could not have been so deeply wounded by anything as by such a command. He, the most distinguished man in Egypt, who might consider himself the true lord of the land, with more right than the imperial Augustalis, before whom the officials as well as the bishops trembled, because he had everything in his hands; must *he* go to Constantinople because of a few insignificant monks, to defend himself there? And before whom? Before strange bishops, whom he did not know? That might be endured—but before Chrysostom, the Archbishop of Constantinople, the rival of Alexandria for the highest ecclesiastical influence in the East, before the Antiochene, whom he had not liked from the first, whose consecration he had been forced to take part in against his will, and to whom he had recently sent a more than uncivil answer! For this man, who thought in terms of pure world-politics, it indeed seemed from the first moment that this summons could only be the secret doing of the Bishop of Constantinople, who, perhaps out of vengeance for the reprimand he had received, now wished to show for the first time that he stood higher than the Alexandrian; indeed, that he was using this whole quarrel of the monks as a welcome opportunity for thoroughly humbling the first Patriarch of the East. So that was the answer to his last letter! A moral challenge to battle for life and death! Theophilus felt that this time it would be blow for blow. Now he would have to dare everything, in order to escape the worst—and there would be no quarter.

And he was determined to overthrow his opponent, no matter what the cost.

The outlook for him in the affair was not so bad. If he had his enemies in Constantinople, he had also long ago learned that he could also find accomplices there, who were ready to take part in any intrigue against the Archbishop. He could reckon on a Severian, Antiochus, Acacius, under any circumstances; on them he built his plan of campaign. As a really angry man, he concentrated thenceforth all the rage and vindictive anger of which he was capable upon the one who was most guiltless in the development of the affair, and who had done his utmost to settle in a friendly manner the conflict which did not touch him personally, and to stand aside from it.

But how to reach his opponent? In regard to this, the resourceful man did not remain long in doubt. Not for nothing did he have in Alexandria the nickname of "Amphallax," which means approximately "the sly fox."[1] It seemed to him that attack was the best defense. So he prepared his offensive as soon as possible. Before all, it seemed to him most important to obtain some material on Chrysostom himself, which could be turned into a legal accusation, or would be sufficient to intimidate him. So he wrote to his Syrian friends in Constantinople, asking them to gather information in Antioch concerning the early life of the Archbishop, especially his youth. What he wished to find is clear enough. His friends acted according to his instructions.[2]

Meanwhile he sharpened a second more dangerous weapon. Chrysostom had sheltered the banished Nitrian monks whom Theophilus had condemned as Origenists. How about giving a hint of accusing the Archbishop of Constantinople of Origenism, or representing him as suspected of heresy?

Those who knew Chrysostom would shake their heads at this idea. But Theophilus took it seriously, or acted as if he believed it. At any rate, this provided for the moment the best and most plausible weapon which he could find. He played with it, in the battle with Chrysostom, as he had done in the strife with the monks, all through the case in the field of dogmatism, and was able to take the field in the grateful role and armor of a fighter against heresy in the person of the Bishop of Constantinople.

But before he entered the lists himself, he tried to send to Chrysostom an opponent to trouble him, an opponent who was known all through the East as a saint, and also as an enemy of heretics, but above all as an enemy of Origenism: namely the holy Epiphanius, Metropolitan of Salamis and Cyprus. Theophilus wrote to him promptly, asking him to hasten to Constantinople at once, for the true faith was in danger there. The Origenist monks, said he, who had come there from Egypt, had already trapped the Archbishop himself, for he was taking the Origenists publicly under his protection.[3]

Theophilus had come to the right man there. Epiphanius had, as it were, devoted his life to the battle against Origenism and every other heresy. Ten years before, in Jerusalem, he had come into bitter conflict with Bishop John there; he wished at any price to force the latter to condemn Origen as a heretic.

On this occasion there had been unedifying scenes in the church, and Epiphanius, in his holy zeal, had even permitted himself to ordain deacons and priests, contrary to the canons, without the permission of the Bishop, and in a strange diocese.[4]

At that time, of course, Patriarch Theophilus did not speak very well of Epiphanius. He even called him a heretic and a disturber of the peace.[5] But now, on the other hand, he could make very good use of the "disturber of the peace," and he needed him, too.

The affair of the Egyptian monks was not new to Epiphanius. Soon after their condemnation by the Synod of Alexandria, Theophilus had sent the report of the Synod to Epiphanius in Cyprus. As soon as he had learned that these monks had gone to Constantinople, he wrote with his own hand to the now "most beloved brother and co-bishop," asking him to summon his bishops as soon as possible to a synod, to condemn Origen, and to send the condemnation, together with that of the Theophilus-synod, to all the bishops of Asia Minor, and above all, to have it brought to Constantinople by special courier. So it was a downright witch-hunt that Theophilus prepared against the Nitrian monks, among whom he named Ammonius, Eusebius, and Euthymius.[6]

So if the Patriarch gave himself so much trouble, as long as he had to do only with defenseless monks, what activity he must have begun when he suddenly received the imperial summons to Constantinople, and saw in Chrysostom himself an enemy of far different caliber.

It might have been about the beginnings of March, 403, when Chrysostom received the news that Archbishop Epiphanius of Cyprus had arrived, and was outside the city in Hebdomon, at the Church of St. John.[7] That was astonishing. There were many nearer places of arrival for those who wished to reach Constantinople. And then also there was an imperial palace near the Church of St. John. Or perhaps had the Empress stopped there, just so Epiphanius could see her first of all, and speak to her? According to the testimony of Chrysostom, or Socrates, Epiphanius had held the Divine Liturgy in the Church of St. John, and even bestowed the diaconate on a candidate there.[8]

Meanwhile Chrysostom had sent some clergy to invite Epiphanius to come and take up his residence in the episcopal palace. The astonishment must have been great when he flatly refused the invitation. He even sent word to the Archbishop that he would not enter his house, indeed he would not even hold ecclesiastical fellowship with him, until he expelled Dioscurus and his companions from the city, and signed with his own hand a condemnation of the writings of Origen.[9]

That was certainly an absolutely illegal proceeding on the part of the 80-year-old Epiphanius. As a visiting bishop, he should not have used such language to the Bishop of the place, for the resolutions of an Egyptian and Cyprian provincial synod were not law for the whole Church. Still less was it suitable to anticipate pending legal proceedings by denouncing the plaintiff simply as a "heretic." In this, of course, Theophilus, who had been summoned months before, had a good hand. And indeed that was the object of the procedure, which Epiphanius did not perceive.

Soon after, Epiphanius came into the city, and took up his residence, not with Bishop John, but in a private house. That was a public insult to Chrysostom, merely because he could not comply with the foolish claims of Epiphanius with the same blind zeal which the latter demanded.

H

But the fighting spirit of Epiphanius was by no means exhausted. Scarcely had he arrived in the city, when he sent out invitations to all the bishops who were in Constantinople at that time, and who were of course guests of Chrysostom. That was another and a still worse breach of tact. But Chrysostom seems not to have informed his episcopal guests of his relations with Epiphanius up to that time. They therefore accepted the invitations. Perhaps it happened with the knowledge and assent of Chrysostom.

Epiphanius then declared to the assembled bishops that Origen had been condemned by several synods; he read aloud to them the judgment of the Synod of Cyprus, and perhaps also that of the Synod of Theophilus, and then demanded of them all that they add their signatures to the sentence of the Synod. Some of the bishops assented to the signing, because of the great age of Epiphanius, and the esteem in which he was held; but the overwhelming majority refused to sign.

The Bishop of the Goths, Theotimus from Scythia, who was respected for his learning, piety and ascetic life, even declared " I do not consider it right to cover with shame the good name of a man who died a holy death so many (a hundred and fifty) years ago, and I consider it a piece of arrogance, insulting to God, to condemn what our ancestors did not condemn. Moreover, I find in general nothing bad in the works of Origen." In proof of this, he brought in a book, from which he read aloud to the bishops, and showed that it agreed perfectly with the teaching of the Church. Perhaps this book was the Philolokalia, which Sts. Basil and Gregory of Nazianzus had put together from the works of Origen. So whoever condemns Origen, said Theotimus in conclusion, he condemns also these teachings.[10]

Epiphanius was apparently not satisfied with this meager success. If Socrates is correct on this point, he allowed himself to be persuaded by the enemies of Chrysostom to a repetition of that which he had done in Jerusalem before. When the Divine Liturgy was about to be celebrated in the Church of the Apostles, he persuaded the Bishop to come forward during the service, and, before all the people, condemn all the works of Origen, and then to exclude Dioscurus and his monks from the fellowship of the Church, and to reproach the Archbishop himself for approving of them.

In fact, Epiphanius wished to carry out his plan the next day. He had already approached the church, when Chrysostom, who had heard about the affair, and wished to avoid a public scandal, sent the priest Serapion to tell him that he was doing a great deal which was forbidden by the canons: first he had performed an ordination in a church which was under the jurisdiction of the Bishop of Constantinople; then he had held the Divine Liturgy there on his own responsibility; so he should guard against arousing disturbance among the people, for it might be dangerous for him.

That made such an impression on Epiphanius that he kept quiet. Also it seems to have gradually become clear to him that he was becoming an object of ridicule on account of his peculiar activities. Sozomen says that he also had a conference with the four Tall Brothers, with the result that his violent urge for persecution was considerably lessened.[11]

The arrival and activities of Epiphanius in Constantinople must have been material for common conversation in the city generally, for even thirty years later, all sorts of stories were told about him.[12] For instance, it was told that the Empress had him summoned, and begged him to pray for the heir to the throne, who was sick. But Epiphanius said the boy would live if she would stop protecting Dioscurus and his heretical monks. Thereupon Eudoxia had answered that if God wanted the life of her child, He could have it. And if Epiphanius had been able to raise the dead to life, said she, his Archdeacon Crispion would not have died shortly before.

Indeed, when Epiphanius at last departed for home, the same Sozomen said that he wrote a farewell letter to Chrysostom with the very unkind wish: "I hope you will not die a Bishop." To which John answered in an equally unfriendly manner: "And I hope that you will never see your home again."

Naturally these stories are not true, but still they show that the unfriendly attitude of Epiphanius toward Chrysostom was well known to the public, and the memory of his public acts remained in the minds of the people. They may also indicate this much, that the clear knowledge of his wrong-doing had not come to Epiphanius. Only a certain dissatis-faction with the result of his journey might be understood from the words which he spoke to the bishops who accom-panied him to the ship: "I gladly give you the city, the court and the whole lot."[13]

Historically reliable, at any rate, is the fact that Epiphanius left Constantinople before Theophilus arrived, and that he died on the way, on the high seas, on the 12th of May, 403.[14]

Later legends felt the necessity of seeking extenuating circumstances for the somewhat compromising conduct of Epiphanius toward Chrysostom. So the romancing Vita Epiphanii of his alleged pupil Polybius [15] places the chief blame on the Empress Eudoxia. She had urged and goaded Epiphanius on; which Socrates obviously relies on when he says that someone had reported to Chrysostom that the Empress had incited Epiphanius against him.[16] On the contrary, from the stories of Sozomen and the remarks of Socrates, it is rather apparent that Eudoxia always stood on the side of the monks, even at the time when Epiphanius was already staying in Constantinople. The personality which animated Epiphanius in his journey to Constantinople, and in his hostile attitude toward Chrysostom, was that of Theophilus, sum-moned before the court. Only he had not been able to accomplish what he wished in this first blow.

Meanwhile, also, news had arrived from Antioch that no one, even with the best will in the world, had been able to find anything evil in the youth of Archbishop John.[17]

So the two first arrows had not reached their mark. New means must be searched for.

But Theophilus had had one success. While his contem-poraries did not take seriously his attempt to label Chrysostom an Origenist, there appeared suddenly, after 700 years, in an inexplicable manner, this information from Anonymus Melli-censis[18] in the twelfth century: "John Chrysostom allowed himself to be deceived, at first by the errors of Origen, but then by the help of God's grace, he improved, and made peace with the Church." How the Anonymus came by this information is not known. But it shows what a tenacious life these calumnies have sometimes.[19]

On the other hand, history concerning Epiphanius himself, following his energetic battle against Origenism and every heresy, gives him only a brief notice, saying that the Metropolitan, who was born of Jewish parents, showed on his part a weak position in regard to orthodoxy. He was, for instance, a very decided opponent of the veneration of images. First, he found in his church at Anablatha, near Jerusalem, a curtain on which an image of Christ or a saint was painted or embroidered. Epiphanius, much irritated, said that it was forbidden by Holy Scripture to place an image of a man in a church; and he seized the curtain and tore it into pieces before the eyes of his startled companions.[20] Might he not have been found among the Iconoclasts three hundred years later?

That Eudoxia, until early in 403, was not an open opponent of the Bishop, and that the friends of Chrysostom still had the upper hand everywhere, may be understood from the fact that the slanderous process which the Theophilus monks had brought against the Nitrian monks had actually been begun in the autumn or winter of 402, and promised an entirely unfavorable outcome for the plaintiffs. At the very first legal proceedings, the ambassadors of the Egyptian Patriarch had to admit that they were not in a position to prove their accusations against the Nitrian monks. Very severe penalties were imposed for calumny. Even capital punishment was decreed for it under certain circumstances. In their trouble, they now acknowledged that the Patriarch Theophilus himself had dictated the points of accusation to them, and that, as accusers, they were only puppets. Then they begged that the affair might be postponed until Theophilus' arrival, and that meanwhile they themselves might go free on bail. But the judges did not agree to this. The not altogether guiltless victims of a conscienceless overlord were kept in prison.

But Theophilus did not hasten his arrival at all, so that in the meantime one or two of the prisoners died.

Chrysostom was accused later, at the Synod of the Ork, of not having done anything for these monks.[21] It was impossible for him to interfere in an impending lawsuit, and Theophilus needed only to hasten his own arrival.

When the Patriarch finally arrived, his monks were no longer in prison. He had lent a hand with money. At the last proceedings, the monks, in spite of their calumny, were "banished" to Proconnesus, which under the existing circumstances amounted to being set free.[22]

FOOTNOTES

1. Palladius, Dial. 6 (47, 21).

2. Palladius (*loc. cit.*) represents the course of events without that exact date, as though the idea were to collect material against Chrysostom, and so with the object of introducing a process against him, begun in the circle of the provincial Bishops Severian and Acacius, and the Abbot Isaac. And then, when they had not been able to find anything, they had inquired of Theophilus what they should really do. It might have been taken thus by an outside observer in Constantinople. Actually, the idea of deposing Chrysostom cannot have originated before the summons of Theophilus to Constantinople, because Eudoxia certainly tried to prevent this summons and the appointment of Chrysostom as judge. On the other hand, still less could these foreign provincial bishops have had this idea, since it was Theophilus who, from the moment of his summons, had a vital interest in destroying Chrysostom. In consideration of the other dealings of the Patriarch, and the fact that he led and organized the entire proceeding against Chrysostom, one scarcely does Theophilus an injustice if one considers him the spiritual author of this investigation into the previous life of Chrysostom, as well as the inspirer of the idea of the falsifying of the sermons, which took place first after the departure of Epiphanius (403). At any rate, the Syrian Bishops in Constantinople worked with Theophilus systematically, toward a common end, and he was always their undisputed leader.

3. Theophilus must have written a letter to this effect, for Letter 90 (ML 22, 756-57) to Epiphanius, was written soon after the arrival of the monks in Constantinople, and said nothing at all about Epiphanius himself coming to Constantinople. Socrates 6, 12 emphasizes expressly that he had made the journey at the urging of Theophilus.

4. F. Cavallera, S. Jérôme 203 ff.; Rauschen, Jahrbücher 404-405.

5. Palladius, Dial. 16 (56). At any rate, Epiphanius was far more a man of emotions than of understanding. His literary activity is criticised by Photius (Bibl. 122-103, 404) as "insignificant linguistically, and weak in content."

6. Epist. 90 ad. Epiphanium (ML 22, 756-57).

7. So according to Socrates 6, 12 (67, 701).

8. HE 6, 12 and 14 (701 and 705). It is not correct, as Dyobouniotis Συμμετοχὴ *loc. cit.* 71-72 says, that Socrates simply produced here a copy of the ordination of Paulinian in Bethlehem.

9. Socrates 6, 14 (705).

10. Socrates 6, 12 (701); Sozomen 8, 14 (1553). Concerning Theotimus and his works, see Archbishop R. Netzhammer O.S.B., Die altchristliche Kirchenprovinz Skythien *loc. cit.* 402-403.

11. HE 8, 15 (1556).—Dyobouniotis, Συμμετοχὴ *loc. cit.*

12. Also Dyobouniotis Συμμετοχὴ, *loc. cit.* 73 ff. at any rate finds the reports concerning this by Socrates and especially Sozomen quite incredible.

13. Sozomen 8, 15 (1556): Ἀφίημι ὑμῖν τὴν πόλιν καὶ τὰ βασίλεια καὶ την ὑπόκρισιν. For the historicity of this expression, naturally no guarantee can be given; still less for the representation of the Synaxarium of Constantinople for the 12th of May (ASS Nov. Prop. 677 no. 2) or the Annals of the Patriarch Eutychus of Alexandria (111, 1029-30).

14. G. Becker mentions in his Catalogus Bibliothecarum antiquarum p. 97, that in a Codex from the tenth century from the cloister of Lauresheim n. 221 and 243 b, there are letters of St. Epiphanius ad Ioannem Constantinopolitanum, which were translated into Latin by St. Jerome. But this treats of a letter of Epiphanius to Bishop John of Jerusalem (ML 22, 517-527 and MG 43, 379-392). Cf. S. Vailhé, Notes de littérature eccl., in: Echos d'Orient 9 (1906) 222-23.

15. No. 62 (41, 104 ff.); ed. Dindorf (Leipzig 1859-1862) I, 1-81 and XXXI-XXXVI.

16. HE 6, 15 (67, 708).

17. Palladius 6 (21).

18. De scriptoribus ecclesiasticis 1, 12 (ML 213, 965-66; ed. Ettlinger [Karlsruhe 1896] 51).

19. Once more after 700 years has Aloisius Vincenzi counted St. Chrysostom, among others, among the "patrons" of Origen, of course not in order to accuse him of Origenism, but to vindicate Origen as orthodox. See A. Vincenzi, In S. Gregorii Nysseni et Origenis scripta et doctrinam nova rescensio cum Appendice de actis Synodi V. oecumenicae. vol. III: Historia critica, quaestiones inter Theophilum, Epiphanium, Hieronymum, adversarios Ori-

genis et inter Origenis Patronos Jo. Chrysostomum, Theotimum, Rufinum et monachos Nitriensis, Romae 1865. p. 102, 221-235.

20. St. Jerome, Letters 51, 9 (ML 22, 526).
21. Cf. Ch. 22; Synod of the Oak p. 247.
22. Palladius 8 (26).

CHAPTER XXI

THE GREAT REVERSAL
(EARLY IN 403)

So the first open attack on Chrysostom spent itself in vain. The cunning of Theophilus had devised it, the simplicity of Epiphanius had executed it, but his honesty had broken it up. They had not been able to expel the Nitrian monks from Constantinople, nor to free the Patriarch of Alexandria from his accusers, and still less had they been able to entangle the Bishop of Constantinople in a suit for heresy, and thereby do away with his future judge. On the contrary, the presence of the Metropolitan of Cyprus, and the publicity, had made Chrysostom mindful of the intrigues whose author could only be the one who would utilize them in the end, and that was the Patriarch of Alexandria. The sympathy of the people had been all on the side of Chrysostom.

So what was to be done, since the investigation in Antioch had not brought anything useful to light? One thing was perfectly clear to the Patriarch: there was only one power in the Empire which was able to give the affair a different turn: the Empress Eudoxia. If it was not possible to win her, then there was no escape for Theophilus from the lawsuit which must bring him, if not deposition, at least a difficult humiliation—for a man of his proud character, an unendurable one. Already, writs of accusation had been handed in against him which included not less than seventy points.

But Theophilus did not lose courage. His supply of ideas and plans was not yet exhausted. All his mind and his aims were henceforth directed toward this, if not to win the Empress to his side, at least to turn her against Chrysostom, to the point where she would willingly agree to his deposition.

But how was the affair to be managed practically? History offers here no positive and express proof that it was Theo-

philus who introduced the idea, as criminal as it was daring,
of bringing about the longed-for end by deception: to get the
help and co-operation of the Empress.   But it is a fact that
just then, at the critical moment, the decisive change was
brought about by a common deception in favor of Theophilus.   In his hand lay the entire management from the
beginning.

For Theophilus was not accustomed to waiting supinely
until the favor of chance came to his help.   So then he was
the first and principal beneficiary of the new action.   Actually
this deception saved his patriarchal see for him, and cost
Chrysostom his episcopal see.   And Theophilus did not
accept the Emperor's invitation until he knew for certain
that the villainous stroke would have the wished-for result.
History commits no wrong in ascribing to him the moral
responsibility for what Severian of Gabala and his friends
now did.   They got together at this time, to search through
the sermons of Chrysostom, in order to find some suitable
point to serve their purpose.   And when they did not find it,
*they falsified some of his sermons, so as to make it appear that
he had slandered the Empress and other persons of the court.*
So Palladius says expressly,[1] and Socrates[2] and Sozomen[3] say
the same.

Unfortunately Chrysostom himself supplied them with the
most useful piece for falsification; he supplied it in a somewhat temperamental sermon about this time, all unsuspecting as he was; he was preaching on the vanity of the devout
sex, and their love of adornment in dress.   Unfortunately the
text of this sermon has not survived, so the method of falsification cannot be demonstrated.[4]   One can only suppose that
Eudoxia and Eugraphia read malicious allusions into the
ambiguity of the words, and that the text, thus distorted, was
spread about by both of them.   Such is the best explanation
of Palladius' statement that someone had falsified his sermons
in such a way as to give the impression that he had " slandered
the Empress and other persons of the court."   At any rate,
among the companions of the Empress, Eugraphia fell into
the most violent rage.

However, it was nothing new or special for Chrysostom to
preach on the vanity or luxury of women.   He had done that

often enough in Antioch too.[5] He had even described women's love of power in his treatise On the Priesthood, in such a way as if he had been a prophet at that time: "The law of God," said he, "has excluded women from the priesthood, but they seek by force to bring themselves to power. And if they cannot accomplish it personally, they attempt it through others. Indeed, often they are able to win such influence that they can install or depose priests at their pleasure . . . I have even heard that some carry their impudence so far that they themselves blame and reproach bishops more arrogantly than lords reproach their own servants."[6]

If Chrysostom had said such a thing in Constantinople in 403, the reference would point very clearly to Eudoxia and her court ladies and bishops. As a matter of fact, John the priest did not at all suspect that he himself would one day be a living witness of the truth of his words. The actual fact stands, that they even grasped at falsification of the sermons in order to set the Empress against the Bishop; and that fact is of the highest importance in the question of placing the blame in the tragedy of Chrysostom. It allows the conclusion that Eudoxia was far more the led than the leader, in the whole affair. Severian and his accomplices went to the young Empress with the product of their malice. And with that, she was caught in her most sensitive side, her womanly vanity. The villainous stroke actually had its full success on the sanguine temperament of the Empress. Her already existing displeasure with Chrysostom flamed up into violent wrath. Her court ladies, Eugraphia, Marsa, Castricia, and others, helped to pour oil on the flames, exactly according to the plans of the ringleaders.

That was the decisive turning point in the fate of St. Chrysostom.

In order to give the affair still more emphasis, and the better to insure its success, the Empress was informed that the Archbishop had called her Jezebel, which must have sounded plausible because of the earlier story of the vineyard or the estate.[7] One must admit that Eudoxia need not be overweeningly proud, or sensitive over her imperial dignity, to feel deeply insulted over such a comparison with her infamous colleague of the Old Testament. She had a right to be insulted, if she believed the story. And her easily irritated disposition inclined her to believe it. The opponents of Chrysostom knew this, and based their calculations on it.

All these incidents and intrigues were naturally kept a deep secret from Chrysostom. He knew nothing else than that the Patriarch of Egypt was to defend himself in Constantinople, before a synod of bishops, at which synod he (Chrysostom) as Archbishop of the city, was to preside. His assent to this was obtained by nobody. A large number of bishops had already appeared; they had been summoned by imperial rescript.[8] About forty of these were assembled about Chrysostom, to wait for the opening of the synod which was to decide the dispute between the Patriarchs.

Meanwhile, however, month after month of fruitless waiting went by. The bishops invited to the synod were there, but the accused, the Patriarch of Alexandria, was not there. The Metropolitan of Cyprus, Epiphanius, who had not been called, was there, but Theophilus, who had been called, was not. June and July passed, and August came, and still he did not appear in Constantinople.

At last, it seems to have been in the second half of August, 403, it was said that the Patriarch had arrived at Chalcedon in Bithynia.[9] It was true. He had purposely delayed his departure from Egypt. He did not start until he had received dependable reports on some secret undermining projects which his friends and helpers were working on. It was only when he knew that the Empress was finally on their side, and had only one wish, to get rid of the embarrassing Archbishop, that he had started to move.

How well the Patriarch was prepared for this affair is proved by the boastful statement which he made in Alexandria before his departure: "I am going," he said to his entourage, "to depose Bishop John."[10] This expression pleased him, for he repeated it during his journey, to a bishop in Lycia.

The plan of Theophilus, who knew very well how to place authority and law in the service of unrighteousness, was very simple: he would oppose the synod which was to judge him, with another synod which should judge Chrysostom. Here a question raises itself. Where was he to get the bishops he needed for his synod? With the exception of Severian, Antiochus, and Acacius, there were at best but a few on whose co-operation he could count. But Theophilus knew an expedient in the matter. He simply brought the necessary bishops with him from Egypt, not less than 29 in number,[11] although it was expressly stipulated in the imperial summons that he should come alone.

Moreover, he thought that a good many of the bishops who were already assembled about Chrysostom could be brought to his side by personal persuasion and other helps, so that he could reckon on a certain majority of bishops for his synod. He could trust his Egyptians, under any circumstances. He had appointed and consecrated all of them himself, and had chosen "the best" to accompany him on this journey. And at the worst, the authority of the secular power was at his disposal in the person of the Empress. So he had nothing to fear.

Over and above all this, he had also brought a multitude of costly gifts with him, especially Egyptian and Indian perfumes. These offerings were intended for the court circle, not the least for the feminine confederates at the court.[12]

So everything was very well taken care of. Sozomen[13] says that the Patriarch made the journey by land. But since he, according to Chrysostom or Palladius,[14] touched at the province of Lycia in the journey, he would have had to make a very long detour, which is not probable. The truth might be that he took his followers to Lycia by sea, and, from there on, sent the others by ship to Chalcedon, and came on after them himself by the land route. Probably he wished to pick up on the way still more accusers and confederates against Chrysostom, and take them along. Actually at least two of the deposed Asiatic Bishops were present at the Synod of the Oak.[15]

The meeting place of all of Theophilus' friends was Chalcedon. There was a secret reason for this. The Bishop there, Cyrinus, was a countryman of the Patriarch, and, what is more significant, a raging enemy of Chrysostom, against whom he gave out at every opportunity with the most insulting expressions. Unfortunately, we do not know what was the true cause of his hatred. He called Chrysostom a godless, arrogant, stubborn man.[16]

When at last the party of Theophilus was more or less fully collected, he decided to make his solemn entry into Constantinople. The only one who had to remain behind was Cyrinus, the Bishop of Chalcedon. Through an accident, Bishop Maruthas of Maipharkat (in Persia) who happened to be present, had trod on his foot, and so injured him that he had to remain at home. With all the rest of the crowd, Theophilus boarded an Egyptian ship, and entered like a triumphing general into the city, on a Thursday about noon, with loud cries of greeting from the crews of the numerous Egyptian merchant ships and grain ships.[17]

Chrysostom had scarcely learned of the arrival of the Patriarch in Chalcedon when he sent him a message at once, to invite him to take up his dwelling in the episcopal palace; the invitation was addressed to him and to all his companions.[18] What answer Theophilus gave, is unknown. At any rate, however, his speech and his behavior soon made it known that he had come not as a guest, but as an enemy. So it happened that at the landing place in Constantinople, no deputy of Bishop John was present.[19] So then Theophilus ignored both the Bishop's Palace and the Cathedral, and went to a palace lying outside the city, called Placidiana.[20] It was the special palace of the Empress.[21] That was a bad sign.

Whether the Empress was in the palace herself at the time, was not certain. But the three Bishops, Severian, Antiochus, and Acacius, were now openly guests of the before-mentioned Eugraphia. Theophilus stayed fully three weeks in Constantinople, without once approaching Chrysostom. He never even entered the church during all that time. Instead of that, he went very often to the palace of Eugraphia, to meet his three fellow-plotting friends, where they took counsel together as to how and with what legal formalities they could pursue the suit against Chrysostom.[22]

In vain the latter sent again to Theophilus, and begged him at least to come and talk with him, and communicate to him the reasons why he had manifested such an unfriendly spirit toward him from the beginning, for it was giving scandal to the whole city. Theophilus gave him no answer, and refused to meet him. He did not wish to come to an understanding.[23]

On the contrary. The Patriarch and his fellow-conspirators worked feverishly and by means of bribes, flattery, and rich entertainments and promises of high ecclesiastical dignities, to win over Chrysostom's clergy, and to find among them accusers against their Bishop.[24] Unfortunately they had only too much success in this. When they noticed the development of affairs, the majority of the clergy forsook their Bishop in the hour of need. The archdeacon of Chrysostom, the successor of Serapion, had been the first to practise treachery and to go over to the enemy; he gradually drew almost all the clergy after him.[25]

Naturally, all this could not remain a secret from Chrysostom and his bishops. An indescribable tumult and uncertainty seized on their spirits. How was it possible that the accused, summoned by the Emperor himself to appear before the court, could enter Constantinople like this, and let it be clearly understood that he was there to depose Chrysostom?[26] The greatest anxiety seized Dioscurus and the Nitrian monks. What would become of them, who had occasioned the summons of Theophilus by their accusations, if the Patriarch could come in like this? In their distress they begged for another audience of the Emperor, and the extraordinary happened: the Emperor, who had had no suspicion of all these events, sent for Chrysostom, and gave him, all over again, the order to receive the accusation against Theophilus,[27] to preside over the synod convened for that purpose, and carry through the whole process. That was the kind of double-faced politics which was carried on in the court at that time.[28]

If Chrysostom had been a less distinguished character, had he been a man of the type of a Theophilus or a Severian, he would have cultivated power politics; and as a "diplomat" he would have played off one against the other; he would now, in this last and highest moment, have had it in his power to compass the downfall of the Patriarch and his following, which the latter intended for Chrysostom himself. But it was to the honor of his character and his Christian thought, that he did not do it.   Open quarreling between bishops was to him an outrage, on account of the scandal to the people.

He did not yield to the request of the Emperor.   With respect to the canons, as well as to the person and the office of the Patriarch, he refused to give judgment on Theophilus.[29]   He referred to the letter in which Theophilus himself had protested against having accusations handled outside the church province to which they belonged.   Theophilus had, until that time, not been willing to take a judgment from the hand of Chrysostom.   He had come to Constantinople now, because the Emperor had commanded it, but much more because he knew that the Empress was inclined toward him—or rather, against Chrysostom.

So the way of justice could not be followed, and it did not lie in the character of Chrysostom to walk on the way of power and appeal to worldly might.[30]

His magnanimity had, humanly speaking, destroyed him.

FOOTNOTES

1. Dial. 6 (21).
2. HE 6, 15 (67, 708-709).
3. HE 8, 16 (1557).
4. Socrates 6, 15 (708) represents the affair thus: Some one had informed Chrysostom secretly that the attack of Epiphanius on him had been occasioned by Eudoxia, and on account of anger over this, Chrysostom had issued a general philippic against women, in which his listeners had seen a reference to Eudoxia.
5. Catech. 2, 4 ad illum. (49, 238); In Ps. 48, 17: Ne timueris n. 5 (55, 507); In Isaiam cp. 3, n. 8 (56, 50-51); Hom. 17, 3 and 30, 5 in Matt. (57, 257-58 and 368); Hom. 41, 4 in Joh. (59, 340-41).
6. De Sacerdotio 3, 9 (48, 646).
7. Cf. Ch. 15: Quarrel with Empress Eudoxia.   In this connection, an explanation of the insulting expression will enable the course of events to be better understood.

In Palladius, cp. 8, col. 30, the Jezebel first appears at the Synod of the Oak, without a date.   Palladius is often not very clear in regard to the chronology and actual sequence of events.   Very often he does not give dates at all. One could only assume from his representation (Ch. 6) that the idea of spying out his former life, and the forging of the sermons, came from Severian. However, the wheels of the plot mesh together too well, even though Theophilus was not the man to leave the results of his actions to a chance idea of his friends, to whom he had made everything clear before his arrival in Constantinople.

8. Socrates 6, 15 (67, 709 A).

9. Socrates 6, 15; Sozomen 8, 16.

10. Palladius 8 (29).

11. Palladius 8 (29). The Synod of Chrysostom alleges that Theophilus said: "You are the thirty-sixth from the same province."

12. Palladius 8 (26) here transgresses the bounds of good taste, when he says that Theophilus had come thither like a heavily-loaded dung beetle, and had covered over with the perfume of his gifts the stink of his malicious envy.

13. Sozomen 8, 14 (1552).

14. Dial. 8 (29).

15. Socrates 6, 15 (709) and Sozomen 8, 16 (1557). According to Photius, Bibl. 59 (103, 108 D), the Lycian Bishop Prohairesius must have specially come into conflict earlier with Chrysostom; so he would explain it, when Theophilus visited Lycia.

The length of the sea journey from Alexandria to Constantinople must have depended on wind and water and the amount of trading done. The Abbot Victor, ambassador of St. Cyril, had to spend 24 days on the sea (Copt. Akten z. ephes. Konzil = T. u. U. NF. XI. 2 (1904) 4 and 136, N.1). But to go by land required 75 days = Pall. Dial. 7 (col. 25).

16. Socrates 6, 15 (709); Sozomen 8, 16 (1557).

17. Palladius 8 (26); Socrates 6, 15; Sozomen 8, 17 (1560).

18. Chrysostom, Letter to Pope Innocent = Palladius 2 (8).

19. Socrates 6, 15 (709); Sozomen 8, 17 (1557-59).

20. Socrates *loc. cit.*

21. Cf. Ch. 3, p. 22.

22. Palladius 8 (27).

23. Chrysostom, Letter to Pope Innocent = Pall. 2 (9).

24. Palladius 8 (26).

25. Letter of Chrysostom to Pope Innocent = Pall. 2 (9). Perhaps this Archdeacon is identical with the Archdeacon Martyrius, of whom Point 26 of the Synod of the Oak says, that Chrysostom had been in his case both the judge, accuser and witness (Photius, Bibl. 59 = 103, 108 D). This Martyrius could also have been the predecessor of Martyrion.

26. Palladius 8 (27).

27. Palladius 2 (9). The Greek text says: The Emperor called me and commanded πέραν, ἔνθα διέτριβεν, ἀπιέναι = to go over to where he (Theophilus) was staying, and listen to the complaint against him.

28. According to the wording of this letter, which Chrysostom wrote to Pope Innocent (Pall. 2, col. 9), there can be no doubt that this order went out to Chrysostom at a time when Theophilus was already staying at the Palace of Placidiana, and indeed at the time of a renewed oppression of the Nitrian monks, who had obviously been much upset over the doings of the Patriarch.

29. Chrysostom, Letter to Pope Innocent, Pall. Dial. 2 (col. 9).

30. One may ask why neither the Nitrian monks nor the Alexandrian accusers against Theophilus went to Rome. That is understandable on several grounds. The first court of judgment against a bishop was the provincial synod. The second was actually the Emperor, and then, if all else failed, the Pope or a general council. Pope and Council together in this case actually formed the court of appeal. Ubaldi (p. 64-65) expresses the suspicion that it was just the refusal of Chrysostom to conduct the Process against Theophilus, at the command of the Emperor, which prejudiced the court against Chrysostom, because the court had made use of every opportunity to get him immersed in ecclesiastical affairs and to demonstrate the overlordship of the secular power against the Church. That is essentially and chronologically incorrect. Here, as in a hundred other cases, it was always ecclesiastical personalities who brought Church questions before the forum of the Emperor. Byzantine Caesaropapism originated in the Greek Bishops. Further, Eudoxia was on the side of Theophilus, long before the latter came to Constantinople, and not on political grounds, but out of purely personal malice.

CHAPTER XXII

THE SYNOD OF THE OAK
(AUTUMN OF 403)

WITH Chrysostom's refusal to act as judge over Theophilus, the stroke of fate fell. Legally considered, the affair had now come to a dead end. Theophilus would have been able to return home, with his Egyptian Bishops. But he was not of a mind to do that. He had come there to depose Chrysostom, and he was in absolute earnest about it. Now the Emperor had only to promise, and the game was won. But it appears that Arcadius always agreed with the one who spoke to him last. So while the one party remained completely passive, the other set every means going to attain by force what was not to be had by law. Theophilus preserved in this, at least, the dignity of a statesman. Severian and Antiochus, on the contrary, allowed their agitation to appear so openly and rudely that even actors ridiculed them on the stage, to the joy of their very mixed audiences.[1] The quarrel among the Bishops had already grown into a public scandal.

After three weeks' work, Theophilus' efforts had finally so far prospered that he could pass over into an open attack. The most important ones, the judges, he had brought with him; accusers he had meanwhile sought for, and found. Even in regard to the points of accusation, after all the deliberation, they had become unanimous; although it mattered little about them, since the judgment was fore-ordained.

Two men came forward as accusers, who brought little honor upon themselves in the affair of the Egyptian Patriarch: they were the two deacons whom Chrysostom, just at the beginning of his episcopate, had expelled from the ranks of the clergy, for grave sins. The fact that Theophilus was not ashamed to let these two gentlemen come in as accusers of their Bishop, shows not only the evil of his own

affair, but it is a brilliant proof of the irreproachable conduct of Chrysostom, in whose life and dealings one would not
have been able to find anything which, to a reasonable man,
would have sufficed for an accusation. Here a criminal must
be brought in against the innocent, and the Egyptian high
priest shrank not at all from soiling his hands with such tools.

As a reward, both these men were promised that they would
be again installed in their offices as soon as there was a new
bishop.

So now everything was ready for the comedy, or tragedy, to
begin. The question of place was still to be solved. It was
not advisable to summon Chrysostom before the court within
the jurisdiction of the City; they feared the people, who had
long since showed themselves upset over the dark rumors
which had partly come into the open. So they decided to
meet at a "court of justice" outside the city, on the other
side of the Bosporus. There lay (near the modern Djadi-
Bostan) the splendid estate called "At the Oak," with a large,
roomy villa, built by the former minister Rufinus in 394, and
which had been an imperial property since his murder in 395.
It had always borne the name of Rufinianai, but was also
called The Oak because of the great oak tree which stood
near it.[2] Nearby was the large and spacious Peter and Paul's
Church, which had been consecrated by Nectarius nine years
before, in the presence of many Bishops, among whom was
Theophilus. Rufinus had received baptism there the same
day.[3] In this Apostles' Church Chrysostom had preached,
for example on the 7th of April, 399, when he led the pilgrimage from Constantinople to Rufinianai to honor the relics of
the Apostles there.[4] Near the church was a building which
served as a monastery for Egyptian monks, but which had
been abandoned by them after the murder of Rufinus. About
three years before, St. Hypatius had set in order the neglected
and devastated rooms, and had gathered together a small
number of pupils about him.[5]

The church and the place belonged to the Diocese of Chalcedon, where Cyrinus was Bishop, the only neighboring
Bishop who would tolerate a synod against Chrysostom in his
diocese.

The "synod" could occupy the palace of Rufinus only with

the permission of the court. That was the first certain proof of open hostility to Chrysostom on the part of the Empress. The cards revealed themselves ever more clearly, and those who knew the state of affairs might well from that moment have had no more real doubts about the outcome of the affair.

So Theophilus journeyed across the Bosporus for the second time, with his Egyptian Bishops, Severian, Antiochus, and Acacius, Maruthas of Maipharkat, and Macarius of Magnesia.[6] Also Cyrinus of Chalcedon joined him later. In all there were about thirty-six bishops, whom he had gathered about him.[7] That was quite an impressive number.

Besides these bishops, who alone formed the real synod, there were other figures animating the halls of the palace of Rufinus. There were the deposed simoniacal bishops from Asia, who were waiting to be re-installed in their dioceses; as deposed bishops, they could not take part in the synod actively. The most outstanding figure there was the father of the monks, the Abbot Isaac. He might well have given the Synod the ascetical consecration in the eyes of the people. He saw the time arriving for the revenge on his long-held grudge against the Bishop who had dared to criticize him and his monks. Beside him, one might meet a considerable number of clergy from Constantinople, who, in anticipation of the coming affair, had already lined up on the side of the Alexandrians—the Archdeacon, the two deacons, accusers, and others. Also came clergy, secretaries, monks, servants, cooks and other people. Suddenly a rich and brilliant life had come into the forsaken halls.

Meanwhile, it had naturally become clear to Chrysostom, and also to the bishops gathered about him, to their astonishment and dread, what an unexpected turn the affair threatened to take. Forty of them had come together, from various provinces of the Empire, in expectation of judging the accusations against Theophilus. And now, suddenly, Theophilus enters as judge himself, and judge of Chrysostom! In the great dining-room of the Bishop's Palace, they assembled together, and earnestly discussed the case. Palladius too, Chrysostom's later biographer, was among them.[8]

Some complained that Theophilus had brought along his suffragan Bishops, whereas the Emperor had commanded him to come alone. Others wondered how it had been possible to change the commands and decisions of the Emperor and the highest officials so quickly to the contrary; and still others wondered how he had been able to get the majority of the clergy on his side. All of them were in forced accord. The sacrificial victim himself was firm and calm. He said to the bishops: "Pray, brothers, and if John is dear to you, let no one for my sake be a traitor to his Church. I have known many bitter things, and I see that my days are numbered. The devil does not wish that I should fight him any longer with the Word of God. Show me your sympathy in this way, by remembering me in your prayers." These short and simple words made a deep impression. Many wept for grief; they embraced and kissed the man who might never appear greater in their eyes than now. Others left the hall, sobbing. Chrysostom sent to beg them to return, and said: "Sit down, and do not weep, or you will weaken me. The present life is but a road; the good and the evil pass over it. Or are we better than the patriarchs, the prophets, or the apostles, that we should wish to live in this world forever?" One of those present said a voice choked with tears, "We grieve over this, that this Church shall be destitute, and that the laws of the Church shall be so trodden under foot; it pains us to see how ambition, that knows not the fear of God, strives after episcopal seats, how the poor shall be left desolate, and zeal for the office of preaching shall be forgotten."

Meanwhile Chrysostom had struck his right forefinger into his left hand, as he used to do when he was being critical; now he interrupted the speaker: "That is enough, brother; speak no more; do only one thing; do not be traitors to your Church. The preaching office did not begin with me, and it will not end with me. Moses is dead too, and Josue came in his place; Samuel is dead, and David came in his place. Jeremias departed, and left Baruch behind him; Elias went to heaven and the prophetic office went to Eliseus. St. Paul departed, and there remained Timothy, Titus, Apollo, and many others."

Then Eulysius, the Bishop of Apamea in Bithynia, said: "If we wish to keep our bishoprics, we will be forced to keep ecclesiastical fellowship with our opponents, and sign the decree for your banishment." Chrysostom gave him this advice: "Keep fellowship with them in order not to give rise to heresy; only do not sign the decree. I am not conscious of any deeds for which I deserve to be deposed."[9]

The Summons

While they were still speaking, the news came: the ambassadors of Theophilus stood at the doors.[10]

Chrysostom at once gave the order to admit them. A deep silence reigned in the hall. The messengers entered. They were three men; two of them in clerical garments. Chrysostom asked them what ecclesiastical rank they held. They answered: "We are bishops." They were in fact two young and newly consecrated bishops from Libya (Egypt). So Chrysostom invited them to sit down and declare the reason for their coming. They said: "We only came to deliver a document. So give order that it be read aloud." Chrysostom agreed. They called on the secretary of Theophilus, who had accompanied them, to read the document aloud. He read: "The holy synod, which is assembled at The Oak, to John." The address was significant. It lacked the title of Bishop.[11] He continued: "We have received a writ of accusation against you, which shows innumerable errors on your part. So present yourself to the Synod, and bring the priests Serapion and Tigrius with you.[12] They must be present likewise." With this, the messengers left the hall and the palace.

The bishops at once began to deliberate. They decided to send ambassadors to Theophilus and his "holy synod." The choice fell upon the following three Bishops: Luppicianus of Appiaria, Demetrius of Pessinus, and Eulysius of Apamea; also two priests, Germanus and Severus.[13] They had a letter to bring to Theophilus, which ran as follows: Do not destroy ecclesiastical order and call down heresy upon the Church, for the sake of which God became man. But if you, against all law, disregard the canons of the 318 Bishops of Nicaea, and sit in judgment in a diocese other than your own, then come to us in this city, where the laws are valid, and do not call Abel out into the field like a new Cain; after that we will hear you. In our hands is an accusation against you, which numbers seventy points, all of them signifying public lapses. Moreover, we are more numerous than your synod, and are assembled with the grace of God, not for the destruction of the Church, but for the restoration of peace. You are 36 Bishops from one single province;[14] we are 40, from various provinces, and among us are not fewer than 11 Metropolitans. It is right and just that the smaller part should be judged by the larger and the more distinguished.[15] We also have a letter from you, in which you warn our fellow Bishop John not to accept any accusations from any other provinces. Then obey the church statutes yourself, and produce your accusers, that they may either desist from the accusation against you, or cease applying to him (Chrysostom).

That was a well deserved, but dignified and manly answer. To Chrysostom the tone might have appeared somewhat too quarrelsome. He said, full of deep feeling, to the bishops: "Give the answer which you consider right and good; I must answer that which has been written to me." So he sent to Theophilus, for himself personally, and for his bishops, the following letter: "Until this hour I had never yet learned that anyone had reason to bring an accusation against me. But if anyone has complained of me, and I must appear before you, then first expel from your midst my open enemies, who of their own fault have let themselves be prejudiced against me. Those whom I decline to have as judges are: Theophilus, whom I accuse of having said in Alexandria and in Lycia, *I am going to the Residence (that is, Constantinople) to depose John.* That this is founded on truth is shown by the fact that he has never met with me since his arrival here, and has held no fellowship with me. So if he has allowed such a spirit of enmity toward me to appear before the hearing, what will he do in the court? In the same way I decline Acacius, who uttered this expression: 'I will soon burn his soup for him.' Of Severian and Antiochus (whom Divine justice will seize only too soon) I do not need to speak. Their rabble-rousing conduct has already been an object of scorn in the worldly theaters. So if you really wish me to appear, then please remove these four, at least as judges, from your midst. If they wish to enter as accusers, let them appear before the court. But I wish to know beforehand whether I am to have them as judges or accusers, if I set foot on the battlefield. I am quite resolved to appear, not merely before you, but before any synod you wish, wherever it may be. But know that you will get no other answer from me, though you send to me ever so often."

This clear and resolute speech gives evidence of the absolute confidence which Chrysostom had in the righteousness of his cause, and in his own innocence. That was his point of view, the only right one in his case, and he adhered to it during the whole time.

When the messengers from the Synod of the Oak returned with this answer to the worthies who had sent them, good advice was much needed. From a legal standpoint, the conduct of Chrysostom could not be objected to. As it is today, also in those times every accused person had the right to reject as judges those of whose impartial judgment he entertained doubts. But if the four ringleaders departed, what would the others be able to do?

The crafty Theophilus had, however, considered the possibility of Chrysostom's rejection. He had just before, probably through Eudoxia's mediation, obtained an order from the Emperor, by which Chrysostom was compelled to appear against his will before the Synod, just as it was. God alone knows whether Arcadius knew what paper he set his signature to. Shortly after Chrysostom's answer to the Synod, an imperial notary brought him a summons to appear before the Synod. The corresponding petition of the Synod to the Emperor was enclosed with the document, or incorporated in it. What answer Chrysostom gave to the imperial notary Palladius does not say: it may have been essentially the same as the one he sent to the Synod. With this, the entire affair became concerned with a dead issue. Chrysostom had, through the position he had taken, broken off the point of the sword which was to pierce him. What would happen now?

Neither the Emperor nor the Synod was able to move the Archbishop from his perfectly legal position. The members of the Synod felt the painfulness, not to say the ridiculousness of their position. Their mood became irritable. Two who were present decided, either on their own responsibility or with the consent of the others, to go to the Archbishop.

These two had been subjects of Chrysostom: one was the priest Eugenius, who later was made Bishop of Heraclea for his treachery, and the other was Isaac, the father of the monks. They spoke harshly to their bishop: "The synod has written to you; come before us and defend yourself against these accusations brought against you!" At that, Chrysostom sent three more bishops to the synod with this answer: "By what right do you judge me, since you not only do not exclude my enemies, but have me summoned by my own clergy?"

Chrysostom was not really obliged to yield to such a summons from his own subordinates. Some members of the Synod fell into downright fury, which they presently vented in the most public way on the ambassadors of their hated victim. They assailed the three bishops like bandits, struck one until he bled, tore the clothing off another, and put an iron chain about the neck of the third. It was said that these things were meant for Chrysostom, should he appear. It had been intended to bring him on board a ship immediately after the condemnation, to load him with chains, and take him away to some place unknown to the public.[16]

The three evilly-treated victims of Egyptian hot-bloodedness returned to the Archbishop's palace. Their appearance spoke louder than words. Chrysostom and his friends now knew what spirit ruled in the palace of Rufinus, and what he had to expect, if these people managed to obtain the imperial *placet* for their ends and aims. To obtain this would not be difficult, in the present state of affairs. Under the circumstances, nothing else remained for him but, defenseless and powerless, to let things take their course. One single way of rescue might be possible for him: namely, flight. St. Athanasius had chosen this way in times past; and it was good, that he thus preserved himself from his own enemies and those of the Church. But Chrysostom did not think of flight. A personal conversation with the Emperor would perhaps have brought about a change. Arcadius was not malicious; but the way to him was obstructed by Eudoxia, and she was herself the unwitting victim of malicious plots and intrigues.

The tragedy pursued its course. Theophilus saw that he would never have the satisfaction of seeing the Archbishop of Constantinople before his judgment seat. He therefore decided to go ahead without him, and to condemn him *in contumaciam*.[17] So the Synod assembled for a solemn judgment. Whether from prudence or spite, or both, Theophilus did not take over the presidency himself, but allowed the Metropolitan of Heraclea to preside.[18]

Photius[19] says that the Bishop of Heraclea at that time was that Paul who had accompanied Chrysostom two years before in his journey to Asia. So Paul might have stood well with Chrysostom at that time. But, if Photius is right, one must assume that Paul, for reasons of opportunity, let himself be directed by the wind from the imperial palace. At any rate, he must have died shortly after the Synod of the Oak, for in late autumn of 403, Chrysostom consecrated his priest Serapion as Bishop of Heraclea. He was, in turn, deposed the following year, in the Johnite persecution, and in his place entered the priest Eugene, as a reward for his treachery to Chrysostom.[20]

On the part of Theophilus a double malice lay in the fact that he turned over the presidency to the Metropolitan of Heraclea. The proud Patriarch could thus express the fact that canon 3 of the Council of Constantinople (381), which set this bishop next lower in rank to the Bishop of Rome, for him did not exist; so that by law, the Bishop of Constantinople would only be a suffragan of the Metropolitan of Heraclea, as had actually been the case earlier.

Lübeck[21] believes that Theophilus had, by his own earlier presidency of the Synod, wished to give the Synod "as legitimate a stamp as possible," and, on Chrysostom's refusal to recognize him as judge (on account of his inimical attitude), to give over the presidency to Paul of Heraclea, as the only chief Metropolitan present. But since the Bishop of Constantinople, through the Council of 381, actually took away the jurisdiction of Heraclea, and that of the Patriarch of Alexandria was never placed under it, the legitimate stamp could not be arrived at. The purpose of Theophilus went much deeper. He wished by this to bring out the fact that *he* did not recognize the canon of the Council in general, and considered himself always the first of the hierarchy in the East. Thereby also, in his design, the Bishop of the capital reverted to the position he held before 381, although all the other

Eastern Bishops had ratified or recognized this canon of the Council.[22]

So after the Presidium was settled, the first accuser appeared. It was the deacon John,[23] whom Chrysostom, just at the beginning of his rule, had expelled from the ranks of the clergy for murder or manslaughter, so he was a very respectable fellow. His complaint ran thus:

1. Chrysostom had treated him unjustly, in that he deposed him; because he himself had "struck" his own servant, or slave, Eulalius, evidently so that the poor man had died as a result.

2. At the command of the Archbishop, the monk John was struck, and even (in prison) was burdened and loaded with chains like a madman. This John was one of the monks who had come forward as accusers of the Tall Brothers, and had been taken into custody. (Chrysostom had nothing to do with that affair. This same John had come forward in the Synod as accuser against Heraclidus of Ephesus and Bishop Palladius of Helenopolis.)

3. He had sold a large number of jewels (from the Church treasury).

4. He had sold marble which the Patriarch Nectarius had intended for the adornment of the Church of the Resurrection. (Naturally, Chrysostom, by the same right with which Nectarius had bought it, could sell it again, and use the money for the building of his hospitals.)

5. He had called fellow members of the clergy dishonorable, evil men, who were capable of anything, and not worth three obols.

6. He had called St. Epiphanius a gossiper and a fanatic.

7. He had made trouble for Bishop Severian, by setting the deacons on him.

8. He had written a book against the clergy, in which he had slandered them and made insinuations against them. (Probably by this was meant the book against the *Syneisaktai*.)

9. He had, in full assembly of the clergy, accused the three deacons Acacius, Edaphius and John, of stealing his maphorion (mantle), and said that they had perhaps taken it for a very different purpose.

10. He had consecrated Antonius bishop, although this man was accused of being a grave-robber. (At any rate, Chrysostom himself was convinced of the falseness of this accusation.)

11. He had betrayed the hiding place of Count John during a military revolt.

12. He had neglected to offer a prayer, either on the way to the Church or on entering the same.

13. He had ordained priests and deacons without the altar.

14. He had once consecrated four bishops in a single ceremony.

15. He had allowed women to visit him, without having anyone else present. (As Bishop, he did not need to have underlings as witnesses and spies on his virtue.)

16. He had sold an inheritance which a certain Thecla had left to him, or to the Church.[23a]

17. No one knew for what purposes he used the income of the Church.

18. He had ordained the deacon Serapion to the priesthood while he was under accusation.

19. He had had people thrown into prison who were in ecclesiastical fellowship with the whole world; and he did not bother about those who died in prison, and not once did he have their bodies brought out of the prison. (This point, again, obviously concerns the imprisoned monks of Theophilus.)

20. He had insulted the most holy Bishop Acacius, and never spoke to him afterwards.

21. He had had the priest Porphyrius exiled through Eutropius.

22. He had also caused the priest Venerius to be exposed to much shame.

23. He had the bath (in the bishop's palace) warmed for himself alone, and when he was ready, Serapion closed the doors, so that no one else could take a bath.

24. He had conducted ordinations without witnesses.

25. He ate alone, and gorged like a Cyclop.

26. When he presided as judge, he was the same time accuser and witness, as in the case of the Deacon Martyrius, and also of Bishop Prohairesius, in Lycia.

27. He had given Memnon a blow in the face, in the Church of the Apostles, so that blood flowed from his mouth, whereupon he nevertheless offered the Holy Mysteries.[24]

28. He put on and took off his liturgical garments at the throne, and ate (after Communion) a little piece of bread.[25]

29. He gave money to the bishops who had been consecrated by him, in order to bring the clergy under his sway.[26]

In this last point, the idea of Theophilus is not to be misjudged. If Chrysostom helped poor newly-consecrated bishops with money, it must have been to bring them into dependence on him, in order to enlarge his power in the Church!

So these were the accusations of the Synod of the Oak against the Archbishop of Constantinople. For many of the points, one does not know whether to blush or to laugh. Even Socrates calls them simply "stupid."[27] The points lack all organization, and seem to have been written down just as one or another had interrupted in the general conference. Theophilus must have checked them at the last. If the whole gives an impression of being a frivolous, far-fetched and even forced attempt at accusation, and often bore on the face of it the stamp of spiteful misunderstanding, yet it is to be regretted that the information at hand is not sufficient to examine each point for inconsistency. However, all these accusations, even had they been less dishonest, would not have been enough to depose a Bishop of Constantinople. Therefore the accusers wished to compensate by a large number of points for what they lacked in importance and significance.

But the members of the Synod had only arrived at the second point when they were interrupted by another quarrel. Bishop Macarius of Magnesia[28] and the monk John,[29] who were mentioned in the second point against Chrysostom, brought an accusation against Heraclidus, Metropolitan of Ephesus, and Palladius, Bishop of Helenopolis. He accused the first of being an Origenist and a thief; he had stolen the garments of the deacon Aquilinus at Caesarea in Palestine, and, nevertheless, Chrysostom had made him Bishop of Ephesus! The last was doubtless the real crime of Heraclidus.[30]

But John also accused Chrysostom himself of being to blame, because he (John) had had to suffer much malice from Serapion on account of the Origenists. It is not clear whether the synod also discussed the deposition of these two bishops; at any rate, there remained no time for carrying it into effect. After these accusations had been heard, and perhaps decided on, the Synod went on with the examination of the points against Chrysostom; there were too many of them to discuss thoroughly. They chose the ninth and the twenty-seventh for discussion. Then came another interruption. The Abbot Isaac began to blame the same Heraclidus for being an Origenist, and for having kept fellowship with St. Epiphanius neither in the church nor at table.

Not satisfied with this, or with the writ of accusation of the deacon John, the pious man (Isaac) read aloud to the Synod a special and individual writ of accusation against Chrysostom. To the 29 previous points he now added 17 further lapses, for which his Archbishop should be brought to the reckoning.

1. First, the document read, the before-mentioned monk John had been beaten and put in chains on account of the Origenists.

2. St. Epiphanius had not wished to hold fellowship with Chrysostom, by order of the Origenists Ammonius, Euthymius and Eusebius, and also Heraclidus and Palladius.

3. Chrysostom broke the laws of hospitality by always eating alone.

4. He had said in the church that the altar was full of Erinnyes (goddesses of vengeance).

5. He had said in the church, "I am entirely beside myself," and he should have explained who the Erinnyes were and what he meant by saying "I am entirely beside myself," for his listeners did not understand it.[31]

6. He misled sinners into criminal over-confidence by saying: "If you sin yet again, repent of it yet again, and as often as you fall, come to me and I will heal you."

7. He uttered blasphemy in the church when he said: "Christ's prayers (in the Garden of Olives?) were not heard because He did not pray in the right way."

8. He incited the people secretly to oppose the Synod of the Oak.

9. He had taken in pagans who had done the Church much evil; he had tolerated them and taken them under his protection. (Perhaps the Goths under Gainas were meant.)

10. He went into other dioceses and consecrated bishops there.

11. He insulted bishops by (ἐκπιγγάτους) ordering them out of his house.

12. He also insults the clergy by new and unheard-of humiliations.

13. He has taken foreign deposits (of money?) by force.

14. He had performed ordinations without consulting the clergy, even against their wishes.

15. He has had dealings with the Origenists; but those who were in good standing in the Church, and had come with letters of recommendation (from Theophilus) he had not liberated when they were thrown into prison, and when one of them died there he did not concern himself about it.

16. He had consecrated, as bishops, men who were slaves, and had not been freed, even those who were under accusation.

17. He himself, Isaac, had suffered much from him.

Of these remarkable accusations of Isaac, only the second and the seventh were proved. Then came the third point in deacon John's series. Here the aged Arsacius, Archpriest of Constantinople, figured, likewise the priest Atticus, as witnesses against their own Archbishop. Arsacius was the brother of Nectarius, the predecessor of Chrysostom. It was said of him that he had refused all bishoprics all his life, in order only to be able to become the successor of his brother.[32] His ambition was to be fulfilled for a short time. A very dangerous character was the much younger Atticus, an Armenian by birth. Palladius says of him, perhaps with exaggeration, that he had been the chief instigator of most of the intrigues against Chrysostom, and had constantly worked against him from ambush.[33] Atticus, indeed, may have been the secret clerical leader of the enemy group in Constantinople. In the principal affair, however, the leadership of the whole lay doubtless in the hands of Patriarch Theophilus, who surely did not need to learn anything of intrigue from the priest Atticus.

However, Atticus now came out into the open as an opponent of his Bishop, and that as a witness, not as an accuser. Apparently he was not motivated by hatred against Chrysostom, but by an excessive ambition, to enter into his place as soon as possible. His wish was also to be fulfilled. The cunning Armenian was actually the successor of his fellow-witness and fellow-betrayer Arsacius in the See of Constantinople.

The priest Elpidius was associated with this group as a third member. He also entered as witness for the third point of accusation. For the fourth point (of the deacon John) came as fourth witness the priest Acacius. Twelve sittings had been held already over these.[34]

The Judgment

At last it seemed to the members of the Synod that they had done enough for the pacification of their consciences and for the benefit of law. The above-named four priests, to whom were added Eudaimon and Onesimus, now made the proposal that the Synod should hasten to conclude its business and pronounce a judgment. This was applauded. The presiding officer of the Synod, Paul of Heraclea, proposed that each one should give his own judgment. And so it was done. The Bishop Gymnasius was first.

When the turn of Bishop Acacius came, he felt, in the consciousness of his wrongdoing, the necessity of vindicating his conduct. "If I knew," he said, "that John would reform himself, if we grant him pardon, and if he would leave off his hardness and rudeness, I would have interceded for him with you all." So obviously he believed that he had to doubt Chrysostom's ability to reform, and considered himself thenceforth justified in voting for his deposition, without further ado. It is noteworthy that St. Cyril of Alexandria spoke in the year 432 of this speech of Acacius as an "admirable judgment," since "his holiness (Acacius) had spoken the truth at that time.[35] So even non-participants and highly placed people could not judge it objectively. St. Cyril was

I

the nephew and later successor of the Patriarch Theophilus. His uncle had brought him to Constantinople with him, and so the young Cyril was a witness of the proceedings at the Synod of the Oak, even though he could take no actual part in it, as he was not a bishop.[36]

The voting on Chrysostom took its course, which from the beginning showed all the participants to be of the same mind. One after another voted guilty and for deposition. The last who gave his vote was Theophilus.[37]

So he had at last attained his ardently desired goal. His wrath and thirst for revenge were satisfied. Thirty-six and more signatures stood under the deposition judgment against him before whose court he was to have appeared.

The Synod sent at once to the Imperial Majesty the news of what had been done, and also in a special letter informed the clergy of Constantinople that their Bishop had been deposed.

In their message to the Emperor the Bishops explained: " John is accused of some misdemeanors, but, in consciousness of his faults, refused to appear. On this the canons set the punishment of deposition. This sentence has been passed. But the writ also includes the accusation of treason against the Emperor. So Your Serenity might command that he be deposed against his will, and punished as one guilty of high treason. It is not in our power to judge this crime."[38]

O you thrice miserable ones! Palladius exclaims here, you speak not from the fear of God, but from fear of men!

For the crime of treason against the Emperor, the punishment was death. Theophilus scarcely believed in earnest that this could happen. But in public it was already being spoken of. Indeed, there were people who already knew absolutely that Bishop John was to be executed by the axe.[39]

*　　　*　　　*

At last, when it was all ended, three more Bishops appeared; Gerontius of Nicomedia, Faustinus and Eugnomonius; they complained that they had been unlawfully deposed by Chrysostom. Perhaps the Synod restored them to their offices and dignities. At any rate, after Chrysostom's second banishment, they took possession of their sees again without further legal proceedings.

From the imperial court, in a short time, the verdict of deposition, probably prepared beforehand, was promulgated. But there was no further mention of treason. Eudoxia would not take such odium upon herself. She was prudent enough to remain in the background and to pass on to others the responsibility of the Synod of the Oak.

With this the Synod concluded its ignoble activities. It had assembled in defiance of the ecclesiastical canons, and had proceeded in defiance of them. Injustice and foul play were its consequences.

Theophilus himself had later done everything that he declared illegal, and his "synod" had done everything for which he had reproached Chrysostom. He had saved himself from being judged outside his diocese by a bishop not belonging to it. He himself had gone from Egypt to Thrace, and had sat in judgment on the Bishop of Constantinople, outside his own diocese. He had accused Chrysostom of ordaining people who were under accusation. He himself had received complaints from accused and convicted clergy, and those deposed by their own bishops, and he had restored them again, illegally, to their ecclesiastical rank, and had made at least one of them a bishop.[40]

Openly, clearly, and at the same time cynically, the Patriarch could not condemn himself and his doings. The haste with which he had carried out the whole affair proved that they were only concerned with the importance of form, and with outward appearances.

After they saw that their victim was not to be brought to appear before them, they dispatched the whole affair, both lawsuit and judgment, against Chrysostom, and also that against Heraclidus, in a single day.[41] There is in the history of the Church a synod in which another Patriarch of Alexandria was opposed to another Archbishop or Patriarch of Constantinople, in hate and enmity, in the year 449. It bears the significant title of the "robber synod." The Synod of the Oak is a worthy model and counterpart of this.[41a]

So the chief business of the Synod was thereby dispatched.

As a mere side-issue, the affair of the Egyptian monks was now taken up. Since Theophilus felt himself the victor in the principal issue, he must have been in a very good mood. That worked for the good of the Egyptian monks. Without Chrysostom, they were certainly not at all to be feared any more. So the Patriarch treated them like ill-bred children, who had done something stupid, and who would be pardoned, if they would ask for it.

The poor monks must have been shocked and overwhelmed enough at the course of events. They had sought in vain, from every possible bishop, protection and justice against the Patriarch of Egypt; in vain they had turned to Chrysostom, in vain to the Emperor and Empress. The best and the most powerful had become, in the main, the victim of their appearance. It seemed as if the powers of earth and hell had conspired against them. Now they stood, after all the tumult, trouble and sorrow of the past months and years, just as helpless and perplexed as they had been at the beginning. To fill up the measure of their unhappiness, they had lost their most distinguished leaders, one after another. First, their ninety-year-old Bishop Dioscurus had sunk into the grave. The corporal and spiritual austerities and the tumult of the past two or three years had broken his already weak vital powers. He was buried before the gates of Constantinople, in the chapel of a martyr. The respect which the people felt for this honorable old man was so great that the memory of the martyr was entirely overshadowed by the brilliance of the new guest, so that henceforth the fine ladies of the neighborhood swore no more by the name of the martyr, but much more often by the "prayers of Dioscurus."[42]

Ammonius, also, had his health ruined by the pressure of the physical and moral sufferings which he endured. The course of affairs before and during the Synod of the Oak had taken from him every hope of finding right and justice in this world. He died before the Synod came to an end. At the sight of the noble dead, even Theophilus seems to have become soft-hearted for a moment. At least Sozomen says that the Patriarch shed tears of honest emotion at the deathbed of Ammonius, and declared that all his life long he had never found a monk equal to him.[43] The monks of the mon-

astery of Rufinus buried him in their oratory near the Church
of the Apostles.[44] Miracles occurred at his grave.[45]

The third victim of death in this unhappy year seems to
have been the priest and guestmaster Isidore, with whom the
whole quarrel had had its beginning. According to Palladius,[46] Isidore was already sixty years old in 388, and he lived
15 years longer. So he must have died about 403.

And finally a fourth, one of the two Hieraxes, who had
lived entirely in the desert for 29 years, and had first come
to Constantinople because of Theophilus' quarrel; he found
that he had had enough of the world. After the death of
Ammonius, he sought out the most remote place in the desert
waste, in order at last to close his days in peace with God.[47]
So it is not surprising that the men who were left, these men
of the desert who were dogged by misfortune, at last did not
know what to make of this hopeless affair, and they suffered
a loss of morale.

That was the favorable moment for Theophilus. The
monks were led before the Assembly of Bishops who had just
been practising all sorts of sleight-of-hand against their own
colleagues.

The chief question of the whole dispute, the condemnation
of the writings of Origen, was passed over now in silence, a
clear proof that Theophilus himself did not believe in the
" Origenism " of the monks whom he had persecuted.[48] On
the other hand, the Patriarch began to speak, and invited
them in a friendly tone to retire into themselves henceforth,
and to do penance, saying that he was ready to forgive everything and to forget what had gone before. The Egyptian
Bishops spoke to them presently to the same effect, and acted
as though the other Bishops had begged them for clemency
for the monks. So much kindness and sympathy from a party
from which for a long time they had received only violence
and persecution perplexed the monks, and softened their
hearts: they, the victims, begged Theophilus, their persecutor, for pardon and clemency! And Theophilus, gener-
ously, pardoned them; this was also a "moral" victory on
his part!

With this, the question seems to have been settled. The
all-powerful Patriarch had come to Constantinople as a defen-

dant; now he could leave it as a victor over all his actual and presumed enemies. From henceforth no one would ever dare bring an accusation against him again. He had beaten the whole troop of monks, he was victorious over the first Bishop of the Empire. He had come to depose him, and he had kept his word. He, the Patriarch of Alexandria, had hurled from his throne the Bishop of the capital city, the celebrated, much admired Chrysostom. Theophilus really stood at the height of his power, and also of his conceit.[49]

FOOTNOTES

1. Palladius 8 (29).

2. Today the place is called Djadi-Bostan, according to the conclusive researches of J. Pargoire, Rufinianes = Byz. Zeitschrift 8 (1899) 462 ff. and 11 (1902) 333-357 and idem, L'Eglise Sainte-Euphémie et Rufinianes à Chalcédoine = Echos d'Orient 14 (1911) 107-110; R. Janin, La banlieue asiatique = Echos d'Orient 22 (1923) 57 and 182-190.

3. Palladius. Hist. Laus. 11 (ed. Butler 2, 34; Pargoire, Rufinianes Byz. Zeitschrift 8 (1899) 436.

4. Hom. contra Judos et theatra n. 1 (56, 265).

5. Vita Hypatii of Callinicus AA. SS. Junii III 308-349; 3 a ed. Junii IV 247-82; ed. Sodal. Bonn (1895) 3-110. Should there not be a causal connection between the visit of Chrysostom and the re-colonization of the monastery? Callinicus, the biographer of St. Hypatius, always speaks with great reverence of Chrysostom, whereas he mentions for instance Theophilus not even once, not even for the Synod of the Oak.

6. According to Photius (Bibl. 59), Paul of Heraclea was also present. The question of the exact date of the beginning of the Synod of the Oak can only be answered with a certain probability. In any case, the Synod began quite a while after the departure of St. Epiphanius from Constantinople (at the beginning of May 403) and about a month after the arrival of Theophilus in Chalcedon. Tillemont, Mémoires 11, 194, Art. 70 sets this arrival, at the latest, on the 18th of June. After that, in July, the Synod began. Montfaucon follows him in this (Vita = 47. 195). On the other hand, Stilting dates the arrival of Theophilus on or near the beginning of August, and the beginning of the Synod in the first days of September (*loc. cit.* no. 958 f., p. 591). This method of procedure is not very probable, judging by the previous course of

events. Ubaldi also follows him, La Sinodo 63. As a matter of fact, Epiphanius left Constantinople at the beginning of May 403. Soon after, Chrysostom preached the sermon on the women, whose falsified text made the Empress so angry that she decided to get rid of the troublesome preacher of morals, once and for all. So this sermon must not have been spoken until after Alexandria. Then came the journey of Theophilus to Constantinople; at least part of the journey was by land. For all this, the space of time of five or six weeks would be decidedly too short. Palladius also says (Ch. 9, col. 32), as does Stilting (n. 958), that between the return of Chrysostom and the second banishment "nine or ten" months elapsed. But the second banishment followed on the 20th of June 404, when the time of the first banishment is given as about the end of September 403. Maruthas, who had been a doctor, then a priest and bishop in Greater Armenia, came repeatedly to Constantinople as a mediator between the Emperor and the King of Persia, in ecclesiastical affairs. So it may well have been only consideration for the Court that brought the otherwise zealous bishop to the side of Theophilus. Concerning his other activities, cf. Ralph Marcus, The Armenian Life of Marutha, p. 51.

7. In regard to the number of bishops, Palladius contradicts himself. In Ch. 3 (12) he says that Chrysostom was condemned in a public process by 36 bishops, of whom 29 were Egyptians, while 7 others came from other regions. In Ch. 8 (29) on the other hand, he claims that the ambassadors of the Chrysostom-synod said to Theophilus: " You are the 36th out of the same eparchy," which can only mean that the 36 came out of Egypt, while they themselves, the bishops about Chrysostom, were not only numerous—namely 40—but they came from various eparchies. Photius (Bibl. 59) finally gives the number of bishops at the Oak as 45. The total number of 36 may be correct, since Palladius emphasizes it twice, and Marcellinus Comes confirmed it in the year 403, when there was an inexactitude in regard to the arrival of the bishops. On the other hand, probably later, other bishops who had not been present at the Synod of the Oak appeared, to set their additional signatures to the decree of deposition. Bishop Eulysius of Apamea spoke out in the presence of Chrysostom the fear that they would probably be forced, if they wished to keep their bishoprics, not only to hold ecclesiastical fellowship with his victorious opponents, but to set their signatures under the decree of deposition. Chrysostom then said to them, You can hold fellowship; but sign you shall not. (Palladius 8, col. 28.) S. Vailhé, Le droit d'appel *loc. cit.* 143 has recognized the juridical

side of the question, when he says that through the imperial order to Theophilus to judge Chrysostom, the earlier command to Chrysostom to judge Theophilus was annulled, wherefore the Synod of the Oak was essentially in the right when the Tall Brothers recalled their complaint against Theophilus. They did this after the deposition of Chrysostom. Also the Synod of the Oak traced back its legal title against Chrysostom to the command of the Emperor. And last, it really expected from the Emperor the execution of their judgment. Still less is it correct to say that the friends of Chrysostom had insisted on a continuation of the Process against Theophilus. Chrysostom had even refused in the presence of the Emperor to begin the process. Only after the Synod of the Oak had he himself asked for a new synod for re-integration and restitution; to this he had a perfect right.

8. Dial. 8 (27).

9. Palladius 8 (28).

10. Palladius could write so, even though Theophilus himself did not preside at the Synod.

11. That was absolutely contrary to law, because it was an indirect condemnation before the judgment.

12. Socrates 6, 15 (709) says they also invited the Lector Paul.

13. Cf. Chrysostom, Letter to Pope Innocent, in Pall. 2 (9).

14. That was not entirely correct. Only 29 out of 36 were Egyptians. That mistake may be laid to the reckoning of Palladius, who reports here from memory.

15. This "principle of the majority," on which the bishops called, reveals also that to them the Primacy of Rome had not entered very vigorously into their consciences as yet.

16. Pall. Dial. 8 (29).

17. Socrates 6, 15 (712), and, supported by him, also Photius, says that Chrysostom was invited four times.

18. Photius Bibl. 59 (103, 113).

19. Bibl. 59 (103, 113).

20. Pall. Dial. 8 (29); Tillemont (Mém. 11, 603-604) gets out of this difficulty by assuming that there was a second Heraclea, whose bishop was named Paul. Such multiplication of places and persons out of mere embarrassment does not do. Either one must also assume that Photius erred by reason of a mere conjecture, or that Theopilus himself presided, as he was also the Spiritus rector of the Synod. At any rate, Palladius represents Theophilus as the leading figure in the Synod.

21. Reichseinteilung p. 212.

22. A very interesting confirmation of this struggle, which lasted for three decades more, which Alexandria made to prevent Con-

stantinople's elevation in rank from being recognized, is found in the Coptic Acts of the Council of Ephesus (German by Kraatz = T. u. U. NF. XI. 2 [1904] 9-10). According to this, the Emperor sent his message to the Council, addressed: To the holy Nestorius and Cyrillus. At once the Apa Victor, Cyril's ambassador, protested and said: In conformity with rank and episcopal dignity, it is fitting to give the first place to the seat of Alexandria; and as far as time was concerned, Apa Cyril had been Bishop long before Nestorius. But the best way was to name no names, and simply to address the letter to the Synod.

However, there are some doubts of the account of Photius. First, Palladius says not a word of the fact that the Metropolitan Paulus had gone over to the opponents of Chrysostom; although he had had occasion to speak of him. For Paulus must have died soon after the Synod, because Chrysostom, at the end of 403 or the beginning of 404, consecrated his priest Serapion as Bishop of Heraclea. Palladius himself designates (Ch. 8, c. 28) the messengers of the Synod of the Oak as "ambassadors of Theophilus," and also the answer of Chrysostom is addressed to Theophilus. This shows that Theophilus was the real inspiring spirit of the Synod, and Paul solely the presiding business leader. It has practically the same meaning, when Photius himself (*loc. cit.* 105) says that the κατάρχοντες of the Synod were Theophilus, Acacius, Antiochus, etc.

23. The two letters of accusation against Chrysostom were given by Photius (Bibl. 59). Their authenticity is defended by Stilting n. 897 against Baronius, whom Tillemont, *loc. cit.* note 68, had disputed.

23a. Probably meaning the holy Thecla of Seleucia, whom Gregory Nazianzus mentioned in his Carmen II, 2 v. 102 (37, 1550 A); see Holl, Amphilochius p. 11, note 1.

24. This is so much opposed to the whole nature and character of Chrysostom that this point of accusation must have appeared very improbable from the first. Moreover, unfortunately nothing is known of this Memnon or of any such scene in the church. On the other hand, it is known of Nestorius that he once gave palpable proof of his patriarchal displeasure to an overzealous monk who wished to prevent him from celebrating the Eucharist on the ground of heresy. (Mansi 4, 1104.)

25. The Greeks to this day distribute little pieces of bread at the end of the Divine Liturgy, the ἀντίδωτον which they eat in their places. And the bishops put on and take off their pontifical vestments at the throne.

26. The δι' αὐτῶν I relate to χρήματο.

27. Ἀτόπους HE 6, 15 (67, 709).

28. Photius, Bibl. 59 (105).

29. *Ibid.* col. 109. Socrates 6, 17 is certainly in error when he says that the proceeding against Heraclidus did not take place until after the return of Chrysostom from exile.

30. Ubaldi, p. 92 (60) establishes the proceeding against Heraclidus entirely on the conclusion that Photius says that this proceeding had been the thirteenth, while against Chrysostom twelve sittings had been held. However, Photius says expressly (*loc. cit.* col. 109) that the proceeding against Heraclidus was interpolated between the discussion of the second and ninth points of accusation against Chrysostom. So it is clear that only on archival grounds was the protocol on the twelve sittings against Chrysostom stored up in a bundle as πρᾶξις 1-12, while the protocol on the proceeding against Heraclidus was attached separately as πρᾶξις 13.

31. The edition of Hoeschel (MG 103, 112) makes two points out of Point 5, and therefore eighteen altogether.

32. Palladius 11 (36).

33. Dialogus 11 (37).

34. Photius *loc. cit.* (113).

35. Epist. 33 ad Acacium Ber. ep. (77, 159). Unfortunately St. Cyril forgot that the Arians also reproached his great predecessor, St. Athanasius, with being "arrogant and presumptuous, the author of quarrels and riots." Sozomen HE II, 31 = 67, 1025.

36. At the Council of Ephesus, which shows externally many similarities with the Synod of the Oak, Cyril must have allowed himself to say that he now persecuted Nestorius with the same "mania" with which Theophilus had persecuted John. Also the Abbot Dalmatius was there, the successor of Isaac, one of the chief opponents of Nestorius, while the role which had been played earlier by Severian was taken this time by Proclus, a better man. Unfortunately, Nestorius himself was not so guiltless as Chrysostom. (78, 361.)

37. Photius, Bibl. 59 (103, 113).

38. Palladius 8 (30).

39. Palladius 8 (27).

40. Cf. Chrysostom, Letter to Pope Innocent, in Palladius 2 (9).

41. Palladius 8 (30).

41a. Also Chrysostomus Papadopoulos, the later orthodox Bishop of Athens, in Eccles. Pharos 4 (1909) 327, calls the Synod of the Oak a "robber synod."

42. Palladius 17 (59). According to Sozomen 8, 17 (1560) Dioscurus was buried in the Church of St. Mokion. Perhaps this did

not happen until afterward. Cf. Pargoire, Rufinianes = Byz. Zeit-schrift 8 (1899) 447-49.

43. Pargoire, Rufinianes *loc. cit.* 8 (1899) 448.
44. Palladius 17 (59); Hist. Laus. 11 (Butler 34).
45. HE 8, 17 (1560).
46. Hist. Laus. 1 (Butler 15).
47. Palladius 17 (59).
48. However, Theophilus seems to have had a broad mind, when something was of importance to him. So in the year 411, he consecrated the philosopher Synesius of Cyrene as Bishop and Metropolitan of Ptolemais in Libya (Cyrenaica), although he him-self expressly stipulated that he might keep (1) his wife, and (2) his neoplatonic ideas (for example, belief in the pre-existence of the soul; the allegorical meaning of the Resurrection, and other things). Only his hunting dogs was he ready to sacrifice. Furthermore, Synesius was not even baptized. H. Koch, Synesius of Cyrene = Hist. Jahrbüch. der Görresges. 23 (1902) 751-74; v. Christ, *loc. cit.* 1397; G. Grützmacher, Synesius von Kyrene p. 134 ff.

49. According to Photius, Bibl. 59, the Synod held thirteen sittings. So it might, including the various embassies, have lasted eight or ten days. When Palladius 8 (c. 30) says that the deposi-tion of Bishop John was finished in only one day, that explains how the first eleven sessions were dedicated to preparations, pro-ceedings on other affairs (such as those of the Asian Bishops). In the twelfth, Chrysostom was dispossessed, and in the thirteenth, the reconciliation with the monks took place.

CHAPTER XXIII

FIRST BANISHMENT AND RETURN

So the sentence of deposition of the Synod of the Oak was sent to the imperial palace for ratification and practical execution. Whether Chrysostom was also officially notified of the judgment of the synod is not known. But Theophilus would hardly have denied himself this satisfaction. Furthermore, the members of the Synod, or else Theophilus, gave the Emperor the decisive advice to condemn Chrysostom as guilty of high treason. As has been said before, this was punishable by death. But the Emperor, and still more the Empress, shrank from this. Her religious scruples were stronger than the malicious hatred of her clerical advisers. The Bishop was only to be deposed, and sent into exile. Of course the affair was not so simple. These occurrences in the Church had for a long time been fermenting deeply in the hearts of the people. While treachery and apostasy showed themselves about the chief shepherd, and even within the circle of those who had had to remain true to him, the mass of the people sided with their Bishop, who, from the time of his assumption of office, had spoken, acted and done so much for the poor and the suffering. In the eyes of the simple people it was no treason to sell jewels and marble, and use the money for hospitals; it seemed to them only right and just that he told the truth in the pulpit, not only to the little people, but also to the rich and the great. Already threats against the Synod of the Oak had been uttered here and there, and certainly this conduct of the people was the reason why the affair at the palace of Rufinus was finally carried out with such precipitate haste.

But Bishop Severian had had the audacity to hasten to the Cathedral and announce the Synod's verdict of deposition to the waiting people from the pulpit. He could not let the opportunity pass without once more airing his malice and hatred against Chrysostom. "If John," he cried, "had been condemned for no other reason, his arrogance alone would have been sufficient to justify his deposition. For God pardons all the sins of men, but He hates arrogance, as Holy Scripture teaches! "[1]

The people were angry at this impudence and tactlessness. They streamed in a crowd to the Bishop's Palace, in order to oppose by force the removal of their chief shepherd. Many voices among the people called out: "Let a general council judge in this affair! "[2] Others were still bolder: they openly insulted and cursed the Emperor and the whole Synod, especially Theophilus and Severian.[3]

It was already late in the evening and completely dark[4] when a military division appeared with the leader of the imperial courier service at its head.[5] The multitude made way, and the officer with his soldiers demanded entrance into the episcopal palace. He was led to the Archbishop, and notified him that he was to follow him at once. Chrysostom was placed in the midst of the soldiers, and they went away through the streets of the city to the harbor. A multitude of men accompanied the procession, amid lamentations, and cursing of the Bishops of the Synod.[6] When they had arrived at the harbor the Archbishop entered a ship that lay ready there; the sails were hoisted, and so Chrysostom was taken away into the darkness of the night, out of the city, by the same way on which he had made his solemn entry almost six years before, amid the rejoicings of the people and the welcomes of the court and the highest officials. "So passes the glory of this world."

Slowly the lights of the city faded from the ship, as it sailed away into the darkness of the night.

Arrived at the Asiatic side of the Bosporus, the exile had to go further the same night, to a little estate at Praenethus in Bithynia.[7] Whether the estate was an imperial villa, or something similar, is not known. Here a preliminary stop was made. Perhaps someone in Constantinople was waiting to see what would be the reaction to the accomplished deed. That their Archbishop should be taken away by night, and under military escort at that, proved that, after all, the possibility of a riot among the people must be reckoned with.

With the people of Constantinople that was no joke under any circumstances. When Bishop Paul of Constantinople was taken into exile by the General Hermogenes at the command of the Emperor Constantius, the people were furious; they stormed the general's dwelling, set it on fire, took Hermogenes on foot in the street and murdered him.[8]

And now the worst had happened. Without a court, without an examination, without defense, Chrysostom had been declared deposed by foreign bishops, and had been taken by armed forces into a still unknown place of exile. Gloomy and oppressive the future lay before him, for the rest of his life. A greater number of bishops, who had adhered to Chrysostom, soon left the city, to return to their dioceses.[8a]

But while Chrysostom meditated over the past and the future in Praenethus, Theophilus was in the most exalted mood in the palace of Rufinus. So he had actually reached his goal! He, the Patriarch of Alexandria, had deposed the Bishop of Constantinople, as he had predicted before his arrival. And from this banishment he would never return, as far as human foresight could tell. It was really a very thorough job which had been accomplished. Theophilus triumphed, Severian gave his malicious tongue free reign, and Atticus calculated in his mind how he could best manage to get rid of the other candidates for the office, and become himself the successor to the exile. All enemies of the fallen one, all envious people, all traitors, all deserters, rejoiced.

The Unexpected Return

All this public and private rejoicing lasted for just one day. Then, like a bolt of lightning from a clear sky, came the unexpected news to this gay company: The Archbishop John is coming back! The Empress has called him back! Brison, the chamberlain, has already been sent to seek him and bring him home! He may come into the city at any moment!

The news sounded so improbable that at the first moment it was considered unbelievable by many, but nevertheless it was true.

How was it possible? What had happened?

What the real reason was, which brought about the sudden

change of affairs, and which was so astonishing and so unforeseen, the world has never learned with certainty. Socrates
and Sozomen say that the threatening attitude of the people
worried the Empress.[9] Theodoret says that on the night after
the banishment a severe earthquake frightened Eudoxia.[10]
Later authors bring these motives together, or tell stories in
order to explain what could not be explained.[11] But the
greatest probability attaches itself to the story of Palladius,
when he says that when only a day had passed since the forcible
removal of Chrysostom from his episcopal see, " there occurred
a misfortune (accident) in the imperial chamber."[12] Probably
delicacy or dynastic reasons hindered Palladius from express-
ing himself more clearly. Still its meaning can be understood
in only one way, and that in relation to the Empress, for she
alone enters into the question here; a θραῦσις had occurred,
which usually occurs in a bedchamber; in other words, the
Empress had had a miscarriage. It lies completely within the
sphere of possibility, indeed of probability, that the spiritual
tumults of recent times, the gloomy feelings of heavy responsibility, the religious fear and terror before a court of divine
judgment, had produced such a result for her.[13]

Whatever the cause may have been, Eudoxia connected it
with the unjust banishment of the Archbishop, and perceived
therein the punishment of heaven for her own guilt. In the
anguish of her heart, she decided to have the exile recalled
at once. Of course the Emperor said yes.

Eudoxia sent for her chief chamberlain, the eunuch Brison,
whose reverence for Chrysostom was well known to her.[14] She
gave him the order to go after the exile at once, in an imperial
ship, and to bring him back without delay.[15]

One can imagine what wretched terror now shook the limbs
of Chrysostom's enemies. Most of them went abroad at once,
or hid themselves in the city, wherever and however they
could. Naturally, the situation was no end painful for that
part of the Constantinople clergy who had been faithless, for
the clergy of the Patriarchal church who had left their
allegiance to their Bishop. How could they greet their chief
shepherd again as Bishop, after all that had happened? How
could they come again before his eyes, without begging and
receiving his pardon for their disgraceful conduct? The

chief offenders preferred rather to remain invisible, and wait.

Socrates,[16] and after him, Sozomen,[17] claim that Chrysostom made no haste about returning. On the contrary. He may actually have delayed in taking possession again of his episcopal see, before an impartial synod had passed judgment upon the accusations of his opponents. Meanwhile, he stayed at a villa belonging to the Empress, named Marianai. Not until the pressure brought to bear by the people, who threatened to riot, did he return.

Such a demand for Chrysostom, as placed conditions on his return, is very possible and even probable. In this lay absolutely no recognition of the legality of the Synod of the Oak. He had already appealed to an impartial synod before his banishment, and he demanded such a synod when he wrote to Pope Innocent, and demanded it repeatedly after his return.[18]

That on this account a slight delay ensued before his return is quite possible, even if neither Chrysostom himself nor Palladius expressly mention it. But not in any case can the delay in his immediate return have been caused by the Archbishop's consideration of canon 4 of the Synod of Antioch in the year 341, which will be spoken of in the following chapter. A delay in his return for such a cause would certainly not have been passed over in silence by Palladius, since he himself says that this canon was used soon afterward by the opponents of the saint, as a weapon against him, and he also tells what answer the friends of Chrysostom gave to this.[19]

It may be still more probable that, since he had been sent into exile at the command of the Emperor, by an imperial officer, he may have had misgivings about returning at the mere invitation of the Empress, without having the formal edict of banishment rescinded by the Emperor. So that would be best explained by supposing that first Brison and then a special notary (adjutant) of the Emperor had been sent to him.[19a]

The news of their Archbishop's summons to return electrified all Constantinople, and set it into a tumult. Some trembled, some rejoiced. The people came together in crowds, and showed themselves full of impatience to see their beloved Bishop again. For them it was not happening fast enough. The slightest delay made the people mistrustful. Soon they began to complain and to say that the court was not playing an honest game.[20]

Then, finally, it was announced that the Archbishop was on the way, and would arrive in a very short time. An enormous crowd of people gathered to meet him, and greeted and welcomed him with heartfelt gladness and indescribable joy.

He returned to the capital city like a triumphing general. An imperial notary stepped forward[21] to bring him back in the name of the Emperor; thirty bishops followed him, who had held out for him in Constantinople until the last. They were all surrounded and followed by an enormous, inspired multitude of people, who sang psalms and songs of rejoicing, and carried lighted candles.[22] All the city appeared there on foot, although horse races were taking place in the Circus.[23] The way to the episcopal palace led past the Church of the Apostles.[24] There the Archbishop was persuaded to mount the pulpit and say a few words to the people. His short word of greeting still survives.

"What shall I say," he began, "of what shall I speak? God be praised! This was my last word before my departure, and it is my first after my return. With Job I said before: *May the name of the Lord be praised for all eternity.* With Job I now repeat these words: God be praised, Who allowed me to be led into exile; God be praised, Who has led me back again, Who has allowed the quiet warmth of summer to follow the harshness of winter. Many and various things have happened, but one and the same Divine Will, one and the same Divine Providence have guided us. The storm has not disunited us, but has bound us more closely together. Not in vain have I said to you that whoever bears affliction manfully will derive great benefit from it. The apostles, too, had to bear great misfortunes and afflictions. Therefore I have summoned you to them. The church will scarcely hold the multitude of sheep, since the wolves have fled, the robbers and adulterers[25] are dispersed. I did not need to grasp lance, sword or shield. You have driven them away by your tears and your prayers. Therefore they are now in affliction, given over to their evil consciences, but we are full of joy. The Lord bless you and your children, and let us thank the loving God, to Whom be honor for all eternity. Amen.''[26]

So Chrysostom returned as a moral victor to his episcopal see, from which before many days he was to be driven away by military force. The wheel of fortune rolled rapidly at the court of Constantinople. Did Chrysostom believe in its constancy?

On the following Sunday the Archbishop is said to have preached a sermon, the text of which is preserved in George Alexandrinus,[27] and concerning which Sozomen admiringly writes that "in a piquant and delicate way" he compares Theophilus to the Egyptian Pharaoh, who took possession of Abraham's legal wife, and was punished by God for it. But the sermon in the given form can hardly be genuine; still less the one on the Canaanite woman.[28]

But meanwhile where was the Patriarch of Alexandria keeping himself? He had also made himself invisible at the approach of his victim of yesterday. But when he heard that Chrysostom had demanded a new synod to judge between himself and his accusers, and that the Emperor had agreed to his request, he thought his cause was lost. And when it was said that the people of Constantinople were hunting for him, and that they threatened to throw him into the sea,[29] then he lost, if not his presence of mind, at least his feeling of personal security. Because of the threatened involuntary bath, and the responsibility of eluding an impartial synod, the Patriarch prepared for departure, together with his suffragan bishops, as quickly as possible, and under the protection of night, boarded an Alexandrian ship, and fled away from there, in the direction of Egypt.

So departed the man who had earlier boasted that he came to Constantinople to depose Chrysostom; in his party was also the Abbot Isaac, who had found the ground too hot in the capital city.[30]

On his arrival at Alexandria, Theophilus was the object of hostile demonstrations on the part of the people.[31]

So Chrysostom was again installed in office and in his dignities. The storm had passed. The opponents had fled, and Eudoxia, the Empress, at least had to put a good face on the matter.

However, there still remained Chrysostom's chief worry, the calling of a new synod. Above all, he had to get a reversal of judgment on all the accusations publicly brought against him by the Synod of the Oak. This he believed himself bound to do, for his own honor and further security, as well as for his standing as a Bishop.

So he went once more to the Emperor, and besought of him the calling of this synod.[32] Arcadius, who was equally easy to persuade either to good or to bad, without having merit for one, or responsibility for the other, gave his assent without further ado. So once more messengers hastened to the four winds with imperial letters, to call the Bishops of the Empire to a new synod. Theophilus also received a special invitation, summoning him to return without delay, together with his earlier companions, and saying that he was not to believe that his illegal proceedings were hidden under the name of the Synod of the Oak.[33] But Theophilus was not the man to let himself be disconcerted by a letter, even though it bore the Emperor's signature. It seems like sarcasm, when he wrote back saying that he could not possibly come, because the people of Alexandria threatened to riot if he went away, and also that his friends were keeping him back. Actually the people of Alexandria would not have objected if their Patriarch had left for good. The truth might well have been that Theophilus was afraid Chrysostom might now return him like for like, which of course would not have been difficult for him, had he been a character like Theophilus.

So the Patriarch did not come, and Chrysostom, who shortly before had had scarcely a defender at the Synod of the Oak, now could find no accusers. The second official personality of the synod, Paul, the Metropolitan of Heraclea, who had presided over the Synod, need appear no more before any earthly judge. He had died shortly after Chrysostom's return. This gave the Archbishop the most favorable opportunity for taking a step which was forgiving toward his enemies, and honorable for all concerned. He named and consecrated, as successor to Paul, Serapion, whom his enemies hated as a firebrand and cried down as a troublemaker.[34] Through his removal a chief stumbling-block appears to have been removed, and through his elevation to the office of Metropolitan every wrong against the true servant of his Bishop had been righted. This measure was doubtless a proof of political tact, and at least removed a cause of provocation. Unfortunately, other causes were soon found.

Meanwhile, about thirty more bishops had accepted the imperial summons, so that altogether about sixty bishops were assembled in Constantinople. It was probably about the end of October or the beginning of November. These bishops now declared: Everything that the Synod of the Oak had done or decided was null and void; Chrysostom was in legal possession of his episcopal see, and could therefore carry out all the functions of a Bishop, especially "to celebrate the Divine Liturgy, officiate at ordinations, and rule the diocese."[35] So by this he was at least to a certain extent rehabilitated and protected. But a formal and judicial decision between him and his opponents was not made, because the opponents did not appear.

There was also a good reason for that.

FOOTNOTES

1. So it is doubtless to be understood, as Socrates 6, 16 (712) says: "When Severian preached in the church."

2. Sozomen 8, 18 (67, 1561).

3. *Ibid.*

4. Socrates 6, 16 (712) and Sozomen 8, 18 (1561) state, that Chrysostom was taken away about midday, not until three days after the verdict of deposition. But Chrysostom himself wrote in his report to Pope Innocent (Pall, 2, col. 9) expressly, that he was taken from his episcopal dwelling late in the evening" (πρὸς ἑσπέραν βαθεῖαν) and that it was night when the ship sailed. Of a difference of three days between judgment and banishment, Chrysostom mentions nothing; neither does Palladius, ch. 8-9 (col. 30).

5. Chrysostom, Letter to Pope Innocent, Pall. 2 (9). Palladius himself, ch. 9 (30) calls him Comes. Κουριοσσὸς means the chief communications official of a province. Cf. Cod. Theod. 6, 29 ed. Mommsen 290-94.

6. Palladius 2 (9); Sozomen 8, 18 (1561). Zosimus 5, 23 says erroneously that Chrysostom left Constantinople of his own free will. Then he relates that the monks of Constantinople had the

churches garrisoned and hindered the people from entering them. Thereupon the soldiers and the people had killed all the monks whom they could get their hands on, even people who were not monks at all, merely because they happened to be dressed in black. Palladius knows nothing of all this. But it is a fact that a large number of monks possessed character enough to follow, not the wrong way of their spiritual father Isaac, but the right way of their bishop. Cf. pp. 335-336 of this volume.

7. Theodoret 5, 34 says: Chrysostom had to leave the city καὶ τὸ ἐν τῷ στόματι τοῦ Πόντου κείμενον κατέλαβεν Ἱερόν. οὕτω γὰρ ἐκεῖνο τὸ ἐπίνειον ὀνομάζουσι. In the night came a severe earthquake, etc.

8. Socrates 2, 13 (208-209).

8a. Palladius 2 (47, 10).

9. Socrates 6, 16 (712); Sozomen 8, 18 (1561-64).

10. HE 5, 34 (82, 1261).

11. Theodore of Trimithus 23 (47, LXXVIII) casually assumes that fire fell from heaven and consumed the Cathedral together with many buildings, that Chrysostom might be called back! George Alexandrinus 49 (Savile 8, 226) says that the Emperor Honorius sent a letter to Arcadius, then an earthquake took place, and finally an accident in the imperial chamber, and besides, the people threatened to riot. Leo Imperator 24 (Savile 8, 286) says that the imperial chamber was partly upset by the earthquake. Anonymous 69 (Savile 8, 352) mentions the earthquake, the hail and the imperial chamber all at once. Symeon Metaphrastes (26; *ibid.* 401) confuses the matter still further.

12. Ch. 9 (30): Συνέβη θραῦσίν τινα γενέσθαι ἐν τῷ κοιτῶνι.

13. On the 10th of February, 403, Marina, her fourth and last child, was born. The Synod of the Oak took place at the end of September.

14. So according to Socrates 6, 16, and Sozomen 8, 18. Palladius 9 (30) says that a special "notary" was sent. At any rate, that excludes the identity of Brison with the notary. According to Babut, La garde impériale = Revue historique 116 (1914) 261, the word notary might have meant an officer from the personal "general staff," of the Emperor, such as a body-adjutant. It would seem suitable that the Empress would first send her chief chamberlain, while the Emperor then sent his special "notary."

15. According to the Sermo post reditum ab exilio (Ὅτε τὴν Σάρραν) n. 4 = 52, 445, which Sozomen knew and completed, the Empress had even given Brison a letter, in which she assured Chrysostom that she had been completely innocent of any part in the plot which had been concocted against him; indeed, that

she felt the greatest respect for him, the Bishop and the baptizer of her children. But Sozomen may only have been relating fiction here. It is unbelievable that Eudoxia, if she had been deceived herself, would have asserted her full innocence to the Archbishop. The execution of the plans of a Theophilus and Severian would not have been possible without her. She knew that as well as Chrysostom.

16. HE 6, 16 (713).

17. HE 8, 18 (1564); Theodoret, HE 5, 34 (82, 1264) says, that not less than three expeditions had been sent, to seek and bring back Chrysostom, and that the Bosporus had been filled with ships seeking him.

18. Palladius 2 (10). Cf. the next chapter.

19. Dial. 9 (30).

19a. Palladius 9 (ed. Norton 51, 18-19) says vaguely that Chrysostom was called back " in a few days."

20. Sozomen 8, 18 (1564).

21. Palladius 2 (10).

22. Sozomen 8, 18 (1564); Theodoret 5, 34 (82, 1264).

23. Sermo post reditum 1 (52, 440).

24. Sermo post reditum 2 : Ideo vos Apostolos vocavi (52, 440).

25. Adulterers, because his enemies had wished to seize his bride, that is, the Church of Constantinople.

26. 52, 439-442. Concerning the authenticity of this speech, extant only in Latin, but in a double text, an absolutely certain judgment is difficult to obtain. The unusually short, broken-off, desultory phrases, especially of the second part, do not sound like Chrysostom. Yet one may see in them the expression of a joyful excitement and an extemporaneity absolutely unprepared. At any rate, the second composition (441-42) is clear and more connected. The double text recension may be explained by the fact that two stenographers had taken it down.

27. 52, 443-448. Savile (8, 262), Tillemont (11, 606; note 73). Montfaucon (52, 438, with notes) and Stilting (note 952) consider this homily authentic. However, the language and the entire content of the speech do not speak of Chrysostom. Even the note " The baptismal bath was filled with blood," (n. 2) reveals a later author, who confuses the proceedings before the second banishment with those before the first. It is equally improbable that the Empress went to meet the returning Bishop herself (n. 3); this cannot be reconciled with the «θραῦσις» in the imperial bedchamber (Pall. 9; col. 30). Neither is it credible that Eudoxia, in a letter to Chrysostom, should have assured him of her absolute innocence and ignorance of what had been going on (n. 4);

further, that in the imperial palace no one should have known
where the officer with Chrysostom had betaken himself (*ibid.*) and
that Eudoxia had first felt the need of falling at the Emperor's
feet, in order to get the Bishop back, and other things.

28. MG 52, 449 ff.: Πολὺς ὁ χειμών. In the Coptic translation (see Budge, Coptic Homilies p. 133 and 275) a homily with
the same beginning is ascribed to Eusebius of Caesarea, while the
Latin translation (ML 66, 116-124 = de muliere Chananaea) names
the author as Bishop Laurentius mellifluus of Novara (Milan?).
Cf. G. Mercati, A supposed homily of Eusebius of Caesarea, in
the Journal of Theological Studies 8 (1907) 114, and S. Haidacher
in the Zeitschr. f. kath. Theologie 30 (1906) 183. This homily
might, from content and language, belong rather to Severian,
who indeed had been banished for a short time (one day).

29. Palladius 9 (30). According to Sozomen 8, 19, it even came
to bloody blows between Alexandrians and Constantinopolitans;
which was not unusual.

30. Sozomen 8, 19 (1565). That Theophilus began the deposition process against Heraclidus of Ephesus after the return
of Chrysostom, and that this had led to blows between the Alexandrians and the people of Constantinople, and that this was the
reason for Theophilus' departure—all this is highly improbable.
Under the "Monk Isaac" the accusers of Chrysostom would be
secure at the Synod of the Oak, and for the moment in Constantinople there was no more need of his presence; for if a new
synod came together, he would be undone.

31. Palladius 2 (10); Chrysostom said in his letter to Pope
Innocent, that when Theophilus returned, the people had reviled
and cursed him.

32. Palladius 2 (10).

33. Palladius *loc. cit.*

34. Socrates 6, 17 (716); Sozomen 8, 19 (1568).

35. Sozomen 8, 19 (1565); Socrates 6, 18 (720) gives the number
as 65. Chrysostom himself, and also Palladius, mention nothing
of such a formal "absolution", which also clearly alluded to the
two Canons of Antioch which had not yet been invoked by Theophilus. But Palladius also says that, following the Emperor's
summons, the bishops came together and gave their allegiance to
Chrysostom; (Pal. 9, col. 30-31). Photius, Interrogationes et Res-
ponsiones 7 (104, 1288) names the Synod of the Oak among those
synodal decrees which were later annulled by other bishops.

CHAPTER XXIV

NEW INTRIGUES

THE only and the deciding motive for Chrysostom's recall was the personal fear and anxiety which Eudoxia was suffering. The court ladies and all other opponents of the Patriarch remained untouched by all this. The only fear which they felt was the fear of the return of the exile, as sudden as it was unexpected. But they recovered from this quite soon, and all the more easily when their episcopal confederates, especially Severian of Gabala, appeared again among them in a short time, in case they had not found protecting shelter among them before. They quickly formed again that kernel of secret, invisible, incomprehensible resistance, which worked under cover, but which was ready at the first opportunity to come out into the light of day. Their influence with the court is probably to be attributed to the fact that a formal synodal decision between the Archbishop and his earlier accusers had not been reached. The opponents, who may have had a sign, simply did not appear, and there was no one who could compel them to do so. By means of delay and evasion, it was possible for them to hinder the crisis, and win time for a new offensive.

One thing was on the side of this inimical group from the first; they did not long consider themselves as finally defeated, and did not give up their cause. On the contrary, they thought only of how and with what they might take up the battle again, and one thing was perfectly clear to them: if they wished to attain their chief end, to get Chrysostom out of the way, then the Empress must be persuaded over again. In view of the sanguine, easily influenced temperament of this lady, that did not appear to be too difficult. As soon as Eudoxia had recovered from her first terror of the judgment of God, her self-love would awake again. Before the public, she stood in a certain sense as the conquered, and Chrysostom as the conqueror, and she must have felt somewhat ashamed over her fall, before her companions, and the dumb, questioning looks of her court ladies. It could not have seemed very difficult for a company of watching court ladies and intriguing bishops to bring the Empress gradually and cautiously over to their side again.

An unfortunate incident came unexpectedly to their help here. The city prefect of Constantinople at that time, Simplicius, wished to gain the favor of the Empress. He asked permission to erect a silver statue in her honor on the most prominent square in Constantinople. The Emperor gave his assent. About the beginning or the middle of November, 403, the solemn dedication took place with great pomp.[1] In front of the Senate House, opposite the church of Hagia Sophia, and separated from it only by the so-called Broad Street, in the square called Pittakia, was raised on a broad plinth the high porphyry pillar on which stood the silver statue of the Empress, clothed in the imperial mantle. The marble base of the monument, with the dedicatory inscription, has survived to this day, and it stands, with many other memorials, in the army museum, the former church of St. Irene,* as the last evidence in a great human tragedy.

The Greek dedicatory inscription, placed on the plinth in four hexameters, reads as follows:

Behold the porphyry pillar and the silver statue of the Empress,
Here where the rulers of the city speak the laws;
Do you wish to know her name?
It is Eudoxia;
and who had the monument erected?
Simplicius, of the race of great consuls,
the excellent city prefect.

Opposite this stands, in Latin capitals, the following inscription:
To our Empress, Aelia Eudoxia,
the ever fortunate,
this statue has been erected
V.C. Simplicius, city prefect.[2]

* Tr. Note: This was probably the Church of Holy Peace (ἄγια εἰρήνη). It is very doubtful if there ever was a St. Irene.

The erection of such a costly monument to the Empress appears to have been an extraordinary honor, since the ecclesiastical historians and the chroniclers unanimously speak of it. So it is obvious that the dedication was the occasion of the most solemn pomp, and the city prefect furnished very thorough-going popular entertainment, and celebrations, including dances, wrestling matches, theatricals and spectacles of all kinds.[3] Even the imperial Sunday prohibition was dispensed with. The Orientals, and the people of Byzantium, had always been noisy people; but in this sort of popular festival their expressions of joy knew no bounds. And this time it was so loud that people in the church on Sunday could scarcely understand the words of the preacher. Vexed at this state of affairs, in consideration of the holiness of the place and of the divine service, Chrysostom allowed himself to be carried away into one of those unforeseen rhetorical sallies which pleased simple people so much, which were almost never misunderstood in Antioch, but which in Constantinople, so near the Emperor's palace, spoken before officials and court people, in certain circumstances could produce the worst consequences, especially if, misquoted and misunderstood, they reached the "divine ears" of their noble Majesties. The Archbishop gave expression to his displeasure over the fact that the noise and disturbance in the street was not once stilled during the divine service.

The wording of this expression has unfortunately not survived. The most unfortunate aspect of it was certainly the circumstance that it consisted of a celebration in honor of the Empress. This was perfectly sufficient to give malicious minds an occasion for new slanders. They reported to the Empress that the Archbishop had spoken slightingly in public against the erection of her statue.[4] That struck Eudoxia on one of her most vulnerable points. Her wrath flared up again. All good purposes were suddenly forgotten again; all thoughts of conscience suppressed; the old grudge awoke, much strengthened, and the Empress' associates hammered the iron while it was hot.

At once new plans were woven. Acacius, Antiochus, and other opponents of the Archbishop, ventured out into the daylight again, and resumed their councils and conferences. It is not improbable that now, in the absence of Theophilus, the priest Atticus played a leading role, and that he led the thought in these first councils and conferences. Nothing certain can be said about this. The secret of those dark dealings has not been entrusted to history. The new opposition, strengthened and encouraged by the imperial support, came forward slowly into public notice. Chrysostom must soon have noted the signs of a change. In order to force his antagonists out of hiding, and into the open, he went to the Emperor again, and asked to have a new synod called. Then, if Theophilus did not come, still some of the other accusers from the Synod of the Oak would be there. In the presence of these, he was ready to prove his complete innocence.[5] It was only necessary to lay before it the acts of the Synod of the Oak, and the accusatory documents of his opponents, and to judge either his deeds or his accusers. But it was in vain. He could not accomplish anything this time.

Soon after this, in Constantinople, or perhaps out at Hebdomon, the feast of the beheading of St. John the Baptist must have been celebrated. The church there was dedicated to him.[6] Feasts of St. John the Baptist were celebrated on January 7, also on February 24 and September 26. The general feast of the beheading of John,[7] celebrated on August 29 is of later origin. The last date does not come into consideration in this case, for at the end of August, 404, Chrysostom was no longer in Constantinople. Perhaps the celebration commemorated the consecration of the Church of the Baptist, or the translation of his relics into it. At any rate, Chrysostom preached the festival sermon. According to the existing form of the text he began with these words: "Again Herodias rages . . . again she demands the head of John the Baptist!" Of course, in a similar way, he and also other Greek orators, had often enough introduced the yearly return of church feasts. At any rate, again it was reported to the Empress that the Archbishop had compared her to Herodias, in a malicious way, not to be misunderstood; Herodias, who had sought the life of the guiltless John.[8] Of all the things that Eudoxia was capable of, her last thought would be to give any one the death-stroke.

Conferences were held again over this. How awkward and

dependent this whole company was, in spite of the Empress'
alliance with them, is shown by the circumstance that they
knew of nothing better to do than to turn again to Theophilus, the Patriarch of Alexandria, asking him to come to
Constantinople again, and take in hand once more the affair
of Chrysostom; or should he have misgivings about the sentiments of the people of Constantinople, he might at least
suggest how they might go about the matter.[9]

Theophilus actually showed no great desire to place himself again in personal danger. Who could tell what Eudoxia
might do this time? On the other hand, he was quite ready
to take part in this new plot from Alexandria, and to lead it
as well as possible from a distance, as long as nothing else
was expected from him. And this time also, he showed himself at no loss for resources. He quickly sent three Egyptian
Bishops to Constantinople: Paul, Poimenes, and a third,
whom he had consecrated shortly before. He gave them a
copy of the canons, which had been decreed by the Synod of
Antioch in 341, by the Arian bishops, against St. Athanasius,
his own predecessor. But his orders were to the effect that
Chrysostom should be accused and deposed on the ground of
these canons, because of his unauthorized return.[10]

Still, a corresponding court judgment was lacking. So
letters were sent out to the Metropolitans and Bishops of
Cappadocia, Syria, Pontus, and Phrygia, summoning them to
Constantinople. A great number answered the call. Some
of them held fellowship with Chrysostom, as was suitable for
their priestly vocation. But that was not well taken by the
court. When Theodore, Metropolitan of Tyana in Cappadocia, found out what was going on, he would have nothing
to do with the affair, which he saw approaching. Without
greeting or farewell he left the city, and returned to his
diocese. He remained in fellowship with Chrysostom and
with Rome until the end.

But other bishops showed themselves lacking in character.
Pharetrius, the Metropolitan of Caesarea, a man of timid and
servile nature, wrote of his own accord to the opponents of
the Archbishop, and assured them of his partiality for them.
That was pure cowardice toward the court, as no one had
either summoned the old man or asked his opinion.

On the enemy side also were ranged Leontius, Bishop of
Ancyra in Galatia,[11] Ammonius, Bishop of Laodicea adusta,
and Briso, Bishop of Philippi in Thrace. Their choice had
been facilitated partly by threats, and still more by the hope
of rich gifts. Also, in the case of Leontius, personal ill-will
possibly played a part. Perhaps he was that Galatian bishop
who had once preached in Constantinople, but whom the
public did not wish to hear, because it preferred Chrysostom.
At any rate, in the assembly of the opponents of Chrysostom,
Leontius and Ammonius advised Acacius and Antiochus
simply to recognize the judgment of the Synod of the Oak
and of Theophilus, and to declare the Archbishop deposed
on the ground of the above-mentioned canons, *without granting him any opportunity for defense*. But when they came
with this to the Emperor, he seemed not to have agreed to
this simplified procedure. He called a deputation of both
parties.[12] Of the friends of Chrysostom, ten bishops appeared.
Among his opponents were the three inseparables: Acacius,
Antiochus, and Severian. Cyrinus of Chalcedon also came,
hobbling along in spite of his wounded foot. Leontius
appeared with Ammonius, and also the three ambassadors
from Theophilus.

When the deputation was led before the Emperor, Elpidius, the Bishop of Laodicea in Syria, and Tranquillius, the
speaker for Chrysostom's party, came forward and said:
"John cannot be deposed on the ground of these canons,
because, first, he was not deposed before, but simply driven
out of the city; and second, he did not return of his own
accord, but at the command of Your Piety, after a special
notary had been sent to him; and thirdly, we have long ago
proved that these canons originated with the heretics." This
clear, courageous speech irritated the opponents so much that
even the presence of the Emperor could not hold them back.
With loud voices, violent gestures, and angry faces, they
shouted at each other; Chrysostom, they said, was deposed by
a lawful synod, and the canons in question were proclaimed
by orthodox bishops. Elpidius made use of a moment of
comparative quiet to make the following proposal to the
Emperor: "In order that Your Patience may be no longer
imposed on, let this one thing be done: let the adherents of

Acacius and Antiochus certify in writing that they share the
faith of those who were the authors of these canons. This
will bring the whole dispute to an end." This simple proposal pleased Arcadius. He said to Antiochus, smiling:
"That seems to me to be the simplest and best way." He
himself, says Palladius, was altogether innocent of what happened; the conspiracy had been contrived by others. But
over the proposal itself, the opponents were so dumbfounded,
that a moment of the deepest silence ensued. Only their
countenances, pale with rage, betrayed their inner agitation.
By the brilliant idea of Elpidius, they had been suddenly
forced into a blind alley, from which at the moment they
could see no way out. But finally they had to give an explanation, and so they promised, under compulsion, at least this
much, that they would give their ratification later. With
this, they separated.

The enemy attack was parried this time. Elpidius
remained the victor.

The promised ratification of course was never given.
Instead of this, the opponents thought up new ways and
means to attain their end.

Meanwhile, Chrysostom also held conferences with the
forty-two Bishops who were on his side, and preached on
Sundays and feast days before a great concourse of people.

So the two parties stood opposed to each other, Chrysostom's
enemies and his friends; the former unwearied in contriving
new intrigues, and the latter equally persevering in patient
repulse of the attacks.

Outwardly, the tension first came again into public view at
Christmastime or Epiphany of 403 or 404. At that time, the
entire court attended the Divine Liturgy, not in the court
chapel, but in the cathedral. Shortly before the feast, probably at the urging of his wife, the Emperor notified the Archbishop that he would not come to the cathedral, and above
all, that he would no more hold ecclesiastical fellowship with
him, as long as he had not vindicated himself against the
accusations which had been brought against him.[13] That
would really be very difficult, if not impossible, since the
accusers themselves were hindering every possibility of a
vindication.

Unfortunately, no one has told us how that Christmas of 403 or 404 really passed. But, at any rate, events show that the state of affairs had completely changed again, and that the final solution of the question would go, not according to reason and judgment, but according to force.

But the affair did not go well. The opponents still did not dare to have a synod called on the ground of their doubtful canons; and no one knew of any other way which would have observed the juridical forms. Neither the Empress nor the Emperor trusted themselves to assume the responsibility for the use of force. It was clearly seen that the violence and the brutal recklessness of Theophilus had failed this time.

Nine or ten months passed under this nerve-racking tension of spirit. Christmas and Epiphany were long past; a new year had begun, and still no speedy conclusion of the crisis was in sight. Soon Lent of 404 approached. Should the Emperor, and above all the Empress, at the head of the court, receive the Easter Communion from the hand of the Archbishop, and thus recognize him as legitimate Bishop?

Thereupon Antiochus and his adherents decided to go to the Emperor again, but this time privately and alone. It would be easier to attain victory thus. So they represented to Arcadius that Chrysostom was already convinced of being in the wrong, and that his cause was lost. He may have given command to expel the Archbishop, for already Easter was near (it fell on the 17th of April in 404).[14] But indeed, he did not need to expel the Archbishop without further ado. It would be enough simply to forbid him to enter the cathedral. Obviously it must have lain heavily upon the souls of the court ladies, and especially of the Empress, that Easter, when the whole court attended the Divine Liturgy before the Patriarch, and it was difficult to avoid a meeting with him. For a long time the Bishops talked the weak Emperor into it. Finally Arcadius gave in to their urging, in the belief that they were dealing honestly. He signed a decree with the laconic command: *Leave your church*.[15]

This was the beginning of the decisive second act of the drama. It was at least a half success, which certainly at the same time was an expression of the entire lukewarmness and the wretchedness of those who had attained this success.

However, Chrysostom sent, in answer to the Emperor's command, an answer worthy of a bishop, full of character and magnanimity: "This Church, and the care of the spiritual welfare of the people, have been delivered to me by God, the Redeemer; therefore I cannot forsake it. But if it is your will, for the worldly power lies in your hands, then use force, so I can say that I only yielded to force, when I left my place."

If only all of the successors of Chrysostom had spoken thus, the history of Christendom in the East would have had a better development.

Palladius writes that after this manly answer of Chrysostom, that someone, with a certain shame and aversion, had sent a message from the imperial palace, saying that Chrysostom was deposed, but that he could remain in the Bishop's Palace until further notice.[16] That was decidedly something new. Constantine the Great and his successors had indeed banished bishops, but not until after they had been declared heretical, and deposed by other bishops or by synods. It had never happened before that an orthodox bishop had been deposed by a Catholic secular ruler, without any reason being given therefor.

So then Chrysostom was a prisoner in his own palace. Palladius was rightly informed when he said that no one had ventured to step forward vigorously against the Archbishop, because the Empress was so worried that a new judgment of God might fall upon her.[17] In this case they at least had Chrysostom close at hand, and could give him back his church and appease the anger of Heaven. So they wished, as it were, to tempt Heaven, to see if it would perhaps remain quiet this time, and be satisfied with merely looking on. That was a very feminine thought. At any rate, it was enough to calm the Empress.

Meanwhile, time passed and no change took place. Already Holy Week had come, and still the Archbishop sat in his palace as a prisoner. Then came another command from the court: "Leave your church," that is, your diocese. Chrysostom answered in the same spirit as before. The Emperor was urged to see to it that under no circumstances was Chrysostom to appear in the cathedral on the Feast of Easter. But Arcadius had misgivings about issuing a command for banishment, on account of the high feast and the sure prospect of a tumult among the people. Therefore he summoned the Bishops Acacius, Antiochus, Severian and Cyrinus, to come to him, probably for the reason that they had been recommended to him as the best advisers. He requested them to advise him according to their best knowledge and conscience, what to do. They said: "Emperor, the responsibility for the deposition of John fall upon our heads."

As the Jews had said long ago: "His blood be upon us and upon our children."

Nevertheless, they could not get a final decision from the Emperor.

Then the bishops who were still loyal to Chrysostom made a final attempt to save him. To get an audience at court was not to be thought of. On the other hand, they knew that the Emperor and Empress would visit the martyrs' shrines on Good Friday. So the bishops, forty in number, assembled there. When the Emperor and Empress approached, they went up to them, and begged with tears that they would save the Church of Christ, especially in consideration of the Feast of Easter, and of the Catechumens, who were to receive baptism on Easter Eve from the hands of their chief shepherd.

The petition of the forty bishops was not heard. Apparently it was Eudoxia who gave the final blow. It might almost be believed that she threatened to interpose with armed forces, if Chrysostom attempted to conduct the baptismal service. Paul, the Bishop of Kerateia, possessed enough courage to say to the Empress: "Eudoxia, fear God, and have pity on your children; do not desecrate the feast of Christ by the shedding of blood! "

All in vain. The forty bishops had to go back to their lodgings with the affair unsettled. All of them were filled with grief; many of them were bowed down by the moral burden of disaster which could now scarcely be averted.[18]

FOOTNOTES

1. Prosper Aq. and Marcellinus Comes (ML 51, 589 and 922) both expressly give this date as 403. I. Gottwald, La statue de l'Impératrice Eudoxie à Constantinople=Echos d'Orient 10

(1907) 274-76, says the statue was erected in September 403. This statement is probably anticipatory, since the Synod of the Oak began in September.

2. Dr. Fr. Pieper, Zur Geschichte der Kirchenväter aus epigraphischen Quellen in the Zeitschrift für Kirchengeschicht 1 (1877) 216; and J. Gottwald *loc. cit.* 275; Anthologia Palatina, ed. E. Gougny 3, 57 and 92 (Paris 1890). The original text of the inscription is as follows:

> [Κι]ονα πορφυρέην καί ἀργυρέην βασίλειαν
> Δέρκεο, ἔνθα πόληι θεμιστεύουσιν ἄνακτες
> Τ' ὄνομα, δ' εἰ ποθέεις, Εὐδόξια. Τίς ἀνέθεκεν;
> Σιμπλίκιος, μεγάλων ὑπάτων γόνος ἐσθλὸς ὕπαρχος.

On the opposite side is the Latin dedication:

> Dominae Aeliae (?) Eudoxiae semper Augustae
> V. C. Simplicius Praefectus Urbis dedicavit.

3. Socrates 6, 18 (721).

4. Socrates 6, 18; Sozomen 8, 20. Palladius says nothing of the silver statue.

5. Palladius 2 (10).

6. John the Baptist was later celebrated on the 29th of August. At the end of August, Chrysostom was already on his way to exile.

7. Kellner, Heortologie 2nd edition, 161-163.

8. The Homily in MG 59, 485 is certainly not genuine, but had an extraordinary literary success. It is still found in more than 70 Greek manuscripts. The oldest material comes, significantly, from Egypt; it is in an Oxyrynchus papyrus fragment of the British Museum, from the 6th century (see Vol. 13; London 1919, no. 1603; and Rendiconti dell' Istituto reale Lombardo, Ser. II, 52 [1919] 292-96). A. Ehrhard, Überlieferung. I. 65. Also Russian, Bulgarian, Serbian etc., translations exist. Even in the Greek Menology it found admission as a Homily on the beheading of St. John; good evidence that, in later Byzantium, no more was thought about the confounding of Herodias and Eudoxia. See A. Ehrhard, Hagiographische Forschungen 102 and 130. A. Konir, Die Homilie v. Joh. Chrysostomus über Herodias, in: Byzantino-Slavica 1 (Prague 1929) 182-206. A. Ehrhard, in: Byz. Zeitschrift 34 (1934) 99 says further, that in the Herodias sermon, one must differentiate between the value of the sources and the question of authenticity. However, the value of the sources here depends on the question of authenticity. A part of

this sermon is also found among the works of Ephrem Syr., Op. omnia, III, 70. The conclusion of the doubtful Hom. Antequam iret in exilium, 4, (52, 432) is surely of later origin.

Gregory of Nazianzus also uses, in the beginning of a sermon on the Theophany (n. 2) the words: Πάλιν τὸ σκότος λύεται . . . πάλιν Ἀίγυπτος σκότος κολάζεται (36, 373 A.).

9. Palladius 9 (c. 30).

10. In his Easter letter of 404 Theophilus warned against avarice and recommended love of one's neighbor (!) (ML 22, 813 ss.). The fourth Canon of this Synod rules: A bishop deposed by a synod, who arbitrarily returns to his office, shall not be installed again by another synod, nor be heard again; he and all who hold with him shall be cast out of the Church.

As a further elaboration of this, the 12th Canon of the same Synod says: If a bishop deposed by a synod, instead of appealing to a greater synod, betakes himself to the Emperor, he shall incur the same punishment mentioned above. Mansi, 2, 1309 and 1313. Hefele, KG 1, 514 and 517. The point of this ruling was directed against St. Athanasius, whose return to his see they wished to make impossible. The Synod of Antioch consisted chiefly of the adherents of Eusebius, who claimed at that time to be an orthodox Nicaean, but who later came out as a Semi-Arian. So it came about that St. Hilarius named this assembly of bishops the Synodus Sanctorum, while St. Athanasius, who perceived their aim, declared them to be Arians. On account of this circumstance, the vacillation of this synod and its canons is not easy for Catholics to understand.

Canon 4 was of course applicable to Chrysostom, but only on the supposition that the Synod of the Oak must be regarded first as an actual, that is legal, synod, and not as a comedy; and second, that the Canons of Antioch had atttained general binding force. Both may well be disputed. The Catholic Synod of Sardica (Sofia), in the year 343-344, abolished this canon, and itself gave legally deposed bishops the right to appeal to Rome.

The opponents of Chrysostom disputed this; the canon had been laid down by orthodox bishops and was legal. (Palladius 9, 31.) But only malice could make use of this Canon 12 in our case; for it did not turn Chrysostom to the Emperor, but the Emperor to him, with the request that he would again resume the episcopal throne.

But it is and remains an irony of fate, that it was just the successor of this Bishop and Patriarch, who had never recognized the legality of this canon, who in our case soon after gave the advice, to invoke it in order to rid himself, in an easy way, of an opponent whom he could not conquer in open and honourable fight.

Palladius 9 (31) gives this canon again, freely expressed: " If a bishop or a priest is deposed, either lawfully, or unlawfully, and arbitrarily takes possession of his church again, without permission of the synod, he shall be finally deposed again without further recourse to law."

11. According to Socrates 6, 18 (717 C), Leontius may even have been the principal leader.

12. Palladius 9 (31) says indeed this was incited by the opponents of Chrysostom. But that does not agree with their aim of deposing the Archbishop unheard and without any defense.

13. Socrates 6, 18 (717); Sozomen 8, 20 (1568). The possibility that there is a confusion here with the order issued to Chrysostom before Easter is not to be rejected.

14. Palladius 9 (c. 32).

15. Palladius 9 (47, 32).

16. Palladius 9 (32): ἀποστείλαντες . . . ἐξέωσαν αὐτόν. Under this, according to the context, a formal decree of deposition is to be understood.

17. Dialog. 9 (32).

18. Palladius 9 (33).

CHAPTER XXV

BLOODY EASTER AND SECOND
BANISHMENT (404)

So Easter approached; in the year 404 it fell on the 17th
of April.[1] To all appearances, the solemn celebration of
the day by Chrysostom or his clergy had been expressly
forbidden; indeed, in case of refusal, the use of armed force
was threatened. After the letter of Chrysostom to Pope Innocent, according to Sozomen, it must be concluded that the
fearless Bishop, with his friends and adherents, nevertheless
made the attempt to solemnize the baptismal service in the
baptistery of the cathedral, and that this brought about a disturbance and a forced emptying of the church by the military.[2] Still, it is not clear whether the disturbances mentioned
by Chrysostom as taking place " in the church "[3] did not take
place in the thermae, which he did not expressly mention.
On the other hand, Sozomen distinguishes clearly between a
violent disturbance in the baptistery of the cathedral, and a
second one in the thermae.

One thing is certain, that they were determined to prevent
any of the catechumens, of whom there were over three
thousand that year, from being baptized by any bishops or
clergy who were friends of Chrysostom; so it may well have
happened that not merely the cathedral, but all other
churches, were prevented from serving as substitute bap-
tisteries.

So what was to be done with the catechumens? Let them
wait until the strife between the court and the Bishop's
Palace was settled? The end of that was scarcely to be seen.
Quickly, certain priests who still remained loyal to their
Bishop decided to call the catechumens to the public baths,
the so-called Thermae of Constantine, which were near the
Church of the Apostles. There they would officiate at the
Easter baptismal liturgy, for which the churches were closed
to them.

The candidates for baptism, with their friends and acquaintances, gathered there; the divine service began; the lectors read excerpts from Holy Scripture; the priests prepared to begin the baptism of the catechumens. But meanwhile, rumors of these proceedings had come to the ears of the three ringleaders of the enemy coalition—the Bishops Acacius, Antiochus, and Severian. As Judas once hastened to betray the Lord, so now they hurried to the military prefect of Constantinople, and demanded that he disperse the assembly by force. The prefect had misgivings; it is night, said he, and there are a great number of people there; a disaster might result. Yes, answered the three, but if the Emperor sees the empty churches in the morning, he will know that the people are favorable to the Archbishop, and we will be called slanderers, because we have told him that no man would willingly hold fellowship with John, since he is an inconsiderate and irreconcilable man. The general might have retorted to the three that they alone were responsible for their noble deed, and that he had no reason for military interference. Instead of that, he resorted to half measures. Refusing to take any responsibility for the results of his own orders, he sent off a captain named Lucius, who was still a pagan, with the order to go quickly to the baths of Constantine, and order the people to come to the church. The assembly refused. Since entry into the church was forbidden to the Archbishop, the celebration of a liturgical feast there would have seemed like a renunciation of him, and a declaration of fellowship with the opponents.

So Lucius announced to Acacius and his friends the failure of his mission. There was a great multitude of people, he added, and the temper of the crowd was one of excitement. However, the three bishops now pressed Lucius to drive the assembly out by force, if they would not clear the place after another demand. With many flattering speeches, and the promise of a quick promotion, they finally broke down his resistance. He obviously did not possess a new command from his superior officer. On his own responsibility he called together the troops under him, a division of 400 men, noisy young soldiers from Thrace, who had been taken into the army a short time before, people who had no experience with that sort of police work, and to whom it was doubtless the greatest pleasure to have at last an opportunity to knock people about. They marched out with drawn swords, led by clergy who were adherents of Acacius and his fellow-conspirators. It was already past midnight.[4]

Meanwhile, in the baths of Constantine, the baptismal ceremony was already well on its way. Many hundreds of catechumens were already baptized, and many still awaited the healing waters. Then suddenly cries of terror were heard; wild confusion began; the armed soldiers of Lucius forced their way through the crowd to where the priests and deacons were proceeding with the baptisms; they pounced upon these, with the greatest roughness, struck the priests over the heads with clubs, so that the baptismal water was stained with blood, and even desecrated the Holy Mysteries, while they tore away the sacred vessels from the deacons. Meanwhile, the people fled in all directions in wild panic. Over here, one would run wailing, because his hand had been struck and was bleeding; over there, followed a young girl with her clothing torn. Half naked women, who had just come from the baptismal font, all fled, together with men, in terror of being murdered. The soldiers snatched the chalice and the sacred vessels, then they took the priests and deacons who had not escaped, as prisoners in their midst, and led them off to prison. Some distinguished lay people were exiled from the city.[4a]

So began the Feast of Easter in Constantinople in 404.

Where the Emperor and Empress, with their train, attended divine service, on this Feast of Easter, we do not know; probably in the chapel of the palace. It is improbable that Severian stayed away from the feast-day services in the cathedral, since the people knew nothing of the opponents of their Bishop; and the Emperor would not pay any attention to it.

But when Arcadius "on the following day" (Easter Sunday?) was out riding in the Pempton Field,[5] he noticed there, to his great astonishment, a large crowd of people in white garments, about three thousand people in all. Those in the Emperor's entourage, who had heard of what had happened in the night, knew at once that these were the newly baptized, and the adherents of the Archbishop, who had come together here, with a few clergy, to celebrate the Divine Liturgy or to complete the baptismal ceremonies which had been so forcibly interrupted the night before. But this could not be revealed to the Emperor. As Arcadius turned to them and asked what the assembly was about, the answer came: They are heretics. So he commanded at once that they be dispersed. Some officers and people of the guard carried out the order with zeal and devotion. They took prisoner several clerics and a number of lay people; even several distinguished women were arrested. In this, again, the soldiers showed general disregard for the rights of the people. Some were robbed of their mantles; several women had their golden earrings torn off, together with their ear-lobes. The beautiful wife of the rich Eleutherius left her mantle behind, and fled back to the city in the garments of her maid. In the city itself, terror and anxiety ruled.

Many people fled, as though there had been a barbarian invasion. Neither were the provincial bishops who had sided with Chrysostom spared. One might have believed that the times of Diocletian had come again. And all this had been brought about by Christian Bishops, who, in alliance with a few court ladies, under the protection of a deceived Empress, at any cost wished to make it impossible for the lawful Bishop to remain in the city. It was not to be wondered at, that not only Catholics, but even heretics, pagans, and Jews expressed their disgust at these doings.[6] The great scandal that they gave, not only to the catechumens and the newly baptized, but to the whole city, obviously did not much concern these gentlemen. They knew themselves to be protected and encouraged by the court, and that was enough for them.

One might ask why they still left Chrysostom in his palace. Why did they not send him into exile long before? The answer may well be this: because Eudoxia was still under the influence of her earlier terror, and feared another affliction from God. She certainly wished, above all things in the world, that Chrysostom would abandon his post voluntarily; and his opponents did all that was humanly possible to force him to such a decision. Thereby the Empress' conscience was quieted, and, as concerned the people, a moral pretext was found.   But the Archbishop without doubt saw through this design, and held fast to his decision to yield only to force.[7]

Through the scandal on Easter Eve, the discord between the two parties, and the secret intrigues, were brought at one stroke out of the half-darkness of the palace walls into the widest publicity, and they became state business, which was soon to broaden out into an affair of the whole Empire and the world.

The Last Decision[8]

It was clear that things could not go on in this way much longer.   The affair pressed on to a final crisis.   While the adherents and friends of Chrysostom were already being actually persecuted, the Archbishop found himself still continuing to live in his palace in Constantinople.   There must have been weeks and months of mental torment for the sensitive soul of the Archbishop, who had once been so triumphant, and raised to heaven; to have to watch quietly and defenselessly, as outside bishops, in alliance with powerful court circles, revealed an absolutely incomprehensible hatred of him, when part of his clergy perfidiously forsook him, and betrayed him, when the people were torn from him by force, when all his attempts at peace and reconciliation were frustrated by the irreconcilable hatred of a small clique, which, however, was influential in the government of that time.   In vain he had asked for law and justice, in vain he had urged the summoning of a new and impartial synod.   He had accomplished nothing.   Only piercing grief came to the spiritual shepherd over the immense scandal which the clergy themselves had given to the people, before all the world, before Christians, pagans, and Jews, to the infinite damage of souls and of the Christian cause.

But there was worse to come.

The excitement in people's minds had mounted up to a very extraordinary height following these public events, and the hatred for the Archbishop, who was still in the city and in his palace, appeared to shrink from nothing any more.   Of the tumult of these days, Sozomen gives a good account; through Palladius, he finds partial support and ratification, and he illuminates the soul of those days with a glaring and sad light.

Not long after the events of Easter, a man who carried a long dagger, and gave the impression of being insane, tried to force his way into the Bishop's Palace. The people considered him a hired murderer, took his weapons from him, and brought him before the prefect of the city (Optatus). When the occurrence was related to Chrysostom, he at once sent some bishops from his entourage to the perfect, and begged him to let the man go free, before he was put to the torture.

Very serious, because seriously meant, was another murderous attempt, also related by Palladius,[8a] which the servant of the priest Elpidius made on the Archbishop. As told by Palladius, the servant had received fifty gold pieces for his work. Armed with three daggers, he ran fast to the palace. An acquaintance whom he met asked him where he was going in such a hurry; instead of answering him, he pierced him in the breast with his dagger. He did the same to a second man, who, terrified over what had happened to the first man, raised an outcry, and after him, a third. But meanwhile, the Bishop's Palace had been alarmed by the excitement. From all sides the dismayed residents came flocking together, in the greatest agitation, everybody screaming and making such a noise that the mad murderer suddenly got frightened himself, and quickly took to flight. Some people ran after him, and cried out to others to stop him. A man who had just come from the baths tried to stop him; a dagger thrust felled him to the pavement. But at last the multitude became so great that the murderer, surrounded, could not find a way out. With much effort, the raging man was bound and led to the prefect in the imperial palace. The aroused multitude demanded that not only the murderer, but those who had hired him, should be punished. The prefect promised it, and the people dispersed.

So far Sozomen. Palladius gives the number of dead as four, and says that three others who were wounded recovered again. What happened to the murderer is not mentioned; at least nothing happened to those who had hired him. Martyrius (f. 517[1]) says that the prefect had some blows administered to the murderer, in order to appease the people, and that settled the affair. This supposition may well be correct.

So it had come to this, that the hated Archbishop's life was no more safe, even in his own palace. Following this sad incident, the people organized, of their own free action, a watch service around his palace; this watch was kept up day and night.[9]

After this, the affair gradually went on to its climax. This extreme tension could not last long. All the world felt that a final decision must come soon. Also it was clear to Chrysostom that there was nothing more for him to do but to wait and endure until his opponents found the courage for the last stroke, and would come again to open force. But the Emperor obviously would not take the responsibility upon himself. He hesitated for a long time. Finally the inimical bishops pushed him forward again.

On the Thursday after Pentecost, 404, the 9th of June, the four Bishops, Acacius, Severian, Antiochus, and Cyrinus of Chalcedon, with their adherents, went to the imperial palace, and asked for an audience. "You, O Emperor," they said to Arcadius, who was perhaps astonished at hearing such a speech from a bishop's mouth,[10] "you have been placed by God as ruler over us, you are subject to no one, you are Lord over all: you can do what pleases you. Do not be more lenient than the priests, nor more holy than the bishops. We have said to you in the presence of all, that upon our heads falls the responsibility for the deposition of John. So do not spare one man in order to destroy us all! " The striking similarity of this speech to that of the Jewish high priest who demanded the death of Jesus is doubtless to be placed to the account of Palladius, but it corresponds actually to the real state of affairs. These bishops carried on with the same stubborn, cowardly hatred as the Jewish high priests did in their time, against the Divine Saviour, and unfortunately with the same result: but still it was more than a week before the Emperor was brought to a final decision. He felt, this time, the need of declining the responsibility for his doings, and, like Pilate of old, of washing his hands to show his innocence.

The Emperor called his notary Patricius, and gave him

this command: "Go and say to John: *The Bishops, Acacius, Severian, Antiochus, and Cyrinus, and their friends, have taken on themselves the responsibility for your banishment. So yield yourself and your cause to God, and leave your church and your diocese.*" Arcadius did not realize what a wretched thing, and how unworthy of a ruler, such a demand was. Patricius delivered himself of the imperial command, the only merit of which was, that it was clear and to the point.[11]

Chrysostom did not need to give an answer to it. He only entered a protest, that he was being expelled by force, and without due process of law, such as is the privilege of even murderers, robbers and adulterers.[12] But he understood very well, in fact he seemed to be glad, that the period of wearisome uncertainty had finally come to an end; only the thought of his flock filled him with pain and anxiety. His preparations for departure were soon completed. He assembled his faithful bishops in the sacristy, which served as chapter room and council hall. He turned to them and said: "Well, we will say a last prayer now, and bid farewell to the angel of the Church." Then a pious man of high rank made his way to him and informed him: "Lucius (the notorious officer who had been guilty of the bloody Easter) is standing ready, with his troops, nearby, at the baths, to expel you from the church by force in case of opposition or delay. The people are already beginning to riot in the city. So hasten and come away secretly, so that the people will not start a fight, and get into a bloody battle with the soldiers."

Then Chrysostom embraced some of the bishops, until his grief overcame him. He tore himself away, and took his farewell of the others with the words: "Stay here a little while, until I have gotten control of myself again." Then he hastened, accompanied by a few of the clergy, into the baptismal chapel, to which he had summoned Olympias, the steadfastly faithful deaconess of the church, together with her fellow deaconesses, Pentadia, Procla, and Silvina, the noble widow of the dead Nebridius. They really belonged with the clergy of the cathedral, and the great services which they had rendered to him and to the Church, as well as the spiritual fellowship which bound him to these noble women, clearly

justified this attention. They already knew what was about
to happen. What with tears, grief, and anguish, they were
hardly able to approach him.

"Come here, my spiritual daughters," said Chrysostom,
"and listen to me. I see that my cause is judged. I have
finished my course, and you will not see me again. But this
one thing I beg of you: do not cease your love and your zeal
for the Church. Whoever may receive the episcopal consecration after me, if it happens that he does not strive after
it, and everyone deems him worthy of it, then obey him, just
as you would obey me. For the Church cannot be without
a Bishop. So you will work out your salvation; and remember
me in your prayers!"[13]

That was the farewell of the Archbishop to Olympias and
her companions. They threw themselves in unspeakable
sorrow at the feet of their shepherd, and wept bitterly. The
Archbishop made a sign to one of the oldest priests, and said
to him, "Take them away, lest the people become upset and
excited at the sight of them." After a short time, they were
calmed again, and they yielded to the wish of the Bishop.

Chrysostom did not return to the sacristy. Neither did he
go into the church, where already thousands were waiting to
see their chief shepherd, for the last time. On the contrary,
he commanded that the animal which he was to use for the
journey should wait for him at the great western door. Meanwhile, he himself came out of the east side of the cathedral,
probably from the baptistery, into the open air. His only
thought was to offer no involuntary cause for disturbance.
Among his attendants were the two Bishops, Cyriacus and
Eulysius, and several clergy. "The angel of the Church also
departed at the same time as the Bishop, for he could not bear
the isolation of the church which had been brought about
by malicious *principalities and powers*."[14] Under military
escort, they went to the harbor. Many people stood on the
road, the friends of the Bishop, some Jews probably well disposed, and pagans hissing, jeering, and ridiculing.[15]

It was Monday, the 20th of June, 404.[16]

So began the journey of the second banishment, a journey
which, from beginning to bitter end, was an unbroken way
of suffering and of the cross, until death brought release.

Here one may ask whether Chrysostom had dealt rightly in allowing himself to be delivered up to his enemies so defenselessly and without any opposition. St. Athanasius did not do that, but placed himself in safety at an opportune time, in order to keep his friends and enemies at peace. Chrysostom, on the other hand, had resolved from the beginning to yield only to force, so that his opponents might not be able to say afterwards that he had left his position of his own free will, and surrendered; if he did, his successor in the See of Constantinople would be lawful Bishop. Thus the injustime would appear to be legitimized.[16a]

But why was he thus defeated? Had not the great Ambrose prevailed over the opposition of an Arian Empress and her court, and did he not face even the Emperor Theodosius himself? Yes. But in the first case, the court involved was one whose power was already tottering, and the matter concerned the Christian faith, and not one individual person. In the second case, the magnanimous Theodosius stood in opposition to St. Ambrose, instead of his much more insignificant son Arcadius, with whom his entourage did what they would.[17]

FOOTNOTES

1. H. Grotefend, Zeitrechnung 1 (Hanover 1891) p. 106.

2. Palladius 9 (47, 33). The entire story rests on the portrayal of Palladius, who obviously was present.

Chrysostom, in his report to Pope Innocent (Pall. 2) and Palladius, in his own report (Ch. 9) do not agree in all particulars in their story of the proceedings. According to Chrysostom, the baptism of the catechumens took place in the church itself, and the soldiers of Lucius broke into it. Of the Thermae of Constantius, Chrysostom mentions nothing, while Palladius says nothing of the church. It is possible or even probable that the adherents of Chrysostom at first were hunted out of the church, and then assembled at the Thermae, from whence the soldiers expelled them again.

3. Letter to Pope Innocent. Palladius 2 (10).

4. In this also, the report of Chrysostom does not agree with that of Palladius. According to Chrysostom, the forcible expulsion took place in the evening. Yet that applies either only to

the church, or he was not exactly informed on the state of affairs. The Magister Officiorum from the 29th of January to the 30th of July was Anthemius. So he must have been the Magister who sent Lucius to the thermae. (Cod. Theod. 6, 27, 14; 10, 22, 5; 16, 4, 4).

4a. Pall. Dial. op. 9 (ed. Norton 57, 5 s). Palladius seems to mean that already a series of edicts had been issued to intimidate those who would not terminate ecclesiastical relations with Chrysostom. Still, these edicts may not have been issued until after the second effective banishment.

5. Cf. Millingen, Byzant. Constantinople 82.

6. Chrysostom, Letter to Pope Innocent, Pall. 2 (11).

7. According to Palladius, ch. 9 (34) one might believe that the Emperor had already forbidden, by a general edict, fellowship with Chrysostom. Yet he might have interpolated something here before, which did not happen until later, since that was the beginning of the Johnite persecution. For as long as Chrysostom was not deposed, or had no successor, he could not well be refused the right to be treated as a bishop, or refused the right of fellowship.

8. Palladius, Dial. ch. 10 (34 ff.); Sozomen 8, 22.

8a. Dialog 20 (72).

9. Sozomen 8, 22 (1572). Since Chrysostom, in his letter to Pope Innocent, exonerated the Emperor from all blame, and said that what had happened was against his (the Emperor's) will, so Arcadius either yielded only reluctantly, or one must assume that everything happened behind his back or through misuse of his name.

10. Palladius naturally was not there, but he characterized the feelings and behavior of the Bishop excellently in this speech.

11. Palladius 9 (34-35).

12. Sozomen 8, 22 (1572).

13. Palladius 10 (35).

14. Palladius Dial., ch. 10 (35).

15. Palladius *ibid.*; Socrates (6, 18), Sozomen (8, 22) and Chrysostom report unanimously, that he was led away by force (πρὸς βίαν συρόμενος). C. Tillemont 11, 604 n. 70 and 71.

16. In the year 404, Easter fell on the 17th of April. According to this, Pentecost would fall on the 5th of June, and the Thursday after Pentecost τῆς Πεντεκοστῆς δὲ συμπληρωθείσης was the 9th of June. Palladius gives no interval between the Thursday after Pentecost and the day of the second banishment; neither does Sozomen (67, 1572 C). The Chronicon Paschale was not written until 200 years after the death of Chrysostom, and

probably took its narrative from Socrates, who in HE. 6, 18 (67, 721) gives the 20th of June as the day of the second banishment. The Fasti Romani gives the same date (Clinton, Fasti Romani I, 561). Since the events dealt with here (the burning of the Cathedral and the Senate House) were of interest to the public and the State, it is probable that the given dates are correct. So, between the audience of the four bishops with the Emperor and the actual command of expulsion, eleven days elapsed, during which the parties for and against Chrysostom contended for victory.

While in the Byzantine Heortologion the banishment of Chrysostom is given as the 13th of November, this date cannot rest on chronological calculations. (M. Gedeon, Byzantinon Heortologion, 42).

16a. Ch. 11 (ed. Norton 63, 20).

17. O. Seeck, Geschichte des Untergangs 5, 336-337 shows here again his complete lack of understanding of Christian magnanimity, when he writes: " Without doubt Chrysostom would have remained the victor, if he had not proudly disdained the favour of the court, on which the high position of his episcopate alone rested, by his *foolish idealism*." Cf. *ibid*. 341.

CHAPTER XXVI

CHRYSOSTOM WRITES TO ROME

SHORTLY before the last crisis had arisen, and Chrysostom had been sent from Constantinople for the second time, he and his friends had decided to set forth in detail all the events of the last months in a letter to the Pope and the Western Bishops. There was a definite reason for that. The violent deeds which had been perpetrated since Easter, against Chrysostom and his adherents, were being imitated in other cities too. In Asia Minor, in Ephesus and in Heraclea, the bishops who had been installed by Chrysostom soon had to recognize that they were faced with the same fate as their friends and colleagues in the capital city. Also, the other bishops began to have ever stronger and more perceptible pressure exerted on them, to force them to refuse fellowship to Chrysostom. What was more likely than that his opponents would make an attempt to excite the Western Bishops to the same step, by a false account of events? The Archbishop had to meet this danger, to take the lead over them, as soon as possible.

It was therefore decided: the four Bishops, Pansophius of Pisidia, Pappus, Bishop in Syria, Demetrius of Pessinus in Galatia Secunda, and Eugenius, Bishop in Phrygia, should visit Rome in company with the two deacons Paul and Cyriacus. They took three documents with them: one from Chrysostom himself, and one from the 40 Bishops who stood by him to the last, and one from those clergy of Constantinople who had remained loyal to him. All three letters spoke unanimously of the confusion which had been brought about in the city by lawless elements.[1]

The letter of Chrysostom to Pope Innocent I was as follows:

"To my most reverend and most holy Lord, Bishop Innocent, from John, greeting in the Lord.

"Your Piety will have already learned, before this letter gives you the assurance, of the misdeeds which men here have dared to commit. The outrage is too great for the news of the tragedy to have escaped any part of the world. The rumor of it has indeed already penetrated to the uttermost bounds of the earth, and has everywhere called forth grief and sorrow. However, we must not merely grieve over this disaster, we must also try our best to see if we can calm this dreadful storm in the Church. We have considered it necessary to beg the right and honorable and reverend Bishops Demetrius, Pansophius, Pappus and Eugenius to leave their own churches, and to venture the journey over so great a sea, and to take upon themselves so lengthy an absence, and to hasten to Your Goodness, to give you an exact report, and to obtain help from you as soon as may be. We have also sent with them the most reverend and beloved deacons Paulus and Cyriacus. So these will inform you shortly of all these events, with the help of a document in the form of a letter."

Then Chrysostom goes on to relate briefly how Theophilus was accused and summoned to the Emperor; of how Theophilus brought it about that not himself, but Chrysostom, was condemned and deposed. He further related the events since his second deposition (or house arrest) and the scandalous events immediately following, on the Easter Eve of 404. He also mentioned the spreading of unrest in other dioceses.

Then the letter continues: "Since you are now informed of all these things, most reverend and pious sirs, we beg you to show that degree of spirit and zeal which is worthy of you, so that these lawless disturbances which have found entrance into the Church may be abolished. For if such a situation remains uncorrected, anyone who wishes might invade the most distant dioceses ('eparchies'), and depose whomsoever he wishes, and rule and govern according to his own pleasure. You know well that in this way everything will go to ruin, and an inexorable (reciprocal) contest would be brought about all over the world, in which one would overthrow another, and again be overthrown by others. So in order that such chaos may not grip the whole world, I beg you to explain briefly whether this deed which was done in such illegal form, in our absence and by one party alone, although we did not hesitate to appear before a court, whether this has any kind of force or value, which it does not have by nature; that, on the other hand, whether those who allowed such lawless deeds to be committed, are subject to punishment under the canons of the Church. And as for us, who have not been convicted, indeed not even accused, much less proved guilty, let us have, as is customary, your letters, and continue your goodness to us, and all else as before. On the other hand, if those who have already so seriously transgressed against the law, still continue with their accusations, on the grounds for which they deposed us, let them first make known their accusations publicly in writing, and send us a written copy of the same; then an impartial court may be set up; then we can defend ourselves, and prove that we are not guilty of those things which are laid to our charge, of which actually we are not guilty. For that which they have allowed themselves to do transgresses against every law and every right, and is against the canons of the Church.

"Never yet has any one dared such proceedings in the courts of the world, not even in the courts of the barbarians. Neither Scythians nor Sarmatians have ever yet judged anyone so partially and so one-sidedly, in the absence of the accused, who himself did not hesitate at all to appear before a court, who himself summoned a thousand judges, who declared himself innocent, and who was ready before the world to wash himself clean of the accusations with which they burdened him, and to prove that he is innocent in all points.

"Consider all this therefore, and above all, get exact information from my lords our pious brothers, the Bishops. And then I beg you to undertake the affair yourselves with zeal. You will thus not only do us a great favor, but also the whole Church, and God will reward you for it; for nothing is so near to His Heart as peace in the Church.

"This letter is also sent to Venerius, Bishop of Milan, as well as to Chromatius, Bishop of Aquileia.[2]

"Farewell in the Lord."[3]

The note in the record which states that "this letter was also sent to Venerius . . . and Chromatius," cannot first have been added in Rome; so it cannot be that the Pope gave the order to send it to the two Bishops. It must have been thus in the original itself, since Chrysostom speaks to the recipients of the letter in the plural, in the text.[4] That point is important for the question previously touched on, as to whether this letter can be considered a formal proof of the " primacy " of Rome.[5]

The fear of Chrysostom and his trusted friends, that Theophilus would also try to win the West, was first of all not well founded. Theophilus possessed enough political instinct to perceive that in Rome, among the Latin Bishops, who were not under the influence of Eudoxia and the Court of Constantinople, he would not be able to make a very good impression with his Synod of the Oak. Directly after the synod, it had not occurred to him to send news of it to the Pope. The collection of signatures on the common letter of the clerical friends of Chrysostom, as well as the departure of the four Bishops and the two deacons of Constantinople, and their preparations, they had hardly been able to keep a deep secret. Theophilus had indeed not in vain sent the three Egyptian Bishops there as agitators and reporters. There can be no doubt that his partisans in Constantinople found time to send the Patriarch very promptly a message as to the proposed step of the adherents of Chrysostom.

Theophilus must have been dismayed, even downright terrified, at this unexpected and unwelcome information. He sent at once a fast courier, the priest Petrus, back to Constantinople, with an order to bring back from there a copy of the Acts of the Synod of the Oak.[6] In his hasty departure from that city, of the year before, the Patriarch obviously had not found time to interest himself in this important document. But in order to arrive before Chrysostom's ambassadors, he sent a second messenger to Rome, a simple lector, with the command to deliver to Pope Innocent the document which he gave him.

This second messenger carried out his orders as well as could be wished. He arrived in the Eternal City just three days before the arrival of the ambassadors of Chrysostom.[7]

In this first letter of the Patriarch of Alexandria to the Pope, there was nothing further to be read than a brief notice[8] that he, Theophilus, had deposed Bishop John of Constantinople, and, as a result of this, Bishop Innocent was to hold no more ecclesiastical fellowship with him who had been deposed.[9]

As to the reason for the deposition, who concurred in it, how the whole affair had progressed, the Patriarch did not disclose anything. Theophilus represented himself as actually the chief head of the Eastern Church, of whose deeds and decisions the rest of the world simply had to take cognizance.

So that was the first news of the events in Constantinople which had come to Rome and to the West.[10] Until the messenger from Constantinople returned, Theophilus worked out a manuscript which was to vindicate his numerous outrages upon Chrysostom.

FOOTNOTES

1. Ἀπαιδεύτων θόρυβον (Dial. 1; col. 8).

2. Milan and Aquileia were, after Rome, the most distinguished ecclesiastical cities of Italy.

3. Palladius, Dial. 2 (47, 8-12). This letter can only have been written between Easter and Pentecost 404; after Easter, since it portrays the events of the Easter baptism, but *before* the second effective banishment, since it reports nothing of the burning of the cathedral, the imprisonment and persecution of the Johnites, and above all, of the installation of Arsacius. The priest Theoctenus brought these reports much later. (Dial. 3; 13.) Our dating is established through the difference in the way in which Chrysostom speaks of the first and the second deposition. Of the first he says that he is expelled καὶ τῆς πόλεως καὶ τῆς Ἐκκλησίας. (Dial. 2 (9).) Of the second, he writes only: πάλιν ἐξώσθημεν τῆς ἐκκλησίας (col. 10). With this he obviously has the imperial decree in mind, which commanded him strictly before Easter: Ἔξελθε τῆς Ἐκκλησίας (Pall. 9; col. 32). Finally, in the letter of Chrysostom to Pope Innocent, the events on Easter Eve directly after his second deposition are related. (col. 10).

4. κύριοι, τιμιώτατοι . . . ἴστε, ὅτι (col. 11). So it was really addressed to several people. On account of these plurals in the address, an explanatory note is necessary.

5. Cf. vol. I., ch. 27.

6. Cf. ch. 28.

7. Palladius, Dial. 1 (7-8).

8. Προσανέφερε = really, information for the purpose of confirmation. Pall. Dial. 1 (47, 8).

9. This last is shown in the second answering letter of the Pope to Theophilus (Dial. 3; col. 13-14). That this succession of events is causatively and chronologically correct becomes clearer from Ch. 28.

10. That no earlier news came to Rome of the Synod of the Oak and of the first deposition, is a matter of course on the part of Theophilus, who after the sudden reversal in Constantinople in September 403 could have had only one interest, namely, to keep silent and to be glad that no one questioned him or demanded a reckoning of him. That Chrysostom said nothing, can be understood, on the one side, from the fact that his first deposition and exile lasted only one day, and so there was no reason for asking help from the West; and then again, from the fact that the rehabilitation synod requested by him concerned itself only with the Bishops of the Greek Empire; and finally perhaps from this, that the winter of 403 was approaching, when no long journey would be undertaken without a very serious reason. The deacon Eusebius, who at that time was in Rome as ambassador of Chrysostom, must have gone there before the Synod of the Oak; otherwise he would not have asked the Pope, after the receipt of Theophilus' letter, to refuse fellowship to Chrysostom, but would have waited for more reliable information.

CHAPTER XXVII

BURNING OF THE CATHEDRAL IN CONSTANTINOPLE: INSTALLATION OF BISHOP ARSACIUS: PERSECUTION OF THE JOHNITES

WHILE Chrysostom, in the evening twilight, journeyed over the waters of the Bosporus, and looked back in dumb anguish for the last time at Constantinople, his episcopal city, he may have seen, to his astonishment and fear, a great fire lighting up the city; it became ever larger and higher, and at last rose to heaven in tawny sheaves of fire. Was it real, or only a dream? The fire rose exactly from the place where, shortly before, he had bade farewell to his episcopal friends and to the deaconesses. No, it was no deception; the outlines rose up clearly from the fiery background; it was the towering episcopal cathedral, which was on fire. It lighted for its banished lord and shepherd a dreadful and sorrowful farewell, in the beginning night of his exile, which would be followed by no bright morning in this world. It was as though the "angel of the church" were departing with the Bishop, from the holy halls.

But what had actually happened?

Sozomen[1] says: Scarcely was Chrysostom in the hands of the soldiers, when the doors of the cathedral were barricaded by Chrysostom's enemies, so that the multitude could not follow him, and perhaps snatch him away into their own hands. Of those who had waited outside, some had actually hastened down to the sea, in order to give their Bishop a last farewell on the way; others had a foreboding of evil, and they absconded. Naturally, the greatest confusion had originated in the church. The masses pressed against the doors (which apparently opened inward), while some people exerted them-

selves to open or break the locks of the doors with stones.
Only after the utmost exertion did they accomplish this.
Everyone tried to be the first to get out into the open air. So
while the attention of the throng was directed exclusively
upon the exits, and they were perilously overcrowded, some
unknown person took advantage of the general confusion, and
set fire to the church.

The origin of this fire, and the identity of the guilty person,
have never been revealed to this day, and probably never will
be. Only this much has been stated by eye-witnesses, that the
fire seemed to start from the episcopal throne of the cathedral;
it seized on the woodwork and tapestries of the walls, and
from there spread to the timbers of the roof, so that in the
shortest possible time the whole cathedral was a glowing mass
of flame; and in the short space of three hours, it had laid the
splendid work of a century in ashes and ruins.

Unfortunately, a north wind was blowing at the time. The
flames and sparks of the burning church flew over the buildings near it, and across the street, which the people had to
traverse as if under an arch of fire; and they enkindled also
the Senate House, which lay to the south of the cathedral.[2]
This was also a work of Constantine the Great. The whole
Greek and Roman Empires had given their best art treasures
to lend special glory to this rival of the Senate House in
Rome. Now everything was robbed by the flames in a few
hours: lost forever. It was remarkable that the Senate House
was first attacked by the fire on its south side, not nearest to
the cathedral, but nearest to the imperial palace.[3] Several
buildings adjoining the Senate House were ruined by the fire,
at the same time. Both Christians and pagans were filled
with pain and sorrow: the first grieved over the ruin of Constantine's church, the second over the loss of irreplaceable
works of art from the most brilliant period of pagan antiquity.

All this happened on the 20th of June, 404.[4]

The question which, from that time on, formed the daily
conversation for the whole city, was, Who started the fire?
Who inspired the deed?

The enemies of Chrysostom first spoke out with their sus-
picions, and named the guilty party: the Archbishop himself, they said, had had the fire started, in revenge for his

second deposition and banishment, and to make sure that no successor might sit upon his episcopal throne. Of course this infamous slander found but few believers. On the other hand, Socrates, the friend and admirer of Atticus, said that the partisans of Chrysostom had originated it.[5] These again accused their opponents of having themselves started the fire, in order to burn them in and with the cathedral.[6]

The people who were really responsible for it remained undiscovered.

It was a real piece of good fortune for Chrysostom that the treasure chamber of the cathedral remained unharmed by the fire, on account of its situation and manner of building. His enemies, in their malice, spread abroad the report that he had had the fire started in order to cover up the disappearance of the treasures of the church, which he had embezzled.

A similar reproach had been made against him at the Synod of the Oak.[7] But now the two guardians of the treasure, the deacons Germanus and Cassian (the later famed Abbot of Marseilles) were in a position to hand over the entire church treasure, with a full inventory, to the imperial investigating committee, the city prefect Studius, the praetorian prefect Eutychian, the imperial treasurer John, the quaestor Eustathius, and some imperial notaries.[8] By this at least, the common slanders were laid. Soon after, the two deacons brought to Rome a ratification of this surrender of the church treasure to the authorities. There still remained the accusation of arson.

This was taken very seriously, and Chrysostom had to submit himself, on account of it, to the greatest abasement and humiliation. His partisans, the Bishops Cyriacus and Eulysius, together with a number of priests and deacons, had to submit to the disgrace of being put in chains like criminals. According to Palladius,[9] the same outrage was offered to Chrysostom, although nothing of this is mentioned in his letters of consolation to the fellow-prisoners.

Chrysostom was held in custody at Nicaea in Bithynia, while the others were confined in Chalcedon,[10] in a dirty unsanitary prison, under constant threats of more severe punishment, for having allegedly started the fire. But they did not venture to bring Chrysostom back to Constantinople, to bring him before the court there, on account of the people, and perhaps also in consideration of the lack of any proof. Only the two bishops, and the other clerical companions of the exile, remained provisionally in prison, to which Chrysostom sent them two letters of consolation.[11]

Meanwhile Chrysostom had asked to be allowed to send a letter to the court, or to his opponents. In his upright mind, he had always believed that there must still be a right way out, open for him. So he wrote from Nicaea: "Since you have given me no opportunity to defend myself against the other accusations, give me at least permission to speak regarding the church, if I, as you say, started the fire."[12]

But this last request for the maintenance of legal forms also went unanswered and unheard. There was no legal decision on the accusation. In the court circles, it was obviously wished not to place the Archbishop's affair in the center of the uncertain daily events, since the people were unusually excited and irritated. Instead of this, they pondered over what place in the great Empire would be the most suitable and most secure place of banishment for the man who could be so loved and so hated.[13]

Arsacius becomes Bishop

While the partisans of Chrysostom were being examined in large numbers, his opponents hastened to present a *fait accompli* by giving the banished man a successor. Already on the 26th of June,[14] one week after his departure, and the burning of the cathedral, the 80-year-old priest Arsacius[15] was elevated to the position of Bishop of the capital city. He was a brother of Nectarius, the predecessor of Chrysostom, a man "dumb as a fish and inactive as a frog," as Palladius pleases to express himself.[16] Socrates characterizes him with an inclusive expression: "exceedingly mild."[17] The sense of both expressions may be the same. The choice of so old a man shows that he was a dark horse, chosen because they had not been able to agree at the moment on anyone else. He also offered the best security that church discipline would not be so strictly kept. It was not for nothing that Sozomen noted that certain of the clergy under him did "whatever they wished" and that they thereby cast reflections on his

own vocation.[18]   It was told of the new Archbishop that his
brother, the Patriarch Nectarius, had once named him Bishop
of Tarsus, which by right belonged to the Patriarch of
Antioch.   But Arsacius refused the dignity.   So Nectarius
reproached him by saying: "He is waiting for my death, in
order to be my successor in Constantinople."   After that,
Arsacius swore on the Holy Gospels that he would never
accept a bishopric.   If the story were true, he well deserved
the reproach of having made a false oath; which accusation
Palladius makes against him on that account.[19]

Schism

With the elevation of Arsacius, the situation of Chrysostom's friends worsened considerably.   What could they do
now?   Should they and must they recognize Arsacius as lawful Bishop, and participate in the Divine Liturgy with him
and with his clergy?   Many did, in fear and against their will;
others hesitated.   Against these there soon began a persecution, which, in harshness and cruelty, was not far behind the
persecutions of the early Christians, and which also found its
heroic confessors and martyrs.   Many clergy and laity, like
the Christians in Nero's time, were brought before the courts
on account of the fire; others because they would have nothing
to do with the new Bishop and his clergy, but held their own
divine service with their own clergy.

Against these last, a whole stream of imperial orders and
rescripts were issued, so that the secular judges might have
a handle against the partisans of Chrysostom.[20]   In what succession, and at what intervals, the various edicts were issued,
cannot be determined exactly, at least not from Palladius.
Only this is sure, that the persecution of those who hesitated
to enter into ecclesiastical fellowship with Chrysostom's persecutors and successors took on an unusually passionate
character, and went on until the year 408.

According to Palladius, the open persecutions began after
the Easter Eve scandal of 404.[21]   Their real beginning came
after the second banishment and the burning of the cathedral.
It was hardly possible to put a penalty on ecclesiastical fellowship with Chrysostom as long as he was still dwelling in his
episcopal palace, and before Arsacius was installed as his suc-

cessor. The forty foreign bishops also remained with him undisturbed until the moment of his second banishment.

If the date of the imperial decree to the Magister officiorum Anthemius, of the 29th of January, 404, is correct, it may well have been that, by Christmas or Epiphany of 403 and 404, things had already come to a state of unrest and separate church assemblies. The decree says: "All military officials[22] are warned that they are to stay away from tumultuous assemblies. If anyone dares to act contrary to the authority of our Majesty, he will lose his military rank (*cingulum*) and will be punished by the loss of his property."

That such a decree was issued against the Johnites, Palladius verifies, saying that it was ordered by an edict that soldiers who adhered to Chrysostom should lose their "girdles" (τὰς ζωνᾶς).[23]

However, this decree, as far as its contents are concerned, corresponds better to the beginning of the year 405.

On the occasion of the fire, not only bishops and priests were arrested, but also a large number of lay people; a suit now had to be brought against them also.

The investigation of the origin of the fire was, according to Socrates,[24] and Sozomen,[25] turned over to the city prefect Optatus, who was a pagan. But in the year 404 Studius was city prefect, while Optatus first assumed this office in the year 405. Now it is entirely impossible to assume that the trials for the fire first began in 405, since already at the end of 404 an imperial decree stated that the instigator of the fire had not been found yet; wherefore the arrested clergy should be released from prison. So one must assume that Optatus conducted the trials in another capacity in the year 404, and that Socrates made an error when he attributed to him a title in 404 which he did not attain until 405.

In the common prison in Constantinople, there were soon so many " Johnites," that is, true partisans of the Archbishop, that they were said to have "changed the prison into a church." The imprisoned priests celebrated the Holy Mysteries, the believers sang psalms and hymns. On the other hand, in the churches themselves, disgusting scenes were played, giving much scandal to the people. The opponents of Chrysostom had seized the Houses of God, and where once an attentive and inspired congregation listened to the words of the Golden-mouth, now the believers were exhorted, by blustering and insults, to show their faithfulness and obedience to their chief shepherd by speaking the anathema against him.

Optatus went very energetically to work. He was obviously glad for the favorable opportunity of showing his zeal. He attempted to extort confessions by the use of the rack. Socrates says that many people were killed in this way. This is expressly stated by Palladius and Sozomen concerning one person: the young cantor and lector Eutropius.[26] This brave choir singer seems to have remained true enough to Chrysostom to be hated by his enemies.

Eutropius had led a very chaste and virginal life from his youth onwards. He was thrown into prison under suspicion of having started the fire, put on the rack, burned with torches, his flesh torn with iron hooks and combs, like the Christians in the time of Diocletian and Nero. In the midst of the torture on the rack, he breathed out his soul.[27] He had become a martyr for his bishop's cause. His executioner, who was perhaps surprised at the unintentional result of his bloody work, buried him in the middle of the night. In the Roman Martyrology his name stands on the 12th of January. The witnesses and accomplices of this murder were not merely the hangman's helpers of Optatus, but also, according to the express evidence of Palladius,[28] even clerics from among the adherents of Arsacius. So far had hatred and the mania for persecution brought them. Against such a rabble the Archbishop had to pursue his fight for moral reform in the capital city. Criminal natures of that sort were at that time brought under the protection of an abnormal state of affairs in the ranks of the clergy, and they disgraced the Church and the priesthood. Fortunately, this stigma formed only the dark background for a group of worthy and noble figures. Tigrius the priest, who had imagined the revenge of Chrysostom's opponents at the time of the Synod of the Oak,[29] now had to believe it. He had been a slave earlier, and had been set free because of his upright character. He became a cleric and progressed to the priesthood. He ranked as one of the most resolute partisans of Chrysostom.

He was very much loved by the people because of his goodness to the poor and the needy.   But now the police seized
him; he was beaten, and then bound hand and foot to the
rack, and twisted on it until his limbs were torn asunder.   At
last he was banished to Mesopotamia, which was probably
his home.[30]

Not once did these absurd, persecution-loving monsters
spare even defenseless women.   Their arrogant hate and their
sin-laden consciences felt themselves wounded if anyone
stayed aloof from them.   It was clear that the leader of the
deaconesses and virgins of the cathedral, the celebrated Olympias, who was the most sympathetic to the holy Bishop of all
the women in the higher circles of Constantinople, would not
be able, with her convictions and her reputation, to unite with
her persecutors, and to enter into ecclesiastical fellowship
with the unrighteous successors of her honoured spiritual
leader.   She could only see in them a group of unworthy and
worthless intruders and robbers, who had desecrated the holiness of the Church.   Already the fact that Olympias had
taken care of the monks exiled by Theophilus had aroused
the wrath of this violent man and his friends.[31]   Now Olympias was taken before the court, first, because, like many
others, she was suspected of having had something to do with
the fire in the cathedral, and second, because she would have
nothing to do with Arsacius.   Flattery and threats were
equally of no avail against this strong-minded woman.   While
many of her companions let themselves be intimidated, she
stood fast, and even gave some sarcastic answers to the judge.[32]

The judge asked why she had set the church on fire.   She
answered that she was not in the habit of setting churches on
fire; that at least up to that time she had always used her
wealth for the building of churches.   I already know the
habits of your life, answered the judge in a sarcastic and suspicious tone.   Well then, was the sharp and ready answer,
take the role of accuser, and let someone else be the judge.

Optatus saw that he did not prevail anything with attempts
at intimidation.   So then he tried, with winning and gentle
words, to persuade her to give up her adherence to her
banished chief shepherd, and recognize Arsacius as Bishop.
Then she and all her companions would be relieved of all

further trouble. How! rejoined Olympias, first I am arrested on the strength of a slander, then they cannot prove anything against me in the court, and now last must I defend myself against something of which I have not even been accused? Allow me first to arrange for legal counsel against the first accusation. But if anyone will force me illegally to hold fellowship with people with whom it is not allowed, then I will never go against my conscience.

Optatus could not very well refuse this lawful demand. But on the following day he summoned Olympias again before his judgment seat, and when she again refused to recognize Arsacius, he fined her the enormous sum of 200 pounds of gold, and banished her out of the capital.[33]

According to Palladius, still other deaconesses of "consular rank" were given the choice by Optatus, of either recognizing Arsacius, or else paying the same immense sum of 200 gold pounds to the fisc.[34]

Olympias went back to Nicomedia, or else this was assigned to her as a place of banishment. In her near neighborhood was Heraclidus, the former deacon in Constantinople, and now the deposed Metropolitan of Ephesus, in prison.[35] Olympias' parting from her cloister, and from her young associates, must not have been easy. She entrusted their worldly welfare to a secular relative of hers, named Marina, who complied with this request for the time being. Her successor in the office of superior was Elisanthia, also a deaconess and a relative of Olympias.[36]

The heroic steadfastness which Olympias showed did not remain unknown to Chrysostom in his place of banishment. Full of inspiration, he wrote to her and praised her courage and the fine example of fearlessness and fidelity which she had given to all Constantinople. "I am glad, I rejoice, and I am on wings with pleasure! Solitude and all other sorrows are forgotten. I am happy and overjoyed, and very proud of your greatness of soul, and your spiritual victory, and indeed not only for your sake, but also on account of that great and populous city, to which you have become a protecting tower, a haven and a wall. Your own deeds speak a glorious language, your sufferings are an instruction for men and women, so that they may also find themselves prepared for such a struggle, to go down into the arena with manly courage, and willingly bear the toils of such a battle. For this, your conduct deserves the highest admiration. For while so many men, women, and old people, who are in the highest esteem, all together are falling on their faces, and indeed without putting up much of a battle, and without even being faced by superior enemy force, they have been hurled to the ground before the battle even began; they were overcome before the struggle had really started; but you have not let yourself be overthrown in spite of all battles and struggles, you have not let yourself be crushed in spite of your misfortunes. On the contrary, the struggle has made you more powerful, and the battle has made you much stronger. Therefore we are glad, we rejoice and triumph, and we will not cease to repeat this, and make known the reason for our joy."[37]

Another distinguished lady, Nicarete, born in Nicomedia, left voluntarily, like so many others, the city in which she could not remain without conflicts of conscience. Sozomen says of her[38] that she had lived a life of voluntary virginity all her days, and that her life was unusually holy. She also showed exceptional discretion, moderation and order in all things—in her speech, as well as in her whole manner of life. With outstanding piety, she combined great prudence and great strength of character. When she lost her paternal inheritance through injustice, she did not lose her spirit, but was able to bring herself and hers through life. Also, she practised great benevolence, knew the art of healing better than many doctors, and prepared free remedies for the poor.

The wrath of the opponents was also roused against the deaconess Pentadia. For years she had seen nothing but her cloister and the Church. Now she was ordered before the court and arrested. Bribed false witnesses were brought against her. Pentadia shamed them, chiefly by a few short and chilly words. They wished at any price to force her to give evidence against Chrysostom concerning the burning of the Church; she endured the cross-fire of questions and accusations without allowing herself to be confused. She did not once satisfy herself with mere defense, but took over the attack, in which she accused the witnesses of shameless lying and slander, and proved it.[39] When, later on, she thought of leaving the city, the saint wrote to her that she ought to remain, to strengthen the others.[40]

Similarly the deaconess Amprucla, with some companions, had the opportunity of showing great courage and steadfastness, in adhering loyally to the cause of their chief shepherd.[41]

However, all struggles and efforts were in vain. The true origin of the fire could not be discovered. The search continued to be fruitless, in spite of prison, threats, and the rack, to the great rage of the enemies of Chrysostom, who would be only too glad to get something positive and palpable against him into their hands. So at last nothing was left but to drop the investigation and release the prisoners.

On the 29th of August, 404, appeared the imperial decree addressed to the city prefect Studius, which ran thus: Since it had not been possible to discover the origin of the fire, the clergy were to be let out of jail, but put into a ship and sent back to their homes. Whoever henceforth should shelter any foreign bishops or clerics risked the danger of being proscribed, as likewise did those clergy who took it upon themselves to cause tumultuous assemblies outside the churches. It was also the Emperor's will that all foreign bishops and clergy should leave the most holy city (Constantinople).[42]

This edict obviously most nearly concerned the bishops and clergy who had assembled about Chrysostom before his second expulsion, and after this, had represented his interests in Constantinople, insofar as they did not sit on the board of investigation. But it appears that it also had in view the bishops who had come forward as opponents of Chrysostom, and whom they would now be glad to get rid of. At any rate, at the same time, the noble trio, Severian, Antiochus, and Acacius, were sent out of the capital, with an order, the purport of which was kept secret, and which will be discussed later. Actually, the three did not return to the city.

But it also followed from the edict of Aug. 29, that an earlier one had already been released, which was directed against the " Johnites." The latter recognized Chrysostom as their lawful Bishop, instead of Arsacius, and held their separate assemblies for worship. It is understandable that this aroused the wrath of the opponents of Chrysostom. So, then, soon after the elevation of Arsacius, a pardon was offered to

L

the Johnites who could be induced at any price to recognize
Arsacius as the lawful Bishop, and to accept fellowship with
him. But that was a very difficult thing. Only fourteen days
after the above edict, on the 11th of September, 404, a new
decree was issued from the imperial chancellery, likewise
directed to the city prefect Studius, and which ran thus:

"Whoever possesses slaves (servants) in this city, must see
to it that they stay away from riotous assemblies. Otherwise
he will be fined three pounds of gold for every slave who is
found in such a forbidden assembly. But if a member of the
guild of money-changers, or else of a corporation, takes part
in one of these forbidden assemblies, the union (guild) must
pay a fine of fifty pounds of gold."[43]   From both decrees it
can be understood that the assemblies of the Johnites for
divine worship often became riotous, obviously because their
services were often disturbed and rendered impossible by the
opponents.

The first ones who drew the hatred of the opponents were
naturally the clergy in Constantinople, who, after the elevation of Arsacius, refused to enter into fellowship with him,
and those who were known as leaders of the Johnites. So far
as they were not already in prison because of being suspected
of setting fire to the cathedral, they were expelled and banished to the four winds.

Besides the above-mentioned priest Tigrius, who was exiled
to Mesopotamia, the priest Philip also had to leave Constantinople. He died during the flight, in Pontus. Probably he
was the same Philip who had previously held the office of a
military chaplain, and who had had to give up his post,
together with his colleague Euthymius.[44]

One of the most faithful adherents of Chrysostom was the
old priest Hypatius, who, with his two deacons Eusebius and
Lamprotatus, showed themselves steadfast in spite of all persecutions, and strengthened and directed many others through
his example.[45]   Whether they lived in Constantinople, or in
some other province of the country, is not certainly known.

The persecution naturally did not confine itself to the
capital city. In the provinces there were likewise partisans,
bishops and priests who stood for or against Chrysostom or
Arsacius. The bishops who even came to Constantinople to

offer Chrysostom their assistance still held to him, for the most part, and would have nothing to do with his enemies. They would rather give up their bishoprics than their convictions.

Among the first victims of the persecution were some of the bishops whom Chrysostom himself had installed and consecrated. It was not yet a year since he had made Serapion, his former Archdeacon, first a priest, than the Metropolitan of Heraclea. This time also, he was involved in the fall of his former master. After numerous slanders had been spread abroad about him, without any proof, he was brought before a court, mistreated in a very brutal way, had a few teeth pulled, and then banished to his home in Egypt.[46] But he seems to have found little pleasure in his proximity to Theophilus, and in coming into his spiritual keeping. According to a letter which Chrysostom wrote to Olympias from his exile, he preferred to keep himself hidden among the Marses and the Goths.[47]

The same fate overtook the bishops whom Chrysostom installed in Asia Minor in his time, especially the Metropolitan of Ephesus, Heraclidus. He was simply deposed without form or process of law, and arrested in Nicomedia.

The deposition of the Asiatic Bishops took place directly after the second banishment of Chrysostom, or perhaps even preceded it by a short time. The letter which Chrysostom wrote from Nicaea to the priest Constantius proves this. In this letter he remarks: "Unbearable sorrow has seized the churches of Asia, as well as other cities and churches."[48]

So it was. If at least a half-way worthy successor could have come to Ephesus in place of Heraclidus! But it was as if the scum of the clergy, as if the spirit of worldliness and brutalization left over from Arian times had won a last victory over the spirit of renovation, of discipline, of the Church and of real Christianity, as it had been embodied in Chrysostom's program. The respectable element among the clergy in Ephesus must now let it come to pass that a common eunuch, the slave or servant of the military tribune Victor, was elevated to the see of the holy Apostle St. John, and St. Timothy.[49] Perhaps Victor was the garrison commander in Ephesus, and used the opportunity to force his menial upon the Ephesians as bishop in derision. If it were only a matter of finding a new bishop who would suit the opponents of the exile and hold fast to them, then the eunuch was a good choice. He was not only of low birth, but a very depraved and immoral man; arrogant, avaricious, easily bribed. At best, he had an inclination for wine and women. It was even related of him that not only when he was yet a pagan, but after he had become a Christian, he had played the role of Bacchus at a banquet, his head crowned with ivy, a goblet of wine in his hand, and an actress upon his shoulders.[50]

Naturally, the six Bishops also had to fall with Heraclidus; (they who were installed with him at the Synod of Ephesus early in the year 401). Those who at that time had been deposed for simony now re-discovered their spiritual vocations, and all six received their sees again, to the great scandal of believing people. No wonder the churches became empty.[51]

It was a far more grievous blow to the cause of Chrysostom that scarcely two or three months after his second banishment, while he was perhaps still traveling on the thorny road to exile, the last pillar which could still offer him a certain moral support, fell: namely, Patriarch Flavian of Antioch, his fatherly friend, who died in the late summer of 404. He had surely already learned of the unhappy fate of his former cathedral preacher. It might have been the last great sorrow of his life, so richly blessed in labors, trials and merits.

So the kingmakers in Constantinople at once decided to place one of their own in this important patriarchal see. Their candidate was Porphyrius, who for many years had belonged to the clergy of Antioch. He had become deacon and priest, and after apparently good beginnings, had taken a less praiseworthy direction. Worldly sentiments, ambition, and flattering place-hunting became a commonplace with him. Clowns, charioteers from the circus, and actors belonged to the circle of his favored friends. According to report, he had even become a sodomite.[52]

Gossip and slander proliferate, indeed, in small and large cities, at any time. But that Porphyrius was not a worthy priest is best shown by the way in which he became a patriarch.

The people of Antioch, after the death of Flavian, would have preferred to have Constantius for their Bishop and Patri-

arch; he had served in their sanctuary from his youth.   He
was first a secretary, probably under the Patriarch Meletius,
and in this position he had proved himself absolutely inacces-
sible to gifts and bribes.   Then he became lector and deacon,
and distinguished himself especially for purity of life.   With
an unusually gentle character, he united an ascetic manner
of life, and, besides, had a clear and brilliant mind, was slow
to blame, prudent and considerate in his dealings; just in his
judgments; he possessed the gift of speaking in a penetrating
and convincing way.   He gave gladly to the poor, indeed he
himself was often still fasting in the evening because he had
spent the whole day in the service of his neighbors.   His
countenance inspired respect; his eyes had an earnest and
austere glance, his step was quick, and in spite of his age, he
had a youthful and fresh countenance.

While in the city and Patriarchate of Antioch they were
preparing for a successor, in Constantinople, where, under
the weak Arcadius and the now sick Eudoxia, spiritual and
temporal plotters were holding high revel, it was resolved to
anticipate the hopes of the people of Antioch, and to present
them with a *fait accompli*.

In order to kill two birds with one stone, the worthy triple
stars, Severian, Acacius, and Antiochus, were sent from the
capital of the East.   So favorable an opportunity of getting rid
of the three trouble-makers, after the work was finished, would
not easily offer itself again.   All three of them belonged to the
Patriarchate of Antioch.   Their appearance at the choosing
of a Patriarch would look legitimate and honorable, even
though they had dishonorable purposes in their hearts.   Their
departure from Constantinople may well have taken place
before the appearance of that imperial decree of August 29,
which ordered all foreign bishops and clergy to leave Constantinople.   At any rate, it appeared at the right time to
prevent the three from returning to the capital city.

But their actual business was nothing less than simply to
make Porphyrius Bishop and Patriarch of Antioch, although
the people knew nothing of him.   Actually, the business was
not so easy.   It was not to be accomplished in a direct and
honorable way.   But the three cared little for that.   They
had decided beforehand to proceed in a crooked and dis-

honorable way.   Indeed, in Constantinople, three decades
before, the Alexandrians had shown how that had to be done.
It was at that time that the affair of Maximus had misfired.
But here one could always call on the Emperor, even though
he did not know anything about the affair.

So what was to be done?   In Antioch, the Olympic Games,
which were celebrated every four years, were at hand.
Already it was the first day of the festivities.   Everyone, from
children to old people, went out to Daphne full of joy and
curiosity, to see the wrestling matches, races and other spectacles.   The city itself seemed dead.   Hardly anyone stayed
behind, except the sick, and thieves, who would make use of
this favorable time.

Then several men slunk into the patriarchal church of
Antioch.   Some clergy, who had been bribed, opened the
doors, and closed them again carefully.   While the people
enjoyed themselves with the spectacles at Daphne, the three
provincial Bishops, Acacius, Severian, and Antiochus, consecrated the worthless Porphyrius, with the assistance of some
of the clergy, as Patriarch of Antioch.   In secret, like thieves,
with the greatest haste, so that no spies would have the time
or opportunity to call the people in, they carried out the consecration ceremony.   They even shortened the consecration
prayers; and scarcely had they finished the ceremony—more
unholy than holy—when the three Bishops left the city, as
soon as possible, for fear the people would start a riot on their
return, and make trouble.   In this they had guessed correctly.
When the people streamed back into the city in the evening,
some of them found out what had happened, and they spread
the news during the night: Porphyrius had had himself consecrated Bishop!

Scarcely had the morning dawned, when a great crowd of
people came together, armed with torches and bundles of
kindling wood.

They were not intending to kindle a bonfire, however, but
to burn Porphyrius in his own house.   But the sly fellow
had had a foreboding of this, and had fled long before the
people came.   Valentinus, the military prefect, offered him
protection and shelter.   The more pious element among the
people now went to the church; some took the great cross and

bore it on their shoulders outdoors in a suppliant procession. Then Valentinus sent soldiers over, who dispersed the people by force, while some soldiers, probably pagans, even trampled the cross under foot. So Valentinus spilled the blood of his own fellow citizens; while outside the city, a few hours away, the Isaurian pirates[53] were laying waste Rosos and Seleucia. Porphyrius even obtained from the court a man acceptable to him for prefect of police.[54]

But he wished to revenge himself for the rousing fright they had given him. Through officials in Constantinople who were under his orders, he had his rival Constantius accused, to the most prominent bishops, of having incited the people to rebellion. In answer came an imperial rescript from the court: Constantius was banished to an Egyptian oasis. Some friends warned him in time, advised him to leave Antioch as soon as possible, and helped him to get to Cyprus, which, apparently, was his home.

Two other priests, Cyriacus and Diophantes, as well as some clerics to whom Porphyrius was not friendly, were let off more easily. The city prefect simply had to jail them as suspected of rioting, and keep them in custody until the publicity incident to the affair had somewhat quieted down.[55]

The whole affair did not succeed any better in Constantinople than in Antioch. The most eminent and most respected members of the clergy, as well as part of the Catholic public, did not wish to have any dealings with the unworthy Porphyrius, who had been forced on them illegally. So they took no part in his Divine Liturgy, but held their own assemblies for worship in secret. The others went to the cathedral, for fear of the authorities, who protected Porphyrius. Secretly, however, they cursed their new Patriarch, and hoped that the judgment of God would soon overtake him.

All these things were suspicious signs in the bosom of the Oriental Church. The first and third cities of the Empire were now, both inwardly and outwardly, torn and rent by schism. And even if one cannot grant in principle the justification of a schism on account of an unworthy chief shepherd, still one can justify and understand the feelings and motives of the friends of Chrysostom. At any rate, the

moral blame for the schism lay on the opposing side. The
respectable Catholics considered Arsacius and his successors,
and also Porphyrius, not merely unworthy, but above all as
unlawful, bishops. That was actually the case in Constantinople, at least during the lifetime of Chrysostom. But also
in Antioch, the attitude of the opponents of Porphyrius found
a powerful support in the attitude of the highest ecclesiastical
authority, that of Rome.

The clergy of Antioch had sent to Rome, to Pope Innocent,
a letter of complaint about the whole proceeding, and the
Pope understandably refused to recognize Porphyrius.[56] So
the partisans of Chrysostom were themselves disclosed, and at
the same time encouraged, by the attitude and example of
Rome.

The Pope indeed did the same thing in regard to Arsacius;
soon Rome broke off fellowship with Chrysostom's chief opponents, and placed itself on the side of the Johnites, whose
attitude it had sanctioned throughout.

So from a division in the capital, came a schism in the
Empire, and from that, a schism between the Latin and the
Greek Churches.

The attempts at persecution by the opponents of Chrysostom gradually spread this schism over the entire Eastern
Empire. These opponents sent messengers out from Constantinople through the Empire in all directions, to persuade the
Bishops to come over to their side. An ambassador came to
Palestine, Phoenicia, and Cilicia. He was rejected almost
everywhere. Only the Bishop of Aegae and the Metropolitan
of Tarsus gave in at last to the pressure which had been put
on from Constantinople, and made their peace with
Arsacius.[57] They even sought to make the Gothic clergy
deny Chrysostom. But here they had no success, at least at
first. Above all, the Gothic monks on the estate of Promotus
appear to have pledged themselves very decidedly to Chrysostom, for which he sent them hearty thanks.[58]

In order to break up the opposition more easily, the court
issued a new edict, on the 18th of November, 404. It ran as
follows:

"The Emperors Arcadius and Honorius, to Eutychius, the
pretorian prefect.

"The city prefects of the provinces are warned to prevent forbidden assemblies of those who, although orthodox, yet despise the Holy Church, and attempt to hold divine services in other places. In all cases, those who will not keep fellowship with the most reverend Bishops Arsacius, Theophilus and Porphyrius are to be sent away from the churches."[59]

About the same time, to make it impossible for the deposed bishops to regain their sees, a new law was published on the 4th of February, 405, in the names of Honorius, Arcadius, and Theodosius II. This decreed that such bishops should be held in custody, far from their episcopal cities, and any appeal to the Emperor was forbidden to them.[60]

FOOTNOTES

1. HE 8, 22 (67, 1573).
2. Palladius 10 (36).
3. Palladius 10 (36).
4. Socrates 6, 18 (721): says the 20th. In regard to the date, the same applies as in regard to the day of the second banishment.
5. HE 6, 18 (67, 721).
6. Sozomen 8, 22 (1573).
7. Palladius Dial. 10 (36); Photius Bibl. 59 (103, 108).
8. Palladius Dial. 3 (14).
9. Dial. 11 (36).
10. Chrysostom, Letter 174 (52, 711).
11. Letters 118 and 174 (52, 673 and 711).
12. Palladius Dial. 11 (36).
13. Chrysostom was kept in Nicaea about three weeks.
14. So according to the Chronicon Paschale for the year 404. (MG 92, 781).
15. Socrates 6, 19 (721-726).
16. Dial. 11 (36).
17. HE 6, 19 (724); Sozomen (8, 23) says he was mild and gentle.
18. HE 8, 23 (1573).
19. Palladius, Dial. 11 (36).
20. Palladius 9 (34): Διατάγματα ἀλλεπάλληλα κατὰ τόπον προετίθεντο. Cf. *ibid.* Ch. 11 (37).
21. *Ibid.*
22. Codex Theod. 16, 44 (ed. Mommsen 854).
23. Dial. 11 (37). It appears to Palladius that such an edict was first published in the time of Atticus.

24. Socrates 6, 18 (67, 721).

25. Sozomen 8, 23 (1576). Palladius 3 (14) refers to Optatus only as " a certain prefect," while at the same time he calls Studius " prefect of the city."

26. Palladius Dial. 20 (col. 72); Sozomen 8, 24 (1577).

27. So according to Palladius 20 (72); Sozomen 8, 24 says he died only as a result of mistreatment in prison.

28. Dialog. cp. 20 (72).

29. Socrates 6, 15 (709 C).

30. Sozomen 8, 24 (1580) and Palladius 20 (71). Tigrius is also in the Roman Martyrology on the 12th of January.

31. Palladius, Dial. 16 (47, 56 f.).

32. Sozomen 8, 24 (1577).

33. Sozomen 8, 24 (1578 f.).

34. Dial. 3 (14). It is also possible that the sum of two hundred pounds of gold had to be paid by the whole body of deaconesses in general.

35. According to the Vita Olympiadis 11. Sozomen 8, 24 (1580) says that the place of banishment was Cyzicus.

36. Vita Olympiadis 10 and 12.

37. Letter 6 (52, 599-601).

38. HE 8, 23 (1576). Cf. p. 101.

39. Chrysostom, Letter 94 (657-659).

40. Letter 104 (663-664).

41. Letter 103 (662-663).

42. Cod. Theod. 16, 2, 37; ed. Mommsen, p. 847-848. Mommsen-Meyer I, 2.

43. Cod. Theod. 16, 4, 5; ed. Mommsen, p. 854. Mommsen Meyer, I, 2.

44. Palladius Dial. 20 (72) and Chrysostom, Letter 213 and 218 (52, 729 and 731).

45. Letter 180 (713).

46. Palladius Dial. 20 (71).

47. Letter 14, 5 (52, 618). Provided the same Serapion is meant here.

48. Letter 221 (52, 733) and the letter to Pope Innocent (47, 8).

49. Brockhoff, Studien zur Geschichte der Stadt Ephesus, p. 13, note 2, says that the eunuch may perhaps have been that Castinus of whom it was said, in the eleventh session of the Council of Ephesus, that he was in Constantinople to be consecrated Bishop of Ephesus (Mansi 7, 293). There is no proof for this supposition.

50. Palladius Dial. 15 (c. 51-52).

51. *Ibid.* col. 52.

52. Palladius Dial. 16 (53).

53. Palladius 16 (55).

54. Νυκτέπαρχος (Palladius 16 [55]).

55. Palladius Dial. 16 (c. 54) states the case as though the banishment of Constantius and the arrest of the other clergy took place before the consecration of Porphyrius. But this is certainly a confusion of times. According to the way the accusation of rioting reads, it can only have meant the rioting after the consecration day of Porphyrius, since nothing is known of an earlier riot, nor any cause for it brought forward.

56. Palladius Dial. 16 (55) and 3 (14). H. Honigmann considers it necessary and possible to defend Porphyrius and to represent his ordination as legal (in: Academie Royale de Belgique, Cl. des Lettres et des Sciences Morales et Politiques. Coll. 8, vol. 46, fasc. 2. Brussels 1950. p. 33).

57. Letter 204 (725).

58. Letter 207 (726-727) and 206 (726).

59. Cod. Theod. 16, 4, 6. Ed. Mommsen, 854-855. Cf. Sozomen 8, 24, (67, 1580). Mommsen = Meyer I, 2.

60. Cod. Theod. 16, 2, 35 (ed. Mommsen 846-847) and *ibid.* Constitutiones Sirmondianae, *loc. cit.* 909. Mommsen-Meyer, I, 2.

CHAPTER XXVIII

THEOPHILUS REPORTS TO ROME

THE things which had been happening in the Eastern part of the Empire at last began to draw the attention of the Latin West. Not only had Chrysostom himself reported from Constantinople, in a letter of explanation to Pope Innocent, concerning these events, but a whole stream of courtiers, bishops, priests, and monks were moving to the West to find help and protection there. On their way they related everything concerning the unlawful and violent doings which had been carried on against Chrysostom and his partisans, in Constantinople and throughout the Empire.

However, the first authentic report which was received in Rome and Italy, of the deposition and second banishment of Chrysostom, had not come from Chrysostom himself but from Theophilus, as has been said before.

The statement of Palladius is quite understandable and credible, namely, that Pope Innocent was not only surprised by the content, as well as the style, of the Egyptian Patriarch's letter, but he was also very indignant. He even openly expressed to his entourage his anger over this "usurpation and arrogance" of the Patriarch.[1]

When the deacon Eusebius, who was Chrysostom's agent in ecclesiastical affairs, had already been in Rome a long time, learned for the first time about the letter of Theophilus concerning the deposition of his master—he probably learned it from a messenger of the Pope himself—he betook himself at once to Innocent, and delivered to him a suppliant letter,[2] in which he besought the Pope to wait a little longer; then he would surely receive a more detailed explanation of the affair. So Eusebius obviously knew nothing himself, yet, of the events which had transpired in Constantinople during the past year.

The Pope actually did not have to wait long. Three days after the messenger of Theophilus, perhaps at the beginning of June, 404, the six-man commission of Chrysostom arrived, with the three long letters which they had brought with them.

The contents of Chrysostom's letter have already been given.[3] But if Theophilus had expected that the Pope would renounce fellowship with Chrysostom at once after reading his first letter, without further ado, and consequently even refuse to receive his (Chrysostom's) embassy, he was very much mistaken.

On the contrary, the letter of the Archbishop of Constantinople could scarcely fail of its effect on the Pope and the Bishops of the West. It made clear to them for the first time an affair in which they had hitherto been in complete darkness. The unemotional, calm, and yet convincing representation of the simple facts, the point of view, completely unobjectionable canonically, which Chrysostom had taken from beginning to end of the matter in dispute, as well as his demand for a new and impartial court of judgment, the very prudent and discreet manner in which he did not mention the Empress in his letter, and defended the doings of the Emperor, and finally, the modest request, almost a matter of course under the circumstances, that ecclesiastical fellowship with him be not abandoned because of his deposition, but that the deposition itself be declared illegal, all these things must have facilitated very much the Pope's intervention in favor of the deposed and banished Archbishop. He could still less disregard this appeal to his zeal for the welfare of the Church when the highest authorities of the Eastern Church were in dispute with one another, and both sides had turned to him in the same affair. Added to this was the fact that the discord had spread to other dioceses.

A purely external comparison between the conduct of the Patriarch and that of Chrysostom in regard to Rome itself might have been an indication to the Pope as to the side on which right and wrong stood in this affair.

However, the Pope would not allow himself to be hurried into any over-hasty steps. The action of Theophilus, for which he himself had offered no reasons at all, he naturally could not sanction, and therefore could not refuse ecclesiastical fellowship to Chrysostom, who, to all appearances, had been unlawfully deposed. On the other hand, he could not treat the accusations brought against Theophilus in the letters of Chrysostom, and by the Eastern Bishops, as already proved facts; hence he could not give a judgment on Theophilus.

So Innocent did the only thing he could do under the circumstances: he did not refuse fellowship to either one, but he sent a letter to each, in which he laid down his strictly legal position on the disputed question in the following manner: First of all, he pronounced illegal the judgment that Theophilus *"appeared* to have passed."[4] Then he demanded that a new and impartial synod should be called, in which should be substituted such Orientals and Occidentals as had shown themselves completely impartial on the question at issue. So neither the outspoken friends and partisans of Chrysostom, nor his open enemies, might take part in it.

This was strictly objective. However, the Pope's position showed a clear disapproval of Theophilus, and realized at the same time the perfectly justified request of Chrysostom for a new and impartial judgment. As a preliminary measure, Innocent would not be able to decide otherwise.

A few days later, before either of the letters had reached their destinations, the second messenger of Theophilus entered Rome, the priest Petrus.[5] He came in the company of the deacon Martyrius, who was one of the clerics of Constantinople, but adhered openly to the party of the Bishop's enemies. The two messengers brought with them the Acts of the Synod of the Oak, together with a second letter from Theophilus.[6]

Palladius says of this letter[7] that in it Theophilus extenuated and covered up his own usurpation, and on this account had reproached the blessed John, for having through love of power deposed sixteen bishops in one day.[8] The entire letter was, in its principal points, an accusation against Chrysostom, and more, a lying accusation.[9] He had accused him not only of love of power, but of arrogance, and of "sacrilegious" dealings.[10] In short, the entire document bore the character of a "smear."[11]

It may speak further for the honesty or sincerity of Theophilus, that earlier, in a letter to Pope Damasus or Siricius, he had called Bishop Epiphanius of Cyprus a heretic or schismatic; but now, when it paid to play off Epiphanius against Chrysostom, he called him the "most holy." This letter from the Patriarch of Alexandria obviously contained a statement of the whole question in dispute, as Theophilus saw it, or rather, as he wished the world to see it. It must therefore have been quite a long letter, for Theophilus had had plenty of time, until his priest Petrus returned from Constantinople. It can therefore be considered very probable, indeed certain, that this second lengthy letter of his was identical with the "liber ennormis," the "monstrous document" of which Bishop Facundus of Hermiane speaks in his "Pro defensione trium Capitulorum," which was translated into Latin soon after by St. Jerome, "so that the Latins might know (according to the purpose of Theophilus) what sort of a man John was."[12] In this letter of defense of Theophilus appeared that sort of insane invective, insult and accusation against the Bishop of Constantinople which made it difficult to believe in their genuineness. Facundus himself admits that only the necessity of vindication could justify his mentioning such a document.

"John," wrote Theophilus, "persecuted his brothers, driven by the same malicious spirit by which King Saul was possessed.[13] He murdered the servants of the saints.[14] He is a mangy (contaminatus), godless,[15] plague-stricken, insane, raging tyrant, who in his folly asserts that he has promised his soul to the devil for adultery." So it is stated literally in the letter of Theophilus, asserts Facundus. Furthermore, he called him an enemy of mankind, who had outstripped the boldness of robbers by his crimes, the ringleader of the despoilers of the sanctuary, a priest of godlessness who made sacrilegious offerings; a shameless man with brazen face. "The chains in which John is bound are not such as can ever be loosed; rather he will sometime, on account of his crimes, threaten the Lord Himself on account of his crimes, and hear Him say: *Judge between me and John.*[16] I had expected that he would do right, but he does injustice and not justice.[17] So as Satan changed himself into an angel of light,[18] so also John was not what he seemed to be; on the contrary, he was a malicious demon, whose speech pours out like a torrent, dirtied with filth. He has even insulted Christ, and he will share in the fate of Judas the betrayer." "He dared to say in the church, that Christ prayed, but was not heard because He did not pray rightly." "With the Jews, he will one day hear: *Your malice has become too great.*"[19] "The Arians and Eunomians use with joy the blasphemies of John against Christ. The Jews and pagans are vindicated in comparison with you." "John is not only no Christian, he is much worse than the King of Babylon,[20] more criminal than Balthasar. John is worse than the servants of the gods and the pagans." "In this world, he says, shame is your lot, and in the next world, expect for yourself eternal damnation." "The Redeemer cried: *Seize John and cast him into exterior darkness.*"[21] Also, "Through his fire[22] he has plenty of tinder ready for himself before the judgment seat of God."

And all that, continues Facundus, still did not satisfy the wrath and fury of Theophilus; he even said of the holy John, that another punishment must be sought for him, since no torture was great enough for his crimes.

And Facundus concludes his report by saying that "whoever reads this atrocious document—atrocious not merely because of the insults it contains, but because of its heaped-up and ever repeated curses and maledictions (saepe repetitia maledictorum capitulatione) will be convinced that I have quoted this, not merely according to the meaning, but word for word, and will see how often the same expressions are repeated. The priest Jerome has translated it into Latin, for Theophilus wished that the Latins should learn from it, what sort of man John was."

The Greek original, from which this unbelievable anthology of theological polemics is taken, is unfortunately lost. A fragment of the Latin translation still survives, however, as an alleged letter in the works of St. Jerome.[23]

What must Pope Innocent himself have thought, when he read this document? Facundus said, in his touching love of peace, that this letter showed neither what John was like, who had deserved nothing of the sort, nor what Theophilus was like, whose virtue had proved itself in many other affairs, and was not to be judged by this accidental complaint; but it only showed how pitiful human life is.[24]

At any rate, the letter shows to what extent passion had

taken captive the intellect of the choleric and irritable Patriarch of Alexandria, and made him flatly incapable of essential calm reflection. It also shows what human judgment could be worth under certain circumstances, even when it came from the mouth of a patriarch.[25]

Pope Innocent did not allow himself to be disturbed by the wild railing of Theophilus, in spite of all the Bible quotations with which the Patriarch seasoned his overflow of wrath. A completely impartial study of the accompanying Acts of the Synod of the Oak showed him, better than anything else, what had really happened, and how, and on what legal grounds Chrysostom had been deposed.

From the Acts, the Pope could conclude that Chrysostom had been condemned by 36 bishops. But on a closer inspection, he must of course have established the fact that of the 36 bishops who signed, not less than 29 were from Egypt, and these also were suffragans and subjects of the Patriarch of Alexandria. And what it meant to provoke his wrath by opposition, he could also clearly see from this document.

Only seven bishops belonged to non-Egyptian dioceses. This discovery, to which the Greek Bishops and the ambassadors of Chrysostom had doubtless contributed their share, was certainly not calculated to throw a favorable light on the judgment of the synod and on the person of Theophilus. And still less so, when the Pope noticed two further important items in the Acts themselves: first, that among the complaints against Chrysostom, not one was of a "serious and important" nature,[26] and second, that Chrysostom had actually not been present at the synod at all, but had been condemned in his absence.

With this, the Pope had the first concrete proof at hand for the illegal proceedings of Theophilus and his partisans. Theophilus himself had supplied this proof. So, this time, Innocent could take a more serious tone. He gave the two messengers of Theophilus a letter, of which Palladius has given us the contents.[27] It ran as follows:

"Brother[28] Theophilus! As we read your first letter, we considered ourselves to be in fellowship with you, as well as with our brother John. We do not now wish to retreat from this position, and therefore we repeat the same once more,

now and as often as you may write to us, namely: As long
as an actual judgment has not been pronounced on that which
was only a mock trial, so long is it impossible for us to
renounce without reason the fellowship with John.   So if
you believe in the righteousness of your cause, then call a
synod, which should assemble in the spirit of Christ, and lay
your cause before it, appealing to the canons of the
Council of Nicaea; for the Roman Church does not recognize
any other law.   Thus you can be perfectly sure of your
cause."

That this letter, in its brevity and its juridical plainness,
had a certain ironical smack, can scarcely fail to be appreciated.   If the Pope said that he recognized only the canons
of Nicaea, he wished by this to reject the legality of the
(Arian) Synod of Antioch, which had served as an excuse for
the second deposition of Chrysostom.   By this means, Theophilus and his cause were placed in an extremely uncertain
position, from the start.   Theophilus had borne himself so
barbarously and conceitedly in his letter of justification, that
if it actually came to the perfectly impartial synod demanded
by Innocent and Chrysostom, he would have much, if not
everything, to fear.   The Patriarch knew this.

Meanwhile, the state of affairs in Constantinople had once
more changed, in Chrysostom's disfavor.   A short time after
the sending of the two letters to Theophilus, the priest Theoctenus entered Rome, from Constantinople, with a letter
signed by about 25 bishops and friends of Chrysostom; this
letter informed the Pope that Bishop John had been sent out
of the city by military force, and sent to exile in Cucusus.
And also that the episcopal cathedral on this occasion had
become a prey to the flames.[28a]   Innocent gave the messengers
two letters, one for Chrysostom, and one addressed to the 25
bishops who had remained loyal to him.   He begged them
with tears, as he said, to endure in patience; he was not in a
condition to help them at present, since powerful and influential persons were working against it.   He probably referred
to Eudoxia, and some of the court circles.

But neither did the opponents of Chrysostom give up their
efforts to draw the Pope to their side.   The most prominent
among them, Acacius, Paulus, Antiochus, Cyrinus, and

Severian, with some others, sent one Paternus to Rome; he announced himself as a priest of the church of Constantinople. Palladius characterizes him as an odious man, hard to understand, a man full of passionate excitement, whose malignant disposition could be read on his face. He launched forth into the wildest abuse of, and insults against, his bishop, and produced a letter from his superior, in which Chrysostom was openly accused of being the instigator of the cathedral fire.[29] That appeared even to the indifferent Romans as an all too obvious lie, and they thought that Chrysostom should have defended himself in the synod against this accusation.[30] The Pope vouchsafed no answer to the writer of this letter.

A few days after that, came Cyriacus, Bishop of Synada, to Rome. He did not bring any letters, but as an eye-witness, he was in a position to give a connected report of all that had happened in Constantinople until then. From him the Romans learned that every bishop who would not acknowledge Theophilus, Arsacius and Porphyrius was punished, by imperial rescript, with deposition and confiscation of his goods.[30a] The sad report of Bishop Cyriacus was soon afterward confirmed and supplemented by two letters which Bishop Eulysius of Apamea in Bithynia brought with him; one of these was signed by 15 bishops, who belonged to Chrysostom's company, while the other had been sent by the aged Bishop Anysius of Saloniki. The latter explained to the Pope that in this dispute he would adhere to the judgment of the Roman Church.

A month later, Bishop Palladius of Helenopolis came to Rome: the probable author of the later chief biography of Chrysostom. He indeed brought no letters, but showed the Pope a copy of the second imperial edict of punishment against the "Johnites"; this threatened with the loss of his own house anyone who would dare give concealment to any partisan of Chrysostom.

Now the Romans had to give up the last doubt of the unusual seriousness of this affair in the East. These edicts spoke in very clear language what had not been heard since the time of Diocletian. The number of refugees from the East who sought protection and refuge in Rome increased from day to day. According to Palladius, the priest Germanus appeared, with the deacon Cassian, "two pious men," Palladius says, and they were Latins besides.[31] This Cassian is none other than he who later became famous as the abbot and founder of two cloisters in Marseilles. In the history of ascetic literature and the spiritual orientation and development of Western monasticism, he attained special significance through the authorship of two documents which have become standard: "Concerning the establishment of the cloister," in twelve books,[32] and a second with the title "Conferences,"[33] namely, with Egyptian monks and hermits. Cassian had visited a large number of cloisters and monks in Egypt with his friend Germanus, and had then gone with him to Constantinople, where Chrysostom had made him a deacon.[34]

Now the two friends had come to Rome as partisans and defenders of the interests of their former Bishop. They brought the Pope a new collective letter from the clergy of Constantinople, among whom were some bishops. At any rate, it included a report on the events already known up to the second banishment, which had resulted from the "doings of the Bishops Acacius of Beroea, Theophilus of Alexandria, Antiochus of Ptolemais, and Severian of Gabala," as well as a report on the beginnings of the persecution of the partisans of Chrysostom.[35] Besides, the two produced a copy of the protocol on the surrender of the gold and silver sacred vessels, and liturgical vestments, which were turned over to an imperial commission by the clergy of the burned cathedral, before court witnesses. Members of this commission, among others, were the City prefect Studius, and the Finance Minister John. The clergy of the cathedral who remained loyal obviously supposed that the opponents of Chrysostom might be unscrupulous enough to repeat in Rome the perfidious accusation of the thievery of the sacred vessels by Chrysostom, since this lie was quickly and easily disproved in Constantinople itself.

This document, together with the protocol, is unfortunately lost, while the Pope's answer is still in existence.

After these two messengers, appeared the Greek Archbishop Demetrius of Pessinus, in the Province of Galatia secunda. He had previously hastened through the whole East, to show the letter which Pope Innocent had sent to

Chrysostom and the clergy of Constantinople, and made it known everywhere that Rome remained in fellowship with the lawful Bishop of Constantinople. Now he brought letters from the Bishops of the Province of Caria, in Asia Minor, which declared that they held fast to fellowship with Chrysostom; and he also brought a letter from the clergy of Antioch, who declared for solidarity with Rome,[36] and entered a protest against the consecration and installation of Porphyrius, which had been done against law and right.

And last came the priest Domitian, steward of church property in Constantinople, in company with a certain Villagas, priest of Nisibis in Mesopotamia. From this last, the Pope learned that ecclesiastical dissension in the East had brought confusion even into the cloisters of Mesopotamia. Domitian produced a protocol which stated that even honorable women of consular rank, deaconesses of the Church, had been brought publicly before Optatus, and compelled either to recognize Bishop Arsacius,[37] or to pay 200 pounds of gold[38] into the fisc. Also monks and religious women had fled to Rome. A great number of these fugitives were cared for and sheltered by the noble Melania the Younger, and her husband Albinus.[39] Some of the monks could even show the traces of torture endured on the rack, and the scars of scourging on their backs, by which they had saved the honor of their position, and atoned for the injustice of their father Isaac.

As an answer to all these written and verbal reports, Pope Innocent sent two letters to the East: one to the exile in Cucusus, and one to the clergy in Constantinople who had remained faithful to him.[40]

The letter to Chrysostom runs thus: "Innocent to his beloved brother John: One who is guiltless may indeed expect all good, and reckon on the mercy of God; nevertheless, we not only wish to exhort you to patience, but also through the deacon Cyriacus,[41] to send you a letter to that effect, that the arrogance of the oppressor may not be stronger than the hope of a good conscience. However, I do not need to teach you, the teacher and shepherd of so many people, that it is often the best who are tried, to find out whether they keep perfect patience and are not overcome by affliction.

A good conscience is actually the surest support against all
the wrongs which one has to suffer. He who does not conquer
this through patience, gives another reason for malicious
opinions. For he who can rely on God and his own conscience must understand how to bear all. The brave and
right-doing man can be tried in his patience, but not conquered. His spirit will be guarded by the word of Holy
Scripture. Very rich in examples of patience are the holy
books which we read to the people, and which show that
almost all the saints were visited with various and continual
misfortunes, and tried as though in a court, and only so did
they win the victor's crown of patience. So may you, beloved
and honorable Brother, establish your good conscience, which
is the consolation of virtue in misfortune. The clean conscience will be anchored in the haven of peace under the
eyes of God."

In this purely ascetic and sober letter of consolation, two
things at least stand out: that the Pope was already convinced
of the complete innocence of Chrysostom, and second, that
at this time he knew of no other help or consolation for the
exile than *patience*. The complete omission of all mention
of persons or essential circumstances in this letter seems to
indicate that it was written at a time at which Innocent had
not yet openly broken with Theophilus and the other opponents of Chrysostom; perhaps because he reckoned on the
synod being called as planned. After all, the chief wish
which Chrysostom had expressed in his letters to Pope Innocent and the Italian Metropolitans had been more than fulfilled: the Pope remained in fellowship with him, and often
showed him that he considered him absolutely guiltless.
That must have been no small consolation to the poor
exile.

At the same time, with this letter to the exiled Bishop, the
Pope gave to the deacon Cyriacus still another one, much
longer, for the clergy and people of Constantinople, insofar
as they remained loyal to their Bishop. In it he condemned,
openly and without restraint, the unlawful deposition of their
Bishop, rejected the canons of the Synod of Antioch as worthless, and proved the necessity of a new synod.

The important part of the letter ran thus:

"Innocent, Bishop, offers his greetings to the priests and deacons, together with the clergy and people of the Church of Constantinople, who are obedient to Bishop John, our beloved brother.

"From your letter, which you have sent me through the priest Germanus and the deacon Cassian, and which I have read again and again, I could clearly see with pity what misfortunes you have had to suffer. Here only patient endurance, with the help of God, can lead you to your goal. That you are resolved to do this, you have given me to understand by your letter. And we suffer with you. For who could endure to look on calmly while the peace and harmony of the Church are being destroyed by the very ones who are called to protect it in the first place? Guiltless Bishops are now being expelled from their own churches and dioceses. And the first one to whom this happened was our brother and fellow-servant in sanctity, John, your Bishop. He has been deposed unheard, without formal accusation or judicial hearing, and now someone else will be installed in the place of him who is still living. Nothing like that has happened since the time of the Fathers, and it is to be condemned. No one can be Bishop who is installed unlawfully.

"But as far as the canons are concerned, we recognize only those which were proclaimed by the Council of Nicaea. Other canons which are in opposition to those of Nicaea, and which were proclaimed by heretics, are condemned by Catholic Bishops, together with their heretical and schismatic teachings. So it has been ruled by the Bishops before us, at the Synod of Sardica.

"What then is to be done in the case before us? *It is necessary that a synod take up the case*, as we have already requested (as in the first letter). But until then, for the improvement of relations, we must submit ourselves to the decision of God, and the judgment of our Lord Jesus Christ. If we stand fast and trust in God, we may all hope in Him. But we have only one thing in view, that the ecumenical synod may assemble, so that peace may be established again, if God so wills it. So let us wait in patience, and trust in the help of God. Concerning the things which you have to suffer, we have been informed by the Bishops Demetrius, Cyriacus,

Eulysius and Palladius, who have fled hither at various times."[42]

These two letters may have been written in the late autumn of 404, after the great number of fugitives had been able to give the Pope a clear picture of the situation in Constantinople.

The thought of a new general synod, unceasingly called for by Chrysostom, remained thenceforth the chief care of the Pope. It was at the same time the hope of one side and the bugbear of the other.

FOOTNOTES

1. Dial. 1 (8).
2. Ἐντευκτικοὺς λιβέλλους, *loc. cit.*
3. Ch. 26.
4. Palladius 3 (c. 12). The original text is unfortunately lost.
5. The «μετ' ὀλίγας πάλιν ἡμέρας» may be dated first from the day of the Pope's answer. Palladius says nothing of how many days elapsed between the arrival of the ambassadors and the Pope's answer. At any rate, the priest Petrus had time to travel from Alexandria to Constantinople and back. If one wishes to count the "few days" from the *arrival* of the ambassadors of Chrysostom, one must assume that Theophilus had already received news earlier from this planned embassy, to which he sent Peter, and when he first learned of the actual arrival, he sent the courier to Rome.
6. That Theophilus had to send the synodal documents to Rome with his first courier, and that the second courier to Rome, Petrus, appeared suddenly in the company of a deacon from Constantinople, proves clearly that the Patriarch had had the documents brought from Constantinople meanwhile; and with the Alexandrine priest they sent a deputy from the clergy inimical to Chrysostom.
7. Dial. 13 (47). The priest Petrus, with the letter of Theophilus and the acts of the Synod of the Oak, could not well have reached Rome until October or November.
8. Cf. Ch. 13.
9. Dial. 13 (47); γράψας κατὰ Ἰωάννου καὶ ψευδῆ γράψας.
10. Dial. 19 (67) and 20 (81-82).
11. Dial. 16 (56): λοιδορῶν τὸν μακάριον Ἰοάννην.
12. Pro defensione trium Capitulorum 6, 5 (ML 67, 676-78).

Bardenhewer, Gesch, der altk. Lit. III, 117 has acknowledged the existence of the pamphlet and its translation by Jerome.

13. 1. Kg. 16, 23. So Theophilus wished to play for himself the role of the innocently persecuted David.

14. Cf. Synod of the Oak, ch. 22, p. 247-48.

15. " In Ecclesia primitivorum impium " = Hebr. 12, 23.

16. Is. 5, 3.

17. Is. 5, 7.

18. 2 Cor. 11, 14.

19. Ps. 56, 11 or 103, 1.

20. Obviously, because he allegedly robbed the church treasures.

21. Matth. 22, 13.

22. A clear allusion to the burning of the cathedral. It was after this that Petrus first came to Constantinople.

23. His actual arrival and activity I have referred to in: S. Jérôme et S. Chrysostome = Revue Bénédictine 23 (1906) 430-36.

24. *Loc. cit.* (c. 678).

25. Even St. Cyril showed himself so much influenced by the judgment of his uncle that he placed Chrysostom in the same class with the Arian Bishop Eudoxius = Facundus Herm. *loc. cit.* (col. 678 C).

26. Palladius 3 (c. 12): αἰτίας βαρείας.

27. Dial. 3 (12-13).

28. The Pope still addresses Bishops as " Brother."

28a. This letter must have been written after Chrysostom's second banishment and after his departure from Nicaea, so at the earliest, the second half of July 404.

29. Dialog. 3 (13).

30. Ὡς μηδὲ διὰ τοῦτο δοῦναι ἀπολογίαν τὸν Ἰωάννην ἐν ἐπισήμῳ συνόδῳ. *Ibid.* This cannot have meant the Synod of the Oak, but the next synod to be expected.

30a. This misfortune must also have affected Bishop Cyriacus, for in the year 408 Theodosius was already Bishop of Synada. (ASS 13. Jan. 477 C.).

31. Dialog. 3 (13). H. J. Marrou, La patrie de Jean Cassien, in : Orient Chr. Per. 13 (1947) 588-96, considers the name " Cassian " a topographical designation, because Cassian was born in Casincea, north of ancient Tomi. According to this, Cassian was a Scythian-Goth.

32. ML 49, 53-476.

33. Collationes = ML 49, 477-1328.

34. Cassian, De incarnatione Christi 7, 31 (ML 50, 269): " Adoptatus enim a beatissimae memoriae Ioanne episcopo in ministerium sacrum, atque oblatus Deo." While Germanus stayed

in Rome, Cassian later went to Marseilles. He is of such significance in the history of dogma that he is considered the father
of Semipelagianism (Cf. Collatio 13). Later he distinguished
himself again as a fighter against Nestorianism by his third work,
" De Incarnatione Christi, contra Nestorium." (ML 50, 9-272).
Cassian died at an advanced age, and highly respected, in the
year 435. Concerning his life see Butler, The Lausiac History 1,
203 ff.

35. The answer of the Pope = Sozomen 8, 26.

36. ῞Οπου ἐπισπῶνται τὴν ῾Ρωμαίων εὐταξίαν = Pall. 3 (14).

37. George Alexandrinus says Atticus. Palladius shows by his
account that his sources originate from the year 404. The same
terror continued under Atticus.

38. Cf. p. 313.

39. Palladius, Hist. Laus. 62 (ed. Butler 157).

40. Sozomen (8, 26) found, probably in the Patriarchal archive,
a Greek translation of both letters, of whose authenticity there is
no doubt.

41. Very probably the same Cyriacus who brought the letter of
Chrysostom to Pope Innocent (Palladius 2 [8]).

42. Sozomen 8, 26 (67, 1558-89).

CHAPTER XXIX

ON THE ROAD TO EXILE

WHILE the friends and partisans of Chrysostom, bishops, priests, and laity, sat under examination, or fled to the West, to Rome, Chrysostom himself was held for fully three weeks in Nicaea, uncertain as to what his immediate fate was to be. He was not indifferent as to the place whither he would be banished. On account of his weak health and his constant stomach trouble, he had a real dread of long journeys on foot. Exiles were not allowed to travel by the state post. It seems to have taken a long time in Constantinople, either for them to persuade themselves that the Archbishop was not responsible for the fire, or else to decide on the final place for his banishment.

Finally, however, it was decided at court to send him to Cucusus, in Armenia Secunda.[1] That was a bitter disappointment for him. He had hoped to be allowed to go to a larger city, which would at least possess a healthy climate, and the most important requirements for the life of a civilized Greek. Especially, warm baths were an indispensable necessity for him. To all appearances Sebaste, the chief city of Armenia, had been mentioned; for a rich friend of his, named Arabius, had already offered him his villa there to dwell in.[2] But *Cucusus*—a little unknown border town, with a garrison, somewhere in Armenia, in the neighborhood of the dreaded Isaurian mountains; a village which did not have a market or even a little shop,[3] where scarcely half a dozen educated men were living. How could that be endured?

Cucusus in Armenia—the name was not new to Chrysostom. He must have heard it before somewhere. Indeed, in the Theodosius Church in Constantinople, a martyr lay buried, one of his own predecessors: Bishop Paulus of Constantinople. The Emperor Constantius had sent him into exile 53 years before (in the year 351) on account of his faith;

and the place of his exile had been Cucusus in Armenia. Then, in his place, Macedonius had been made Bishop, while Paulus himself had been strangled by the soldiers who took him into exile, doubtless by order of the higher command.[4]

Was perhaps the same thing to happen to him? Was the choice of the place of exile to be a quiet answering sign for the soldiers who were to bring him to Cucusus? The thought must have obtruded itself upon his mind, and surely was not to be rejected without further consideration. He knew, ever since the Synod of the Oak, that there were a large number of influential people, even among the clergy, who would rather see him dead than alive. At any rate, that was not a tranquilizing prospect for the future, and much which he saw on the journey and in Cucusus itself could only confirm his possible fears.

In the first half of July the traveling party reached Nicaea.[5] Before the departure, Chrysostom sent a farewell greeting to Olympias. He besought her not to have any unnecessary worries about his journey: "The stop for rest in Nicaea and the fresh air have done me much good, and I have been very well and kindly treated by my escort. Only send me news of yourself and of your health very often, for it pains me each time when people come here who could have brought letters from you and did not bring any."

From these lines speaks the noble, religious fellowship of soul which united these two personalities.

As to the route which the little caravan took through Asia Minor, nothing is known with certainty. Only some of the stops are known: Nicaea, Ancyra, Caesarea. The way was not only long, but also dangerous. Further on in the southeast, in Pisidia, Cilicia, and Cappadocia, dwelt wild tribes of robbers, who had their seats and strongholds in the Taurus mountain chain, and bore the name of Isaurians. For the surrounding provinces in the fourth and fifth centuries, these were about what the Turks were for half of Europe from the fifteenth to the seventeenth centuries; they lived by armed piratical sallies, by land and water, by which they kept Syria and half of Asia Minor in fear and terror.[6] It was very difficult to come at them by military means. They did not come down to the plains, and in the mountains they were almost impossible to catch.

They first became Christians in the sixth century. One of them mounted the throne as Leo III. In the fifteenth century they were conquered by the Turks, and today Christianity is again lost among them.

It was surely not without a malicious purpose that Chrysostom's place of exile was chosen in this district so greatly afflicted by the invasion of these Isaurians. How easily could he become a victim of a surprise attack by these wild, half- or all-pagan hordes. Theophilus, Arsacius, and their friends, as well as some of the court circles, would scarcely have felt pity for that.

All through the journey the noble exile received the greatest consolation, in being given the most touching sympathy for his fate. The inhabitants, and also strangers from the provinces of Asia Minor, from Bithynia to Cappadocia, or Armenia Secunda, whom they met at each station on the journey, wept abundantly on seeing him, who bore his loss with so much calm and resignation.[7] It gave him a special joy, when he received letters and news from the friends and partisans whom he had left behind. He also took advantage of every such opportunity to answer them as soon as possible. Unfortunately, most of these letters were lost, either through fate or through the delicate feelings of the recipients. Some of the latter collected and preserved them as dear memorials of their author; others were not so careful. Probably many of the letters never reached their destination.[8]

Olympias preserved the letters of her spiritual father and director most faithfully. The disaster which had come upon the Church of Constantinople, the indescribable scandal, which spread from clerical circles and remained outwardly victorious, all this was obviously too much for that noble and deeply religious woman, whose heart was so zealous for the honor of the Church and the good of souls. The experience was a too cruel deception for her sensitive spirit. She fell into such a deep depression that apparently she never completely recovered from it all the rest of her life. It was just toward this that Chrysostom's letters to her were directed, with a specially warm sympathy and sincerity. With incomparable delicacy of feeling, he sought to represent his own pain and suffering as something insignificant; he spoke of everything that might bring consolation to her, and urged her always to bear her misfortunes courageously and with resignation to God's will. He never forgot to say, in conclusion, that she must write to him often, that he would be very glad to answer, if only she assured him that his letters were really a consolation and a relief to her.[9]

Chrysostom appears to have been well treated on the way to Cucusus by the soldiers who formed his escort. At least he writes to this effect, to Olympias, and compliments them for being so ready to serve him that he did not need or miss any other servants.[10] With the head of the escort, who was named Theodore, he stood on very good footing. The same Theodore took back his letter to Constantinople from exile.[11]

But in spite of all the sympathy, the journey for the frail Bishop was a continual martyrdom, on account of the physical and spiritual sufferings which he had to bear, alternately, and often both at the same time. While the people and the clergy treated him, almost all through the journey, with touching respect and love, on the other hand he had occasionally to endure from his own episcopal brothers what one can hardly find it possible to believe.

As he came through Galatia, he was threatened with death, at least in Ancyra, by Bishop Leontius, who was his bitter enemy.[12] He was consoled by the expectation of finding a better reception in Caesarea. When he had traversed Galatia, and stepped over the border into Cappadocia, he heard that the Metropolitan Pharetrius had sent out messengers everywhere, even to the monasteries of men and women, saying that if Chrysostom should come through, he should be told that Pharetrius was expecting him, and longed to see him, to show him his love.[13] That cheered the poor exile, all the more since his weak health could hardly endure the difficulties of the journey any longer. The irregularities in food and sleep, the changes in climate, the heat of high summer, the pain and suffering of endless marches, the dangers and tumults, the lack of doctors and medicines, the bad water, hard and mouldy bread, and all the other things that accompanied a long journey in those times, had affected him so much that he was extremely ill with fever, completely worn out and exhausted, so that he came to Caesarea more dead than alive.[14]

Here they brought him as soon as possible to the nearest shelter which they could find, on the outskirts of the city. Doctors were called, and the danger of death proved well-founded: the body of the sufferer was burning with a fiery fever. Their unselfish care, however, succeeded in slowly quenching the fever.[15] The clergy came; also monks and cloistered women, to render every possible service to the sick man. Only one he did not see, Pharetrius, who had apparently longed so greatly to see him. On the contrary, it seemed now that the Metropolitan expected and wished that Chrysostom would go further on, as soon as possible.

This was a painful and bitter deception for the poor invalid.

But worse was to come. Scarcely had Chrysostom's condition improved somewhat, so that he could think of resuming the journey, when a fearful rumor spread through the city of Caesarea, to the effect that a great mob of Isaurians had broken into the province, devastated the level land, and already set a large village on fire and killed the people. A great excitement seized the inhabitants; it was believed that the enemy was already at the doors; and every one, even the old people, hastened with their weapons to defend the city walls.

But instead of the Isaurians, another enemy came. With the earliest break of day, appeared a horde of fanatical monks,[16] before the house in which Chrysostom was staying; they demanded with loud shouts that Bishop John should depart, otherwise they would burn the house, and either burn him in it, or slay him. No allusion to the threatened danger from the Isaurians was of any avail, nor any begging for consideration of the weak health of the patient; the monks raged and blustered in such a rough and passionate way that even the soldiers of the escort were worried. Indeed, the monks threatened to seize the soldiers themselves, and boasted that they had already thrashed many of the Praetorians disgracefully.[17]

The soldiers of the escort now besought Chrysostom to proceed further: it would be better to be in the hands of the

Isaurians than to fall among those wild beasts! Meanwhile someone had informed the prefect of the city what was going on. He hastened thither, but was no more able to accomplish anything against these hysterical fanatics. He dared not use force, perhaps because he feared that by this he might fall into disfavor in Constantinople. In his helplessness, trying to quiet the monks meanwhile, he sent to the Metropolitan Pharetrius, and begged him to wait a few days, at least, in consideration of the condition of Chrysostom's health, and the danger from the enemy. But all this was of no avail. The day passed in fruitless negotiation. The next morning, the monks appeared again, and acted still more violently and impatiently than they had the night before. The priests and clerics who had previously showed the unfortunate exile so much sympathy did not dare visit him any more, even when he begged them; they kept themselves concealed, and sent him word that Pharetrius was to blame for everything, for it had all happened with his consent.

So at last there remained nothing but to yield to force. About the middle of the day, under a burning sun, the exile, who was again sick with fever from the tumult, and from two sleepless nights, and who seemed followed by misfortune, had to get into a litter once more; for it was impossible for him to travel on foot or on horseback.

They left the inhospitable city, toward an uncertain fate; for perhaps they might yet fall into the hands of the Isaurians. Once more it was the simple people who did not shrink from guarding him. They all wept and grieved, and many hurled curses and threats against those whom they considered responsible for such shameful treatment of an exiled bishop, who moreover was considered holy. "Whither will you lead him then—to manifest death?" asked one, and another, full of bitterness, said to Chrysostom: "Yes, go, I beg of you; you may fall into the hands of the Isaurians, if you only escape ours. Whatever may happen to you, you will be more secure if you escape our hands!" It was not until he had the city walls behind him, that some priests followed him, slowly, and bade him farewell with grief.

Whither should they go now? A distinguished lady named Seleucia, the wife of Rufinus, who had shown him consider-

ation before, earnestly besought him to come and stay at one
of her country houses, which was about five miles from the
city. She even sent some servants and guides to him. So they
traveled the short distance to this place.

Meanwhile, scarcely had Pharetrius heard of Seleucia's
offer, than he sent her a messenger and demanded, with
threats, that she expel from her estate him who had been
expelled from Caesarea. But Seleucia did not allow herself
to be intimidated. She came out herself to her estate, but
did not inform Chrysostom of the demand of Pharetrius. On
the contrary, she ordered her steward to take care of Chrysostom as well as he could; if the monks should come thither
again, in order to injure or mistreat him, he was to call
together as quickly as possible the peasants and tenants of her
other estates, and to battle the monks out and out. Then she
besought Chrysostom to move to her own dwelling, which had
a fortified tower; it was impregnable, and he would be secure
there from Pharetrius and his monks. Unfortunately the
sick man did not take advantage of this invitation. Perhaps
he believed that his persecutors would even let him rest
here.

But the opponents were not sleeping. While it was still
night, some people came, who were sent, it was said, by
Pharetrius; they demanded of Seleucia, with the most violent
threats, that she expel her guest. In her solitude, and with
the impossibility of getting help at the moment, frightened
at the danger and darkness of the night, also perhaps egged
on by her household, Seleucia allowed herself to be intimidated. But she was ashamed to admit her terror, and, according to Chrysostom, grasped at a woman's trick. Also it may
have been possible, after all, that she was not the author but
the victim of the trick. Only this much is certain, that in
the middle of the night, the priest Evethius burst into Chrysostom's sleeping chamber, roused him up, and cried in a loud
voice: "Up! the barbarians are here, they are already upon
us!"

It is a pity that Chrysostom does not tell us whence this
Evethius came, and in whose service he was: whether he
belonged to Pharetrius, or to Seleucia, or to Chrysostom himself. It is understandable that the poor sick man, in the first

M

moment of being awakened, was helpless: "What can we
do?" he asked. "We cannot go back into the city, since we
had to flee out of it, in order to avoid something worse than
the Isaurians." Actually, it was midnight, and pitch dark.
No one was there who could have helped them—everyone
had run away. In anxiety and fear, expecting death at any
moment, tortured with pain, Chrysostom roused himself up
and ordered a light kindled. But Evethius had the light put
out, for fear, he said, that it would allure the barbarians. So
it was decided to flee to the mountains.

But Chrysostom was scarcely able to negotiate the steep,
rough mountain path on foot, so they prepared for him a sort
of little litter or bed on the back of a mule ($\lambda\epsilon\kappa\tau\acute{\iota}\kappa\iota\upsilon\nu$). But
this was the cause of another mishap. In the intense dark-
ness, the mule had a fall, and Chrysostom was thrown out;
he almost fell to his death. With difficulty he picked himself
up. Meanwhile the priest Evethius had also mounted on his
beast, and Chrysostom dragged himself, with Evethius holding his hand, or pulling him further along, as well as he could.
It was not until morning that he and his companion learned
that the invasion of the Isaurians was absolutely an invention,
whose object had been to produce a panic.

What was the reason for the scandalous behavior of the
Metropolitan? Chrysostom asks himself this question in a
letter to Olympias.[18] He believed that it was envy and
jealousy. When Chrysostom had entered the city of Caesarea,
all the officials, professors, tribunes, and all the people had
promised him every day to be of service to him, and to prove
their love and fidelity. That, he believed, had aroused the
envious wrath of Pharetrius.

That was possible—but perhaps less malice and more
cowardice entered into it. It can be clearly observed that in
the question of the treatment of Chrysostom from the beginning, two currents in Constantinople battled with each
other: one wished to have him treated as well and as con-
siderately as possible. This view was that of the circle which
momentarily prevailed at court; at least the escort soldiers
had received such orders, and were obviously treating him
accordingly.

At the same time, another circle sought from the beginning

to make the fate of the exile as difficult as possible, and, if it could be done without observation, to avoid a possibility of his return, by a speedy death which would not look like a murder. Internal and external reasons speak for the existence of such a private circle among those clergy whose tenacious, enduring hatred chiefly brought about the deposition and banishment of the Patriarch. If a corresponding sign, accompanied by threats of disfavor, came to the aged and timorous Pharetrius, that might explain his unworthy and shameful treatment of Chrysostom.

In spite of this, the latter was right, when in his letter to Paeanius he designated the conduct of the Metropolitan as unpardonable and inexcusable.[19] That the barbarous monks could only have been roused against the exile by clerical circles is clear without further explanation. But it is sad that they carried out their orders in such a brutal way. The great Basil, the predecessor of Pharetrius, and spiritual father of monasticism in Cappadocia, would have risen from his grave on that day for shame of Christian Caesarea. But the time of the great and holy men was gone. It was the time of beginning decline, of the little ambitious men, who hunted the great ones out of their own places into exile and death.

Chrysostom, in one of his letters to Olympias, made the terrible remark that he feared no one so much as the bishops, with the exception of a few.[20]

However one may consider this incident in Caesarea, there remains so much scandal-giving that one finds it completely comprehensible if Chrysostom, who was the very one to whom scandal in clerical circles was most painful, begged both Olympias and Paeanius[21] to tell no one about it, but indeed if anyone should mention it, to reprimand him. For himself, the saint took all these things as opportunities of "atoning for his sins," and of "laying up a treasure of merit for himself in heaven." That was reason enough for rejoicing and being glad, and giving thanks to God.

Chrysostom was not to lack similar sad occasions for spiritual joy in days to come. Among continual dangers, fears, and great difficulties, the journey in the direction of Cucusus was continued; finally they arrived there. The entire journey had consumed about 70 days, that is, from

about the 10th of July until about the 20th of September.[22]
It was a half or a whole martyrdom for Chrysostom. " Now,"
he wrote in his first letter to Olympias from Cucusus, " when
the difficulties and sufferings of the journey are past and gone,
I can portray them to you. For a full month and more, I had
to battle with the most fiery fever, and in this condition I had
to continue on the long and difficult way. Furthermore, I
suffered from severe stomach trouble. Only think what that
meant, when there were no doctors, no warm baths, no care,
no comforts of any kind. And with all that, was the constant
fear of the Isaurians, who threatened us from all sides."[23]
One can well feel for him, and understand that he breathed
more freely when he finally had the troublesome journey
behind him, and felt secure again in Cucusus under the protection of the garrison, and now at least could rest.

Cucusus, today Göcksun, is an oasis surrounded by mountains, through which a wide brook (Tölbüzek) flows. In the
warm season the place has a pleasant summer freshness; in
the long winter it is very cold. The village, with the city
hall, stands on a little hill on the plain. Formerly it was
probably the site of a small Greek garrison. It once belonged
to the Province of Cappadocia; in Chrysostom's time, to
Armenia Secunda.

On the same day of Chrysostom's arrival came also the
deaconess Sabiniana, very probably his aunt,[24] who, in spite
of her age, had hastened from Antioch when she heard that
he had been banished to Cucusus. The length and strenu-
ousness of the journey she had taken in her stride. She
declared that, in spite of all, she would never again forsake
him, even though he should be banished to Scythia.[25]

The priest Constantius also wrote him, asking if he might
come and share his exile.[26] He actually did come, likewise
another priest named Evethius.[27] How long the two
remained with him is uncertain. Constantius went from
Cucusus to Phoenicia, and then took his way back to Antioch.
Chrysostom gave him a letter to the four Antiochene priests,
Castus, Valerius, Diophantes, and Cyriacus, with the request
that they would grant every consideration to Constantius,
who had been so much tried and persecuted.[28] Also other
clergy of Constantinople expressed the intention of visiting

their banished Bishop in exile, as soon as they were liberated from prison.[29]

Furthermore, Chrysostom found in his place of exile a good and benevolent reception. Besides the Bishop of the place, there was a wealthy landed proprietor there named Dioscurus; these did all they could to make his stay as pleasant as possible. Dioscurus even sent out his servants from Caesarea to beg the Patriarch to take up his dwelling in no other house but his. He especially saw to it that everything imaginable was taken care of for the coming winter, so that the poor health of the exile would suffer no injury. There were also other gentlemen of Constantinople who ordered their stewards there to care for all his necessities.[30]

Even the prefect of Armenia, Sopater, showed himself extremely benevolent to Chrysostom. The latter wrote in gratitude to Bishop Cyriacus (of Emesa or Synada?), requesting him to show his special attention to the son of Sopater, the prefect of Armenia Secunda, who was studying there.[31]

In the beginning things went very well. The long rest and the feeling of security after the continual struggles and tumults of the long journey allowed him to feel the benefits of Cucusus. The warmth of the late summer, and the clean, fresh mountain air, did their work. He wrote to Olympias that he again felt completely restored to health, indeed stronger and healthier than he had been in Constantinople. The climate was scarcely less beneficial for him than that of Antioch.[32] Indeed, in his joy he forgot so completely the troubles and difficulties of the journey, that he wrote to Firminius that he had endured the journey well and was in good condition.[33]

However, in reality Cucusus was a solitary and forsaken place, "the most forsaken corner of earth," as Chrysostom himself repeatedly expressed it.[34] Its real importance lay in the garrison, always very small, which had to protect the boundary of the Empire against the Isaurians.[35] That offered at least a certain quiet, in so far as it gave protection against sudden attacks. Moreover the Isaurians were snowed in during the winter, in their mountains, and scarcely climbed out each year before Pentecost.[36]

FOOTNOTES

1. Armenia Secunda had earlier belonged to Cappadocia.   Cf. Theodoret, HE 2, 4 (82, 997 A B).
2. Chrysostom, Letter 121 (52, 676).
3. Chrysostom, Letters 13 and 14 to Olympias (610 ff.).
4. Socrates 2, 26 (67, 268).
5. The third, according to Letter 10 to Olympias (52, 608) but on the fourth, according to Letter 221 to Constantius (52, 732).
6. In the Peregrinatio Sylviae-Aetheriae (ed. Ponialowsky p. 37) the Abbess says of the Isaurians " quia satis mali sunt et frequenter latrunculantur."   Cf. also the Syrian biography of St. Simeon Stylites the Younger (died 592) n. 7; ed. by Hilgenfeld = T. u. U. 32 (1908) IV. p. 83 f., and Theodoret, Hist. Rel., ch. 10, 12 and 21 (82, 1392, 1398, 1448); Philostorgius, HE 11, 8 (65, 664-65).
7. Letters 8 and 9 to Olympias (52, 607 and 608).
8. Cf. Letters 179 and 226 (713 and 736).
9. Letters 8, 9, 10 etc. (607 ff.).
10. Letters 10, 11 (608 f.).
11. Letters 672 and 115 (672).   G. Bardy, in Mélanges de sc. rel. 2 (1945) 272, note 1, says that Theodore probably took with him letter 1 and perhaps letter 13.
12. Letter 14, 1 (613).
13. Letter 14, 1 (613).
14. Letter 120 (674).
15. τὸ τριταῖον = the three-day fever (intermittent fever).
16. Δροῦγγος μοναζόντων is the expression which Chrysostom uses and he adds that this word shows the maniacal fury of these men (μανίαν).   Letter 14, 2.
17. Actually, the good or indiscreet zeal of the monks had already interfered with the course of justice, either in court itself, or among the escorts, so that Theodosius I had already been forced to issue prohibitions against it.   The example of the Patriarch Theophilus has shown how often the primitive zeal of the monks, who were uneducated, and came from the lowest classes of the people could degenerate to the border of fanaticism, especially when bishops roused and misled them.   About the year 452, Bishop Xenaias (Philoxenus) of Hierapolis near Antioch, a friend of Dioscurus, wished to compel the Patriarch Flavian II of Antioch to condemn the Council of Chalcedon (451) and the dogmatic letter of Pope Leo I.   He collected a great number of monks around him, told them that the true faith was in danger, and led the whole crowd to Antioch, to the palace of the Patri-

arch Flavian. With great clamor and tumult they presented their
demands. When Flavian, angry at such proceedings, refused, the
monks became more wild and blustering. Then the people of
Antioch lost patience. They grasped their weapons, and attacked
all those who had not had time to get away. The bodies were
thrown into the Orontes. (Evagrius Scholasticus, Historia Eccles.
3, 32 = 86², 2665). Of course the Antiochene clergy themselves
had, more than twenty years before, given a bad example of such
oriental readiness for battle. When the Metropolitan Theodore
of Cyprus was sojourning in Antioch in the year 435, he was
requested by the clergy there to recognize the supremacy of the
Patriarch of Antioch. When he refused, they fell upon him and
beat him as though he were a slave, so that he died soon after
his return. S. Vailhé, Formation de l'église de Chypre 431 = Echos
d'Orient 13 (1910) 9.

18. Letter 14, 3 (616).
19. Letter 204 (724 f.).
20. Letter 14, 4 (617).
21. Letters 14 and 204.
22. Letters 234 to Brison (52, 739-740).
23. Letter 13 (610).
24. Cf. Vol. 1, p. 1.
25. Letter 13 (611).
26. Letter 13 (611).
27. Letter 114 (670). This Evethius is probably identical with
the Evethius mentioned on p. 347.
28. Letter 62 (643).
29. Letter 114 (670).
30. Letter 13; 14, 1 and 75 (610 ff. and 649).
31. Letter 64 (644).
32. Letter 14, 4 (617).
33. Letter 80 (651) and 84 (652).
34. Letters 234-236 (739 ff.).
35. Letter 13 (610).
36. Letter 14, 4 (617).

CHAPTER XXX

DEATH OF THE EMPRESS EUDOXIA

SCARCELY had three weeks passed, since Chrysostom had been buried in his living grave in far-off Cucusus, when the shadow of death touched the imperial palace in Constantinople: Eudoxia, the beautiful and proud young Empress, reached unexpectedly the end of her life. On the 6th of October, 404, she died, and four young children wept at the bier of their unfortunate mother.

A peculiar darkness hovers over the cause and time of her death. From the "accident in the imperial bedchamber," which happened in September, 403, the Empress had recovered, at least so far that, in Lent, 404, she was able to visit the martyrs' shrines with the Emperor.[1] But her feeling against the Archbishop at that time was again so irritated and embittered that she would not listen to the requests of the bishops who came to her on his behalf. However, from the long and continued hesitation in the matter of his banishment, from about Christmas to June, one must draw the conclusion that Eudoxia was actually animated by the fear that another punishment from heaven might come upon her; so she was not so willing to consent to a new banishment.

The leadership of the plot before the second banishment lay visibly in the hands of the three Bishops, Severian, Acacius, and Antiochus, and perhaps the court circle that stood behind them, as well as the Patriarch Theophilus, who indeed had purposely sent the three to Constantinople. The Empress would obviously have much preferred to have Chrysostom renounce his office voluntarily and of his own impulse. Only when he opposed a decided *No* to all kinds of demands and pressures, Eudoxia appears to have yielded gradually, and to have given a free hand to the others. As a consequence of her position as Empress, she was actually the center of attention, in the eyes of the people and her contemporaries, but also apparently an outstanding factor in the whole tragedy of Chrysostom. The actual deception that was played on her by the clergy and the court ladies doubtless decreased her subjective guilt to a significant extent; however, a tragedy of a peculiar kind ordained that her fear or presentiment actually fulfilled itself, and that her name came to stand first on the list of those who may be named under the heading "De mortibus persecutorum."

But it is a strange thing that Palladius, who devoted a special section to the judgment with which many persecutors of Chrysostom were concerned, says no word on the early death of Eudoxia. That may well mean, not so much that he considered her completely innocent, but rather from his policy of drawing the "divine Majesties" as little as possible into the debate, in his Dialog. To be sued for an insult to Majesty was a dangerous thing. In any case, silence does not prove that the Empress was still living at the time of the Dialog (about 408).

Socrates could speak more openly. He was still a young man at the time of Eudoxia's death, and lived in Constantinople himself. So one may trust him to have exact knowledge on this point. This ecclesiastical historian merely says: "On the 30th of September, 404, slightly more than three months after Chrysostom's second banishment, and shortly after his arrival at Cucusus, a dreadful hailstorm fell on all Constantinople and all its suburbs, and did great damage. Then he adds: "This was the punishment of Heaven for the unjust deposition of Bishop John." Then Socrates continues: "*This view was strengthened by the death of the Empress, which followed soon after*; for she died on the fourth day after the hailstorm."[2] So, according to Socrates, Eudoxia died on the 4th of October, 404.

Sozomen[3] offers the same facts, in the same essential succession, and with the same allusion to the people's interpretation of it. Sozomen also lived in Constantinople; so he might easily have corrected Socrates, if he had had any occasion to do so.

Theodoret[4] mentions Eudoxia only twice, and that without mentioning her name. He passes over her death in silence. Philostorgius does the same.[5]

On the other hand, the well-informed Marcellinus Comes (died about 534) speaks quite clearly and distinctly. For the year 404 he makes the laconic observation: "Eudoxia, wife of Arcadius, died"[6] . . . on the day before the Nones of October (the 6th of October), 404, on a Thursday.

The *Chronicon Paschale*[7] joins with Marcellinus in setting the date of Eudoxia's death as 404, on October 6; her burial in the imperial mausoleum in the Church of the Apostles took place on the 11th (three days before the Ides).[8]

Only the much later Byzantine authors say that Eudoxia did not die until after Chrysostom. So says George Alexandrinus[9] and his plagiarist, Anonymus,[10] and also Leo Imperator.[11] Metaphrastes[12] says that Eudoxia was still living when the embassy of Pope Innocent was pounced on at its arrival in Constantinople: he says nothing more of her death. On the other hand, Zonaras[13] and Nicephorus Callistus[14] give the year as 407.

The forged correspondence between the Pope and the Emperor probably formed the ground for these differences, as well as the uncertainty which one must consider as really the cause of the continued persecution of the Johnites and the almost violent death of Chrysostom, if Eudoxia died in 404. Also it works out more dramatically, if one considers the death of Chrysostom to be followed directly by that of his "mortal enemy" Eudoxia.

However, all these later accounts merit no belief in the face of the much older and more reliable sources.

Of the newer historians and biographers, Baronius[15] and Savile[16] have allowed themselves to be misled, in giving the year 407 as the year of Eudoxia's death. They were probably led into error chiefly through the fact that the Dialog of Palladius, composed about 408, does not mention the death of the Empress, and that the forged correspondence between Pope Innocent, the Emperor Arcadius, Honorius, and Eudoxia, from the years 405 to 408, presumes them to be still living.

Concerning the cause of the early death of the young Empress, the oldest sources have no certain information. Socrates and Sozomen mention only the mere fact of her death. The completely unreliable Theodore of Trimithus[17] first relates that the Emperor Arcadius had discovered that he had been deceived by Eudoxia in the affair of Chrysostom. In his wrath he mistreated the Empress in such a way that she died of a hemorrhage. This tale is incredible, because Arcadius would never have had so much energy as to come to such grips with anyone. Besides, he ratified the decree against the Johnites after Eudoxia's death.

George Alexandrinus[18] asserts that the unfortunate woman was consumed by worms, while Anonymus[19] says she died of a hemorrhage together with worms. Martyrius relates in harsh tones that she died of an unborn dead child.[20] In view of the earlier misfortune in the imperial chamber, which occurred almost exactly a year before, this account of Martyrius does not seem improbable.

But one thing is true, that at least the people, who always stood on the side of their rightful Bishop, considered the early death of Eudoxia, who had only been Empress for nine years, as a punishment from God, as was also the dreadful hailstorm which had fallen upon Constantinople just four days before.[21]

That sort of popular interpretation of public events reflects at least the impression which the people had in regard to the question of guilt, and to that extent, they are of relative historical importance. Outwardly, Eudoxia must stand as the chief culprit, and so she stands clearly to this day. Actually, the sources give quite a different picture, through which the unfortunate Empress is really exonerated. She appears far more to be the involuntary victim of unscrupulous intrigues and notorious deceptions on the part of men to whose Christian character and ecclesiastical position she gave more faith and trust than they deserved.

One thing seems certain, that Eudoxia did not possess a malevolent character. Even though she was haughty, credulous and sensitive, a deep attraction toward faithful piety in her nature is not to be denied. Fate placed her at the side of a man whose hands were more fitted for the spindle than for the scepter, and necessitated for her a role to which, in the midst of vileness and court intrigues, she as a woman was not equal.

The earthly remains of the unfortunate Empress were laid in the imperial mausoleum in the Church of the Apostles.

There they probably remained until the destruction of the Church by the Turks in the fifteenth century. Under the Emperor Constantine Porphyrogenitus, her tomb, a sarcophagus of porphyry, was listed in the Caeremoniale Aulae Byzantinae;[22] and Anonymus, in the fifteenth century, mentions, among the burial memorials in the Church of the Apostles, three sarcophagi of porphyry, which contained the remains of the Emperor Arcadius, the Empress Eudoxia, and their only son, the Emperor Theodosius II.[23]

Since then their ashes have been scattered to the four winds, like those of the great Emperors Constantine and Theodosius.

The base of the vanished silver statue, which has been mentioned before, with the inscription of the city prefect Simplicius, together with an ordinary and almost forgotten romance by the Countess Ida von Hahn-Hahn,[24] constitute the only remaining monumental and literary memorials of Eudoxia, the first German to occupy the East Roman imperial throne.

FOOTNOTES

1. Palladius, Dial. 9 (47, 32-33).
2. HE 6, 19 (724).
3. HE 8, 27 (1589); but Socrates did not recall that in October the Nones fell on the 7th, so Eudoxia must have died on the 6th.
4. HE 5, 28 and 34 (82, 1256 and 1261 f.).
5. HE 11, 6 (65, 600 f.).
6. Ed. Mommsen, MG Auct. Ant. XI, Chron. min. II, 68. Prosper of Aquitaine in his Epitoma Chronicon (MG Auct. Ant. IX, 465) apparently did not mention Eudoxia's death. On the other hand, in some manuscripts of the year 404 the note is found: "Death of Eudoxia, the wife of Arcadius." See ML 51, 589.
7. Ad ann. 404; (92, 781).
8. The Arian church historian Philostorgius, XI 6 (ed. Bidez 136) has nothing good to say of Eudoxia. He reproaches her for "barbarian wildness"; and in the 12th cent., George Cedrenus, (Compendium 121, 636) repeats it after him.
9. Ch. 70 (Savile 8, 251).
10. Ch. ρλή (*ibid.* 368).
11. Ch. 30 (*ibid.* 290) and 107, 292 A B.

12. Ch. 47 (*ibid.* 426) and 114, 1201 (n. 57).

13. Annal, 13, 20 (134, 1181): "Scarcely three months after the *death* of Chrysostom." A clear proof that here is a confusion with the second banishment, to Pityus, for the 6th of October, 407, was only three weeks after the death of Chrysostom.

14. E. H. 13, 38 (145, 1053).

15. Annales ad annum 407, no. 29; cf. ad ann. 404. no. 120-23 (ed. Lucae 1740; vol. 6, 472); on the other hand, Pagi ad 404, no. 28.

16. MG 47, XXX. Also the Roman Breviary for Jan. 27.

17. Ch. 29 (47, LXXXV).

18. Ch. 67 (Savile 8, 246).

19. Ch. 138 (*Ibid.* 368).

20. Cod. Paris. B. N. 1519 p. 532 f.

21. Socrates 6, 19 (67, 724); Sozomen 8, 27 (1589); Chronicon Paschale ad an. 404 (92, 781).

22. Lib. 2, 42; MG 112, 1204 B.

23. MG 157, 736. Perhaps the author only drew from the "Caeremoniale" without himself being an eyewitness.

24. Eudoxia die Kaiserin. Ein Zeitgemälde aus dem 5. Jahrh. by the Countess Ida von Hahn-Hahn. Mainz (Frz. Kirchheim) 1866.

CHAPTER XXXI

ATTICUS BECOMES BISHOP

IN the midst of the confusions of the persecutions of the Johnites, the aged Arsacius died, in the 82nd year of his age. He had had but fourteen months to load himself and his age with a responsibility which must have been difficult enough for him. His ambition had been greater than his ability.

As always, the usual struggle over the succession began. The choice among the many who coveted the chief spiritual dignity in Constantinople appears to have been difficult. At last appeared as a victor in the struggle Atticus, a priest of the cathedral in Constantinople. The sources do not agree as to the exact date on which he became Bishop. According to Palladius,[1] Arsacius was Bishop for only fourteen months. Since he came to the episcopal throne in June 404, he would have died in July or August 405. This would agree with the other accounts of Socrates, who says that Atticus died on the 10th of October 425, in the 21st year of his episcopal office.[2] So Atticus must have been Bishop at the latest, in September 405. Socrates contradicts himself here, and also Palladius, when they say that Arsacius died on the 11th of October, 405.

Besides, Socrates writes[3] that after the death of Arsacius, a long time passed before Atticus was made Bishop, in the following consulate, the sixth of Arcadius, and that of Probus, in the year 406. Finally Socrates notes[4] that the eighth year of the life of Theodosius the Second (born in April 401) coincided with the third year of the bishopric of Atticus. But the eighth year of Theodosius ran from the 10th of April, 405, to the 9th of April, 409. Accordingly, the first episcopal year of Atticus fell approximately in the time between April 406 and April 407.

On the other hand, Sozomen says[5] that Atticus was made

Bishop four months after the death of Arsacius. Unfortunately he gives no dates for the latter. So if he followed the account of Socrates (= the 11th of November), Atticus would have been made Bishop in February or March of 406.[6] But if Arsacius died in July or August, Atticus would have become Bishop in November or December of 403.

So if it is not possible to find a sure way out of the confusion of these accounts, at least it may be considered certain that Atticus was already Bishop at the beginning of the year 406.

This fact is important for the fixing of the responsibility for the events which took place in the year 406.

Atticus was born in Sebaste, and so was a near countryman of the holy Meletius, the Patriarch of Antioch, who had baptized St. Chrysostom. Like most Armenians, he was very intelligent, and with it he was unusually sly and cunning. Nicolas Mesarites portrays the Armenians, in quite unjust generalizations, as shameless, cunning, sly, flattering betrayers.[7] Atticus came to the cloister of Sebaste when he had scarcely outgrown boyhood.[8] According to Sozomen,[9] the monks there were the Macedonian monks, so-called because their founder, Bishop Eustathius (died 380) of Sebaste, would not recognize the divinity of the Holy Ghost, hence subscribed to a heresy whose real champion and leader had been Macedonius, Bishop of Constantinople. It is difficult to make out whether Atticus had been a Macedonian earlier, or whether his lack of theological training had kept him from it; Sozomen says at least that he possessed more intellect than education and knowledge; while Socrates says that as a priest and bishop he had taken great trouble to complete his faulty youthful education by strenuous study.[10] At any rate, when and why Atticus came to Constantinople has remained a personal secret. One thing only is certain, that what he had already become under Nectarius, that he brought to his priesthood at the cathedral church in the capital city. An unusually large share of ambition and place-hunting characterized him; it was stronger than his love of ecclesiastical discipline or his zeal for souls. He had successfully hidden his opposition to Chrysostom for a long time. When he first considered his Bishop's cause lost, he appeared openly as an opposition wit-

ness at the Synod of the Oak, apparently quite unexpectedly.
Obviously Atticus wished at that time to secure the favor of
the court.[11] His outwardly winning, flattering manner helped
him in his association with men; he knew how to make himself popular with those whose favor he wished to win.[12]

On the contrary, it was never granted him to pluck the
laurels of an orator and preacher. None of his sermons was
considered worthy of record. As a priest, says Socrates, he
learned his sermons by heart, before he spoke them in the
church. Only later did he begin to speak extempore. Still,
his hearers never applauded him, never wrote down his sermons.[13] On the other hand, he tried to be a writer. Gennadius says that he wrote a treatise for the imperial princesses
"On the faith and on virginity."[14] Socrates knows only good
of him. But this shadowless character certainly does not
correspond to the historical truth. Atticus belonged rather
to that class of ambitious and lordly characters who will walk
unscrupulously over a dead body if they strike obstacles to
their personal aims and wishes, but who will show themselves
very humane, even benevolent and magnanimous, to those
whose opposition or concurrence they do not need to fear.
To this extent, Atticus seems to have resembled the Patriarch
Theophilus. At any rate, Palladius shows evidence that,
among the clergy of Constantinople, he was the "chief plotter
against Chrysostom."[14a]

The adherents of the exile in Cucusus would naturally
have known less of Atticus, the open enemy and opponent of
Chrysostom, than they did of Arsacius. Neither the Bishops
of the East, nor the people of Constantinople, entered into
fellowship with him, or took part in his divine service. Atticus
was not now the man who would take the silent opposition
of the Johnites quietly. Palladius even insists that he persuaded the Emperor to issue more decrees of persecution,
sharper than before: every priest who refused to hold fellowship with Porphyrius, Theophilus, and Atticus should lose
his office and his possessions. An official was to lose his office
for the same offense, and a soldier his girdle (that is, he would
be expelled from the army); and a citizen or tradesman would
be assessed a heavy fine and sent into banishment.[15] It is of
course not probable that an entirely new edict is concerned

here, first published under Atticus, and worded almost the same as that of 404, but which was altogether omitted from the Codex Theodosianus. Rather, Palladius included the chief contents of all the persecution edicts, and thereby at least gave the impression that they were first issued under Atticus, whom he considered the chief intriguer against Chrysostom. It was indeed possible that Atticus, as arch-priest and influential member of the anti-Johnite party, had helped to inspire the decrees in question before his elevation to the bishopric; but it is more probable that he invested them with new force in the beginning of his pontificate. But surely the court in Constantinople would not have waited a whole year before it proceeded through edicts against the Johnites, the opposition against Arsacius and against the official policy of the Church. Palladius himself also says that edict after edict was published after the Easter riots in 404.[16] On the other hand, at the end of 405 and the beginning of 406, so just at the time when Atticus became bishop, the new synod demanded by Pope Innocent and Emperor Honorius for the investigation of the whole Chrysostom affair was at hand; so that more vigorous activities against the Johnites appear more understandable—and also they actually took place.

One thing is certain, that Atticus never did or attempted anything to bring about a change or mitigation of the condition of his unfortunate predecessor and victim. On the contrary, as long as Chrysostom still lived, he could not enjoy his own fortune, and what he had attained with so much trouble and sacrifice he wished to hold at any price, as is shown by the following.

When Chrysostom was already dead, and Atticus did not need to fear for his spiritual throne, he resisted for a long time the insertion of his predecessor's name in the ecclesiastical diptychs, as a sign of reconciliation and fellowship. And then he put it in, far less from the need of expiating past injustice and to do right again, but from political considerations, to do away with schism in his diocese and to facilitate reconciliation with the Johnites.

The character of Atticus also revealed itself in his treatment of heretics. According to the statement of Socrates, his policy consisted of instilling fear into them. Then as soon as they had shown themselves yielding, he treated them with mildness and kindness.

So if we disregard his inexcusable behavior against his Bishop and predecessor, whom he sacrificed to his own ambition and love of power, one can show proof that he attended to his office and his church in other things with that measure of prudence and success for which his natural gifts qualified him. The historian Socrates has nothing but good to say of Atticus, under whose rule the Church made such great progress, who was so friendly and winning in his relations with the people, who cherished the afflicted with such deep sympathy, and gladly helped the poor. In a word, he was, according to the expression of the Apostle, all things to all men; indeed once he worked a half miracle, and predicted the time of his death.[17]

This hymn of praise for Atticus is perhaps to be explained by this fact: that Socrates, as a younger man, had come into personal relations with Atticus, and had developed a friendship with him. Surely it is not the case that the same Socrates showed himself prejudiced against Chrysostom, and more than once unfriendly, making fault-finding remarks about him. They may be the echo of the speeches which were made in the house of Atticus about his predecessor.

FOOTNOTES

1. Dial. 11 (36).
2. HE 7, 25 (67, 797).
3. 6, 20 (725).
4. HE 7, 2 (741).
5. HE 8, 27 (1589).
6. So, for instance, is assumed by Pagi (ad ann. 408, No. 8= ed. Lucae 1740. Vol. 6, 486).
7. Description of the Church of the Apostles, in Heisenberg 2. 43-44.
8. Socrates 6, 20 (67, 725).
9. HE 8, 27 (1589).
10. HE 7, 2 (741).

11. Dial. 11 (37); Πάσης μηχανῆς τεχνίτης κατὰ τοῦ Ἰωάννου.
12. Socrates 7, 2 (741); Sozomen 8, 27 (1589).
13. Some of the sermons written by himself must still have been in circulation; cf. Bardenhewer, GAL 3, 361-62.
14. De Viris Illustribus 52; ed. Bernoulli 79.
14a. Dial. 11 (47, 37).
15. Palladius, Dial. 11 (37).
16. Dial. 9 (34).
17. Socrates 7, 2 and 4, and 25 (67, 741, 745, 793).

CHAPTER XXXII

CHRYSOSTOM IN EXILE

WHILE all these things were happening in Constantinople and the Empire, and one injustice followed
another, he whom half the world appeared to have
forsworn sat in far-off Cappadocia-Armenia, and spent the
hardest winter there he had ever experienced.

As has been mentioned before, ever since Chrysostom had
suffered from cold and illness in the hermit's cave on Mt.
Sylpios above Antioch, he had been extremely sensitive to
cold. In Antioch itself, on the flat land, a warm and sunny
climate prevailed, and he could protect himself against the
cold in winter. Such was also the case in Constantinople,
where all the comforts and helps of the great city were at his
disposal whenever he wished them.

But now he suddenly found himself set down in a cold
mountain region high in altitude, in a desolate land, where
every convenience of the great city was lacking. The cold
here reached such intensity that Chrysostom scarcely dared
go out into the open air, without at once beginning to feel
sick.

Then he would usually begin to have headaches, fever, and
pains in his stomach, accompanied by nausea, and also
insomnia. In the first winter, this situation lasted for two
full months, uninterruptedly, so that the poor invalid believed
himself to be at the gates of death.[1] Nothing was left for
him but to stay confined in his dwelling like a prisoner, with
doors and windows carefully closed, muffled up in warm
clothing and coverings.[2]

Just after the first winter he wrote to Olympias: "I am
coming back actually from the gates of death. It was fortunate that your messengers did not see me in this condition.
The winter this time was unusually severe, so my stomach
trouble was worse. In the last two months I have been worse

than a dead man. I had only just enough life left in me to perceive the suffering that was going on around me. Otherwise everything was dark night around me. . . . I was constantly chained to my bed. I have tried every imaginable means, but cannot escape the disastrous effects of the cold. I had a fire kindled, and endured the thickest smoke, was muffled up in countless coverings, never dared leave the house, and still I had to endure the greatest pain, suffering from constant headache, nausea, loss of appetite, and insomnia. . . . Scarcely did warmer weather begin, when all this ceased of itself."[3]

After such a miserable winter, he rejoiced like a child when spring came and the first warm air burst open the door of his prison. Then he quickly recovered his health. Not in vain did he write again and again to Olympias, that bodily pain may often be worse and more difficult to bear than death itself, and the depression and discouragement that often follow bodily suffering are worse than the pain itself.

To conclude from the fourteenth letter, there was a Bishop residing in Cucusus at that time. However, Cucusus was a little mountain town, lying at a height of over 4600 feet in the Cilician Taurus, completely surrounded by mountains. In winter it was extremely cold, in summer it might become very hot. Chrysostom thus very clearly explained his situation.

"I enjoy much quiet and leisure here, and find myself well in body, although there are many things here which are not conducive to health. There are seldom any doctors here, and often the necessities are lacking; one cannot buy anything here, even medicines are not to be had. Moreover, there is the rude climate. The heat of summer is as difficult for me as the cold of winter. Besides, we are continually surrounded by enemies, and live in continual fear of the Isaurians. That and many other things prey on my strength."[4]

Also the lack of a regular occupation may have been especially difficult for him. Outside activity was not possible, and there were not many books for study in this place forsaken by the world.

So he reflected gladly upon the Book of Job, as can be understood from his letters to Olympias. It is understandable that under these circumstances it was for him a day of festival, when after a long winter season, in which all the roads were snowed under, a messenger came again with letters from Constantinople or Antioch. He always waited with longing for fresh news, and scarcely ever wrote a letter himself without regularly asking at the end that letters might be sent to him as often as possible. Most of his friends did this. And they sent him not only letters, but money and medicines and other things from Constantinople. The women especially took care of this. Syncletia, apparently the wife of the Count Theophilus, once sent him a remarkably efficient medicine for his stomach trouble. He thanked her through Olympias, and asked to have some more of it sent to him.[5] Carteria wrote to him, saying that, as a proof of his trust, he should dispose of her property as though it were his own.[6] At the same time she sent him various things. Others also did the same. Still, he seldom or never accepted these things, but wrote that he was sufficiently cared for; he preferred not to have anything sent to him, unless he needed it and asked for it.

The solitude and isolation of the place in which he had to live appeared, to the child of the great city, the unwearied apostle and shepherd of souls, to be especially difficult to bear. In a large number of letters, he speaks of the "great" and "very painful" solitude, which did not have the advantage of promoting rest for the soul. The place was not merely solitary, but also extremely unsafe. In the better time of the year, it was never certain when the dreaded Isaurians might make an unexpected raid. The roads and ways were harassed year in and year out by robbers and brigands. This uncertainty was the cause of many restless hours to the exile.

Chrysostom remained in Cucusus just one year,[7] until the late summer of 405. For him it was a year of severe trials and painful experiences, bodily privation and illness. But in spite of his own sufferings of soul and body, he found time for a word of consolation and encouragement for everyone else. The people were thankful to him for this, and honored him as a father and benefactor, especially as the exile could occasionally bestow abundant alms, for which Olympias and his other friends of Constantinople and Antioch furnished the means.[8]

The need was great at that time. Unfortunately, there had been a bad harvest over wide sections of the country in the year 405, and this had resulted in hunger. The rougher and less fruitful areas of the mountain lands were just the districts which had to suffer most from hunger. So it is understandable that the always wild and warlike and mostly pagan mountain peoples, the Isaurians, came down from their mountains in the autumn, and robbed and stole in the cities and villages of the plains and valleys, to get what they could. As a matter of fact, in this year they came in such multitudes, to harass and plunder the surrounding provinces to such great extent that the historians, after decades, still designated the year 405 as the year of the Isaurian invasions.

Besides Palladius[9] and Sozomen,[10] Philostorgius also says, that the Isaurians had brought much disaster to the Romans. "In the East, they overflowed Cilicia and neighboring Syria, even to the borders of Persia; they invaded Pamphylia and laid waste Lycia. Likewise they took possession of the island of Cyprus, and conquered Lycaonia and Pisidia. In Cappadocia (Armenia) they took a multitude of prisoners of war, and even threatened Pontus."[11] Likewise Marcellinus Comes writes in his chronicle of the year 405 that the Isaurians had caused much damage by their invasions into the country, but he added that the imperial legate Narbazaicus had damaged them still more.[12] This last had probably happened in the years 406 and 407, and was at any rate no easy thing. The Isaurians understood very well the art of border warfare. They were always at their very swiftest there, where none expected them; they seldom presented themselves in open battle, and they always found rest and protection in their widespread mountains, full of chasms. A region similar to the Pyrenees, like Macedonia or Albania, it could be conquered or kept in check against a resolute, warlike people, only by perseverance and great expense in money and military forces. For this a Theodosius was needed, and not an Arcadius.

At any rate, Asia Minor in the year 405 was practically without protection against the sudden and massive invasions of the Isaurian plunderers, and burning and murdering bands. Not merely the flat land and open cities were plundered and laid waste by fire, but even the smaller border towns, defended by military garrisons, could not hold out against them. The small military division in Cucusus had apparently carried out a strategic retreat when the first news came that the Isaurians were coming. At any rate, the civilian population felt that they were not secure. Whoever had legs, fled into the forests and solitudes. Many were frozen to death, others were murdered by the invaders or carried away into slavery. So, for the exiled Archbishop, there was nothing left but to flee. In the middle of winter, he had to leave his house suddenly, with no other object than to avoid falling into the hands of the Isaurians.[13] In his letters he tells how he had had to flee from one place to another,[14] how he had had to seek protection in wintertime now in cities, now in ravines and forests, everywhere frightened away by the approach of the Isaurians. "There is no one left who dares remain in his house. Everyone flees. . . . In the cities there are only the houses left; on the other hand, the ravines and forests are changed into cities."[15]

At last he was able, with his companions, to reach the border fortress of Arabissus, about 46 miles distant from Cucusus, where he found security for the time being.[16]

Arabissus, today called Yarpus, is the chief place of a Turkish *sanjak* of the same name, and lies three thousand feet high in the midst of the mountain chain of Amanus, which in this part is especially inhospitable. On the surrounding heights, the remains of ancient fortifications are visible, and "to judge from the numerous ancient ruins converted into modern buildings, the region must once have been well built up, and possessed highly developed cities."[17]

Moreover, Arabissus had once given shelter in passing to another exiled bishop, the Arian Patriarch Eudoxius of Antioch, who had even been born in Arabissus. But, more fortunate than his successor, he came into favor again, and soon after, was made Bishop of Constantinople.[18]

The accompanying difficulties of the flight, together with the cold of winter, had again made our poor fugitive extremely ill. He was able to recover but slowly. It seemed

a special sacrifice to him that, on account of the general uncertainty and danger of life, no more letters came, from his
many friends and acquaintances. "No one dares come here
any more, because all the roads are closed."[19] Another danger
was added to that of enemies; the danger of hunger in Arabissus, which was overcrowded by the large number of fugitives. What sort of anarchic conditions prevailed at that time
in the Empire under Arcadius, and what daring the Isaurians
possessed, is shown by the circumstance that early in the year
406, by a sudden night raid, Arabissus fell into the hands of
a band of only 300 Isaurians. The terror of the exile would
surely have been great, had it not been for a favorable incident; he did not hear any of the noise. Not until the next
morning did he hear of the nocturnal adventure.[20]

Naturally only a few dared to come as far as Arabissus
under these circumstances, and Chrysostom wrote to the
deacon Theodotus that he was caught in the fortress as in a
noose.[21] Moreover, a dwelling had been assigned to him in
the fortress, which, according to his own statement, was
"smaller than the worst prison cell."[22] How long he was
forced to live in this prison cell is unfortunately not evident
from his letters. However, we learn from his letter to Bishop
Elpidius that he longingly awaited the day when he might
escape from his imprisonment in Arabissus.[23] That is quite
comprehensible.

Among the many privations and precarious conditions of
life in Arabissus, the poor fugitive could recover only slowly
and with difficulty. It took until the early part of 406 for
him to recover from the effects of his illness.[24]

But Arabissus was not only a border fortress—it was also
an episcopal city. According to Letter 126 of Chrysostom, the
Bishop at that time was named Otreius. To his honor it
must be said that Otreius treated his exiled colleague with
all fraternal charity, and showed him every imaginable attention.[25] After the great danger was past and gone, the Bishop
offered his unfortunate colleague his own house to dwell in.

As to how long Chrysostom remained in Arabissus, or
whether he perhaps did not return to Cucusus at all, cannot
be said with certainty. But since he himself often said in his
letters that one was never safe from the Isaurians, one may

well assume that he remained in Arabissus, in the neighborhood of the protecting garrison.[26]

The Isaurian invasions and predatory sallies were repeated, if not to so large an extent, in the years 406 and 407. They had at least the effect of making the district constantly unsafe. But if anyone in Constantinople had cherished the hope that Chrysostom would perhaps fall a victim to "accident on the highway" in one of these robbing expeditions, their expectations did not come to fulfillment. Palladius has expressed the suspicion that the Archbishop had been purposely banished to Arabissus by the scheming of the clerical circle, so that he might fall into the hands of the Isaurians on the way.[27] It was also true that an exile might not leave his place of banishment without permission. But probably he had been later permitted to remain in Arabissus, at a time when he feared nothing so much as traveling.

FOOTNOTES

1. Letter 6, 1 (52, 593).
2. Letter 4, 1 (590); cf. letter 146 (698-99).
3. Letter 6, 1 (598-99). Cucusus, which I visited in May 1932, usually has a temperature of from –10° to –25° in winter. (See C. Baur, Im Christ. Orient, p. 120).
4. Letter 146 (698-99).
5. Letter 4, 1 (590).
6. Letter 232 (738).
7. Palladius 11 (37).
8. Palladius, Dial. 11 (37). Sozomen 8, 27 (1592).
9. Dial. 11 (36); 16 (55); 20 (72).
10. HE 8, 25 (1581 A).
11. MG 65, (604-605).
12. MGH., Auct. ant. 11, 68 and ML 51, 922.
13. Letter 127 (687).
14. Letter 61 (642).
15. Letter 127 (687). So it is not correct, as Palladius says, that the change from Cucusus to Arabissus was arranged by Chrysostom's opponents in Constantinople; for they would not have endured that he should win the sympathy of the people by his sermons and his kindness.
16. Letter 69 (646).

17. Schaffer, Cilicia p. 95. Today there are two places called "Yarpus." The one is in Cappadocia, north of Cucusus (Göcksun), the other further south, between Osmanje and Hassanbeg, near the Gulf of Iskenderun. In his letter 4, 1 and 4 (52, 590 and 593), Chrysostom writes that he had spent the winter in "Armenia," which could only have meant Lesser Armenia. That would point to Cucusus and the more northerly Yarpus. Since the final banishment of Chrysostom, to Pityus, was occasioned by the fact that the "church" (that is, the faithful) made pilgrimages from Antioch to "Armenia" to see him, (Dial. 11, 37-38; ed. Norton, p. 66, 12), therefore only the northern Arabissus can have been meant, where there was an episcopal see and a large garrison. Only it is difficult to understand, considering the nearness of this Arabissus to Cucusus, why it should have taken Chrysostom and his companions 3 months to make the journey between them. Also, since the banishment to Pityus was ordered because he had to many visitors from Antioch, who could reach the southern Yarpus much more easily, one might believe that the southern Yarpus is meant. Whether the latter was an episcopal see in 405, or had a garrison, or whether it was called "Arabissus" at that time and belonged to "Armenia" or to Cilicia, I have not been able to find out.

18. Philostorgius, HE 4, 4 and 8 (ed. Bidez 60-62).

19. Letter 69 (646) and 67 (645).

20. Letter 135 (693).

21. Letter 135 (693).

22. Letter 69 (646).

23. Letter 131 (690).

24. Letter 135 (693); Letter 70 (647).

25. 52, 685-687.

26. Tillemont, Mémoires 11, 621-22 (Note 101) says that Chrysostom returned again from Arabissus to Cucusus, but only for this reason, that his journey from Arabissus to Comana Pontica took three months, which is easier to understand than a start from Cucusus. Tillemont's view follows Neander (2, 241, Note 1). However, the period of three months is far too long for that extent of country, under normal conditions. So one must assume that a spurious variation is involved, in regard to the given position of Palladius, and that weeks are meant instead of months, or that Chrysostom had to break the journey, on account of illness, oftener than appears probable, in view of the lack of consideration of his escorting soldiers. Cf. Ch. 37.

27. Dial. 11 (37).

CHAPTER XXXIII

LETTERS FROM THE EXILE[1]

D URING all this time in Constantinople, not only the enemies of Chrysostom had been active, but his friends also. Olympias felt the deepest and most sincere sorrow over his undeserved fate. In the beginning it was for her a consolation and a diversion to be able to suffer for the good cause, and to be brought before the court. Then she found sufficient energy to take every imaginable step in order at least to obtain a better, and if possible, a nearer place of banishment for her holy spiritual director. Obviously she had, in her first letters, informed him of her purpose, and of her steps to realize it. But Chrysostom was so exhausted still, by the pain and trouble of his first journey into exile, that the mere thought of having to take another journey, even to a more favorable place, filled him with more fear than joy. So already in his first letter, which he wrote to her in 404 from Cucusus,[2] he purposely emphasized how well he was resting in Cucusus after that frightfully difficult journey; and how a whole troop of friends and well-disposed people there had taken every possible care to see to his wants in every way. So then he adds, " No efforts should be made to remove me from Cucusus, unless the free choice of a place of exile be given me; on the other hand, I would rather not have a new place of exile arranged for me; for in the first place, it might be worse than Cucusus, and in the second place, I fear the misery of another journey more than a thousand exiles. For the other journey certainly brought me to the edge of the grave. So do not trouble yourself about another dwelling place for me. But if you discover that they want to take me to a city on the sea, or somewhere near Cyzicus or Nicomedia (to which Olympias herself had been banished), accept it; but not to a more remote or distant place; for the journey is dreadfully difficult for me."

He wrote in a similar vein to a certain Paeanius, whom Olympias had obviously won over to the same plan; he said, God be praised for all things, but no new changes of place.[3]

It was brought to pass by the saint's opponents at the imperial court, that the efforts of Olympias were frustrated. The malicious afterthought which had determined the choice of such a distant, rude and dangerous frontier town, still ruled, and was still victorious. Chrysostom was not to obtain either a better or a nearer place of exile.

Olympias was deeply pained by this. Every hope and possibility of being able to do something for the exile appeared to be gone. No wonder that the poor woman, who had suffered so much in late years, at last gave way in spirit, and was seized by a discouragement and sadness which is made all too clear in her letters: "From your letter, which was brought by Patricius," Chrysostom wrote to her, "I see how infinitely sad you are, and that you have left nothing undone to obtain a better place of banishment for me. Do not be so sad about not having accomplished it. Everything goes well with me here. The quiet and stillness do me good, and all necessities are given me in abundance. The Bishop of the place, and my friend Dioscurus, give me the best of care. The good Patricius, when he returns, will be able to confirm all this to you."[4]

Did Olympias believe this optimistic picture of the situation? At any rate, Chrysostom was still far away, and her sorrow continued.

He writes to her in another letter:[5] "How is this? You are still ever sad, and you say: I cannot be otherwise! This unmeasured sorrow is injurious. To sorrow for your sins, that is right, but to sorrow immoderately for other things is imprudent. You have no real sins, and therefore you have no reason to fear. For, although you were married, you now belong to the band of wise virgins, for you were always mindful of the things of God, through almsgiving and patience in suffering, through self-control in eating and sleeping, and in all other things, but especially through modest simplicity in dress. It is in these things that true virginity lies, and that is something infinitely great. God has laid on men many difficult things, but not virginity.

Moses, Abraham and Job were great men of God, and they
showed heroic virtues; but they did not practice virginity.
And yet there are many young women who are strong enough
to observe it; but yet they are not prepared to renounce fine
clothes. Think therefore on the heavenly reward which
awaits you, while the scandal-givers and the ravishers of the
Church must come to a fearful judgment. Yes, you say, but
I miss your personal presence and your conversation. Now,
it is certainly hard, if two affectionate souls are parted; however, only practice patience, and think of the heavenly
reward! "

However, even this praise from the mouth of her episcopal
consoler, amounting almost to a canonization, was not able
to soothe Olympias. Patience and resignation, in the face of
the victory of the wicked, and the defeat of the good, were
hard demands for her intimidated spirit. She was sick from
grief and sorrow, and longed for death, so as no longer to have
to be a witness to victorious injustice.[6] Repeatedly the
Bishop, who himself had to suffer superhuman things, tried
to console and comfort the poor soul; God sends sorrow, and
then again joy. Therefore do not weep, but be strong![7]
Then he praised her again for her courageous spirit and her
greatness of soul in persecution, by which she had shamed
even men.[8] For the rest, he said: The good must always
suffer, and there is really but *one* misfortune, and that is sin.[9]

Chrysostom amplified these thoughts in a special composition, which he wrote for her consolation, probably in
Arabissus, and sent to her from there. This is the treatise
" Nemo laeditur nisi seipso."[9a] He means by this the spiritual
harm which can only be accomplished by sin: No earthly
misfortune can harm the soul, but benefits it if we bear it in
the right way.

He soon followed this treatise with another: To all those
who were scandalized at the happenings of the years 403 and
404, and who could not understand how God could permit
such things to happen.[9b]

To inquire minutely into God's decrees, laws and dispositions, says he, has no purpose, because we mere men will
never thoroughly understand God our Creator, nor be able
to comprehend Him. Not even the angels and archangels

can do that. Also among created things there is so much
which we do not know or understand, and for man, the
greatest riddle is man. Although the world is so full of malice
and wickedness, still the love and care of God for us is shown
in all things, and His creation shows the most beautiful order.
To inquire minutely into the Why and How of all things is
unprofitable. We do not inquire of the doctor why he orders
for us this medicine or that, or why he occasionally cuts or
burns us. So trust in God and wait patiently for the end.
Thus did Abraham and the Egyptian Joseph; so did the
Apostles and all the martyrs. Gaze on the Cross, the most
sublime proof of Divine Providence and love. Do not be
scandalized, neither at a bad priest or bishop, nor at those in
high places and those who rule over us. The gold will be
refined in the furnace, and the soul in trial and misfortune.
Whosoever bears these in resignation, will one day have his
place beside the martyrs, the apostles, the saints. So remain
faithful and strong; God will richly reward you.[9c]

Truly, he writes in another letter to Olympias, a sick body,
and a storm-whipped sea, need a long time before they can
become calm again, after illness and storm. So it is also with
you. Even although the sorrow has already passed away, still
the perfect calm and steadfast peace have not yet come. In
order to find them, you must wish for them, and work with
them. So be brave, and thank God for all.[10]

These practical letters of consolation unfortunately did not
fully accomplish their end with Olympias. But she was not
the only one who was in correspondence with the exiled
Bishop. Her fellow-deaconesses at the cathedral, Pentadia,[11]
Amprucla (Procla?),[12] Asyncritia,[13] and Chalcidia,[14] sent and
received letters repeatedly. All of them had had more or less
to suffer during the persecution, but had remained steadfast.
Pentadia had also distinguished herself in this.[15] For this,
Chrysostom also bestowed the most direct praise in his
genuine Greek manner. " I rejoice and am glad, and find the
greatest consolation in my solitude, in the fact that you have
been so manly and steadfast, and that you have not allowed
yourself to do wrong, but have shamed the opponents by your
prudence, innocence and openness, and have given the devil
a mortal blow; by this time also, you have encouraged the

others to fight for the truth, and, like a valiant hero in battle, you have carried off the victory. Be glad therefore, and rejoice over your victory. For they have done everything they could against you. You, who knew only the Church and your cell, they have dragged out into the public eye, from there to the court, and from court to prison. They have bought false witnesses, have slandered, murdered, shed streams of blood, raged with fire and sword against the lives of youths, and left nothing undone to inspire you with fear, and obtain from you an untrue statement regarding the burning of the church. But you have brought them all to shame. If we are sick, your love is the best means for making us healthy again. Write us, therefore, as often as you can."[16]

When Chrysostom learned that Pentadia was thinking of leaving Constantinople, as it appeared, to come to Cucusus, he urgently besought her not to do so: your very presence in Constantinople, said he, is a support and encouragement to the others; and, moreover, the time of year, the middle of winter, is a very unfavorable season for travel, and it is dangerous for your weak health. The Isaurians are a continual danger for travelers. So in the meantime, stay there. Somewhat later, he complained to Pentadia that she wrote to him so seldom, and said that a rumor of her heroic conduct had spread to the borders of the world. Unfortunately, we do not know anything of her fate.

Also a number of distinguished society women entered into correspondence with the exiled Bishop. It must not have been the easiest business for him, in his solitary and uneventful existence, to answer all the letters he received, even if he could get paper for it. However, in a certain sense, it was often the only pleasure and change in his monotonous existence, if now and again a messenger came with letters. Often, also, they brought along some very necessary things. The before-mentioned Carteria sent him some medicine, which she had prepared herself.[17] Only the fact that she was ill herself prevented her from visiting Chrysostom in his exile.[18] She once sent to him a certain Libanius, and besought him in an accompanying letter, that if he ever needed anything, he would show his trust by considering her property as his own. However, this time he sent the accompanying gift back to her, because he really did not need it, and begged her, at the same time, to show him by writing often that she did not think badly of him for doing this.[19] In all, about 55 of his letters are addressed to 19 different women. The names of some who were near to him in Constantinople are lacking; for example, Silvina, who was present at the last farewell in the cathedral; likewise Procla, in case she was not identical with Amprucla.[20]

All the other letters are addressed to men, laity and chiefly clergy; 43 of them to bishops: 29 to single bishops and 14 to groups of bishops. Among these is included his letter to Pope Innocent I. Some letters are directed to other Latin Metropolitans, and have, in part, the object of begging their moral support in his cause, and in part of thanking them for the steps they had taken, in union with Pope Innocent, in his cause.[21]

Among the bishops known by name, who had earlier decided for him, only seven appear in the exchange of letters. The Metropolitan Elpidius of Laodicea in Syria received most of these.[22] This honorable old man had not ceased in any way, especially by letters, to assert the justice of his friend's cause. He had written to Cucusus promptly, to inform Chrysostom himself as to how things were with him, who was with him, and especially how Chrysostom's own cause was going. Chrysostom answered him with the warmest expressions of thanks; he was well, he said, and had recovered from the illness from which he suffered on the way; the rest, and the feeling of security from the Isaurians, were doing him so much good that he scarcely felt the extraordinary solitude of the place.[23]

In his company at that time were the priests Constantius and Evethius; others were expected soon, who had previously been in prison, but who had already been released. This Constantius is doubtless the same priest (from Antioch?) to whom Chrysostom had turned in the affair of the mission to the Phoenicians.[24] Chrysostom also wrote to him from Arabissus, and described to him the great need to which he and all the country had been reduced by the Isaurians.[25]

There are a number of letters to simple priests, as well as deacons and monks; the rest are to members of the laity:

N

nobles, officials, doctors, etc. There are only two addressed to the chamberlain Brison. Chrysostom sent the first[26] soon after his arrival at Cucusus; I was on the road, he said, about 70 days. From this, your Excellency can understand how much hardship I had to suffer, on the one hand from fear of the Isaurians, who threatened us all, and then from the unendurable fever from which I also had to suffer. Finally, I have arrived in Cucusus, which is about the most forsaken place in the world. I do not say this so that you will take steps to bring me somewhere else (for the worst part, the sufferings of the journey are all over), but so that you may write me often; for indeed you know how much joy that will be to me.

Unfortunately Brison, the chamberlain and choir director, was not in a position to give this pleasure to his exiled friend. Chrysostom sent him after some time another letter,[27] in which he said: "How does it happen that you never write me? In Constantinople you showed me so much love and friendship that the whole world spoke of it. And now you have not written me one single time, although you know with what impatience I await your letters. This is not a reproach. I know very well that you still keep your good will for me, whether you write or not. But it always rejoices me when I hear from others that you are well. But if I am not asking anything too difficult, give me this pleasure, and send me some news of yourself." But, to all appearances, Chrysostom waited in vain. No other letter from him to Brison is known. Was it the fickleness of a musician, or the characteristic prudence of a courtier, who feared to lose the favor of the court, or a third and unknown reason? The earlier conduct of Brison justifies the last assumption.

Chrysostom begged Bishop Cyriacus[28] to visit the son of the Prefect of Armenia, who was carrying on his studies there; he wished thereby to show his gratitude for the kindness which the Prefect had shown him.[29] Whether Cyriacus complied with the request is not certain. At any rate, Chrysostom wrote to him several times (and never received an answer), asking whether Cyriacus was in good health. Finally Chrysostom sent him a very emphatic letter of complaint. "Is this to be endured? Is it to be borne? Do you think that you have the shadow of an excuse? I sit here in the utmost abandon-

ment, for this long while, in the midst of the greatest confusion and agitation, in misery and need, and you will not
even take the trouble to write to me just once! I have written
once and twice and repeatedly, and you keep silent the whole
time, and you think it is only a trivial oversight, to lack consideration for us. I do not know any more what I am to
think. I am not able to find a reason for your silence. You
have always shown us such warm and sincere love. The
reason cannot be love of ease, for I know your zeal; still less
can it be cowardice, for I also know your courage; nor slow-
ness, for you are vigorous and quick. Neither is illness the
cause, for that would not have hindered you from writing.
And furthermore, I have heard from other people that you
are well and healthy. So I do not know what the real reason
is; I only know that I feel pain and sorrow. Therefore, do all
you can to free us from this grief. If you do not answer this
letter, you will be giving us the utmost grief and sorrow."[30]

But Chrysostom was not to be spared even this sorrow. No
further letter to Bishop Cyriacus exists, so one may reason-
ably assume that the Bishop left unanswered even this appeal
from his unfortunate colleague. We cannot explain the conduct of Chrysostom's former friends and partisans, any more
than he could.

Not in vain did Chrysostom praise, in many of his corres-
pondents, the unchanging, faithful, steadfast, sincere love
which they showed him.

Among the bishops who had stood at his side before his
banishment, and remained true to him until death, the
following kept up a correspondence with him: Palladius,[31]
very probably the same man to whom the Dialog is ascribed.
The latter was in hiding somewhere at that time, and sent
out from his hiding place a letter of consolation to Chrysostom. It is stated in the Dialog that Palladius was held
prisoner at Syene, on the border of Ethiopia.[32]

Also a letter exists from Bishop Tranquillinus,[33] possibly
identical with the Bishop Tranquillius mentioned in Palladius, who in his time stood up so valiantly for Chrysostom's
rights, together with Elpidius of Laodicea, in the presence of
the Emperor and the inimical bishops.[34] Bishop Theodore,
to whom Letter 112 is addressed, may have been Bishop of

Tyana before he was Bishop of Mopsuestia.[34a] Whether Bishop Aurelius (Letter 149) is the same person as the Aurelius in Palladius 17 (58), is not certain. The collective Letter 148 is to the following Bishops, known to Palladius: Cyriacus of Emesa, Demetrius of Pessinus, Palladius of Helenopolis, and Eulysius of Apamea, who belonged among the most outstanding and enduring friends of Chrysostom.

Strange to say, not a single letter to Serapion exists: he was the former faithful deacon, and later Metropolitan of Heraclea. That is all the more inexplicable in view of the fact that Marcian and Gothic monks, among whom Serapion had hidden himself, came to Cucusus.[35] Also absent among the recipients of letters are Heraclidus, Metropolitan of Ephesus, and Bishops Pansophius, Pappus, Eugenius, Lupician, Paulus, Hilarius, Rhodon, Gregory, Lampetius, and others, as well as a group of priests and deacons who were mentioned in Palladius as partisans of Chrysostom, but who, probably as a result of the persecutions, or partly because of banishment, either could not write, or did not dare to write because they were afraid. Also many letters have certainly been lost.

Therefore his joy was all the greater, when not only lay people, but deacons and priests, indeed even bishops, disregarded the considerable trouble and cost, and the still greater danger of the journey, and came to visit the exile personally in Cucusus or Arabissus. It has already been mentioned that the Deaconess Sabiniana, just at the beginning, come from Antioch to Cucusus, and offered him her care and service. A certain deacon named Theodotus, with a lector of the same name, had the courage to visit him in Arabissus, in spite of ice and snow and danger of Isaurians, in the midst of the winter of 405-406.[36]

Also a bishop named Seleucus appeared one day before his exiled colleague. The poor man had almost frozen on the way, and Chrysostom gave him a letter of recommendation to Bishop Tranquillinus, and to the physician Hymnetius.[37]

Priests also must have come fairly often to visit him, as can be seen from various letters.[38]

Then again come special messengers, sent by good friends with letters and gifts.[39]

Sozomen also testifies[40] that Chrysostom in his exile had

received from his friends, and especially from Olympias, so much money that he was in a position to ransom many people who had been taken prisoner by the Isaurians, and to give them back to their relatives. He also supported a number of poor and needy.

This much is doubtless true, that the exile, as in the days of his good fortune, so in those of misfortune, reached a helping hand to other unfortunates as far as he could.

When the priest Domitian complained to him of his need, because he could no more support the poor widows and maids committed to his care, Chrysostom begged a certain Valentinian to give him the necessary means to provide for them.[41]

Occasionally, also, people came to him with very peculiar requests. A certain Theodotus, of a consular family, sent to him a lector of the same name, with the request that Chrysostom, who he obviously believed had nothing else to do, should educate him in spiritual and ecclesiastical affairs, and prepare him for higher consecration and dignities. Chrysostom felt himself compelled to send back the pupil, on the ground that the Isaurians made the region too unsafe.[42]

Another time came the servant of a certain Theodora; his mistress had driven him away, for an unknown reason. Chrysostom did what St. Paul once did for the runaway slave Onesimus; he gave the servant a letter to Theodora, and begged her to take him back.[43]

If one of the narrow circle of friends and acquaintances had not written him, or not for a long time, Chrysostom did not hesitate to inquire as to why he had not written, or why he wrote so seldom.[44]

But he also kept his people in mind in other ways. He wrote, full of sorrow, to the priests Sallustius and Theophilus, to ask why the former had preached only five times in three months, and the latter never preached any more.[45] Then he turned to Theodore, the friend of Sallustius, with the request that he would try to help kindle his zeal somewhat.[46]

If Palladius is well informed, the visits to Arabissus from the not far distant Antioch seem gradually to have become so numerous that the impression was "as if the Church of Antioch had emigrated to Armenia, and as if from there the pleasing voice of John resounded in Antioch."[47]

The exile could not cease preaching and caring for souls even in Arabissus. Palladius even says that he awakened by his words the whole neighborhood of Arabissus from the sleep of ignorance and indifference.[48]

FOOTNOTES

1. As far as the dating of the letters is concerned, Montfaucon, or his collaborators, consider no less than 114 out of 242 letters, or almost half, to have been written in the year 404. But Chrysostom had come to Cucusus, sick unto death, in the middle of September, and so needed a few weeks to recover somewhat; after the beginning of winter, about the middle of November, if not earlier, there were very few messengers or travelers in these regions. So it is obvious that Montfaucon's assumption cannot be correct, and rests on a doubtful supposition. In a great number of the letters there is not the slightest chronological clue, while Montfaucon allows of only 26 letters which have no indication of the year.

The letters 18 to 173 give a uniform impression all the way through that they are all of the same stamp; one must occasionally almost believe that he has a school exercise in letter writing before him. What does this mean?

The second collection of letters (174 to 242) are different in language and richer in content, and give a far better impression of authenticity than the first group. An exact philological examination of both collections is much to be desired.

Most of the letters are short, and surprisingly contain almost no real inquiries or information, but only assurances of love, wishes of good health to the recipients, and requests to write him often—indeed, to send him " clouds of letters," so that his solitude may be more tolerable. (Cf. Letters 18, 19, 20 ff., 47 ff.). The letters to Olympias are the only ones which differ in tone and contents from the others, and strike a more personal note.

Chrysostom begged pardon of Bishop Elpidius (of Laodicea?) for his long silence: there were few people whom one could use as messengers, and among those few, not all could be trusted. (Letter 138.)

2. Letter 13 (52, 610).

3. Letter 193 (720); cf. letter 204 and 220.

4. Letter 14, 1 (612).

5. Letter 2 (556 ff.).

6. Letter 4 (589 ff.).

7. Letter 16 (620).

8. Letters 4, 7, 17 (589 ff., 601, 621).

9. Letter 1 (549 ff.).

9a. 52, 459-480.

9b. 52, 479-528. Cf. letter 4, 4 to Olympias (52, 595, lines 22-26).

9c. There can scarcely be any doubt that this letter, perhaps the last one of his life, was written during the banishment, and probably from Arabissus. Especially in the last part, there are obvious allusions to the Johnite persecutions and to Olympias herself. Chrysostom wished to console and comfort his true friends with this letter. Probably the treatise was the same as Cassian's Collatio VI, 4: Quod malum nulli invito possit inferri. (PL 49, 651).

10. Letter 3 (572).

11. Letters 94, 104, 185 (657 ff.). Cf. Palladius 10 (35).

12. Letter 96 (659).

13. Letters 39, 60, 77, 99 (631 ff.).

14. Letters 60, 76, 98 (642 ff.).

15. This Pentadia is at any rate identical with the Pentadia who was the wife of Timasius, whom Eutropius banished into the oasis of Egypt, where he perished in the desert. Sozomen 8, 7 (1533). Cf. p. 44.

16. Letter 94 (658 f.).

17. Letter 34 (629); cf. letter 18 (623).

18. Letter 227 (736).

19. Letter 232 (738).

20. Palladius 10 (35).

21. See the following chapter.

22. Letters 25, 114, 131, 138, 142, 230 (626 ff.).

23. But that lasted only until his strength and health returned.

24. Cf. p. 388 ff. and letter 13 (610).

25. Letter 131 (690).

26. Letter 234 (739).

27. Letter 190 (718).

28. Who this Bishop Cyriacus was is hard to determine. At any rate, at the time of Chrysostom's banishment he was in quiet possession of his bishopric, and enjoyed good health. Cyriacus of Synada, on the contrary, had fled to Rome, and, as a member of the Roman synodal embassy, was sent to Constantinople. Cyriacus of Emesa, on the other hand, was an exile in the fortress of Palmyra. So these two scarcely come into consideration as recipients of letters.

29. Letter 64 (644).
30. Letter 202 (723).
31. Letter 113 (669) and 148 (699-700).
32. Cf. Introduction I.
33. Letter 37 (630-631).
34. Dialog. 9 (31).
34a. The Syrian-Nestorian Chronicle of Seert (Patrol. Orient. V, 320) says that Theodore of Mopsuestia wrote a beautiful letter to Arcadius in favor of Chrysostom. But Eudoxia prevented the success of his intervention. This is not known otherwise, and the report is of very late date.
35. Letter 14, 5 (618).
36. Letters 135 and 136 (693-694).
37. Letters 37 and 38 (630-631).
38. For example, letters 26, 27, 28, 104, 127, 128 (626 ff.).
39. Letters 225, 229, 230-232 (735 ff.).
40. Letter 24 (629).
41. HE 8, 27 (1592).
42. Letter 217 (730); it is doubtful.
43. Letter 61 (642-643).
44. Letter 117 (672-673).
45. Cf. Letters 185, 190, 195, 198, 202, 208 (716 ff.).
46. Letter 203 (721) and 212 (729).
47. Letter 210 (728).
48. Dial. 11 (37).

CHAPTER XXXIV

CHRYSOSTOM AND THE PAGAN MISSIONS[1]

PALLADIUS, Socrates and Sozomen are silent about the missionary activity of Chrysostom among the pagans. Theodoret, on the other hand, says that Chrysostom already had, as Bishop of Constantinople, not only brought about reforms in Thrace, Asia, and Pontus, but also had promoted the missions, that is the conversion of the pagans, to the best of his ability, especially in Phoenicia, Scythia, and Syria.[2] George Alexandrinus copied this from Theodoret, and added the Celts to the list,[3] and even said that while Chrysostom was in Cucusus, he had converted the whole of Armenia to Christianity, and even had the New Testament and the Psalter translated into Armenian.[4] Then Leo Imperator,[5] Anonymous,[6] and Metaphrastes[7] copied this from George. Anonymous even knew exactly which cities and peoples were benefited by the missionary zeal of Chrysostom; they were Tyre and Sidon, Berytus, Heliopolis, Damascus, Emesa, and Cyzicus; also the Persians, Iberians, Alani and Abasci.* However, these splendid deeds may be traced back more to the later Byzantine urge to date back as far as possible the motives and signs of the legality of Chrysostom's ecclesiastical overlordship. Martyrius[8] names only the Persians and the Goths.

It has already been emphasized that Chrysostom, when he was Bishop of Constantinople, possessed influence far over the boundaries of his diocese, and gave proof of this. He interested himself especially in the Arian or pagan Germans, who were chiefly represented by the Goths.

Unfortunately, we do not possess any further information as to whether he found the possibility or the opportunity of interesting himself also in the spreading of Christianity in a

* Tr. Note. The Iberians, Alani and Abasci were barbarian tribes around the Black Sea.

real mission to the pagans outside the borders of the Empire. At any rate, nothing is reported of a systematic greater mission undertaking during the period of his office as Bishop. Only once did he come into relations with the affairs of the pagans, and that was at the time when Bishop Porphyrius of Gaza traveled to Constantinople to ask help from the Emperor against the pagans in Gaza of Phoenicia.

Now it seems that just about the time when Chrysostom had to go into exile for the second time, in the summer of 404, disturbing conditions arose again in Phoenicia, and they were of quite a serious nature. We do not know whether the deposition of the Bishop of Constantinople encouraged the pagans, or whether some other occasion arose. At any rate, affairs so stood, in the summer of 404, that the missionaries there were near to losing their courage, indeed to giving up the mission entirely.[9]

No help could be hoped for from the old Bishop Arsacius, in regard to ecclesiastical or religious affairs. He was not able to keep his own church in order, much less interest himself in foreign churches. And Bishop Antiochus of Ptolemais in Phoenicia, the opponent of Chrysostom, had more important things to do than dedicating himself to the conversion of the pagans. So it may be understood that Chrysostom interested himself voluntarily in the Church in Phoenicia, through pure religious enthusiasm. It is also not at all impossible that, for his part, the journey of Porphyrius was the cause of Chrysostom's giving special attention to the conversion of the pagans in Phoenicia. It is comprehensible that he still kept up his interest in the mission when he was in exile. It is a fact that while he was in Nicaea, directly after his banishment, he was interested in the Phoenician mission.

In Nicaea he met a monk who had lived for long years as a recluse, in complete seclusion from the world and from all human relations. Chrysostom, who, according to Palladius, said that a virtuous man who lived in the world was worth more than a sluggard in a monk's habit,[10] visited the hermit, and represented to him that he had been living in solitude long enough for his own soul's health. He should now begin to be of some use to others, for instance, to go on a mission to Phoenicia, and work for souls there under the direction of the priest Constantius. Fortunately, the hermit showed him-self not intractable to this apostolic idea, and allowed himself to be persuaded to something better; he forsook contempla-tion and the cell he had lived in so long, and went to Phoenicia.[11]

The priest Constantius seems to have exercised a sort of superintendence of the pagan missions in Phoenicia, Arabia and the Orient. At least, Chrysostom hastened to write to him from Nicaea that he would have a monk sent to him, and he was to let him know if the monk was acceptable. He also exhorted him, in spite of all the storms in his post, which he had understood from the beginning, that he was to hold out, and to let the victory over paganism, the erection of new churches, and the care for souls, be the most important thing. "The more violently the storm bursts, the more firmly the steersman must take the rudder in his hands, and the worse an illness is, the more the doctor must devote himself to the sick person. So leave nothing undone in caring for the churches of Phoenicia, Arabia and the Orient."

Who this priest Constantius was, and what ecclesiastical position he occupied, is unfortunately not easy to say. It would not be impossible that he was identical with the priest Constantius of Antioch.[12] On the other hand, naturally it is just as possible, indeed very probable, that in the chief city of Constantine there were many people who were called Constantine or Constantius, and that Chrysostom delegated a cleric of this name to work especially in the mission sphere. So the very personal sympathy which Chrysostom showed for these missions is naturally explained.

How much he really had these things at heart is shown by the fact that he begged Constantius to inform him regularly as to how many new churches were being built, who had gone to the mission in Phoenicia, and what sort of progress was being made there. Also, he was not to let anything discour-age him from sending him letters, as often as possible.[13]

From the same letter (221) we also learn that, about the same time, the Marcionite sect at Salamis in Cyprus was troubling the Catholics, and that Chrysostom, in the very last days of his Bishopric in Constantinople, had entered into correspondence with the proper authorities there about this;

but the affair could not be carried through. "If you should learn," he wrote to Constantius, "that Bishop Cyriacus is still in Constantinople, write to him about this affair. He can take care of everything."[14]

Chrysostom did not let the matter drop with the simple recluse in Nicaea and the letter to Constantius. He sent from Cucusus a letter of thanks to a certain Alphius, because he had sent the priest John to Phoenicia and supported him with money.[15]

He was greatly inspired by the fact that a certain priest Nicholas, who was superior of a monastery, had not only sent monks to the missions before, but even now, in spite of the unrest, he had them remain. And if the priest Gerontius should regain his health, he would send him to Phoenicia again soon. The priest John might go with him then, as a traveling companion. He knew that Nicholas would do everything, and make every effort, to send qualified men to Phoenicia, and to encourage those who were already there to persevere; and then, too, to send thither those who lived in the neighborhood.[16]

He wrote to Gerontius himself, asking him to try to inspire others to go with him. To make such apostolic journeys was better and more useful than sitting at home. They could also practice fasting, night-watching, and other virtues there, and thereby save many souls. The priest Constantius would take care of all their other needs.[17]

Finally, Chrysostom sent a letter to the monks' chaplains, Symeon and Mares, in Apamea, saying that if they knew any virtuous people anywhere who were prepared to work with the priest John in Phoenicia, they should make every effort to send them there.[18]

Also a priest named Basilius showed himself enthusiastic for the conversion of the pagans. Although Chrysostom did not know him personally, he wrote to him anyhow, to give expression to his friendship, love and honor.[19]

But the continual reinforcement of the spiritual armies does not seem to have attracted the pagans very much. Possibly the monks who hastened there in the beginning did not show much experience in missionary teaching. Theodoret, inexact as usual, in writing of the blame or merit of

Chrysostom, says that he destroyed the pagan temples in Phoenicia through the monks, and under the protection of an imperial decree (in the year 405 or 406).[20]   Perhaps here is a faint indication that the monks in their zeal had gone too far, and brought on themselves the revenge of the pagans. It is a fact that, in the year 405 or 406, the pagans had fallen upon the monastic missionaries and wounded many of them; they even made martyrs of some of them.   When Chrysostom learned of it, he wrote at once, in evident distress, to a priest named Rufinus, asking him to hasten as soon as possible to the Phoenician battlefield; the mere sight of his calmness and gentleness would be sufficient to calm the pagans, and encourage their own people.

So he was to travel with the greatest possible speed, as if to save a burning house.   And on the way he should have news brought to him, from every city, for he could not be calm until he knew that he (Rufinus) was in Phoenicia.   If necessary, he was ready to write to Constantinople, and, if he needed it, he would send him more help, at the same time with the martyrs' relics he had asked for, which he had begged from Bishop Otreius of Arabissus.   The church of Arabissus possessed many relics, which were indeed absolutely authentic.   Rufinus was also to strive to get the new churches roofed before the beginning of winter.[21]

He wrote in the same vein to another group of priests and monks, urging them not to be discouraged or frightened.   He had received letters from the priest Constantius; it seemed, from them, that the situation had improved again.   The Apostles had endured chains and prisons, and, in spite of them, they had not lost their apostolic zeal.   Therefore he had sent the pious priest John to them, to strengthen and fortify them.[22]

Another priest, Elpidius by name, had taken upon himself the task of winning to Christianity the pagan dwellers in the Amanus mountain chain; they were Isaurians.[23]   After endless trouble and difficulty, this was actually partly accomplished.   Several small churches and colonies of monks cared for what had been acquired.   There Chrysostom gladly gave to Elpidius, who it seems was again afflicted by a money shortage, a letter of recommendation to a certain Agapetus, whom he begged to show in deeds that the recommendation from him had not been in vain.[24]

From one of the letters to Olympias, one may conclude that Chrysostom's care for the missions in his exile extended even to Persia. At least he begged Olympias to show kindness to Bishop Maruthas (who had come into such painful contact with Bishop Cyrinus of Chalcedon at the Synod of the Oak), because he needed him badly for the Persian affair. Also he wished to know what Maruthas had accomplished in Persia, why he had come back to Constantinople, and whether he had received the two letters which Chrysostom had sent him.[25]

Finally, Chrysostom showed himself much concerned that the Goths should get a worthy new bishop. When he himself was in Constantinople, he had given them a distinguished Bishop in the person of the priest Unilas. Now the Gothic king had sent a certain deacon Moduarius (to Constantinople?) begging for a new bishop. This appointment would have to be delayed until the winter was over. Otherwise he feared two things: first, that his opponents would name a new bishop, and second, that they would choose someone unworthy. He wished very much that Moduarius, the deacon, might come to him, if possible.[26]

Unfortunately, we do not know of the outcome of this affair. In later letters Chrysostom spoke no more of it.

From all these particulars, one may rightly assume that Chrysostom, while he was Bishop of Constantinople, had given his deepest attention to the outposts of Christianity, and that he did everything possible to lead the way to an enduring missionary activity in the lands near Constantinople. One may define it as the great tragedy of the Orient, that this missionary spirit did not live again in his successors. One cannot imagine what might have become of the Greek Byzantine Empire, if 200 years later, at the time of Mohammed, Arabia and Persia had already become Christian, when the storm of Islam burst over the Christian world; if from the gates which led to Asia, India, and China, the Cross of Christ had traveled into the eastern pagan lands.

If Chrysostom had had time to accomplish religious and moral reforms among his clergy, and to form them according to his heart, and had it been possible for him to bring into the Greek episcopate of his time a great number of men who were filled with his spirit and his fiery apostolic zeal, the Greek Church would have been in a position to accomplish the most splendid world mission ever allotted to any people. It would have been allotted to him, in infinitely higher measure, if only through his classics, to unite under the spiritual hegemony of his name an enduring union of peoples.

That this did not happen is the most tragic part of the Chrysostom-tragedy. That his apostolic and missionary activity was not carried on further—indeed, scarcely an earnest and lasting effort to this end was made—that instead of this, the Greek-Byzantine clergy bogged down in mutual intrigues and exhausted themselves in continual theological quarrels, and that Oriental monasticism allowed itself to acquiesce in a one-sided flight from the world, instead of remembering world conquest and world renovation—all that can be considered as the great tragic fault, as is shown by the resulting sad loss suffered by the Orient and the Occident until this day, through which the Byzantine Empire, together with Constantinople itself, went down to ruin together.

FOOTNOTES

1. Cf. P. Romuald Heiss, Mönchtum, Seelsorge und Mission nach dem heiligen Johannes Chrysostomus, in: "Lumen Caecis" (St. Ottilien 1928) p. 1-23. P. Andres, O.M.J., Der Missionsgedanke in den Homilien des Joh. Chrysostomus, zur Apostelgeschichte, in: Ztschr. f. Missions wesen 19 (1921) 201-225; Edm. Hartung, Joh. Chrys. und die Heidenmission, in: Allgem. Missionsztschr . . . 21 (1894) 310-26.

2. HE 5, 28-31 (82, 1256-1260). The account of Theodoret is evidently based on recollections from the collection of Chrysostom's letters, which must have been already known at that time in Antioch and its environs.

3. Ch. 23 (Savile 8, 189).

4. Ch. 59 (*ibid.* 235-236). Actually the Armenian translation of the Bible (of Sahak the Great?) originates in the first half of the fifth century, and it was made from the Greek. (Moses of

Khoren, Historia Armen. 3, 57). So it is not impossible that the Armenian translation was made at the urging of a Greek. That this Greek was St. Chrysostom, banished to Armenia Secunda, is certified only by George Alexandrinus, as far as my knowledge goes. About the year 404, Mesrop found the Armenian manuscript. That year is reckoned as the birth year of Armenian literature. Armenia at that time was for the most part under the rule of the Persians. That Chrysostom had relations with the "Persians" during his exile, we have seen from his letter 14, 5 (52, 618). However, that is not sufficient for serious proof. S. Weber, Die Katholische Kirche in Armenien, Freiburg 1903, p. 406-407, mentions this information concerning Chrysostom, without investigating it further.

5. Ch. 13 (Savile 8, 276).

6. Ch. 42-52 (*ibid.* 320 ff.).

7. Ch. 18 (*ibid.* 390-391).

8. P. 471, l. 2.

9. Letter 53 (637); 123 (676); 221 (733).

10. Dial. 19 (47, 69).

11. Chrysostom, Letter 221 (52, 733).

12. In spite of Palladius Dial. 16 (54).

13. Letter 221 (733).

14. This letter gives rise to more than one idea. 1. Could Chrysostom have learned from Nicaea, more easily than Constantius from Phoenicia, whether Cyriacus was in Constantinople, and could he not have written to him himself? Or which Cyriacus was meant here? Scarcely an open defender of Chrysostom. 2. Should Constantius not have known that Salamis is a "place in Cyprus"? 3. How could Chrysostom charge a mere priest to take care of "the churches of Phoenicia, Arabia and the Orient"? However, I dare not designate the letter as unauthentic.

15. Letter 21 (624).

16. Letter 53 (637).

17. Letter 54 (638-639).

18. Letter 55 (639-640).

19. Letter 28 (627).

20. HE 5, 29 (82, 1257 B-C); Thierry, Chrysostome 336, copies it without criticism; as does also O. Gruppe, Griechische Mythologie und Religionsgeschichte 1672 and 1674, note 4.

21. Letter 126 (685-687).

22. Letter 123 (676-678).

23. The mountain chain which separates Syria from Asia Minor and from the Taurus mountains toward the south runs

along the shore of the bay of İskenderun, and in the southwest, it ends with the steeply sloping Ras-el-Chansir at the edge of the sea. Its greatest height is 7,800 feet.

24. Letter 175 (711-712). Theodoret relates something similar in his *Historia religiosa* (Ch. 17) of Abraames, who converted the pagans on the Libanon, if Theodoret is not fictionizing.

25. Letter 14, 5 (618).

26. Letter 14, 5 (618-19).

CHAPTER XXXV

THE FRUSTRATED COUNCIL

IN all the time during which Chrysostom had dwelt in Cucusus and Arabissus he was not forgotten by his friends nor, above all, in the West. Pope Innocent had become convinced that no progress was to be hoped for in his cause by mere patience and waiting. With the death of the Empress Eudoxia he believed, as many others did, that the chief hindrance to the contemplated synod had been done away with. Naturally, nothing was to be hoped for in the affair from the Bishops of the Orient, least of all from the three great Patriarchs. But after the whole ugly persecution of Chrysostom and his partisans by their episcopal opponents, in the name of the Emperor of the East, and on the ground of his decrees, had taken place, no other way remained open but to call for the mediation of the Western Emperor Honorius, who, as brother of Arcadius and coregent of the entire Roman Empire, appeared to be the next in line to soothe the party strife.

So then Innocent wrote, probably early in 405, to the Emperor Honorius at Ravenna, and at the same time enclosed copies of the various letters which had been sent to him from the East. These letters actually did not fail to make their impression on Honorius. However, he did not wish to interfere decidedly in the course of the affair, but expressed to the Pope the wish that a synod of Italian bishops should first examine the entire affair, and give their judgment on it. But meanwhile he wrote to Arcadius and begged him to see to it that justice was done to Bishop John. Honorius received no answer. Neither did a second letter receive any answer.[1]

Meanwhile, the Synod of Latin Bishops which Honorius had wished for convened in Rome. A significant number of Italian bishops took part in it. This synod concluded, in regard to the Oriental ecclesiastical dispute, that the Emperor

Honorius should be requested to write to his brother and co-Emperor Arcadius, and ask him to call a general synod of Greeks and Latins at Saloniki, because the favorable situation of this city facilitated the attendance of Orientals as well as Occidentals. At this council, not numbers but law was to be decisive; for only thus could a really impartial judgment be expected. Also, Chrysostom was to appear before this council, but only under the condition that his diocese and the ecclesiastical fellowship were to be given back to him before the council convened. He was to appear before the clerical court in full possession of his rights and dignities.[2]

Therewith the Roman synod, under the presidency of the Pope, pronounced a formal declaration of invalidity on the judgment of the Synod of the Oak. Previously, in the same way, a Latin synod under Pope Julius had pronounced invalid the deposition of St. Athanasius and Bishop Paul of Constantinople; this deposition had been pronounced by Greek Arian bishops.[3]

Emperor Honorius agreed to the proposition, provided that the Pope would be the chief negotiator. He would send an embassy of five bishops, two priests and one deacon, to Constantinople, and there, among other letters, they would hand over the one which Honorius would send with them.

The imperial letter to Arcadius read as follows:

"For the third time I write to Your Serenity with the request that the cause of John, Bishop of Constantinople, be rectified. For apparently this has not yet been done. For this reason I am sending a new letter through bishops and priests, entirely on account of concern for ecclesiastical peace, through which the peace of our Empire is guaranteed. Vouchsafe them to command that the Bishops of the Orient meet in Saloniki. For our Western Bishops have also chosen men who are incapable of malice or lying, namely, five bishops, two priests, and a deacon of the great Roman Church.[4] Therefore show them all honor, and if they are convinced that Bishop John was lawfully deposed, they are to inform me, so that I may abstain from fellowship with him. On the other hand, if they find that the Oriental Bishops are responsible for an injustice being done, then they will have you announce the fellowship. As to how the Western Bishops think concerning the case of Bishop John, the same is disclosed in a number of letters, which have been sent to me in regard to this affair. Two of them I enclose, which make all the others unnecessary: the letters of the Bishops of Rome and of Aquileia. But this one thing I beg you especially to attend to, namely, that Theophilus of Alexandria is also to appear, even though it is against his will; for he appears to be the chief cause of all the trouble. So thus the assembly will be able to secure peace unhindered, of which the present time is much in need."[5]

For bringing these letters to the Emperor Arcadius, the Pope named the following: Bishops Aemilius of Benevento, Cythegius, Gaudentius of Brescia, as well as the priests Valentinian and Bonifacius, and the deacon Paulus.[6] Of the Greeks, the four earlier mentioned Bishops Cyriacus, Demetrius, Palladius, and Eulysius, together with their retinue, traveled back with the embassy. Also a Bishop Marianus appeared among the ambassadors, as a bearer of important documents.[7] Besides the letters of the Emperor Honorius, they also brought along some letters from Pope Innocent, from the Italian Bishops Chromatius of Aquileia and Venerius of Milan, to whom Chrysostom had also written. But, as an important legal document, they brought the official proceedings of the Western Roman synod in the affair of Chrysostom, which stated that the Bishop of Constantinople should be reinstated in his offices and dignities before he appeared in court at Saloniki. They also wished to send letters to Anysius, the Bishop of this city, on the way.

So departed the embassy for Constantinople, early in 406, accompanied by the most fervent wishes of the Pope and the Latin Bishops for a happy outcome, in the name and under the protection of the highest religious and secular authorities of the West.[8] Justice, afflicted and ill-treated, seemed about to have her resurrection; the partisans of these legitimate bishops of the chief city of " East Rome," who had been expelled, felt new courage and confidence.

The one around whom all these dealings, synods, ambassadors, and letter-exchanges revolved learned, from a priest who visited him, of the state of affairs and of the delegation of the bishops, who were coming to Constantinople in the name of the Pope and of the Western Church, in order to represent his cause.   One may imagine what happy feelings of hope must have risen in the heart of the far-off exile, when he heard that the Pope and the Western Emperor were interceding for him.   He wrote several letters to the Western Bishops as soon as possible, in which he thanked them for their zeal and their efforts; he begged them to continue to the end the work they had begun; the heavenly reward would surely not be lacking to them for their efforts toward the restoration of peace to the Church.[9]

From about this time originates the fourth letter to Olympias, in which he expresses to his faithful deaconess and companion in suffering the happy hope that the time of his exile might soon come to an end.[10]   This hope seemed all the more justified in that the exiled Bishop still had many friends, in Constantinople itself, who would intercede for him.   For instance, a certain Anatolius, of an eparchal family, worked very zealously for him.[11]   The eunuch chamberlain Brison seems to have possessed no more influence after the death of Eudoxia, while Anthemius, city prefect and consul for the year 405, was at least not unfavorably disposed toward Chrysostom.[12]   Also a certain Theodotus, of a consular family,[13] the city prefect Studius,[14] and others, belonged among his friends.

To this same priest Chrysostom gave letters to individual bishops of the Greek and Latin halves of the Empire, of whom he knew that they were in some way interceding for him and for his cause.   Thus he wrote to Bishop Maximus of Turin, Venerius of Milan, a Bishop of an unknown diocese who bore the unassuming name of Asellus; then Gaudentius of Brescia, Chromatius of Aquileia, Hesychius of Salona, and even Aurelius, Archbishop of Carthage.[15]   In all these letters he thanked the recipients for their efforts toward the peace of the Church, deplored the fact that in his solitude he so seldom had the opportunity to write, and begged them for further activity toward the restoration of law and order, for which the heavenly reward would not be lacking.

In the same vein he wrote to several Greek Bishops and

Metropolitans; to Anysius of Saloniki, whom the Roman embassy expected to visit first; to various bishops of his Macedonian province, and to Alexander of Corinth.[16] Unfortunately we find in these letters almost no enrichment of our knowledge concerning the succession of individual events.

Reception of the Embassy in the Orient
Return and Report of the Latins

Actually, the cause of the persecuted Patriarch seemed more favorable and hopeful than ever before, since his second banishment. He himself waited in joyful expectation, and so did every one who had remained loyal to him; the whole Western Church awaited the fortunate outcome of the negotiations, and the speedy restoration of peace and concord in the Greek Church.

At last the news of all the resolutions and proceedings in Rome and Italy reached the East. In the hearts of one group they awakened joyful and happy hope, and in those of the other, fear and dread.

If it actually came to this, that the synod assembled according to plan, what would be the easily foreseen result of it? First, Atticus would have to descend from his long-striven-for and scarcely-won throne, before the synod had even held its first meeting. The Pope, with the entire Roman Synod (405) had declared that the judgment of the Synod of the Oak was illegal, and even demanded that Chrysostom must be reinstated in his office and dignities before the meeting of the synod. Thus Atticus was disposed of before all. At the most, he would have to be satisfied with a provincial bishopric. Naturally, he had no taste for such a bitter pill. It is, humanly speaking, easy to understand that the sly man, unscrupulous in case of necessity, brought into play all his diplomatic arts, and used all his influence with the court circles to hinder the assembling of the dreaded synod.

The same was true of Theophilus. The Patriarch of Alexandria was doubtless the chief originator of the entire Chrysostom tragedy. The Synod of the Oak was his work exclusively. And then he had given out a "lawful reason" for Chrysostom's second banishment (namely, his forbidden return in spite of the Synod of the Oak), and, besides, he had sent three Egyptian

Bishops to Constantinople, to see that the proceedings were carried out. Therefore he seemed, in the eyes of the world, to be the chief culprit, and the Emperor Honorius had openly expressed this conviction of his contemporaries, when he wrote his third letter to his brother Arcadius, asking him especially to see to it that Theophilus would also appear at the coming synod, "for he appears to be the chief cause of all the trouble." That Theophilus, in the bottom of his heart, held the same opinion, is shown by the incredibly furious tone of the "Liber ennormis," against Bishop John. But the same document must also have made clear to all sensible people that Theophilus would not be frightened away by any violent means from protecting and defending his work against any attack. The Patriarch knew very well what would happen to his patriarchal seat if the synod assembled. With the quick decision with which he was accustomed to act, he had doubtless also sent suitable advice to Constantinople, with which he found full understanding in Atticus.

Another man whose patriarchal existence was threatened by the meeting of the synod was Porphyrius, the unlawful usurper of the episcopal seat in Antioch.

If one includes the new Metropolitans of Ephesus and Heraclea, the guilty bishops Severian, Antiochus, and Acacius, the simoniacs of Asia Minor, and all others who had intrigued against Chrysostom, and finally the unfaithful group among the clerics of Constantinople, one would understand that the Western embassy faced an almost unanimous, resolute and decided phalanx of bishops who would almost give their lives to prevent the meeting of that synod.

Under these circumstances, it must have seemed easy enough for the most nearly threatened heads of the Eastern episcopates to get the necessary powers of the State into their service, and to take every measure which seemed most opportune, to provide a little comfort for their fearful hearts.

In Rome nothing was heard of the great embassy for a long time. Weeks and months passed by, and no news came. Then finally, after fully four months of anxious waiting, still no news had come, but the Archbishop Aemilius of Benevento, the leader of the embassy, appeared in Rome himself with his companions. Grief and disillusion, perhaps also shame and

despair, spoke in their actions and words. They reported to
the Pope concerning the "Babylonian treatment" they had
received in the East. "When we sailed along the Greek
coasts, in the direction of Athens," they related, "we were
suddenly stopped by an insignificant officer (a chiliarch). He
turned us over to a subordinate (a hecatontarch) and forbade
us to land in Saloniki. We had some letters to deliver to
Bishop Anysius there.[17] Instead of that, we had to get into
two other boats and proceed further. Soon after that, a great
storm came up from the southwest, and for three days, without being able to eat anything, we had to sail through the
Aegean Sea and the Dardanelles. Fnally, at noon on the third
day, we landed before Constantinople, near the suburb of
Victor.[18] Here we were detained again, by the harbor authorities, and commanded to go back. No one told us from whom
the command came. We were locked up in a fortress called
Athyra, on the Thracian coast.[19] Then we Romans were
separated from the Greeks, and interned in a small building,
where we had no one to serve us, while Cyriacus and his
companions were lodged in various places.

"Then they demanded our letters and documents. We
refused to give them up, and said: We cannot, in our capacity
as ambassadors, give the letters of our Emperor and the
Bishops to anyone but the Emperor. Since we persevered in
our refusal, the notary Patricius came to us, and then some
others, and at last an officer named Valerian, a Cappadocian,
with a troop of soldiers. He used force against Bishop
Marianus, even broke his thumbs, and tore from him the
sealed letters of the Emperor Honorius, and the other
letters.

"On the second day ambassadors came to us, whether from
the court or from Atticus we did not know; the latter, they
told us, was in possession of the episcopal throne. They
offered us three thousand gold pieces, and sought to persuade
us that we should extend fellowship to Atticus, and be silent
about Bishop John and the demand for a new synod. We
rejected these demands; and since we could do nothing for
the restoration of peace, we began to beg perseveringly that
we might, in the face of such fury and brutality on the part
of our opponents, be allowed at least to go home safely again

to our own dioceses. At last the same tribune Valerian returned, and brought us to an old rotten boat, in which we were under guard by twenty soldiers from various garrisons. They even told us that the tribune had given the captain money to let the bishops die on the journey. It was a fact. Scarcely had we gone a few miles (and reached the north entrance to the Dardanelles), when the boat threatened to sink. Then we landed at Lampsacus (the modern Lapsaki), opposite Gallipoli, there entered another boat, and twenty days later landed at Hydrus in Calabria."[20]

Such was the report of the returning ambassadors. But as to how things stood with Chrysostom, and as to the whereabouts of Demetrius, Cyriacus, Eulysius, Palladius, and the other bishops and their companions, who had taken part in the journey, they knew nothing.

Such was the sad end of the embassy which had been prepared with so much effort and expense, and which had set out with such fair hopes. Thus were treated these bishops and priests who had come in the name of the Emperor of the West, and of the Pope, to establish a peace which the people of power and influence did not want. So thus right and justice were further away than ever, mishandled by external brute power, and to the old wrong a new injustice was added.

It has naturally been asked, in all times, who the politically powerful personage could have been who dared perpetrate such an insult and a challenge to the whole political and ecclesiastical West. The legends concerning the affair could not explain it except by lengthening the Empress Eudoxia's life by three years. This was the best way to explain everything, and it was not necessary to malign anyone.

But at any rate, history has passed a significant judgment upon him in whose name all these misdeeds were done, namely, the Emperor Arcadius. It has unanimously pronounced him guilty, although he was not fully informed in regard to the affair. Sozomen even assigns a motive by which the whole affair was made acceptable to him, a motive which, for the ecclesiastical manner of thought of the Greek-Byzantine bishops, was very significant, indeed of long-range significance in world history. It was represented to the Emperor that it would be an outrage[21] upon the imperial dignity of

East Rome if the Bishop of West Rome should send an embassy thither, to demand a summoning of an Eastern synod, and perhaps even depose some of the distinguished Bishops of the Empire. So spoke those who shortly before had turned to the Pope themselves. The Emperor fell in with this appeal to his self-glorification without further ado.

But this alleged motive appears for this reason to be significant in world history, because, as far as I can see, here, for the first time, among the Catholic Bishops of the East, a moment of nationalistic and imperialistic feeling was misused as a political weapon, which carried in itself the embryo of schism between the East and the West, and which actually led, some centuries later, to the final separation, the unfortunate Eastern schism. But it meant still more than the first lightning-flash of the coming schism between the Greek and the Latin Churches. This appeal of the Greek Bishops, of the highest spiritual authority of the Church, to the secular power, shows also the beginning of that unworthy subjugation of the Greek Church to the Greek-Byzantine imperium, which has been so strikingly characterized as Byzantine *caesaropapism*.

This challenge of the secular power against the Church authority had indeed been practiced by the Arian Bishops almost as a customary thing, and thereby the foundation was laid for this Byzantine caesaropapism. But on the part of the Catholic Bishops, such a case as this had not yet come up. It had been worthily introduced. Shortly before Chrysostom's second banishment, the Bishops Acacius, Severian, Antiochus, and Cyrinus, said to the Emperor: " *You have been set over us all by God, as ruler; you can do whatever pleases you.*"[22] This speech, so unworthy of a Bishop, was the signal for a tragedy, in which a hated colleague was betrayed by handing him over to the secular power. In order to attain this end, the Church had basically and practically been betrayed, and delivered over to the secular power. That was the beginning of Byzantine caesaropapism. It derived, not from the Emperor, but from the Greek Bishops. On their shoulders lies the responsibility for the development of the ecclesiastical relations of the East which were to have such unhappy results, not only for the East itself, but for Christianity and for the whole Church.

So if the Empress Eudoxia bears no blame for the last events of the Chrysostom tragedy, because she was already dead, and the Emperor Arcadius none, because he lacked the intellectual requirements for blame and sin, then, in the face of history, the whole responsibility for the atrocious perfidy and disloyalty rests upon the few Greek Bishops. But the spirit which animated them had not only paved the way for the coming great schism, but it had also led to an actual separation between Rome and the Catholic Orient; the first such separation known in the history of the Church.

The Pope could not submit in silence to such an insult against his authority, such an unheard-of outrage against ecclesiastical law. But while the Patriarch of Alexandria, in his first letter, demanded of him that he give up ecclesiastical fellowship with Chrysostom, now *Pope Innocent broke off all ecclesiastical relations with Theophilus, Atticus, Porphyrius, and all of the other chief opponents of Chrysostom.* Thereby a schism between the Orient and the Occident was actually introduced, and so a tragic fate ordained that he whose first official action accomplished the settlement of a partial schism between Antioch and Rome henceforth became the apple of discord and the unwitting cause of a schism between Rome and the entire Orient.

But in spite of the momentary failure, it contributed to the enduring honor of Rome that it, almost alone with the Latin West, vindicated the lost honor of a Greek Bishop of Constantinople, against the opposition of the influential Greek bishops. And also it would have helped to obtain victory for the law, if these bishops had not prevented it with the help of secular power.

For the moment, injustice had conquered in the Orient, and had maintained itself in possession of power. But in spite of this Rome did not give up the idea of a synod, in which justice and injustice would be defined. Even after Chrysostom was already dead, it held fast to this idea. Palladius says (in the year 408) in his Dialog: "The Roman Church firmly refuses to maintain fellowship with the Oriental bishops, especially with Theophilus, until, by the help of God, a general council can be called, in order that those who have dared to do such things will be cut off as unprofitable members. For even though John is dead, the truth still lives, and that is the question.[23]

But even if the council did not meet, the final moral victory would still be on the side of right and innocence.

FOOTNOTES

1. That resulted from the letter of Honorius to Arcadius which follows below. Cf. Palladius 3 (14).

2. Palladius, Dial. 4 (15).

3. At that time Constantius' brother threatened, if he did not re-install both of them, to come himself and bring them back. That got results. (=Socrates 2, 22=67, 245; Sozomen 3, 8 and 10 (1052 and 1057). In regard to this, later Byzantine biographers of Chrysostom have similarly portrayed the events of 405-406.

4. Τῆς μεγίστης Ἐκκλησίας Ῥωμαίων (Palladius 3. col. 14).

5. Palladius 3 (14-15).

6. Sozomen 8, 28 says that the Pope, with (besides?) the Greek Bishops who had come from the Orient, sent five Bishops and two Roman priests to Honorius *and* Arcadius, and thus did not keep the embassies apart. The reliable report is doubtless that of Palladius. The deacon Paulus is probably the deacon of the Bishop Emmelius. (Pall. 4 [16]).

7. Also Sozomen 8, 28 says that there were five bishops.

8. One can only assume that 406 was the year of this embassy. Since the Pope had received the first news of the deposition of Chrysostom about the beginning of June 404, several months passed in the exchange of letters between Rome, Constantinople and Alexandria. The result was that the Pope declared that in the meantime he could do nothing. But at last he turned to the Emperor Honorius. Many Latin Bishops did the same. Then Honorius wrote twice to his brother, and both times he waited in vain for an answer. Meanwhile the Pope summoned a synod in Rome. This took place, and proposed the summoning of a Greek-Latin synod in Saloniki. The Emperor Honorius acquiesced, and asked the Pope to name an embassy. All these events must have abundantly occupied most of the year 405, and, just at the beginning of winter, the embassy for summoning the Oriental Bishops to Saloniki would not yet have departed. Furthermore, it appears from Palladius, Dial 4 (col. 15) (15) that, at the time of the arrival of the embassy in Constantinople, Atticus was already Bishop. But Atticus was very probably made Bishop

in December 405 or early in 406. So the embassy cannot have departed before the early part of 406.

9. Letters 152-154; 156-159 (52, 701 ff.).

10. Letter 4, 4 (594).

11. Letter 205 (726).

12. Letter 147 (699). Cf. Schultze, Konstantinopel, p. 136 ff. This Anthemius is perhaps identical with the Antimus of Marcus Diaconus.

13. Letters 61 and 141 (642 and 696).

14. Letter 197 (721); cf. letter 139, 236.

15. Letters 149-151, 155, 182-184.

16. Letters 162-164.

17. The Bishop of Saloniki was subject to the Pope, and was at the same time the papal vicar for all of Illyria. He possessed also, since 383, spiritual jurisdiction in this whole province, and, since 402, the right to consecrate its Bishops. S. Janin in Echos d'Orient 13 (1910) 138.

18. Palladius Dial. 4 (15): «Πρὸ τῆς πόλεως πλησίον τῶν Βίκτορος προαστείων.» This designation is not mentioned by Paspatis (=Σύλλογος 12 [1879] 33 ff.).

19. Palladius 4 (15); Paspatis *loc. cit.* 36 identifies Athyra with the modern Turkish Bugiuk-Tzekmetze, which lies a few miles west of Constantinople. The ancient fortress is completely destroyed.

20. Palladius Dial. 4 (15-16). Palladius (4, 16) adds here that God the Redeemer had made the ambassadors aware of their fate by means of various manifestations beforehand. So to Paul, deacon of the holy Bishop Emmelius, an unusually gentle and prudent man, was vouchsafed a vision of St. Paul, during the journey; the holy Apostle quoted to him the words of the Epistle to the Ephesians: "See therefore, brethren, how you walk circumspectly, not as unwise, but as wise, redeeming the time, because the days are evil" (Eph. 5, 15-16). By this dream was signified the various kinds of attempts at bribery by which they would be persuaded through gifts and flattery to betray truth and right. Thus far Palladius. It is indeed credible that uneasy forebodings and dreams came to the ambassadors after their first experience on the heights of Athens.

21. Ὡς ἐπὶ ὕβρει τῆς ἐνταῦθα βασιλείας. HE 8, 28 (67, 1591 C).

22. Ἔξεστι σοι ὁ θέλεις ποιῆσαι. Palladius Dial. 10 (34).

23. Ch. 20 (78).

CHAPTER XXXVI

FINAL ANNIHILATION OF THE
ADHERENTS OF ST. CHRYSOSTOM[1]

So the plot against the council had succeeded. What cunning and bribery had not been able to do, force had accomplished. In regard to that, the opponents were sure that no new attempt would be made very soon. The Emperor Honorius was too much occupied with political worries over the continuance of his Empire, at the doors of which Alaric and his Goths were now pounding, to be able to undertake anything, and no one need fear the clergy of Rome, as long as one was under the protection of the secular power.

The Latin members of the Roman embassy might well be glad that they had only been sent home. It had gone much worse with the Greeks. They had to do penance for having called on the Latins, and for having been the cause of the whole wretched story.

First of all, it seemed as though they had disappeared from off the earth. No man knew what had happened to them. Among the people it was said that they had drowned themselves in the ocean, or, what was more probable, that some one else had drowned them.[2] As a matter of fact, they had been very quietly banished by the "administration" to various regions on the extreme borders of the Empire. There some of them were held prisoner for years, under military guard.

Their leader, Cyriacus, Bishop of Emesa, was banished to Palmyra, a border fortress near Arabia, more than eighty miles from his episcopal see. Eulysius, the Bishop of Bostra in Arabia, was imprisoned in a fortress called "Misphas," on the border of the Saracen lands, three days' journey from his home. Palladius, who had his servant taken away from him, and who was robbed of his letters, arrived at a fortified place in Syene, in the neighborhood of the Blemmyes,* or the Ethiopian boundary.[3] Demetrius was removed to an oasis near the tribe of the Mazices.

The worst of this was not so much the banishment, but the treatment during the journey thither. They went under military escort. At that time the military had to fulfill the duties of state police, and the degree of culture of soldiers and officers at the beginning of the fifth century can scarcely bear comparison with that of our time, which has experienced much. It went much worst with the poor bishops when their escorts received a hint to torture them and mistreat them as much as possible. They did it with a good will.

They began their noble business by taking away all money from their victims, and dividing it among themselves. Then they put as many pressures as they could devise upon their prisoners, some of whom were old men, and increased the speed to such a degree that they covered in one single day the distance which ordinarily required two days. They always forced the prisoners to start at the earliest dawn, and did not stop until evening. Some of them developed stomach trouble, on account of the nervous strain and the miserable food. Neither were they spared insults and filthy speech. If they passed a church the soldiers would not allow the Bishops to visit it, or even to take shelter overnight in the church hospice. For this purpose they used common inns, or imprisoned them overnight in Jewish or Samaritan synagogues. In Tarsus, the birthplace of St. Paul, they carried their malice and vulgarity so far as to take the bishops into a den of the lowest sort, merely a public brothel.[3a] "Why are you sad?" one of the exiles exhorted his unhappy companions. "We did not come here of our own free will. That too will be to the glory of God. Who knows but what some of these dissolute women, when they see how we are insulted and mistreated, will repent and be converted?"

But it was rash to be irritated over the brutality of these soldiers. A sad and scandalous contribution was afforded here

* Tr. Note. The Blemmyes were a tribe of barbarians in upper Egypt; they often harassed the Roman settlements, and several Roman Emperors sent expeditions to subdue them.

by those clergy and bishops who belonged to the party of Theophilus and Atticus. Whether it was through cowardice, or lip service, or peculiar malice and hatred, some of them not only showed no sympathy with the fate of their brothers, imprisoned in exile, nor offered them any hospitality, if the escorts came through their place of residence; but on the contrary, they even gave the soldiers money to persuade them to get out again as soon as possible. Among these sad creatures belonged the man who was Bishop of Tarsus at that time, the successor of Diodorus, who would not recognize his colleagues in any way; also the intruder Porphyrius, Patriarch of Antioch, and Eulogius, Metropolitan of Caesarea in Palestine. Those who showed themselves most hateful were Leontius, Bishop of Ancyra in Galatia, and Ammonius, Bishop of Pelusium.[4]

Both of these forced the soldiers, partly by money and partly by threats of denunciation, to be more cruel and brutal to their prisoners than they had been before; indeed, they even prevented compassionate people from giving them shelter. No wonder that some of these unfortunate people said they would rather die than remain longer in the hands of their tormentors.[5] Punishment overtook one of these policemen on his feet. The soldier who had tormented Bishop Demetrius the most was suddenly seized by illness, and died the same day, in dreadful pain. The onlookers saw this as a judgment of God.[6]

A spiritual alleviation for so much infamy and malice in high places was offered by the fact that other bishops happily showed more consideration. The bishops of the second province of Cappadocia, in which Cucusus and Arabissus lay, showed the prisoners, who were passing through, the most sincere sympathy, and proved their compassion with tears. In particular, the famous Bishop Theodore of Tyana and the aged Bishop Bosporius of Colonia, distinguished themselves by their kindness; the latter had held the shepherd's staff for 48 years. Even in Egypt, in spite of the nearness of the powerful Theophilus, the aged Serapion, Bishop of Ostracine, with much courage, treated the exiles with love and care. He also had been bishop for 45 years, and had been consecrated by the great Athanasius.[7] So even here, some rays of light shine out among dark shadows, noble and manly figures beside miserable cowards, heroic confessors and martyrs beside malicious and persecution-minded clerical policemen.

Thus ended the great attempt at Chrysostom's rescue, which had begun with so many joyous hopes, and which the West and a number of heroic Eastern bishops had undertaken. But the unhappy result of this attempt had at least one good feature: it had shown the whole world on which side stood those who did not have good consciences, and who dared not expect anything good in the event of justice being done.

Almost one might presume the frustration of the council to have been, for the opponents of Chrysostom, the occasion for proceeding against the remaining Johnites with renewed rigor. At least so Palladius says, in joining the fate of the Greek members of the embassy to that of the whole number of the other partisans and friends of Chrysostom, in which of course he makes no distinction between those who were mistreated and persecuted in the beginning, and those who were persecuted later. At any rate, in the year 408 he could report on the following victims of the Johnite persecution: a certain Hilarius, who may have been a bishop, an honorable old man, who was considered a saint, and had not eaten bread for 18 years, but lived only on vegetables and the Holy Sacrament, was banished to the furthest regions of Pontus. He bore scars of wounds which had been given him, not by judges, but by clerics.[8] Perhaps this is the same Hilarius to whom St. Chrysostom had sent a letter through Olympias, soon after his arrival in Cucusus.[9]

Another man (a bishop?) named Antonius, had retired to a cave somewhere in Palestine, obviously to live there as a hermit. Also Silvanus, the heroic bishop, had gone to Traos, where he, like St. Peter in olden times, lived as a fisherman.[10]

Of Timotheus, Bishop of Maronea (in Thrace) and John, Bishop of Lydia, it was said that they were staying in Macedonia. Rhodon, Bishop in Asia, went back to Mitylene. Gregory, also Bishop in Lydia, was supposed to be in Phrygia. Brisson, the brother of Palladius, willingly renounced his bishopric, went back to his estate, and thenceforth planted cabbage and turnips. Lampetius, it was said, was staying in a certain place in Lydia, with the assistance of a certain Eleutherus, and there he devoted himself to study. Eugenius

o

had gone to his home. Elipidius, the aged and great Bishop of Laodicea in Syria, who for his part had brought the opponents of Chrysostom into such difficulty before the Emperor,[11] devoted himself to prayer, in union with Pappus. For three years neither of them had crossed the threshold of their house. Palladius did not know anything about where the other bishops were. Only of Bishop Anatolius was it said that he had gone to Gaul.

So all these bishops, together with those who have been mentioned before,[12] had remained faithful to their colleagues of Constantinople, through all this time, through pure love of justice. They had not only sacrificed their bishoprics, but some of them had endured mistreatment and persecution, for his sake. For this they deserved not only honor and recognition for themselves, but they had saved the honor of the Oriental episcopate. And for the historian, it is a joy to be able to tell of these shining and heroic forms among so many dark shadows.

Unfortunately not all the bishops who stood at Chrysostom's side at the beginning persevered to the end. Some, among them Palladius, wearied of the unsuccessful and discouraging battle, gave up, and entered into fellowship with Atticus. As visible reward, they received new bishoprics in Thrace.[13]

On the other hand, some simple priests, deacons, and monks became victims of persecution. The priest Tigrius "sat and wept by the rivers of Babylon;" he was banished to Mesopotamia. The priest Philip died in exile in Pontus. The priest Theophilus remained in Paphlagonia. John, the son of Aithrius,[14] fled to Caesarea, where he later founded a monastery.

Stephanus was to be deported to Arabia. But on the way the Isaurians snatched him from the hands of his guards, and sent him to the Taurus. Of Sallustius it was said that he was in Crete. The priest and monk Philip, military chaplain of the garrison in Constantinople, had fled to the Italian Campagna, where he lay sick in 408.[15] The deacon Sophronius was kept prisoner in the Egyptian Thebaid. The deacon Paulus, vice-steward in Constantinople, was in North Africa, so it was said. Another Paulus, deacon at the Anastasia Church, lived thenceforth in Jerusalem.

The priest Helladius, son of Palatius, went back to a little estate which he fortunately possessed in Bithynia.[16]   Other clerics had fled to their home lands.   Only a few had kept themselves hidden in Constantinople all this time.

Even a soldier of the imperial guard, one Probicialus,[17] had confessed himself a partisan of the exiled Archbishop, had been accused, scourged, tortured, and racked, and finally banished to Petra in Arabia.

Special malice had been endured by the monk Stephanus. He had once taken letters to Rome, was questioned about it, and spent ten months in prison.   Then he was offered his freedom if he would recognize Atticus.   He refused, was then placed on the rack, and his breast and side horribly torn with sharp irons.   But he did not waver.   After he lay for ten months in a hospital, he was finally exiled to Pelusium.   Of the famous monk John of Lycopolis in Egypt, who was probably ordained by Chrysostom, Palladius says[18] that he had stayed hidden for eleven months in a dark cave ($\kappa\epsilon\lambda\lambda\iota o\nu$), and it came to pass as Chrysostom had foretold to him, that he would in this way become fond of solitude, which had possibly not been the case before.   So these were the means by which Atticus and Theophilus secured their rule.   Through cunning, terrorism, and rough external force, they had asserted themselves, had overthrown every opposition, and expelled or ruined the congregation and dependents of their hated and feared victim.

But this victim himself was still living, as a constant danger and cause of unrest to his persecutors.

FOOTNOTES

1. Palladius, Dial. 20 (70 ff.).
2. Dial. 20 (71): $\epsilon \grave{\iota}\varsigma \ \theta \acute{a}\lambda a\sigma\sigma a\nu \ \grave{\epsilon}\pi o\nu\tau\acute{\omega}\theta\eta\sigma a\nu$.
3. Palladius 20 (c. 72). Cf. Vol. I, p. XXV.   Either this information served only as concealment of fact, or the author of the Dialog is not the same as this Palladius.   Concerning the Blemmyes and Syene, see J. Maspero, Organisation militaire de l'Egypte, 13, 17 and 24.
3a. Cf. Friedländer, Sittengeschichte Roms (8th. ed. II Leipzig 1900) 44 f.

4. Dial 20 (73); according to ch 9 (31) one would rather expect Ammonius of Laodicea adusta.

5. Palladius 20 (72).

6. Palladius *loc. cit.*

7. Palladius, Dial. 20 (73-74).

8. Dial. 20 (71).

9. Letter 14, 5 (52, 618).

10. Dial. 20 (72).

11. Cf. Vol. II, p. 279.

12. Ch. 27: Persecution of the Johnites.

13. Dial. 20 (71).

14. Or should it be: "built the Aithrios monastery in Caesarea"? In which Caesarea, is not mentioned.

15. The epitaph of a Hypatia from Constantinople is found in St. Paul-outside-the-Walls; in Rome:

τριάκοντα πέντε ἔτης ἐνθάδε κεῖται Ὑπάτι[ν]α
θυγατὴρ Ἀντωνίου κωνσταντινουπολιτίσσα
τῇ πρὸ δέκα καλανδ[ί]ων φεβραρίων ὑπάτια ἀνικίῳ
βάσσου καὶ φιλίππου τῶν λαμπροτάτων.

anni 408.

Whether she also belonged among the fugitives, is not known.

16. Ὁ τοῦ παλατίου (or = priest to the court church?) = Palladius 20 (72).

17. Dial. 20 (72) = Provincialis?

18. In the Historia Lausiaca 35 (ed. Butler p. 105).

CHAPTER XXXVII

DEATH OF THE MARTYR

WHEN St. Chrysostom learned of the unfortunate outcome of the embassy from the West, which was to have been a rescue expedition for him, he felt that there was scarcely any doubt of the vanishing of all human hopes of his return to Constantinople. With his keen and delicate perceptions, it doubtless pained him very much, although no visible expression of this is to be found in his surviving letters. Perhaps gloomy forebodings and thoughts arose in his soul. If his opponents went so far as to treat so shamefully and insultingly, against all laws of Church and people, an embassy which came in the name of, and had letters from, the Pope and the Emperor, then what would they not dare to do in case of need, against him, who on the one hand was the center and cause of all these hopes, and on the other, of all those fears? Must not a foreboding have risen slowly in his heart, connected with thoughts of death?

There is no doubt that the occupants of the three highest and most influential episcopal sees of the Orient could no more enjoy their lives, as long as this exile was alive in far Cappadocia. They would have to be in constant fear of a change of fortune, or else expect that Rome would again take up its efforts to convoke a new synod at the earliest opportunity.

To this was added the fact that the sympathy of the people and the public was turning to the exiled Archbishop in ever increasing measure, and ever more openly.

Already in Cucusus the attraction of the people to the holy Bishop was great, especially since the generosity to him of his friends had enabled him to do a great deal of good, which was felt as a double benefit in that year of hunger. But, also, it seems that he was sought out in various kinds of spiritual anxieties and troubles of conscience, as one who could give consolation and encouragement. At least, Palladius says that he helped the poor still more by his words than he did with bread.[1]

In Arabissus, one may conclude that Otreius, the Bishop of the place, offered him the opportunity to preach, since there, on account of better facilities of communication, the attendance of the people must have been significantly greater.

Real pilgrim crowds came to Arabissus, especially from Antioch, which lay somewhat nearer to the place of banishment, in order to see their famous former preacher once more. Palladius, who of course knew only by hearsay of the events of the banishment, writes that the enemies of the Church must notice "how the Church of Antioch is making pilgrimage to Armenia, and from there the ringing tones of the sweet philosophy of John are resounding back in Antioch." The opponents had felt this news like the stroke of a whip, and even their own adherents among the clergy had noticed this and said: "See that! A half-dead man frightens them, and those who are still living, and have the power in their hands, are as frightened before him as children before a ghost! Indeed, those who have at their disposal the power of the state, and the rule of the Church, in fullest measure, they fear and tremble in pale terror before a Bishop who is alone and forsaken, homeless, sick, and in exile!"[2] "And there," Palladius adds, "arose the desire in them to see him dead."[3]

Here, unfortunately, Palladius does not utter mere suspicion. The objective situation, as well as the following events, only too clearly prove that in Constantinople and in other places there were those who ardently longed for the death of the exile—and indeed even wished to hasten it by force.

The wish to be quietly rid of the disturbing rival had indeed been the determining point in the choice of his first place of exile. But since neither the long journey, nor the wild Isaurians, nor three icy winters, had fulfilled their hopes, so new measures must be contrived, in order to dissipate the nightmare which weighed on them continually.

As to who gave the first impulse, God alone knows. But certainly everyone assented, and at last they were all at one in this, to obtain a new imperial decree, by which their victim might be banished to the last and furthest corner of the Eastern Empire. Then, if he survived the rigors of the journey—and everything would be done to prevent his survival—he would be so cut off from human relations and influence that nothing more could be feared from him, for some time at least.

So there actually appeared, early in 407, an imperial command, under threat of punishment by the pretorian prefect, the minister of war, and the minister of police, which ordered Bishop John to be taken, as soon and as quickly as possible, to Pityus, a solitary and forsaken place on the shores of the Black Sea, the modern Pitsunda.[4] There, according to Theodoret, lived, in the mountains near the Caucasus, a primitive people, who surpassed even the warlike Isaurians in savagery.[5] The pretorian prefect delegated, as soon as possible, a small military party, to bear the imperial command to Arabissus, and to bring it at once into effect. The subordinate who commanded the party received a secret instruction to the effect that he should force the Archbishop to the utmost haste. But if he died on the way, there was a promotion in sight. So Palladius says, whose assertion alone on this point many may not perhaps find full credence, were it not confirmed by the following events.

The death journey

When the military party from Constantinople arrived in Arabissus, and informed the exile of their orders, the knowledge must have struck through Chrysostom's soul like a lightning flash, that this journey would be for him the journey to eternity. He was a sick man, weakened by privations and the severity of the climate. The journey, the long and weary marches on foot in all kinds of weather, the primitive and often bad lodgings at night, the irregular and often unpleasant food, the lack of any kind of care or ministration, in the midst of an escort of rude, uneducated soldiers—all these things would have been enough to undermine the strength of a healthy and robust man. For him, it meant an almost certain death.

And as to Pityus, it was at the foot of the Caucasus mountain range. If he ever reached it, he would be simply buried

alive.   Only a few ships and merchants visited it in the course
of a year, although it was at the opposite end of the Black Sea,
almost exactly opposite Constantinople, but separated from it
by more than 600 miles of sea.

The departure from Arabissus meant a farewell for life
from all the friends and well-wishers whom he had found
there, and above all, to his friends and acquaintances in
Antioch, who had followed him into exile, or who had visited
him there often.   It must have been very difficult for him.
He must have felt like a sacrificial lamb being led to the
shambles.

In the desperate heat of high summer, the middle of July[6]
or August, 407, they departed from Arabissus.   It was brutal
that the Archbishop, already weakened by the severe illnesses
of the years of exile, did not dare make at least part of the
journey in a chariot or on horseback, but was forced to go on
foot over at least six mountain ranges, two great rivers, and
nine tributaries.   The purpose of his persecutors was made
very clear when the leader of the escort took not the slightest
consideration of the state of health of the exile, but, on the
contrary, purposely did everything possible to increase the
difficulty of the journey, to exhaust the strength of the unfortunate Archbishop as soon as possible.   No matter how hot
the burning sun, which especially gave Chrysostom headaches,
he was not allowed to seek the shade.   If it rained in streams,
with the water "running down like a brook from one's back
and breast," he was not allowed to take shelter under a roof.
If they came through a city or a village, where there were
warm baths, which had become a necessity for Chrysostom,
he drove his victim remorselessly on.   If Chrysostom could
scarcely stay on his feet for weariness, he granted him no rest
or quiet; in short, he appeared to have only one thought, to
drive his prisoner to death as quickly as possible.

One of the soldiers of the guard sympathized with the tortured one; but he dared not let him find it out, except in
secret.   In the stopping places, or in going through the cities,
the people often showed compassion for the wretched state of
the traveler, and begged the leader and his companions to let
themselves be ruled by consideration and humanity; they got
only insults and curses, and the rude answer: "If he falls on

the road, so much the better; then we will get better wages, and such are our orders."[7]

So Chrysostom knew what fate was in store for him. He must have suspected it long since.

At the end of his tenth homily on the Gospel of St. Matthew, he had once written: "To this alone should we train ourselves, to bear all trials with courage, and not inquire as to the How or Why of them. It is God's affair alone, to know when our sufferings will come to an end. It is our duty to bear with gratitude the affliction which God ordains for us. . . . So let us put all discouragement aside, and give glory in all things to God, who directs all things for our best good."[8]

Now the time had come when he must fulfill literally his own words. The road from Arabissus brought the caravan to a road leading almost directly north, a military road which in part is still existing,[9] and which went through Asia Minor, over Tanadaris, Gauraina, Euspoena (Ispa), and Blandus, toward Sebaste (Sivas), the home of the Patriarch Meletius, and the onetime place of exile of St. Eustathius of Antioch. Sebaste itself lay at a height of 4,030 feet. From here, the road led over an undulating solitary plateau, of the average height of 5,000 feet, to Siara and Verisa (Tiflis).

Cumont, who traveled in this region, writes: "The climate of this plateau was severe even in the middle of May. We were surprised by stormy weather with hail, and after sunset it became piercingly cold. A violent attack of fever with which one of us was seized caused us to seek a milder climate as soon as possible."[10]

After Verisa, the road sank to the fruitful plain of Art-Ova, which was famous in antiquity for its rich grain-fields. Before they descended from the plateau and its bordering mountain chain (Chamlu-Bel), into the Iris valley, a view opened out before them of Dazimon and the entire valley of the Iris. But on the other side of the river, a little city greeted them: Comana Pontica. Through the narrow pass of Ak-Sou they arrived finally at Tokat, the ancient Dazimon.[11] This city, on the River Iris, lying in the rocky and forested river valley, owed its importance to its mild climate, and the fruitfulness of the surrounding region. Before the Second World War, it had about 20,000 inhabitants, of whom more than three-fourths were Christians. Not far from there, toward the west, lay the hill of Zela, at whose foot Caesar, in 47 B.C., conquered the last king of Pontus, Pharnaces, the son of Mithradates. His account of this battle was told in the famous three words: Veni, vidi, vici.

If Palladius is rightly informed here, the journey from Arabissus or Cucusus to Dazimon lasted not less than three months. So Chrysostom had traveled only about two and a half miles on an average day. Three years earlier, on the road from Constantinople to Cucusus, he had come, on the average, up to almost seven miles a day. Tillemont believes he can assume, on this ground, that the point of departure for this journey must have been Cucusus, which is somewhat south of Arabissus. However, this distance is not enough to explain the long duration of the journey. So one must either assume that Chrysostom was not able to travel on account of weakness, or that Palladius was misinformed here, and said months instead of weeks.

However it was, when the caravan arrived at Dazimon, the Archbishop's strength was so completely exhausted that he could scarcely go further. Until then, he had borne with unexampled patience and courage the bodily and moral hardships of the long journey. About a fourth of the way still lay before them, the road through Neocaesarea to Polemonium on the Black Sea. From thence, in all probability, they would have to use a ship for the last leg of the journey to Pityus.

Chrysostom desperately needed some time for rest and recovery in Dazimon. His face was burned by the sun, and glowing with fever, and looked, as Palladius forcibly expresses it, like the sunny side of a ripe apple.[12] Everyone could see that he was in a serious condition. But even then, the leader of the escort would not show him any consideration. He ordered the journey to continue. It was the 13th of September, 407.

Summoning his last powers, wasted with fever and wearied unto death, the prisoner dragged himself on. About five miles from Dazimon was the little city of Comana Pontica.[13] It had attained a sad fame in antiquity, because of the goddess Anahita, who played about the same role in Pontus as Astarte in Phoenicia. In her temple, in those times, lived about 6,000 priests of the goddess, and temple slaves. The chief priest enjoyed the highest honors, after the king. In the fourth century, however, all this sad splendor was past and gone. The ancient temple and its buildings had had to serve for the beautifying and enlarging of Dazimon. Today, at Comana, there are only ruins to recall the ancient Pontic national sanctuary. But at the end of the fourth century, Comana was a fortified place, in a condition to offer protection against the invasions of the Scythians.[14]

Here in Comana, the leader again refused to halt. They simply marched through or past the city, and over the Iris River bridge. Obviously he thought that the day's performance since Dazimon was too insignificant. About five miles beyond Comana, and so after a day's march of about ten miles, they halted. There, in a village called Bizeri today,[15] stood the chapel of the martyr St. Basiliscus, with the dwelling of the priest, and a few other houses.

Here they were to spend the night. Palladius relates: "St. Basiliscus, who had once been Bishop of Comana, and who had suffered martyrdom in 311, in Nicomedia in Bithynia, together with the priest Lucian of Antioch, under Maximin Daza the fierce persecutor of Christians[16]—appeared to the priest at the martyr's chapel, and said to him: "Prepare for Brother John; he is on the way."

And that very night, Basiliscus appeared also to St. Chrysostom, and said to him: "Be of good courage, Brother John; for tomorrow we shall be together."

There is no doubt that Chrysostom was so exhausted with the toils of the journey that he not only suspected the nearness of death, but felt it clearly. The next morning, the poor soul begged the leader to wait until the fifth hour. But the inhuman brute refused even this last request. Like a beast hunted to death, the saint dragged himself painfully on. But after he had covered about three and a half miles, Chrysostom suffered such an attack of weakness that his companions realized the seriousness of the situation. They brought the dying man back to the chapel of the martyr Basiliscus; there he prayed them to put upon him the white garments of death, according to an old custom of the Romans. He gave his own garments to those around him. When he was clothed, except for shoes, the priest brought him the Holy Sacrament of the Eucharist, and he received for the last time that which he had so often spoken of in life with words of holy inspiration and glowing love. Then he offered, in the presence of the by-standers, his last prayer of gratitude, which was his dying prayer. In the last moment left to him in life, he uttered the words:

"Glory to God for all things. Amen."

And, with the Sign of the Cross, that strong and mighty soul returned to its Creator.

The body fell back; the famous preacher, the great bishop and teacher, had ceased to suffer.[17]

So passed John Chrysostom. He who had always lived in great cities, who was accustomed to seeing thousands of people around him, who were charmed by his word and his glance; he who had the greatest number of friends and enemies in the whole Empire, departed from the world in this solitary, far-off place, alone and forsaken by the world. But he died a "victorious athlete,"[17a] a hero and a martyr, without inner bitterness, with a prayer of gratitude on his lips to God, who had tried and purified and sanctified him through three years of the most extreme bodily and spiritual sufferings. In that frail body dwelt a truly great heroic soul, which had stood steadfast under trial.

It was the 14th of September, 407, about three years and three months since his second banishment.[18]

With the speed of the wind, the news spread about that John, the former Bishop of Constantinople, had died on the journey, near Comana. The news caused universal sorrow and sympathy. From all sides the Christians streamed in, to see, at least in death, the man who for four years had kept the Empire breathless, and of whom all the world spoke so much; who was honored by some as a saint and a martyr, and by others was hated and persecuted to death. Now at least they all would give him the last honors.

His burial was celebrated in the place where he died, in the chapel of the martyr St. Basiliscus, and beside his grave.[19] Thus one grave united two martyrs, of whom one was the victim of the pagans, the other of the Christians; indeed, of his own clerical brothers in office. A great number of people gathered there. As if they had come by appointment made long ago, there were present monks, nuns, and lay people from Syria and Cilicia, from Pontus and Armenia. This general grief and sympathy for the fate of the exile was a solemn protest of the people against the clerical and worldly rulers and leaders of the people who had sinned against the departed.

Now he lay in the quiet grave, having been literally hunted to death by his own brethren. At last he had found eternal peace. At the new grave the Christian people mourned, the Church mourned, even heaven may well have mourned over the scandal which cried to heaven, and the unheard-of insult which had been offered to the departed. There were only three men who breathed more easily when they heard the news of Bishop John's death: the three Patriarchs, of Alexandria, Constantinople, and Antioch.

They did not need to fear any more their episcopal sees: their opponent would return no more; and a synod in his favor was now improbable. Theophilus had the satisfaction of standing outwardly before the world as victor in the battles. The facts, he might perhaps say Providence, had proved him right to a certain extent. Bishop John, apparently forsaken by God and man, vanquished and ruined, had died in distant Pontus in distress and misery, while he continued to rule as Patriarch over Christian Egypt.[20]

And yet Palladius says rightly that the actual *victor* in the battle, the real hero of the day, was not Theophilus, nor yet Atticus nor Porphyrius, not Acacius nor Severian, but the one who to all outward appearances had been conquered, but who still remained the spiritual victor, whose shining victorious vindication had forced a path for itself after his own death and that of his adversary: John, the "victorious athlete,"[21] in his lonely matryr's grave in Comana Pontica.

But Theodoret, the Bishop of Cyrrhus, said a few years later in a sermon: "You are not dead, Holy Father, but only gone down, like the sun. We do not grieve as for one of the dead, but as for one who is hidden from us. We do not seek you among the dead, but among the blest in heaven."[22]

*　　　*　　　*

Here arises the question: Why was Chrysostom actually frustrated, in spite of his brilliant talents, his good intentions, all his virtues and the political shrewdness which he had repeatedly shown? The men of antiquity asked this question also.

One may well say that a special destiny rules the lives of such men. What if fate had so ordered that Chrysostom had been placed at the side of the religious-minded and strong-souled Theodosius, twenty years earlier, instead of Nectarius? What a splendid combination these two great men would have made; doubtless they would have mutually completed and strengthened each other. It was not to be. First a great Emperor had an insignificant Bishop beside him; then a great Bishop had an insignificant, indeed an incapable, emperor at his side.

On the monument of Pope Adrian VI, the last German pope (d. 1523), in Rome, at Santa Maria dell' Anima, are found these words:

"Oh, how much depends in what times the deeds of the best men are performed! "[22a]

These words might also be very suitably used as a memorial inscription for St. Chrysostom.

How differently affairs might have shaped themselves, if Chrysostom had become Bishop in Constantinople only a few years later, in the time after 414, when the youthful, genial and pious Pulcheria held the reins of Empire in her hands. What might have been attained in brilliant cooperation by the clerical and secular powers for the reform of the Eastern clergy! But Pulcheria was saddled with Nestorius.

So failed the episcopal activity of Chrysostom in a time of political decadence, in which a eunuch and a woman ruled, together with their effeminate court. And if Eudoxia was really pious in the depths of her soul, still she did not show herself independent enough in relation to the artful flattery and tale-bearing of those about her. Certainly she was not blameless in the tragedy of Chrysostom; but the legends have done her great injustice when they burdened her with the chief responsibility for all the wrong which had been done.

Though she failed through womanly self-love, she atoned by an early death.

The chief offenders were elsewhere. History must place the Patriarch Theophilus of Alexandria in the first place in the dock. Without him the whole discontented crowd of women and clerics would never have had the courage or the power to depose the Bishop of Constantinople and to send him to exile. Without his counsel and his management, neither would the second banishment have come to pass. And even then Theophilus had the audacity to write to Pope Innocent that Chrysostom deserved still more punishment. Who could believe that he, in the consciousness of his guilt, and in the face of the attempt by the West to rehabilitate Chrysostom, could have been guiltless in the matter of the last banishment to Pityus, and in the purpose for which it was done? As has been mentioned before, Palladius declared Theophilus to be chiefly to blame,[23] and likewise the letter of the Emperor Honorius to Arcadius.[24] Likewise, both St. Nilus[25] and St. Isidore[26] of Pelusium have shown that Chrysostom was the victim of the envy of the bishops. They all give only the collected impressions and convictions of the contemporaries.

Atticus must be placed beside Theophilus. He was naturally the one most likely to be threatened if Chrysostom returned, and his right to the see of Constantinople remained uncertain, and contested, as long as Chrysostom remained alive. There is no doubt that Atticus had it in his power to alleviate the hardships of exile for the banished Bishop. But he did not do it. On the contrary, one may very rightly assume that the banishment to Pityus would not have taken place without his wish and consent, or perhaps his urging and demand.

To what degree Porphyrius of Antioch participated in the last part of the tragedy cannot be determined exactly. At any rate, it is significant that the immediate cause of the second banishment to Pityus is said by Palladius to have been the fact that Chrysostom had too many visitors from Antioch. That would scarcely have happened to Porphyrius.

Of course a shocking measure of blame attaches to Bishops Severian, Acacius and Antiochus. In the case of Severian, a decisive factor may originally have been his vanity and his jealous envy of Chrysostom's oratorical gifts, while Antiochus, to all appearances, simply let himself be taken in tow by Severian and the external advantages he hoped for.   But what is completely incomprehensible is the conduct of Bishop Acacius of Beroea, who was in many respects so ascetic and so meritorious, both before and after the tragedy of Chrysostom. Acacius had previously been a monk, and was made a bishop because of his strict asceticism.   He was reckoned to be a pillar of orthodoxy, enjoying everywhere the greatest respect, and was even chosen by Chrysostom as a mediator between the Pope and Patriarch Flavian, and sent to Rome.   And, after all that, a little supposed neglect and humiliation was sufficient to awaken in this man a hatred and desire for revenge against Bishop John; a hatred which did not shrink even from the fratricidal alliance with Theophilus, Severian, and Antiochus.   Acacius took part in all the intrigues before the second banishment, and at last he lent his cooperation to the illegal elevation of the unworthy Porphyrius to the Patriarchate of Antioch.

That the few old women of the court, such as Marsa, Castricia, and Eugraphia, on account of their fault-finding vanity and love of show, were egged on in their anger to insult him and intrigue against him would not of itself alone have hurt Chrysostom very much, and the fact that he lost their favor can scarcely have been considered a special fault in him.

But one thing is possible, that on account of his stomach trouble, perhaps also on account of the increasing opposition (not always by open or honest means) against his reform of the clergy, occasionally a certain amount of irritation was roused in him, especially by those of the clergy who failed to correspond to his ideal for priests or bishops.

However, this would be only a partial excuse for his opponents.   When bishops who often had the simplest and most primitive origins stayed in Constantinople for weeks and months, claiming the hospitality of the Archbishop, asking his intercession with the Emperor in all their affairs, not giving themselves any concern about the order of the house, going in and out every day and every night—moreover, being presumptuous, and speaking tactlessly and disapprovingly

about their host, etc.,—one can understand how the patience
of the "housemaster," the deacon Serapion, would be exhausted, and also that even Chrysostom himself might request
such a disturber of the peace to return to his diocese and,
like a good shepherd, to look after his own flock. Not without
good reason did the patriarchs and even the Emperor himself,
again and again forbid the bishops to come to Constantinople
without the consent of the Patriarch, or to stay there any
longer than necessary.

That Severian and others were angry at Chrysostom, and
in their anger accused him of "hardness and arrogance" is
humanly understandable, but regrettable, since their reproaches have always found credulous ears, even in modern
times. However, St. Nilus called it foolishness to accuse
Chrysostom of being "irascible and faultfinding." If that is
so, says he, then John the Baptist, St. Paul, and even Christ
Himself must endure the same accusation.[26a]

Also, the Synod of the Oak brought up only such points
of accusation throughout, which, if true in general, were either
ridiculously insignificant, or else such as did not concern
Theophilus or his satellites.

And so it went. St. Augustine, in his Letter 21,1 to Bishop
Valerius, has given the only right point of view for judging
the conduct of Chrysostom, as for all bishops and priests in
general: "In this life, and especially in our time, there is
nothing easier than for a bishop, priest, or deacon to conduct
his office in such a way as to please men; but in the sight of
God there is nothing sadder, more piteous, or more worthy
of condemnation. So also it is in this world, and especially
in our time, nothing more difficult, painful and dangerous,
but also in the sight of God more meritorious (*beatius*), as
when one so serves Him, as He as almighty Lord would
wish."[26b] But Palladius says, "Of those who have committed
such misdeeds in the Church, one may rightly ask: Where is
the priestly dignity here? Where is the holiness? Where the
natural gentleness and brotherly love? Where is the command of God, 'If you wish to offer your gift and you remember
that your brother has anything against you, first go and be
reconciled with your brother, and then come and offer your
gift'? Where is the word: 'If anyone strikes you on one

cheek, offer him the other'?   Where is the Scripture which
says: 'See how sweet and pleasant it is for brethren to dwell
together in unity'? . . . How could you thrice-wretched
people have done such a thing, as though it were a good
work?   What moved you to think murderous thoughts against
him, as though he were your enemy?   How were you able to
rage so against one another? [27]

"But God, who has glorified these gentle and holy shepherds, these lights of uprightness, may also make us participants and joint heirs of the fearful day of judgment; He, to
whom all glory, honor, greatness, and fame, to the Father,
and to the Son, and to the Holy Spirit, now and for all eternity.
Amen."[28]

FOOTNOTES

1. Dial. 11 (37).
2. Dial. 11 (37-38).
3. Ηὔχοντο καὶ τὸ ζῆν ἀπποῤῥῆξαι (*ibid.* c. 37).   Sozomen brings
the new banishment to Pityus into causative connection with the
new synod striven for by Rome. (HE 8, 28 = 67, 1592).
4. J. J. Egli, Nomina geographica. 2. A. Leipzig 1893, p. 727.
5. HE 5, 34 (82, 1264).
6. If Palladius 11 (38) is actually right that the journey lasted
three months.
7. Palladius 11 (38).
8. 57, 192.
9. Ramsey, p. 266 (map of Cappadocia); Munro, Roads in
Pontus = Journal of Hellen. Studies 21 (1901) 66-67; Fr. and Eug.
Cumont, Voyage d'exploration archéologique (Studia Pontica II)
237 ff.
10. Cumont *loc. cit.* 237 ff.
11. The Turkish name Tokat first occurs in the twelfth
century.   Concerning Dazimon, see Jerphanion, Une nouvelle
méthode, *loc. cit.* 261 and 269, and C. Ritter, Die Erdkunde, vol.
IX, 1, p. 116-24.
12. Dial. 11 (38).
13. Anderson, A journey, p. 60 ff.   Today Comana (Turkish
Gümenek) is only a field of ruins.   The name of the ancient
Comana is preserved in a village some distance away.
14. S. Gregor Nyss., De baptismo (46, 424).   The sermon seems
to have been given in Comana.

15. Anderson, *loc. cit.* 63. Cf. p. 25, note 1.

16. Concerning St. Basiliscus, see Acta Sanctorum Mart. I, 237-241 and Synaxarium Constantinopolitanum (A SS. Nov. tom. Prodromus ed. Delehaye) for the 22nd of May, p. 669 ff. Bibliotheca hagiograph. graeca 2. A., S. 37 and H. Delehaye, Les légendes grecques des saints militaires (Paris 1909) 202-13. According to that, Basiliscus was not a Bishop, but a simple layman or soldier under Maximin, and is alleged to have been killed with Eutropius and Cleonicus in Comana Pontica under the general Agrippa. The Menologium Basilii imp. says (probably from George Alexandrinus) the same about the death and apparition of Basiliscus as Palladius does. In the Historia Lausiaca, ch. 60 (ed. Butler p. 154) Palladius relates a similar death scene, in which the holy martyr Kolluthos appeared to a pious recluse in his shrine before her death. P. Dörfler, Die Anfänge der Heiligenverehrung nach den römischen Inschriften und Bildwerken (Munich 1913) 70-85, shows how often such appearances first led to the discovery of the wished-for graves of the martyrs.

17. Palladius, Dial. 11 (47, 38): Εἰπὼν τὸ ἐξ ἔθους ῥῆμα. Δόξα τῷ θεῷ πάντων ἕνεκεν ἐπισφραγισαμενός τε τὸ ὕστερον ἀμὴν, ἐξῆρε τοὺς πόδας.

17a. Pall. 11 (ed. Norton 69, 1-2).

18. Socrates 6, 21 (67, 726). About 6 miles behind Comana, to the left of the road, which leads to Neocaesarea, lies the village of Bizeri, with a church and Armenian cloister. In the church there is a grave, with marble cover, which is considered the honorary tomb of St. Chrysostom. Since Palladius gives a distance of about 5 miles, this tradition is not improbable. (Anderson *loc. cit.* p. 63). At any rate, the memory of the death of Chrysostom has been kept there until this day. Also the bridge which spans the Iris river at Comana is visible today, probably the same as when Chrysostom walked over it.

19. Theodoret 5, 34 (p. 336). When I visited Bizeri in 1932, the Armenian monks there had been expelled or killed, and their little ancient cloister of "St. John Chrysostom" had been changed into a barracks for gendarmes. In the church I saw an open, empty grave. According to the Armenian tradition of the place, Chrysostom was buried there, and his body brought from there to Constantinople in 438. Cf. Chr. Baur, Im christl. Orient. Reiseerlebnisse. (Seckau 1934) p. 137.

20. Dial. 11 (39).

21. Palladius 11 (39).

22. Photius, Bibliotheca 273 (104, 232). But when Arcadius once wrote to St. Nilus, asking him to pray that the capital city might be spared from earthquake and fire, Nilus answered: "How can

you expect that Constantinople will be spared numerous earth-quakes and fires, a place where so much injustice prevails . . . since you have banished the pillar of the Church, the light of truth, the trumpet of Christ, the holy Bishop John! " (Epist. II, 265-79). The authenticity of this letter has never been questioned. Was Arcadius allowed to read it?

22a. Proh dolor! Quantum refert in quae tempora vel optimi cuiusque virtus incidat! " See E. Hocks, Der letzte deutsche Papst: Hadrian VI, 1522-23. Freiburg 1939, p. 9.

23. Dial. 20 (78).

24. *Ibid.* 3 (16) = Θεόφιλον, δι᾿ ὅν μάλιστα λέγεται ἅπαντα τὰ κακὰ γεγενῆσθαι.

25. Letter 3, 199 to the ex-consul Severus (79, 475 B-C).

26. Letter 1, 152 (78, 284-285).

26a. Epist. I, 309 (79, 193).

26b. ML 33, 88.

27. Palladius, Dial. 20 (78); George Alexandrinus 74 (Savile 8, 255).

28. Palladius, concluding words of the Dialog.

CHAPTER XXXVIII

CHRYSOSTOM AS A "MARTYR"

THERE can be no doubt, from what has been related, that Chrysostom was designedly hunted to death, and his life forcibly shortened. Likewise, it is certain that he died in a holy and righteous cause. On account of his efforts toward ecclesiastical discipline among monks, priests, and bishops, and for the sake of Christian behavior among the laity he had drawn to himself the disfavor of those who were not of good will. He had, by his remonstrances, even in the highest places, lost the favor of an Empress. Through his well-meant and quite unobjectionable welcome for the persecuted monks from Egypt, and in spite of his refusal to function as judge over Theophilus, he had roused the jealous hate and unscrupulous longing for revenge of the Patriarch of Alexandria. And finally, the fear of his return, on the part of three Patriarchs and a number of bishops, to his episcopal see, had delivered him to an early and painful death. One may therefore rightly say that Chrysostom entered into eternity with the palm of martyrdom in his hand.

Among all the great teachers of the Greek Church, St. Chrysostom suffered the most bitter death. The great St. Athanasius was sent into banishment five times; but he died at last as Patriarch of Alexandria, surrounded by the love and veneration of his whole diocese. St. Basil endured much suffering in his life, but he remained to the end the celebrated Metropolitan of Caesarea. Gregory of Nazianzus relinquished his See of Constantinople voluntarily, and died in peaceful retirement in his ancestral home at Arianzus. Chrysostom alone ended his life deposed and exiled, slandered, hated and feared, tortured to death like an outlawed criminal at the slightest whim of a brutal soldiery.

" A man is not a martyr only if he is commanded to sacrifice to the gods, and then dies rather than sacrifice; but he is also a martyr if he obeys any commandment which is likely to lead to his death; this is obviously martyrdom."[1] Thus had Chrysostom preached in his early years in the priesthood.

It was the almost unanimous conviction of his contemporaries that Chrysostom was a martyr.

Palladius, in his Dialog, emphasizes not less than five times that his opponents had had the purpose of killing Chrysostom, and that without including the two attempts that had been made upon his life in Constantinople.[2]   And then he says expressly to the deacon Theodore: "As the Apostles were at first cried down as demagogues, and now are honored as saints, so you will live to see that, after the present generation, John Chrysostom will be venerated as a martyr."[3]

Likewise Martyrius writes: "If John has actually departed into another world, then we have in him a martyr who will intercede for us."[4]

Theodore of Trimithus has Pope Innocent writing a letter to Arcadius and Eudoxia, after Chrysostom's death; it begins with these words: "The voice of the blood of my brother John cries to God, and his blood will find vengeance."[5]   He also regarded the dead as a martyr.   George Alexandrinus calls Chrysostom a "hieromartyr."[5a]

Callinicus, the biographer of St. Hypatius, writes: "After several years his bones (Chrysostom's), like those of the great and holy martyrs, were brought back with great pomp, at the command of the blessed Emperor Theodosius."[6]

In the document concerning the "Martyrium" of the holy monks of the great Laura of St. Sabas, who were taken by the Saracens and murdered, because they had refused to hand over some brothers, the author of the Martyrium wishes to prove that these monks were really martyrs.   Therefore, he calls on the example of John the Baptist, of the Maccabees, of the murdered monks of Mt. Sinai, and of Rhaitu, and continues thus: "But John Chrysostom, the shining star of the Church, the teacher of the whole world, was he not condemned to exile on account of his heroic virtue, and did he not endure many trials, even unto death?   Shall we then deny to him the honor and reward of a martyr, because he was not attacked on account of the faith?   No, no reasonable person will do that; only a fool could think so."[7]

Even in the fourteenth century, Nicephorus Callistus declared Chrysostom to be "a martyr, though an unbloody one."[8]   And in the twentieth century, the Greek Orthodox Metropolitan of Athens, Chrysostomus Papadopoulos, writes that Chrysostom "died a martyr's death."[8a]

The official Greek Liturgy, in its Vespers for the 27th of January, calls him "companion of the martyrs," and reads a lesson from Sapientia Salomonis 2 ff. the following passage: "We will condemn him to a shameful death," and "he has given his life for his sheep."   One may rightly say that Chrysostom is officially recognized as a "martyr" by the Greek Church.

The Syrians were also of the same view.   The Syrian "History of the Barhadbesabba Arbaia" says that Atticus had pressed St. Cyril to entitle him "Teacher of the whole Church" and "Martyr of Christ."

The Latin authors agreed with the Greek. Cassian, Chrysostom's former deacon, writes: "Hear what John, the ornament of the Bishops of Constantinople, whose holiness triumphed over the storm of pagan persecution to the reward of martyrdom—hear what he thinks of the Incarnation."[9]

Leo Clericus speaks in the prologue to his Life, of the virtues "of our most holy and blessed Father and martyr John," and further on he expressly insists: "That you may be able to recognize surely that he is a martyr."[10]

As a matter of fact, the Church has declared several saints to be martyrs, and honored them to this day as such, whose martyrdom was less direct than that of St. Chrysostom.   Pope Pontianus, whose health was ruined by the privation and mistreatment of his exile in Sardinia, is honored as a martyr. The inscription on his grave, which was found in 1909, reads: "Ponzianus Ep., Martyr."[11]   The same is true of Hippolytus, his contemporary and companion in suffering.[12]

The holy Dionysus of Alexandria (died 265) was honored as a martyr, because he was exiled under Decius and Valerian, and had to bear many trials, although he was able to return later, and died in office and dignity as Patriarch of Alexandria.[13]

Likewise Bishop Eusebius of Vercelli, who had been sent into exile by the Arians, did not die there, but after his return to Vercelli, and he still was honored as a martyr.[14]

Similarly, Popes Marcellus and Martin I were honored as martyrs.[15] Pope Silverius died in exile, after he had spent three months of the greatest misery on the island of Palmaria. In the Roman Martyrology he stands as a martyr, on the 20th of June.

Among the newer authors, Tillemont is one of the first to give Chrysostom the title of martyr: "If one wishes to recognize the full merit of St. Chrysostom, he must honor him as a real martyr."[16]

Similarly, the Bollandist Stilting unhesitatingly calls our saint a martyr.[17] H. Delehaye, S.J., writes thus: "It would be only logical, if one honors bishops as martyrs, to honor those like Meletius, Eustathius of Antioch, and John Chrysostom, who suffered for the faith, without dying a violent death."[18] In the case of Chrysostom, one can even say that he did die a violent death; at least, his life was forcibly shortened, and his death was a direct result of his forced physical overexertion.

The following also declare him a martyr: S. Osgood,[19] E. Martin,[20] A. Thierry,[21] G. Gagniard, S.J.,[22] and H. Kellner.[23]

It would not seem unsuitable for the Church to place the palm of martyrdom officially in the hand of the great Greek ecclesiastical teacher.

FOOTNOTES

1. Hom. 8, 7 adv. Judaeos (48, 939).
2. Dial. 8 (26): Theophilus acted during the Synod of the Oak, "as if he was able to take not only John's church away from him, but even his life." Hence accusations of high treason. Ch. 11 (36). Chrysostom was exiled into that Cucusus threatened by the Isaurians: ἐπὶ τὸ σφαγῆναι. *Ibid.* (37). He is brought to Arabissus: ἵνα τὸ ζῆν ἀπολίπῃ (here the reproach scarcely turned out to be true). *Ibid.* ηὔχοντο καὶ τὸ ζῆν ἀπορρῆξαι; finally (38): the soldiers had the order, etc.
3. Dial. 19 (68).
4. Encomium 4 (47, XLVII) and in Mscr. 247.

5. Vita 26 (47, LXXXI).

5a. Savile 8, 258, l. 42.

6. De Vita Hypatii liber (Leipzig 1898) a. 71 p. 24.

7. Acta SS. Martii III APP. 11 and: Pravosl. Palest. Sbornik 19³ (1907) 30. Also Cosmas Vestitor, Encomium 3 in translationem S. Jo. Chrys. (ed. Dyobouniotis=Epeteris 2 [1925] 69). The meaning is that Chrysostom had not suffered less than the martyrs.

8. HE 14, 43 (146, 1209 C).

8a. Geschichte der Kirche von Alexandrien (1935) p. 293 (Greek); the same in his Historikai meletai, p. 132. 8 b. Menologium gr. (ed. Athens 1896) pp. 237 and 239; and 13 Nov., pp. 99 and 97. 8 c. Patrol. Orient. XXIII, 8. p. 332. M. Briére, Une homélie inédite d'Atticus, Patr. de Constantinople, in: Revue de l'Orient chr. 29 (1933) 160.

9. De incarnatione Christi 7, 30 (ML 50, 267).

10. Catalogus Codicum hagiogr. Bibliothecae Nationalis Paris. III, 18.

11. J. Wilpert, Die Papstgräber und die Cäciliengruft. Freiburg 1909. p. 1 ff. and 17 ff. second copy. The word "martyr" was not added until later. In the Roman Martyrology he stands on Nov. 19.

12. In the Roman Martyrology, on the 13th and the 22nd of August.

13. Martyrologium Rom. 17 Nov. (cf. 3rd October).

14. *Ibid.* Dec. 16th.

15. *Ibid.* Jan. 16 and Nov. 12.

16. Mémoires 11, 346, at the conclusion of the statements of Palladius and Cassian.

17. Acta SS. Sept. IV p. 689 no. 1477: "Si de martyrio quaeritur, ne hanc quidem palmam Chrysostomo deesse videbimus."

18. Les origines du culte . . . p. 116-117.

19. Chrysostom and his style of pulpit eloquence=The North American Review 42 (1846) 29.

20. St. Jean Chrysostome (Montpellier 1860) 1, 25.

21. St. Jean Chrysostome . . . 3rd ed. pp. 21, 509 and 523.

22. Les Saints Pères au tribunal de M. Thierry=Études religieuses 13 (1867) 375.

23. Die Verehrung des heiligen Johannes Chrysostomus=Chrysostomica pp. 1007-1008.

CHAPTER XXXIX

"DE MORTIBUS PERSECUTORUM"

SOME of the enemies and opponents of Chrysostom vanished so quickly from the stage of the world, and under such striking circumstances, that according to the statement of Palladius and many of his contemporaries, they might have formed a supplement to Lactantius' De mortibus persecutorum.[1]

That Eudoxia had to die first, and so early, among the enemies of Chrysostom, seemed to the more pious people among their contemporaries as a judgment of God.[2]

The next one touched by the hand of God was Bishop Cyrinus of Chalcedon. Having had his foot stepped on by Bishop Maruthas of Maipharkat, accidentally, produced a wound which soon developed into caries of the bone. Within a short time he had to have three amputations done, the last one to the knee. He died some time in the year 406.[3]

Only eight months after Chrysostom's death, in the year 408, the Emperor Arcadius also departed this world, perhaps the least guilty of all the guilty ones. He had only reached the age of thirty-one.[4]

Others followed, of whom Palladius does not speak. One of the bishops who had signed the decree of banishment died of dropsy; another rotted away while he was still living; a third became crippled and lay for eight months on a bed of pain, without being able to utter a word. Still another fell from a horse, broke his leg, and died of it. Still another developed an ulcer of the tongue, lost the power of speech, and at last wrote with a stylus the confession of his guilt and remorse.

So far Palladius, whom we cannot re-examine.[5]

If one designates these cases as "judgments" of God, a human judgment lies therein, on the inscrutable design of God, in which He allows human and natural things to happen. That sort of explanation-judgment has a purely human value.

At any rate, one thing is certainly striking, and that is, that God's justice punished only the accessory figures in the great Chrysostom tragedy, and allowed the chief actors to enjoy undisturbed, for the rest of their earthly existence, the fruits of their wicked deeds.

Theophilus died as Patriarch of Alexandria, five years after Chrysostom, in the year 412. He had never atoned for his injustice, did not even recognize it as such, nor ever gave any evidence whatever that he grieved for his conduct.

The later legends set about correcting things in this regard.

St. John Damascene quotes a passage from the otherwise unknown chronography of a deacon named Isidore, in which it is related that Theophilus, when near death, was not able to die on account of his conduct against Chrysostom. Someone brought a picture of Chrysostom to his dying bed, and, after Theophilus had demonstrated his reverence for him, he was able to give up his spirit.[6]

This anecdote proves only that at that time it had already been asked whether Theophilus had passed into eternity with the unexpiated burden of his sin against Chrysostom still upon his soul. Unfortunately, the tales are only invention; otherwise St. Cyril, the nephew of Theophilus, would not have so long refused to give up his uncle in favor of Chrysostom.

The old bishop Acacius of Beroea outlived Chrysostom by almost thirty years. He at least partly atoned for his injustice. At the time of the Council of Ephesus, he is heard of, apparently for the last time. He must have died about 437.

Severian of Gabala, and Antiochus of Ptolemais, appear to have remained in their dioceses after that, without once coming into the notice of history. Both of them had fulfilled their sad business, and played their role.

At length the second successor of Chrysostom, the Armenian Atticus, enjoyed the pleasure of his spiritual overlordship. He died in 425.

What fate eternal justice has reserved for these men is naturally a secret which lies outside the frame of history. The Eastern Churches have given the riddle a simple solution. They see to it, like the public after a spectacle, that all the players, whether they have played well or badly, shall receive

applause. They opened the doors of heaven to all the participants in the Chrysostom tragedy, and placed the nimbus of
holiness on all their heads: Chrysostom, Theophilus, Atticus,
Acacius, Severian, and others, sit in the Eastern heaven
friendly and peaceful together, as if they had been so in life.
The Eastern Church has thereby stated the same spirit of
absolute forgivingness with which they later canonized equally
a St. Ignatius and his opponent and persecutor Photius.[7]

The Patriarch Theophilus was placed among the blessed
in heaven by his grateful nephew, St. Cyril of Alexandria. In
his first Easter sermon (in the year 414) he said of his dead
uncle: "Since our father Theophilus, of glorious and blessed
memory, through God's decree has happily ended his earthly
life, and has soared up to the heavenly dwelling place, his
succession in the episcopal office has fallen upon me, the most
insignificant."[8] So it is not so surprising that Atticus of
Constantinople, in a letter to Cyril of Alexandria, calls
Theophilus, his one-time ally and friend, "the holy father
who is like the Apostles."[9]

Even the Council of Ephesus, over which of course St. Cyril
presided, designated him, above all the other fathers quoted,
as the "most holy bishop" Theophilus.[10] Supported by this,
the fifth general council spoke again of Theophilus "of blessed
memory."[11] One must consider this attribute chiefly only as
a customary title for one who is dead, or for a dignitary, for
whom no "canonizing" significance is intended.[12] However,
Vincent of Lérins also speaks of "the holy Theophilus, a
bishop distinguished by his faith, his life and his knowledge,"[13] and Leo the Great classes him with Sts. Athanasius
and Cyril, among the "most distinguished shepherds" of the
Church of Alexandria.[14]

However, St. Isidore of Pelusium was of another opinion.
He wrote to Cyril: "Many of those who took part in the
council at Ephesus (431) jeer at you, and say that you were
moved by personal enmity, not by love of the true faith; he is
a nephew of Theophilus, they say, and he imitates him. So if
he vents his well-known hate against the God inspired and
God-loving John (Chrysostom) so will he (Cyril) make himself
notorious (through the deposition of Nestorius) since a great
difference exists between these two defendants."[14a]

The Copts in Egypt celebrate Theophilus' feast on the 15th of October,[15] the Syrians on the 17th of October.[16]

Remarkably, the oldest pictorial representation which has survived is of him. A papyrus manuscript which contains an Alexandrian world-chronicle, and which probably dates from the first half of the fifth century, shows the picture of the Patriarch twice.[17] Naturally it is not a historically true portrait, although pictures of the Patriarch may have been plentiful at that time. Only for the dress and the representation of the figure can the pictures be considered typical. Theophilus " is grey-bearded, carries about his neck the short white band (the pallium), and holds in his left hand, covered by the outer garment, a book of the Gospels, which he touches with his free right hand. The undergarment (tunica) is yellow, and the outer garment, a sort of chasuble, is reddish brown." His eyes and nose are turned toward the right, away from the spectator. His face is more long and oval than round. In this rather rough representation, no special expression of the face can be recognized. Above, at the right of the head, stands an inscription: ὁ ἅγιος Θεόφιλος. The same inscription is on the other picture.[18]

As the Alexandrians gave to their Theophilus, so did the Church of Constantinople give to Atticus, and even to Arsacius, a small place among the stars, although a modest one. In a manuscript of the Synaxarium Constantinopolitanum, the memory of the three Patriarchs, Nectarius, Arsacius, and Atticus, is preserved on the 11th of October, while Atticus is again mentioned on the 8th of January.[19] Socrates had already spoken of him as half holy.[20] Then Cassiodorus has derived from him for his Historia tripartita, and so it happened that Atticus, mentioned expressly by name, finds entrance in the Historia tripartita, even in some Western Latin martyrologies, on the 10th of October, at a time when Pope Celestine praised in several letters the " holy Atticus " for his vigilant battle against heresy, and even called him a worthy and true successor of the holy John Chrysostom.[21] One can see how quickly history is forgotten.

Fortune was also favorable to the old Bishop Acacius of Beroea, when in the year 437 he died at the age of 116 years, after having cared for his flock for 58 years. The dark stain

which he had brought upon his name through his evil role
in the Chrysostom tragedy paled, in the memory of the after
world, before the splendor of his later deeds. Sozomen speaks
only in praise of him.[22]   Patriarch John of Antioch counted
him among the holy and distinguished bishops, and called
him " Acacius, who was great and holy in every way," to whose
efforts the unity of the Church was chiefly due.[23]   St. Cyril
of Alexandria gave evidence that he was a " very God-fearing
and holy bishop,"[24] and Theodoret says that "as a hermit, as
well as a bishop, he sent out the brilliant rays of virtue."[25]

These speeches of praise may have been well merited. They
only show that even "a very God-fearing and holy" man
occasionally shows bad blunders and aberrations in the list of
his human qualities.

At least, it is to be understood that even the most malicious
intriguer of the years 402-405, Bishop Severian of Gabala,
found an unnoticed hiding place, not merely among the Copts,
but even in some old Latin martyrologies.[26]   On the other
hand, the official Roman martyrologies, whose revision was
entrusted to the learned Cardinal Baronius, does not include
him in its list of saints, for which one may well feel a sense
of satisfaction.[27]

The friends of the saint, as well as the enemies, gradually
vanished from the theater of the world. Only a little of the
further history of a few of them is known.

Olympias seems to have suffered most over the fate of her
bishop friend, but still more over the immense disillusionment over the public scandal given by the bishops on whom
she was accustomed to look only with holy reverence. Again
and again Chrysostom tried to cheer her from his exile.[28]

She did not outlive her former shepherd for a year. She
died on the 25th of July, 408, at Nicomedia in Bithynia,
among gentle cloistered women, who later, out of gratitude,
left a small literary memorial of her.[29]   The Greek Church,
as well as the Latin, has placed her rightly among the saints.
In the Menologium of Basil, she is remembered on the
25th of July,[30] and in the Roman Martyrology on the 17th of
December.[31]

Palladius, who is almost generally considered the author
of the oldest biography of Chrysostom, that is, the Dialog,

received in the year 417 the Bishopric of Aspona in Galatia. That may well have been a proof that at last, knowing the complete hopelessness of further opposition, he had made his peace with the earlier opponents, at least with Atticus. Doubtless this step was made possible and easier for him by the fact that, shortly before, Atticus had made his ecclesiastical peace with his persecuted predecessor, in which he, yielding to the demand of Rome, and his own political insight, had the name of St. Chrysostom entered in the ecclesiastical diptychs, as proof of fellowship.

On this basis, of course, even Palladius could make peace with him, presuming that Atticus did not know of Palladius' authorship, and of the fine role which he (Palladius) had therein ascribed to him.

Sunk in the sea without a trace, as it were, are the Egyptian monks, who were involuntarily the external cause of the entire Chrysostom tragedy. After the Synod of the Oak, some of them at least returned to their dearly-won Nitrian solitude, while others ended their lives in Palestine or Syria, all with the gnawing conviction that they had nowhere been able to obtain right and justice for the wrong they had suffered, that it was solely the surpassing might and power of the Patriarch of Alexandria which had conquered them, and had forced them, against their inward convictions, to acknowledge themselves the guilty ones, and beg him for pardon.

The great world did not trouble itself about them further, and the monks themselves must have been glad that henceforth they did not have to enter the world of men.

FOOTNOTES

1. Palladius 17 (58) and 20 (81); Socrates 6, 19 (724); Sozomen 8, 27 (1589); Theodoret 5, 34 (82, 1264 C-D); S. Nilus, epist. 3, 199 (79, 475 C).
2. Cf. p. 357: Death of Eudoxia.
3. According to Palladius, Cyrinus died three years after his accident, hence in 406. Socrates 6, 1 (67, 724) gives no date, while Sozomen 8, 27 (1589) says Cyrinus died before Eudoxia. Cf. J. Pargoire, Les prémiers évêques de Chalcédoine = Echos d'Orient 4 (1900-1901) 27-30.

4. Socrates 6, 23 (729-731) represents him as almost a saint, whose intercession could produce an answer to prayer.

5. Dial. 17 (58-59).

6. Oratio 3 De imaginibus (94, 1409).

7. Concerning other remarkable saints in the Byzantine heaven, see A. Fortescue, The Orthodox Eastern Church. London 1920. P. 103-104.

8. Hom. Paschalis 1, 2 (77, 405 C).

9. Cyrill. Al. epist. 75 (77, 349 A). Cf. Tillemont, Mémoires 11, 493 ff.

10. Mansi 4, 1188. The attribute "holy" is lacking in Atticus of Constantinople and in Amphilochius of Iconium, whose citations were probably later additions.

11. Mansi 9, 251. On the other hand, Theophilus is not in the Menaion (Athens 1896); neither is he in the Menologium Basilii imp.

12. H. Delehaye, Sanctus (Subsidia Hagiographica 17). Brussels 1927, p. 38 ff.

13. Commonitorium ch. 30 (ML 50, 680). Petrus Novalis and others place Theophilus among the saints on the 5th of March, perhaps confusing him with Theophilus of Caesarea in Palestine from the second century.

14. Letter 102, 4 (ML 54, 987).

14a. Epist. II, 310 (78, 361).

15. Le Synaxaire Arabe Jacobite (Rédaction Copte) Texte arabe publié traduit et annoté par R. Basset (= Patrologia Orientalis 1, 3). Paris 1907 p. 345-347; he mentions no word of Chrysostom; neither does the "History of the Patriarchs of the Coptic Church of Alexandria." Arabic text ed. . . . by B. Evetts (=*ibid.* 1, 4). p. 425-430.

16. Le Martyrologe Syrien de Rabban Sliba = Analecta Bolland. 27 (1908) 165. Cf. F. G. Hollweck, A Biographical Dictionary of the Saints. London 1924. P. 972.

17. Die Alexandrinische Weltchronik, published by Ad. Bauer and J. Strzygowski. Vienna, 1905. Table VI. The manuscript was found in 1905 in the private possession of W. Goleniscev in St. Petersburg.

18. *Loc. cit.* 721; inventory by Strzygowski.

19. = Bibl. Nation. Paris. 1583 (thirteenth century); see; H. Delehaye: Acta SS. Nov. Propyl. p. 131 and Atticus on the 8th of January *ibid.* p. 378. In the Menaion, which appeared in Athens in 1896, the three Patriarchs appear neither on the 11th of October nor on the 8th of January.

20. HE 6, 20 and 7, 2 and 4 (67, 725, 741 and 745).

21. Epistola ad Maximianum ep. = Mansi 5, 272 and epist. ad Theodosium imp. *ibid.* 270 (ML 50, 469 and 545); cf. epist. ad Nestorium = Mansi 4, 1026; Acta SS. January I 473 to 482; see Tillemont, Mémoires 12, 430. Still in the Acta SS. August I 32-37 = MG 65, 637-650 the holiness of Atticus is defended. Cf. on the other hand Tillemont 12, 416-431.

22. HE 7, 28 (67, 1504).

23. Epistola 1, ad Nestorium (77, 1453 A).

24. Epistola 48 (77, 249 C).

25. Historia Religiosa 2 (82, 1313 C). The Syrian hymn writer Balï wrote four short hymns of praise " to the holy Bishop Mar Akak." Translation in: Bibl. d. Kirchenväter 6 (1913) 78-89. Cf. G. Bardy, Acace de Bérée, in: Revue des Sc. rel. 18 (1938) 44.

26. Among the Copts on the 4th of September. Acta SS. January III, 229. The Coptic-Arabic Menologium mentions only one Severus, not otherwise distinguished (ed. F. Nau = Patrologia Orientalis 10 [1915] 187). A Gabala (now Meude) in Gaul has been mentioned, with a holy Bishop Severian. See H. Quentin, Les Martyrologes historiques p. 479 and 724. There may be a confusion between the two Severians.

27. Tillemont, Mém. 11, 173 (Art. 62) and Acta SS. January III, 229. Cf. Zellinger, Genesishomilien p. 7. J. Forget, Synaxarium Alexandrinum I (1921) 11-14. S. Duchesne, Fastes d'episcopaux de l'ancienne Gaule II, 2 (1910) 53. M. Jugie, Sévérien de Gabala et le symbole Athanasien, in: Echos d'Or. 14 (1911) 195-201 considers Severian, if not the author, at least one of the sources of the Symbolum Athanasianum.

28. Cf. Letters 1, 2, 11; 3, 2; 5-8; 14, 1 (52, 549 ff.).

29. Cf. Vol. I., p. xl.

30. MG 117, 557-560.

31. Martyrologium Romanum. Rome 1902. p. 189.

P

CHAPTER XL

CHRYSOSTOM IN THE DIPTYCHS

THE dispute among the clergy over the grave of the dead in the lonely martyr's tomb in Comana had not yet come to an end. Indeed, Atticus considered the time favorable for making an offer of reconciliation to the Johnites. To conclude from a letter of Synesius of Ptolemais, no less a man than Theophilus had encouraged him to do it.[1]

Theophilus himself seems even to have sought again a union with Rome, by a roundabout way involving the neighboring North African bishops. At least, on the 13th of June, 407, hence while Chrysostom was still living, a synod in Carthage sent a request to Pope Innocent, to grant peace and fellowship again to the Patriarch of Alexandria.[2] These efforts of both sprang from the desire to prevent the schism from becoming permanent in the East and the West, and thus being remembered as the darkest page in their own history. Whatever changes of feeling took place on their side did not enter into the question.

But an unconditional resumption of fellowship with Atticus, Theophilus and Porphyrius was flatly refused by Bishop Alexander of Basilinopolis, and several other Greek bishops, who until then had steadfastly defended the rights of Chrysostom.

Rome, above all, did the same. Pope Innocent, after the forcible prevention of the synod which he had ordered and striven for in 406, had held firmly to his once broken down guide line: no resumption of ecclesiastical fellowship with the guilty patriarchs and bishops, without reparation for past injustice. This course, since the victim was dead, could only be accomplished by at least entering the name of the dead in the *diptychs*, that is, the list of those dead with whom all had continued in peace and fellowship, and whose names were read aloud in the liturgy.[3] The important point was not that his name was entered in the list; that could be done even for the laity, and it meant only that the person so listed had departed this life in peace with God and the Church. The important point was that Chrysostom should be listed as *Bishop*. That would bring out the fact this his deposition was unjust, and that Arsacius, as well as Atticus, were to be considered unlawful bishops, at least during the lifetime of Chrysostom.[4]

The proud Theophilus had never bowed to this demand of Rome and of justice. He died before having renewed fellowship with Rome.

At any rate, it is easy to understand that Atticus struggled as long as possible against the admission of his injustice.

The first outsider to break through the closed ring of opposition was Alexander, the new Patriarch of Antioch. In the latter place, circumstances were specially favorable for Chrysostom. The people of Antioch had always retained a happy memory of their great countryman. The opposition to him there was embodied only in the person of Porphyrius (who had forcibly intruded himself upon the protection of the court), and his personal friends. But Porphyrius had scarcely disappeared from the scene, a year after Theophilus, when his successor Alexander, a pupil of Flavian, and a colleague of Chrysostom, made haste to insert the name of " Bishop John " in the ecclesiastical diptychs.[5] And what was more, he allowed the Bishops Elpidius of Laodicea in Syria, and his friend Pappus, also from Syria, to return to their episcopal sees; they belonged to his patriarchate, and had been deposed as " Johnites."[6]

When Pope Innocent learned of the change in the state of affairs in Antioch, through Alexander and the two reinstated bishops, he promptly sent to the Patriarch a document signed by twenty Italian bishops, in which it was stated: " With true joy we have heard that Alexander has shown himself so forgiving to the remaining adherents of Paulinus and Evagrius, and that the Bishops Elpidius and Pappus are able to return unhindered to their episcopal sees, and also that all the terms will be met which we made in regard to the holy and venerable Bishop John. So we thank God that the fellowship between your church and ours is restored again."[7]

In the joy of his heart. the Pope also hastened to inform his nuncio at the imperial court at that time in Constantinople, the priest Boniface, who was soon after to be his successor, of the fortunate turn of affairs: he told him, he writes, that the Church of Antioch had returned again to fellowship with Rome, after the Patriarch there had unconditionally resumed fellowship with the adherents of Paulinus, as well as those of Bishop John, of happy memory, and had promised to read the name of Bishop John in the list of dead bishops. And he, Boniface, might so inform all persons who had repeatedly interceded for Atticus.[8]

To the latter belonged especially Bishop Maximian from Macedonia, who in Rome had recommended the resumption of fellowship with Atticus. The Pope had expressed to him his surprise that he, without possessing a letter from Atticus, should have made such a request. He was very much inclined to reconciliation, but Atticus had to fulfill the same conditions as Alexander of Antioch had undertaken, "especially in the affair of the most holy John, our former fellow-bishop." So Atticus might send a petition to Rome himself for the granting of fellowship, at the same time with the declaration that he had assumed and fulfilled all the conditions.[9]

But now Atticus could not make up his mind to do this. He may well have wished a resumption of fellowship with Rome, and had evidently repeatedly worked for it, in a roundabout manner. But it was still a bitter pill for him to place his predecessor and former superior in the diptychs, as a man who had died in lawful possession of his episcopal dignities, and had been illegally deposed.

Meanwhile, still another former fellow-conspirator against Chrysostom had to go to Canossa. The old Acacius of Beroea could not, in the long run, evade the example of his Patriarch Alexander. So he also sent thither, at the same time with him, a letter to Rome, with the request for restoration of fellowship. Innocent wrote to Alexander that, if Acacius would declare himself ready to follow in all things his praiseworthy example, then the fellowship would be offered him.[10] At the same time the Pope sent to Acacius a letter of fellowship, which was not to be valid until he had shown it to the Patriarch Alexander, and had made to him a declaration that he assumed all the conditions listed therein. These conditions were the same as those for Alexander himself: namely, peace with the Eustathians, and recognition of the consecrations performed by Paulinus and Evagrius, but above all, reconciliation with the Johnites, by placing "the name of the holy John, the admirable bishop," in the diptychs.[11]

Acacius had doubtless fulfilled the conditions, and so had followed the example of his Patriarch.

Thus peace was brought about between Rome and the entire Patriarchate of the "Orient."[12] By this was made a mighty breach in the union of the inimical three. That must have been of real influence on public opinion in Constantinople. Patriarch Alexander could even soon after venture to come to Constantinople himself, and there, in the very place where he had suffered the injustice of being exiled, the moral rehabilitation of Bishop John was arranged.

But Atticus was not yet ready to yield. To all appearances he expressed himself to the people among whom such great unrest had been aroused. There Alexander himself preached in the church to the people, in order to win them over to make reparation for the injustice done to their former bishop. That could not have been difficult. Even though it was just ten years since Bishop John had been taken by force from his people, and most of them preserved a good memory of him, either openly or secretly.

Atticus himself admitted soon afterward, in a letter to Cyril of Alexandria, that some of the people wished to have the name of Chrysostom placed in the diptychs. He even made, at the same time, the reproachful remark that Alexander of Antioch had been in Constantinople, and had even attempted to stir up the people to force him against his will to enter John's name in the diptychs.[13]

As to how well founded this reproach was, it is difficult to say. The customs and usages of the East in the fourth and fifth centuries are often far from our ideas of tact and discretion. However, it is not otherwise known of Alexander that he possessed the reckless fiery enthusiasm of a St. Epiphanius.

But still he had doubtless become somewhat embarrassing to Atticus with his presumption.

Soon after that the entire course of the reconciliation almost came to a standstill again. Patriarch Alexander died in 416, after ruling only two years. The successor chosen for him was Theodotus, who in all probability had belonged to the party of Porphyrius, or was otherwise near him. At least one must conclude from the before-mentioned letter of Atticus to Cyril, that Theodotus, whether from his own resolution or from outside influence, had originally attempted to assimilate himself more with the Patriarchs of Alexandria and Constantinople, and to leave the name of Bishop John out of the diptychs. Not until he was energetically opposed by the people of Antioch did he agree to enter the much-disputed name in the list again, or let it remain there.[14]

Now Bishop Acacius of Beroea informed Atticus of this, with the request that the Patriarch should not take it amiss, since he had been so treated only out of necessity. At least so Atticus wrote. The priest who brought the letter of Acacius to Constantinople made no secret of its contents, and of the object of his mission. The people were finally impatient, and demanded stormily of Atticus that he place the name of their Bishop John in the diptychs. Now Atticus found it necessary to look more closely into the question. But, as a genuine court bishop, he did not decide it for himself, but first inquired of the "most pious" Emperor, whether he, in the interest of peace and public security, should yield to the demand of the people. The Emperor found that it would be no harm to place the name of the dead in the diptychs for the sake of peace. Then, finally, Atticus yielded, and consented to do justice to his former bishop, and the victim of his ambition.

So the affair went, after the representations of Atticus. But it may not be excluded that the initiative in the affair came from the court itself, which still had the most interest in demanding peace and quiet in the capital and the Empire. With difficulty had Atticus been compelled, by the people alone, to take a step which he had obviously forced on himself with the greatest self-conquest. It really sounds pitiable when, in his letter to the Patriarch Cyril of Alexandria, he assured him repeatedly that he had placed the disputed name in the diptychs against his will and purpose, only from considerations of necessity, and not for reasons of justice. His purpose had really been to assure peace and harmony among the people.[15] In this he had not erred against the canons, for there were not only bishops in the diptychs, but priests too, and deacons and lay people, even women. It had not been considered evil for David to have Saul buried with honor, and it did not injure the Apostles if the Arian Bishop Eudoxius was buried in their church (in Constantinople). Also, in Antioch, the names of Paulinus and Evagrius, who had been the authors of schisms, were placed in the diptychs, for the sake of peace and harmony.[16]

Socrates[17] and Theodoret[18] both confirm that Atticus actually gave the command to speak the name of "Bishop" John at the Divine Liturgy, in order to further reconciliation with the Johnites. Atticus had not entirely reached his aim. Some of the Johnites could not yet forgive him for having once given public evidence against their Bishop. They might well have noted how little his present conversion came from the heart. So a great number of them remained in opposition for twenty years, until Patriarch Proclus placed the keystone in the edifice of reconciliation by having the remains of the saint brought back to Constantinople.

Atticus concluded his letter to Cyril with the challenge that he, for his part, should do the same, and have the name of the dead inscribed in the diptychs, wholly for the sake of peace and harmony. This proposition did not find a good reception with St. Cyril. His uncle Theophilus had been considered, and actually was, the chief originator of the plot against Chrysostom. To place his name in the diptychs, therefore, would be to admit that the Patriarch of Alexandria had committed an injustice that cried to heaven, and that the Synod of the Oak, which Cyril had attended, at least as a spectator, had been a crime. It is humanly understandable that it would be hard for him to be objective in this matter. Cyril, in his answer, called the Synod of the Oak a "holy synod" and even made reproaches to Atticus on account of his complaisance, especially saying that placing John in the diptychs as bishop was contrary to the definitions of the Council of Nicaea. Indeed, he asked him finally to put an end to it, since for a long time all opposition on the part of the Johnites had ceased, and everyone attended the Divine Liturgy with Atticus, except possibly a few.

But while he united himself with the Johnites, he separated himself from all Egypt. If Judas is still recognized as an apostle, what is to be done with Matthew?[19] In regard to this, Facundus of Hermiane noted, in the sixth century: "These bitter words of St. Cyril, injurious to Christian feeling, which he, forgetting himself, uttered against the most beloved Father of the Church, whose words are sweeter than Attic honey, I repeat with sadness, and only because I must. For who can mention without a shudder that Cyril did not shrink from calling John a Judas, a Jechonias, a profane man—and what is still more cruel, John was already dead—and also, he did not shrink from comparing him with the Arian Bishop Eudoxius, and saying that he had been expelled from the Church."[20]

In order the more easily to defend Cyril, Stilting[21] and, following him, Ludwig,[22] declare both the letters in question spurious, for clear internal reasons. But since the testimony of the letters in a polemical work which had become generally known dates back to the sixth century, and the internal doubts brought forward are not difficult to disperse, one cannot pass by the authenticity of these letters.[23]

However, Cyril was not able further to halt the course of the affair. Right and justice demanded satisfaction, and their final victory was only a question of time. When Antioch and Constantinople had once taken the decisive step, and thereby obtained union and peace with Rome and the West, Alexandria could continue to live in splendid isolation. Added to this, that the restoration of general peace was to the best interests of the Empire and the court, and therefore they also wished it. A great part of Byzantine internal politics always exhausted itself through long centuries in the attempt to put out the fires which its quarreling theologians and bishops had kindled in the Empire.

How long St. Cyril continued his opposition is not exactly known. Only this is certain, that he had given up before the year 430. On the 12th of December of that year, Nestorius, the countryman and successor of Chrysostom, in the See of Constantinople, gave a sermon, in which he apostrophized the Patriarch of Alexandria, his opponent. He said: "I say nothing of John, whose ashes you now honor against your will."[24] From this it certainly follows, on the one hand, that that Cyril originally opposed allowing justice to be done to the memory of Chrysostom; and on the other hand, that before 430 he had given up his opposition, at least outwardly.[25]

A certain probability speaks for 418 as the year in which Cyril allowed the name of St. Chrysostom to be placed in the diptychs. At that time, Pope Zosimus sent out a notice of the condemnation of the errors of Celestius and Pelagius; it was sent to Patriarch Cyril, among others, which always seems to presume resumption of ecclesiastical fellowship.[26] Nicephorus Callistus also says that the expiation had been made in the year 418, and that it was St. Isidore of Pelusium who had moved Cyril at last to yield.[27] However, not a word about the entrance of Chrysostom's name into the diptychs is found in the collected letters of St. Isidore, and the letters usually quoted hitherto for this[28] are first applied to the diptych question on the basis of Nicephorus.

One may rightly presume that Cyril, like Atticus, first gave up at a sign from the court of Constantinople, and that this pressure from above may have followed soon after the capitulation of Atticus, and so about the year 418.

In a later time, it has been considered necessary to attribute to Cyril a somewhat holier motive for yielding. According to this, Cyril is supposed to have had a dream, or a vision, in which Chrysostom appeared to him, surrounded by the Heavenly army, with the threatening object of expelling him from the episcopal palace. But then the Mother of God interceded with John for Cyril, who had fought so valiantly for her honor. Cyril had this circumstance to thank for being able to remain, and for making up his mind to conclude peace with such a formidable opponent.[29]

As a matter of fact, Cyril, just like Atticus, had only submitted to external pressure, obviously against his will. No importance should be attached to the fact that in his numerous writings he only quoted Chrysostom one single time, in a treatise intended for the court, and then together with Atticus, Antiochus and Severian,[30] and therefore in doubtful company. Still, he at least calls him Bishop, if one may trust the printed edition. In the year 432, Cyril alone remembered, in a letter (surviving only in Latin) of Bishop Acacius of Beroea, that, at the Synod of the Oak in 403, he had expressed himself as follows: "If I knew that John would now improve himself, if we would grant him pardon, and that he would discontinue his hardness and unfriendliness, I would have interceded with you for him." And Cyril, significantly, continued: "Acacius merits admiration for this judgment, for there he told the truth!"[31]

So also a St. Cyril could not free himself, all his life long, of a prejudice and animosity which was instilled into him in his youth. Obviously he had believed, to the last, that Chrysostom had deserved all this for his vices. Surely he would have been more than disconcerted if he had been able to read what a Western Bishop wrote of him and Chrysostom more than a hundred years later. Facundus of Hermiane asks: "Who would not prefer John of Constantinople to Cyril?"[32] They are not to be compared."[33] Cardinal Newman wrote: "I do not believe that Cyril would agree to it, that one should accept his external acts as the measure of his interior holiness."[34]

However, the healthy understanding of the people, through all weakness and opposition, had maintained that their spiritual leader was right. It was a triumph of justice that, only eleven or twelve years after his death, the much outraged and bitterly hated, deposed and banished Archbishop of Constantinople, whose bones still lay in solitude in distant Pontus, should have been placed in the ecclesiastical diptychs by his former opponents themselves, and even as a bishop. Thus it was indirectly conceded that an injustice had been done to him.

But the first and chief credit, in the victory of justice and truth, belongs without doubt to Pope Innocent I, who, until his death, had made the rehabilitation of Chrysostom the first condition of peace between the East and the West.

Even Photius, whom certainly no one can accuse of partiality in favor of Rome, acknowledges the conduct of the Pope in the affair of St. Chrysostom: " Innocent of Rome made many efforts for the saint, even though his efforts were unavailing. He sent ambassadors who, however, were sent back in an insulting fashion. Likewise, he wrote letters. But all his efforts were in vain."[34a] However, they were not altogether in vain. The victory of righteousness came late, but it came eventually. The first schism between eastern and western lands was thereby brought to an end. The placing of his name in the diptychs was only the first step to greater honors.

In the year 428 a priest of Antioch was once more summoned to Constantinople, and consecrated there as Bishop of the capital city; it was Nestorius. In him, in a remarkable parallel, history and the tragedy of Chrysostom repeated themselves, though from a different cause.[35] Nestorius stood as a countryman at the side of Chrysostom. At any rate, he had also read his Scriptures industriously, and schooled himself in them, for even as a priest Nestorius was known as a good orator. So without further ado, it is understandable and credible that the always well-informed Marcellinus Comes said in the year 428: "In this year, on the 26th of September, for the first time, in the capital city, the memory of the blessed John was celebrated as a church feast."[36] With this, Chrysostom was actually elevated to the honors of the altar, and called holy, after the Eastern manner.

Whether Nestorius had already established such a "Feast of St. Chrysostom" in Antioch, or introduced it first into Constantinople of his own will, cannot be decided. At any rate, it is proved in a eulogy of Chrysostom, attributed to Proclus, that his Church feast was celebrated before the translation of his relics.[37] Indeed, one might almost believe that the celebration of the feast for the entire Eastern Empire was ordered by the Emperor. For two years later Nestorius made to St. Cyril the above-mentioned reproach, that he showed only involuntary honor to the memory of Chrysostom. For the Latin *adorare* certainly stands in the original Greek text as προσκυνεῖν. That means much more than the mere entering of the name in the diptychs, for it signifies showing religious honor. One may also rightly assume that the "Feast of St. John Chrysostom" was generally celebrated in the Greek Church after the year 428. That could not have happened at the command of Nestorius, under the conditions of that time, for Nestorius did not possess this power, but at the command of the Emperor, who yielded to a proposal of Nestorius. The

Byzantine Emperor began, in the fourth and fifth centuries, to play the role of a pope in his Empire.

Unfortunately, the originator of this new "feast" soon had to share the fate of his predecessor, not as a saint, but as a heretic. That may also be the reason why the later biographers and chronographers do not especially mention or bring into prominence this merit of Nestorius. On the other hand, there appears now a later account, perhaps originating in the eleventh century, a Nestorian fragment of church history of the fourth and fifth centuries, which says: "Cyril was very angry with Nestorius, because the latter brought back the relics of St. John Chrysostom to Constantinople, and buried them there."[38]

Perhaps Nestorius actually had this in view. At any rate, his attention was very soon drawn to other things, which occupied him entirely.

The carrying out of this idea was reserved for another.

FOOTNOTES

1. Epist. 66 ad Theophilum 35 (66, 1409 A-B). A "reconciliation" of the Johnites with Atticus *before* the admission of Chrysostom into the diptychs was of course a "submission" and a recognition of the Synod of the Oak.

2. Mansi 4, 502, no. LXVIII, and ML 20, 618, no. 21.

3. The "diptychs" still exist in the form of the Memento vivorum et mortuorum in Holy Mass. Naturally only the most distinguished personalities come into the list, which probably formed the beginning of the Martyrology. Cf. R. Maere in the Catholic Encyclopedia 5, 23; H. Leclercq, Diptyques in the Dictionnaire d'Archéologie Chrétienne et de Liturgie 4 (Paris 1921) 1045-1170.

4. A deposed bishop ranked as a layman in the Orient. If he received another episcopal see, occasionally he even might be consecrated again. (L. Saltet, Les Réordinations 29; 37-38). So a deposed bishop could only be mentioned in the diptychs as a layman, given of course the legality of his deposition.

5. Theodoret 5, 35 (82, 1265; ed. Parmentier p. 338): "This Alexander was the first who entered the name of the great John in the diptychs."

6. Cf. Palladius, Dial. 9 (31-32) and 20 (71); Elpidius was the Bishop who brought the opponents of Chrysostom into such embarrassment in the presence of the Emperor by proving the Arian character of the Synod of 341 and who later, with Pappus, devoted himself to prayer for three years without leaving his house.

7. Epistola 19 ad Alexandrum Ant. ep. (ML 20, 540-542). Like-wise epist. 20 ad Alexandrum (*loc. cit.* 543).

8. Epistola 23 (ML 20, 546-5). Dionysius Exig., Collectio Decretor. Innocentii I. n. 41 (ML 67, 252-253). Pope Boniface recalled later in a letter of March 11, 422, to Rufus and the other Bishops of Macedonia, this reconciliation of the Bishops of the Orient with Rome (ML 20, 783).

9. Epistola 22 (ML 20, 544-546) and Dionysius Exig., Collect. Innocentii I. n. 43 (ML 67, 254).

10. Epistola 19, 2 (ML 20, 542). Cf. Cavallera, Le schisme 295.

11. Epist. 21: Innocentii Pp. ad Acacium Beroeae episc. (ML 20, 543-544).

12. Severian of Gabala and Antiochus of Ptolemais were already dead at that time.

13. Epistola ad Cyrill. 75 (MG 77, 349 C). Cf. Abhdlg. d. bay. Akad. d. wiss. 32, 6. p. 23 f.

14. *Loc. cit.* (77, 349 D). Concerning a surviving mosaic inscription in the Church of St. Babylas, see J. Lassus in: Still-well, Antioch. Excav. II (1938) 42.

15. Cyrilli epist. 75 (77, 348-349 A).

16. *Loc. cit.* (352).

17. HE 7, 25 (67, 793).

18. HE 5, 34 (82, 1265). According to Moses of Khorene, His-toria Armeniae, III ch. LVII, Atticus wrote to Bishop Isaac of Armenia a letter in which he overwhelmed Chrysostom with praise, as " the fountain-head of the Church, our father, the holy John, who is not merely father of these cities of the world; for all Christians, all the world, are enlightened through him." This letter cannot be considered genuine. (Armenian-French edition of P.E. Le Vaillant de Florival. Venice 1841. 2, 155).

19. Cyrilli Al. epist. 76 (77, 352-360). Cf. Photius Patr., Interr. et Resp. V (104, 1224-1225).

20. Pro defensione trium capitulorum 4, 1 (ML 67, 609).

21. A. SS. Sept. IV p. 682 ff.

22. Chrysostomus in seinem Verhältnis zum Byzantinischen Hof, p. 173 Note 3.

23. Nicephorus Callistus has embodied the text of the letter in his Church history. (HE 14, 26 and 27=MG 146, 1137-1149): Cf.

Cyrilli Al. epist. 75 and 76 = MG 77, 348-360). As internal reasons against its authenticity Stilting counts the following:

1. According to his letter, Atticus lied by the statement that he had not entered Chrysostom's name as Bishop. But Atticus expresses himself very ambiguously when he says that the diptychs listed not only the names of bishops, but those of priests, deacons, laity and women (77, 352 A). 2. It is improbable that Atticus did not yield to Bishop Alexander, but to the priest of Acacius. This may have been caused by the fact that meanwhile the voice of the people had become impatient. 3. Socrates is silent concerning the urgency of the people. Naturally that proves nothing against it.

The allusions to David, Saul, Eudoxius and the mere assertion of anxiety as a motive are absurdities; also the letter is absolutely silent about Rome and the Oriental Bishops (Johnites). The allusions and comparisons are very fitting in the mind of Cyril, and Atticus did not need to name Rome and the Johnites, because they did not exert any special influence at that time (417).

Likewise, the objections (n. 1441 ff.) against the authenticity of Cyril's answer are not valid, as is shown for the most part in our representation in the text. That the style of the letter does not specially agree with that of Cyril's other letters must first be shown. That other letters also were forged is correct; but the authenticity of these was already attested to in the sixth century by Facundus of Hermiane.

24. " Cuius cineres nunc *adorando veneraris* invitus " = Marius Mercator, Nestorii Sermo 12, 5 (ML 48, 852); Loofs, Nestoriana n. XVIII. p. 300. Cf. Jugie, Nestorius p. 43.

25. That has eluded Duchesne, Histoire ancienne de l'Église 3, 302.

26. Marius Mercator, Commonitorium I and III = ML 48, 82 and 93. Of course Pope Boniface I wrote (Epist. 15 = ML 20, 783) under his predecessor, Pope Innocent (died 417) that the " Orientalium Ecclesiarum Pontifices " had prayed for peace and had obtained it easily (non difficulter). Still, among the Oriental Churches, the Patriarchate of Antioch is understood to be in the first rank, while the Egyptians are almost always expressly designated only as Egyptians. (Contrary to Stilting *loc. cit.* n. 1448-1449).

27. E. Bouvy, S. Jean Chrysostome et S. Isidore de Péluse = Echos d'Orient 1 (1897) 200.

28. Letters 1, 310 and 370 (78, 361 and 392).

29. George Cedrenus, Compendium Historiarum a. 397 (121, 626) and Nicephorus Callistus HE 14, 28 (146, 1152).

30. De recta fide ad reginas 10 (76, 1216). Cf. Baur, S. Jean Chrysostome 6-8.

31. Cyrilli Al. epist. 33 (77, 159 C). Stilting does not mention this letter.

32. Pro defensione trium capitulorum 8, 7, (ML 67, 736 B).

33. *Ibid.* 8, 6 (col. 730).

34. Theodoret = Historical Sketches 2, 341.

34a. Bibl. 96 (103, 360). Also Chrysostomus Papadopoulos recognized that Pope Innocent was a most decided defender of Chrysostom. (Eccles. Pharos, 4 [1905] 510).

35. The opponents of Cyril cast him out of the Council of Ephesus: "He is the nephew of Theophilus, and imitates his opinions and actions. As the one (Theophilus) gave vent to his fury against the God-loving John, so the other (Cyril) wants to make himself famous here, even though there is a great differ-ence between the two accused (Chrysostom and Nestorius)." (S. Isidore Pelus. epistol. 1, 310 (78, 361). On the polemics of the Nestorian Barhad besabba, against Cyril, see Ztschr. f. neutest. Wiss. 30 (1931) 239.

36. ML 51, 925; ed. Mommsen = MGH Auct. Ant. XI, p. 77. Concerning the day on which the feast was celebrated in the future, see the following chapter. George Cedrenus of course states that the Feast of St. John Chrysostom was first solemnly celebrated in the year 424, so also under Atticus (died 425). (His-toriarum Compendium 2 = MG 121, 644). Still he cannot pre-vail over the authority of Marcellinus Comes. In the Latin Martyrology, Chrysostom has been listed since the ninth century. In the obviously Greek-influenced memorial calendar in the Church of S. Giovanni Maggiore in Naples (s. IX) on the 10th of January is listed: Deposition S. Jo. Chrys. [ostomi]; on the 27th of January, Natalis S. Jo. Chr.; on the 13th of November again the Deposition; see Anal. Boll. 57 (1939) 8 and 39. In the Martyrology of the Archbishop Ado of Vienne (between 850 and 865) the name of Chrysostom is found on the 27th of January (PL. 123, 223). In the Martyrology of the monk Balbulus (end of the ninth century and beginning of the tenth) it also falls on the 27th of January. (ML. 131, 1040).

37. Oratio 20 (65, 827-834). At any rate, the panegyric was given when the bones of St. Chrysostom still rested in the Mar-tyrium of St. Basiliscus: "In Ponto jacet et in orbe terrarum laudatur" (*loc. cit.* 831).

38. E. Goeller = Oriens Christianus 1 (1905) 95. Cf. M. Briére, La legende syriaque de Nestorius = Revue de l'Orient chrétien 15 (1910) 19.

CHAPTER XLI

THE VICTOR'S RETURN

O N the 27th of January, 438,[1] a mood of solemn festival lay on the Empire's chief city on the Bosporus. Half of Constantinople was on its knees. The people did not go in such numbers to the circus, or the theater, or even to the triumphal return of the Emperor, victorious from the wars. They streamed toward the shore of the sea, and an almost religious consecration shone in their faces.

The Bosporus was covered with boats and barques, even to the Propontis, and the many lights of the boats gleamed by thousands in the evening twilight, mirrored on the calm surface of the sea. Everyone gazed toward the sea in expectation. Today a spiritual conqueror was making his entrance, a man who only after his death had vanquished his opponents, through the mere power of right and justice; John, the Golden-mouthed, who long since had been honored by the world as a saint; the former Bishop of Constantinople, he was awaited again today in his episcopal city, thirty-four years after his last banishment. So no one would stay away, if it was possible to join the cortège of the dead shepherd, who was to go in solemn procession on his third and last entrance into Constantinople, and enter into his final resting-place.

What a change in the spirit and in the times! First, he was expelled from the city amid the scorn and derision of Jews, pagans and Christians; that was the triumph of force and wrong. And now the day had come when innocence and nobility of soul had obtained the final victory, when an immense concourse of people came together for the solemn reception of the dead hero, in the great city where none were now living who had been among his enemies. The former mightily heaving waves of passion had had time to become calm again; the chief characters in the tragedy were now no longer living. Eudoxia and Arcadius, Severian, Theophilus, Antiochus,

Cyrinus, Arsacius and Atticus, had all vanished from the stage of the world. His former friends and contemporaries too, the gentle Olympias, the faithful Serapion, and many others who had been persecuted for his sake, had already followed him into eternity. Only a distinguished witness of the proceedings at the Synod of the Oak was still living: Cyril, the successor of Theophilus. But in his church calendar already stood the name of John Chrysostom, as one of the Bishops and Saints.

The court also took part in the joy of the people. Theodosius II, the son of Arcadius, had entered willingly into the plans of the new Patriarch, Proclus,[2] and of his own pious and intelligent sister Pulcheria, and had given the command to have the remains of the saint taken up from the far-off martyr's tomb in Pontus, and brought to Constantinople. The later legends have embellished the facts of the exhumation in their own way. At first, at was absolutely impossible to raise the coffin from its place. Then the Emperor wrote a touching letter " to the oecumenical teacher and spiritual father, the saint and patriarch John Chrysostom," to beg him to forgive all the injustices which had been done to him, and to return. This letter, said the legend, was laid on the breast of the dead, and then the coffin was easily raised.[3]

The fact of the matter is that the Emperor himself, with his court, appeared at the solemn reception. Theodoret even tells that when the coffin, with the beloved remains of the Saint, was borne to land in a boat by the light of uncounted torches, amid the deepest stillness and emotion of the great multitude of people, Theodosius, as the first of his people, knelt down, with eyes and countenance fixed upon the coffin, according to the Eastern custom, and prayed to the dead for pardon for the injustice which his parents had unwittingly done him.[4]

Then the procession moved, with lights, and accompanied by the Emperor and the Patriarch, through the midst of the city, to the Church of St. Irene, the new cathedral, and past his former episcopal palace, to the Church of the Apostles.[5] There, in the imperial mausoleum, beside Constantine the Great, beside Constantius and Theodosius I, Arcadius and Eudoxia had also been buried.[6] Near to them, in the Church itself, beside the Apostles, Chrysostom was to find his last resting-place.[7] So the bones of the Empress and of the Archbishop rested for centuries in the same place, almost under the same roof. Death is a great reconciler.

Chrysostom had once written: "In Rome, the Emperor, the consuls, and the rulers, make pilgrimages to the graves of the Fisherman and the Tent-maker. But in Constantinople, those who once wore the diadem are satisfied if they are buried, not even near the Apostles, but outside in the forecourt. So the Emperors become doorkeepers for the fishermen."[8] "These find themselves inside, like the lords, but those, as though they were servants, consider it a favor if they may find a place by the outer door."[9]

But in the coming centuries, annually on Easter Monday, the Byzantine Emperor approached the Church of the Apostles in solemn procession, in order to pray at the tombs of St. John Chrysostom, St. Gregory of Nazianzus, and Constantine the Great.[10]

Also in the course of the years the Johnites, who had become a very small group, showed themselves reconciled; that perhaps all too steadfast number of faithful adherents of the Saint, who, even after his death, indeed even after his name had been placed in the diptychs and he had been raised to the altars, still refused to enter into fellowship with his successors. Socrates, the contemporary, and perhaps an eyewitness of the translation of the relics, and who wrote his history just after that, about 440, remarks expressly that Proclus, by these prudent measures, had reconciled the last remnants of the Johnites, and led them back to the unity of the Church.[11] In the following century, the Emperor Justinian restored the Church of the Apostles, and enlarged it. Mesarites, in his description of Justinian's Church of the Apostles, says: "Toward the northern side, on the west, the great John, whose speech and understanding were golden, and more valuable than any gold, the true high priest of the Lord, who was the model of the great Shepherd, and gave his life for his sheep, the great wonder of the world, has found the last resting-place for his body in the earth. Myrrh flows from him evermore, which surpasses all the perfume of the world, and bursts forth from his holy body, as from a fast-flowing fountain, and penetrates with a certain divine power through the silver statue made in his image, which lies on his gravestone, and wells forth with rapid flow, descends from his head or his hand, or often from his knees, even to his beard or to the border of his episcopal garment, and overflows to the whole grave. Everyone who has seen it will give testimony to my words, and have already done so, and their testimony is true."[12]

But the people were not satisfied even with simple canonization, and with the miraculous occurrences. Already, in the seventh century, or a little later, one who had chosen the contemplative life as his vocation related that Adelphius, Deacon of Arabissus, had been pained by the thought that Chrysostom, who had so rejoiced the Church of God by his preaching, had died as a deposed bishop. So he wanted to know whether the Saint in heaven had his place among the bishops or among the laity, and he prayed very earnestly to God to allow him to see the Goldenmouth in heaven. And so it was done. One day, in an ecstasy, Adelphius saw the splendid place where the holy teachers were gathered together, in Heavenly blessedness. But he could not discover Chrysostom among them. Then, full of sorrow, he inquired of his Heavenly guide where the Goldenmouth might be. The guide answered him: " A man who still lives in the flesh cannot see Chrysostom, because he is beside the Throne of God."[13]

Indeed apotheosis could go no further.

But his successor in the Patriarchal See of Constantinople henceforth eulogized the greatest and holiest among his predecessors annually on the 13th of November, the day on which the Byzantine Church entered him among the number of its saints. Why this particular day was chosen is not known. The 14th of September, the actual day of his death, was reserved for the Feast of the Exaltation of the Holy Cross.[14] Nestorius established the feast on the 26th of September.[15] The Latin Church, on the other hand, chose the 27th of January, the day of the translation of the relics, as the feast of St. John Chrysostom. And he was honored even a third time, on the 30th of January, which they celebrated as " the feast of the three great hierarchs," Basil, Gregory of Nazianzus, and Chrysostom.[16]

Already the Emperor Leo. V, the Wise, had raised the Feast of St. John to the rank of a public festival day, together with those of Athanasius, Basil, the two Gregories, Epiphanius and Cyril of Alexandria.[17]   On the other hand, Manuel Comnenus (1143-1180) declared, among others, as general Empire holidays, which also had to be observed by the courts: the Feasts of the Blessed Virgin, of the Apostles, of Sts. Athanasius, Cyril, Gregory of Nazianzus and Chrysostom.[18]

So ended the "tragedy" of St. John Chrysostom.

Through almost 800 years, the bones of the great sufferer rested in the Church of the Apostles in Constantinople. During this time, many storms and afflictions passed over the Empire and the capital city.   But when the Venetians conquered the city in 1204, they showed that remarkable mixture of commercial genius and piety which they have always shown: they robbed not merely earthly but also heavenly treasures.   At that time the relics of St. Gregory of Nazianzus and St. John Chrysostom were supposed to have been sent to the West, to Rome, where they were laid in the shadow of St. Peter's.   Their graves are still shown there, in the choir chapel of St. Peter's.[18a]   This account is not improbable.   At least Antoniades, in his account of the Church of St. Sophia, notes concerning the relics of St. Nicholas, John the Almoner, St. Andreas, Gregory of Nazianzus (?), Sts. Catherine, Barbara, Lucia and others, whose bodies, wholly or partly, had been shown in Hagia Sophia, were all in the year 1204 stolen by the Latins.[19]   Hence, it is not quite credible that they should have left the saints of the Apostles' Church quite undisturbed.   As a matter of fact, they also plundered the Church of the Apostles unsparingly.[20]   If the Greeks of that time were justly enraged at this robbery of their sanctuaries, one may find a certain satisfaction in the fact that so many sacred memorials, among them the bones of St. Chrysostom, at least did not fall into the hands of the Turks 250 years later.   As Rome was Chrysostom's last refuge in life, so it became also his last refuge and resting-place in death.[21]

But the Church of the Apostles was destroyed by the Turks in 1460, and in its place the Greek architect Christodoulos built the Mosque of Mohammed II, the conqueror of Constantinople.   Today this towers above all around it, visible

from afar, in the place where Chrysostom was once buried,
and also the first Christian Emperor, Constantine the Great,
and the great Theodosius, and Justinian I.

FOOTNOTES

1. The year 438 is quite well established as the year of the
transfer of the relics. Socrates 7, 45 (67, 836) contradicts himself
in the same chapter in which he says that the transfer took place
in the thirty-fifth year after the (final) banishment, and under the
sixteenth consulate of Theodosius II., both of which give 438;
and then, immediately afterward, he says in the thirty-fifth year
after his *death*, that is, 442. The latter is obviously an inexactitude. Marcellinus Comes (ML 51, 925; ed. Mommsen, p. 77)
gives the 28th of January, 438. The Menologium Basilii (MG
117, 281) says the thirty-third year after his death (440). The
chronography of Theophanes (MG 108, 244 B) says that he was
brought back 32 years (after his death?) and finally laid to rest
a year after that, in the Church of the Apostles; and dates his
burial at the year 430. Nicephorus Callistus, HE 14, 43 (146,
1205-1209) dates the transfer of the body in the fifth year of the
Patriarchate of Proclus (438-439). The two oldest and most
reliable authorities, Socrates and Marcellinus Comes, therefore
testify for 438.
2. Socrates 7, 45 (67, 836). E. Schwartz, Cod. Vatican. 1431,
in: Abhand. d. bayer. Akad. d. Wiss. XXXII, 6, p. 24-25, ascribes
the first initiative to Pulcheria. Proclus had earlier been a lector
and secretary of Bishop Atticus, who ordained him priest and
Bishop.
3. Menologium Basilii Porph. for the 27th of January (117,
281-283) and Nicephorus Callistus, HE 14, 43 (146, 1205-1209).
4. HE 5, 36 (82, 1265-1268). Inwardly, such a proceeding, or
a similar one, does not appear impossible or improbable. In
later centuries, the poetic art of Byzantine writers enriched the
journey over the Bosporus with a miracle. In the midst of a
perfect stillness, suddenly a storm broke, which dispersed all the
ships. Only the ship with the relics of the saint remained
upright, recalling the vineyard for the sake of which Chrysostom
had first clashed with Eudoxia. After that the storm subsided.
Nicephorus Callistus HE 14, 43 (146, 1209).
5. A pictorial representation of the transfer from a Menologium Basilii is to be found in Heisenberg, Grabeskirche und

Apostelkirche II. Table III.b. While Socrates 7, 45 (67, 836) says the burial of the relics took place directly in the Church of the Apostles, later chroniclers and historiographers say that the body was first laid to rest in the Church of St. Thomas τῶν ᾿Αμαντίου, then in St. Irene, and lastly in the Church of the Apostles. Perhaps that did not happen until the time when Justinian I had the Church of the Apostles newly built up from the foundations. Nicephorus Callistus 14, 43 (146, 1209).

6. R. F. Ph. Brunck, Analecta veterum poetarum graecorum 3 (Strasbourg 1776) 297 (n. 684) gives, without any account of the arrival, an epigram, probably purely literary, on Chrysostom and Theodosius:

«ἐνθάδε τύμβος ἔχει θεοειδέας, ἀνέρας ἐσθλοὺς
θεῖον ᾿Ιωάννην, τὸν πάνυ θευδόσιον
ὡς ἀρετὴ πολύολβος ἐς οὐρανοῦ ἄντυγας ἦλθε
καὶ φωτὸς μετόχους δεῖξεν ἀκηρασίου.»

That naturally does not mean that both were buried in one grave, but only that both graves were under the same roof, so to speak, since the imperial mausoleum, even though it was a separate building, was united with the church. The epitaph is repeated in Fried. Jacobs, Anthologia graeca 4 (Leipzig 1794) p. 263 (n. 684 a) and Dr. F. Pieper, Zur Geschichte der Kirchenväter aus epigraphischen Quellen = Zeitschrift für Kirchengeschichte 1 (1877) 218. In the Anthologia Palatina, VIII I, The epigram is wrongly attributed to St. Gregory the Theologian.

7. Already in the year 381 Theodosius (Cod. Theod. 9, 17, 6; ed. Mommsen 465) had forbidden citizens to be buried in or near churches within the city.

8. Contra Judaeos et Gentiles 9 (48, 825).

9. Hom. 26, 5 in 2. Cor. (61, 582).

10. Constantine Porphyrogenitus, De Caerimoniis aulae Byzantinae 1, 10, 5 (112, 280). Cf. O. Wolff, Die sieben Wunder *loc. cit.* 328, and Ebersolt, Le grand Palais 184. Besides Chrysostom, Gregory of Nazianzus, later Patriarch Flavian of Constantinople and Methodius the Confessor, were buried in the Church of the Apostles.

11. HE 7, 45 (67, 836). So one may assume that Nestorius failed in his plan of winning all the Johnites. Also in Antioch, the last remnants of the Eustathians (Paulinians) were reconciled after the Patriarch Kalandion (482) had the relics of St. Eustathius brought back to Antioch. (Cavallera, Le schisme 207-208).

12. Heisenberg, Grabeskirche 2, 80-81.

13. Johannes Moschus, Pratum spirituale 128 (87, 2992-2993);

George Hamartolus, Chronicon lib. IV. CC.III. (110, 737);
George Cedrenus, HC (121, 633-636). Cosmas Vestitor, In translationem S. Jo. Chrys. Encom. 2 (ed. K. J. Dyobouniotis=
Epeteris 2 [1925] 21) says Adelphius was Bishop of Cucusus. A
book with a representation of the death of St. Chrysostom exists
in the Meteora Cloister of St. Barlaam (see A. Xyngopoulos, in:
Epeteris het. byz. Spoudon 9 (1932) 357 and: Oriens chr. 34, 2
(1934) 231. In the Handbuch der Malerei vom Berge Athos, ed.
Dr. Schafer (Trier 1855) p. 238, is a "Darstellung aller himmlis-
chen Geister als Regel": Chrysostom is represented there as the
intercessor of all holy bishops. Also, in Santa Maria Antiqua in
Rome, Chrysostom is represented in the first place among all the
Greek martyrs and bishops represented there. (L. Dieu, La Mari-
ologie de S. Jean Chrysostome, in: Mémoires et Rapports du
Congrès Marial 1921. I, 91 (Brussels 1922).

14. Synaxarium Eccl. Constantinople 217. Menologium Basilii *loc. cit.* (117, 157); Vita S. Georgii Hagioritae n. 98; ed. P.
Peeters in the Anal Boll. 36-37 (1917-1919) 156 (written about
1070); Johannes Chrysostomus "die decimo quarto Septembris
obiit in exaltatione Crucis, qui dies cum vetitus esset, decimum
tertium Novembris assignarunt."

15. So according to Marcellinus Comes in the year 428 (ML
51, 925; ed. Mommsen 77). According to this it might appear
as though the Feast of the Exaltation of the Cross was already
being celebrated in the year 428. Tillemont 11, 623 (note 104)
is of course of the opinion that perhaps an error in copying is
involved here: XXVI instead of XIV. In the festal calendar of
Antioch of the early sixth century, that is, the earliest time of
all, the Feast of St. Chrysostom was celebrated on the 13th of
September, obviously in order to bring it as closely as possible to
his actual death day, the 14th of September. (A. Baumstark, in:
Jahrb. d. Liturgiewiss. 5 [1925] 129). The oldest festal calendar
of Constantinople, which celebrated the death of St. Chrysostom
on the 13th of September, is found in Cod. 2 of the S. Andreas-
Skiti on Mt. Athos, from the ninth century (A. Ehrhard, Überlieferung . . . I, 29).

16. Synaxarium Constantinopol. = Acta SS. Nov. Propyl. 433,
L. 52. The feast of the "Three Hierarchs" was introduced in
the tenth or eleventh century. Cf. Baur, S. Jean Chrysostome 25,
note 2. The Menologium Basilii imp. has, on the 13th of
November, a memorial celebration for the *exile* of St. Chrysostom.
(MG 117, 157). P. Eut. Lamérand, La Fête des trois Hiérarques
dans l'Église grecque, in: Bessarione, anno III, vol. IV (1898)
164-76.

17. Novellae Constitutiones 88 (107, 600-601).

18. Novellae Constitutiones XIII, De diebus feriatis = 133, 760. C. Baur, S. Jean Chrysostome p. 25.

18a. Cascioli, Del corpo di S. Giov. Cris.   Bessarione 33 (1917) 63.

19. *Ἔκφρασις τῆς Ἁγίας Σοφίας*   3, 146.

20. A. Heisenberg, Grabeskirche und Apostelkirche 2, 2 = Nicetas Acom. p. 855 f. ed. Bonn. H. Delehaye, Méthode hagiographique, p. 97.

21. Cf. Riant, Les dépouilles religieuses enlevées à Constantinople, au XIIIe siècle, par les Latins (Paris 1875) 192 and 204 (after Antonius of Novgorod, who died in 1238).

It does not signify much to the contrary that an unknown Russian monk (1424 to 1453) claims to have seen Chrysostom's grave in Hagia Sophia, where his Bishop's staff was also shown. (Antoniades, *Ἔκφρασις* 2, 96).   In the times of unholy treatment of relics, naturally even the name of Chrysostom must occasionally have concealed fraud.   In the year 1251 the Abbot of Clairvaux solicited the permission to celebrate the Feast of St. Chrysostom with two Masses and twelve lessons, since they had come into possession of the Saint's head.   (Martène et Durand, Thesaurus novorum anecdotorum. Paris, 1717. Vol. 4, 1394).   But in the monastery of Vatopädi, on Mt. Athos, the head of St. John Chrysostom was shown, "intact and whole" (Montfaucon, Palaeographia graeca 464), while the monastery of St. Athanasius on Mt. Athos also believed that they possessed a hand of the Saint (*ibid*. 456; cf. 474 and 491) and a Greek monastery on the Island of Patmos counted the entire body of St. Chrysostom among their treasures. (Revue d'Histoire Ecclés. 13 [1912] 786). Even in the year 1284 the Emperor Andronicus II sent to the monastery of Philotheus on the island of Thasos the right hand of the great orator, so says Goldbulle: Παῖδες Ἑλλήνων ἀσεβεῖς = Zachariae of Lingenthal, Jus Graeco-Romanum III, p. XX. See also Gedeon, Byzantinon Heortologion 65-66 and the same, Πατριαρχικοὶ Πίνακες 152-153.

Theodosius I had forbidden, already in 386, the carrying on of dealings in relics (= Cod. Theod. 9, 17, 7; ed. Mommsen 466) and St. Augustine complained: Alii monachi membra martyrum, si tamen martyrum, venditant" (= De opere monachorum ch. 28 = ML 40, 575).

CHAPTER XLII

CHRYSOSTOM IN LATER CENTURIES

THERE is infinite tragedy in the fact that the countries which first received Christianity, and sacrificed and bled for it the first and the most, which have given the Church the greatest and most splendid figures, are the very countries through which the bloody, culture-destroying rule of the Crescent has almost completely lost Christianity—namely, Syria, Asia Minor, Egypt and Palestine. Antioch, the proud Queen of the East, as it were the second cradle of Christianity, the birthplace of Chrysostom, was afflicted with one catastrophe after another, from the sixth century on. In the year 526, under the Emperor Justinian, a fearful earthquake leveled the city almost to the ground. It had scarcely revived again somewhat, when, 14 years later, Chosroes with his wild Persians stormed the city, which was reduced in a few days to a colossal pile of smoking ruins. The king carried off the surviving inhabitants to Persia, as once Nabuchodonosor had carried off the people of Jerusalem. Justinian rebuilt the city for the second time. A century later (638) it became for the first time the victim of the fanatic multitudes of Mohammed, and remained so for more than 300 years, until in 969 it fell back to Byzantium and the Christians. But another century later the Seljuk Turks snatched it for themselves (1084). Fourteen years later the armored Latin Crusaders stormed the city, planted the Cross upon it again, and maintained themselves there for almost 200 years.

But the hour of death for Antioch and Christian Syria struck in the year 1268. Then the Sultan Bibars of Egypt conquered the city, and, in conquering it, he submitted it to a barbarous blood bath.

Antioch never recovered from that blow. No new life has thrived under the gleam of the Crescent. For 700 years the former Queen of the East, the great city of the Orient, which

467

once had half a million inhabitants, has been humbled in the dust. Now a small Turkish city of 15,000 or 20,000 people, Antakya remains today to recall the ancient and once famous Antioch. And the Christianity which was once preached there by Sts. Peter and Paul now drags on a wretched and scarcely endurable existence.[1]

Other Christian cities suffered the same fate as Antioch. Long the victorious banners of Mohammed have waved over the pinnacles of what were once the high citadels of Christian antiquity: Alexandria, the city of St. Athanasius, Theophilus and St. Cyril; Jerusalem, the Holy City; Caesarea, whose most famous shepherd St. Basil had been; Ephesus, the city of the Apostles; and uncounted others; the whole of Christian Asia Minor, with its splendid world of ancient culture, gradually became the spoil of the irresistibly forward-moving Islam, which crushed everything under its bloody footsteps. Slowly but surely, the Crescent embraced at last the chief cities of the once so great and mighty Byzantine Empire. For more than a thousand years Christian Constantinople upheld the banner of the Cross, with changing fortunes, if not always with clean hands, in the midst of all the tumult of peoples. Its greatest religious and national misfortune was the Church schism, with the separation of the Greek East from the Latin West. With this, the consciousness and feeling of religious unity and the alliance of Christian people were finally lost, and the Turkish armies stormed against the last Christian bulwark on the Bosporus, since the unfortunate city lacked the moral and political help of the West. In the year 1453, Constantinople fell, and, with this, after an 800-year battle and struggle, the greatest Christian Empire of the East vanished from the history of Christianity and humankind.

But the schismatic successors of St. Chrysostom, as well as all Greek Christianity, led an always wretched existence under the cruel and avaricious rule of the Turkish Sultans. During the course of the centuries the people turned to Islam in great numbers, under the pressure of the conquerors, and the last remains of Christianity in Asia were murdered by the Turks, during or after the First World War, or forced to emigrate.

So that was the end of a Christian Empire, a great Christian culture.

And yet this great world of culture is not completely lost nor vanished. Its spiritual memorials and monuments have survived the storms of the centuries, having survived the thousand-year Byzantine Empire itself. As Olympias once complained in a letter to the exiled Bishop John, that she missed so much his personal presence, his teachings and his sermons, Chrysostom replied: "In spite of my absence, you can keep in touch with me through my letters."[2]

That is really the greatness of Chrysostom, that he continues to live through his writings. The pulpit from which he first preached in Antioch has actually broadened into a world pulpit.

When he was taken away into exile, his writings, which doubtless were all in the Patriarchal Library in Constantinople, certainly remained behind. Zonaras says that the writings of the Saint were destroyed in 790 in a fire in this library.[3]

However, his works long ago conquered the ancient world, and they were circulated in uncounted manuscripts, not merely in the Eastern Greek Empire, but in the Western Latin Empire. St. Nilus said: "John, Bishop of Constantinople, has become the benefactor of all humanity through the flame of his learning," and Theodore called him "the great light of the world."[3a]

In some old Latin manuscripts of the catalog of authors of St. Jerome, a gloss is found on St. Chrysostom in Chapter 129: "His writings hasten through the world like sudden lightning, as well in the Greek as in the Latin language."[4] And Cassian, in his treatise "On the Incarnation of the Lord," 7, 30, exhorted the clergy of Constantinople: "Think of your former teachers and bishops, a Gregorius . . . a Nectarius . . . and holy John, who is so worthy of admiration on account of his faith and his purity; John, I say, that John, who, like John the Evangelist, as disciple and apostle of Jesus, rested as it were continually on the breast and in the heart of Jesus. Be mindful of him, I say, follow his example! Keep his purity, his faith, his learning, his holiness before your eyes! Never forget this, your teacher and spiritual helper. Under his protection, in his arms, you have, as it were, grown up. He was my teacher and yours; we are his pupils and the cham-

pions of his life. Read his writings, hold fast to his teaching;
make his faith, his merit, your own. If this goal is great, and
difficult to reach, to strive after it is noble and glorious. . . .
So may it always be before your eyes and your senses; may it
live in your feelings and thoughts. May it also recommend
to you what I have written; for what I write, he has taught.
Therefore consider it as written, not by me, but by
him; for the stream flows from the fountain, and what
the pupil produces must be reckoned to the honor of the
master."[4a]

No other Greek ecclesiastical author has so many surviving
manuscripts as Chrysostom.[5] The oldest Greek manuscript
of his hitherto known, containing the Homily on the Gospel
of St. Matthew, from the seventh century, was accidentally
found in Germany, in the library of the former Duke of
Wolfenbüttel.[6]

But people of other cultures also wished to draw from the
golden stream of the works of Chrysostom.

After his tragic fate the attention of the Latin West was
drawn to him, and Western scholars were the first who began
to translate his works into Latin. Greek excerpts of the works
of Chrysostom came at the end of the fourth and the beginning of the fifth century, to the numerous Greeks in Rome
and Italy.[6a] So they made their way into the Latin world.
The first known translator is the Pelagian Deacon Anianus
of Celeda, who between 415 and 419 translated the seven
Homilies on St. Paul, the first twenty-five Homilies on St.
Matthew, and probably a number of other Homilies, which
in the old editions bore the note "incerti interpretis."[7] In
the sixth century the great Cassiodorus (died 563) delegated
his friend (a monk?), Mutian, to translate into Latin the
thirty-four homilies on the Epistle to the Hebrews, and the
Commentary on the Acts of the Apostles. In the twelfth
century, Burgundio of Pisa (died 1194) translated the
Homilies on the Gospel of St. John, and the Explanation of
Genesis.

Also there existed, in the seventh century, translations of
the Opuscula: Ad Theodorum lapsum, De compunctione,
and Neminem laedi nisi a seipso; also De Sacerdotio, and the
Pillar Homilies. A new and augmented translating activity

began again with the invention of printing. The Moors added
to their collected Greek editions the complete Latin translations. In all, about 300 Latin editions, complete and partial,
are known.

Chrysostom was also translated into Syrian, Armenian, Coptic, Slavonic, as well as all modern languages. The French
deserve the most credit for the publication of his works and
their circulation in print.[8] Even the Czar of all the Russias,
Peter the Great, required, in the clerical regulations which he
gave the Russian Church through his Holy Synod, that every
Russian cleric should possess and read the works of Chrysostom.[9] And also A. Archangelsky confirmed that there was no
Church Father whose works had had such success in the old
Russian literature, and were valued so highly by the people,
as the writings of St. John Chrysostom.[10]

As a matter of course, the Germans, English, Italians,
Spanish and others do not remain behind, and so it is a fact
that the former priest of Antioch has become a great world
preacher, who speaks to all people in their own language, as
the Apostles did on Pentecost.

For the sake of his classical Greek, he is also very much
used in school lectures, although critics and grumblers in this
respect are not lacking among his own countrymen. Professors
and teachers of rhetoric have always been a critical group. In
the Byzantine Middle Ages a certain Deacon Constantius
wrote an irritated reply to someone who said that Chrysostom's writings were lacking in art, and did not observe the
rules of rhetoric.[11]

However, all people have given him the tribute of their
admiration. The Greeks have composed eulogies upon him,
have praised his works in inspired poems, and consecrated
churches and cloisters, and named them after him. But as a
special distinction they have given to him, and to him alone,
the name of the "Gold-flowing," or "Goldenmouth," which
has appeared in the literature since the middle of the sixth
century.[12]

The Latins also had their own "golden speaker," St. Peter
Chrysologus. But he could never sustain a comparison with
Chrysostom. He never came anywhere near attaining the
significance of the "prince of orators." On the other hand,

Pope Celestine (432) in a letter to the clergy and people of
Constantinople, praises " Bishop John, of holy memory, whose
writings have already circulated all over the world, and which
support and build up the Catholic faith; his teachings never
fail.   For wherever he is read, there he still preaches today."[13]
St. Augustine praises him as "excellentis gloriae sacer-
dotem;" and Facundus of Hermiane (about 550) calls Chrysostom "the most distinguished teacher of the Church."[14]

One would need to write a special book to collect all the
eulogies and expressions of admiration which have been given
him in the course of the centuries by the best of all people.
The cited testimony of those may suffice who were nearest to
him in time, and who knew best how to value, and how most
keenly to perceive, the spiritual treasure which he gave to his
times.

Their judgment finds its confirmation in all those of our
own time who enter into and occupy themselves with him
sufficiently.   The biographer E. Martin says: "Chrysostom
belongs to that great host of distinguished men whose works,
whose virtues, whose genius had such a great influence on the
history of Christianity, and who filled the fourth century with
such indescribable splendor."[15] And the Anglican J. T. Kings-
mill writes: "The life of Chrysostom was not merely consecrated to the service of Christ, it was Christ's gift of grace
to His Church."[16]

So the Greek-Byzantine Empire and people had not at all
lived in vain.   It had in the course of its many centuries of
history made many bad mistakes and failures, and had wan-
dered into many ways of error, of which the most fateful was
its spiritual and religious separation from the West, from
which its foundation had come.   At the same time, it alone
had poured out gifts and treasures to the world, which had
been for the good of mankind, and to this common treasure
of the noblest spiritual and human culture Chrysostom doubtless contributed a distinguished and valuable share.   Among
all Greek ecclesiastical teachers and authors, he is definitely
the best known and most read, far more than an Athanasius,
a Basil or a Gregory of Nazianzus.[16a]

So he goes on preaching and working, as the great and
shining light of a gifted and vanished people, and, according to

all human foresight, he will continue to preach through his writings as long as Christian culture exists.

But the Papacy has given the last homage to him and to the genius of his people, when it declared Chrysostom the model and official "Patron" of Christian preachers, for the entire Holy Church.[17]

Δόξα τῷ θεῷ πάντων ἔνεκεν.

FOOTNOTES

1. The ancient Antioch, like ancient Rome, lies today under 20 to 40 feet of earth, and masses of buried stones, some from earthquake and some from alluvial deposit (see R. Förster, Antiochia am Orontes, 105-06).

2. Letter 2, 11 to Olympias (52, 568).

3. Annales 15, 12 (134, 1348): 'Εμπρησμοῦ δε συμβάντος ὁ μέγας τρίκλινος τῶν ἱερῶν ἀνακτόρων, ὁ θωμαίτης λεγόμενος, ἔργον γέγονε τοῦ πυρος· ὅτε λέγεται καυθῆναι καὶ τὰ σχεδιάσματα τῶν ἐξηγήσεων τῆς θείας Γραφῆς, ἃ ὁ χρυσοῦς τὴν γλῶτταν συνεγράψατο 'Ιωάννης, ἐκεῖσέ που ἀποκείμενα.

That the autobiography originating from Chrysostom himself is in question here, is proven by the fact that only the σχεδιάσματα of Chrysostom are named, while his writings surely were not the only ones which were found in the Patriarchal library.

3a. S. Nilus, Epist. II, 183 (79, 296); Theodoret, Eranistes Dialog. 1 (83, 77). Cf. Isidore of Pelusium, Epist. IV, 224 (78, 1317-20); Photius, Interrogatio II and III (104, 1221) and IX (1229).

4. Bouvy 200; Feder, Schriftstellerkatalog 159.

4a. ML. 50, 270.

5. The catalog of Greek Chrysostom manuscripts, which I myself compiled, has passed the two thousand mark. Naturally all the manuscripts are included in it which contain at least *one* sermon of Chrysostom. On the other hand, there are, for example, of the writings of St. Athanasius, only about 80 Greek manuscripts surviving.

6. Codex 95 (=75a Helmst.) in the catalog of O. von Heinemann. Wolfenbüttel 1884. Vol. 1, 67.

6a. Pallad. Dial. 12 (ed. Norton 71, 8).

7. Baur, S. Jean Chrysostome 61-63.

8. *Ibid.* 84-88, 91-139 and 199-213.

9. " Every preacher should have the works of St. Chrysostom and read them assiduously, for he will thereby learn to compose pure and clear sermons, although they cannot equal his work. But he must absolutely not read the frivolous Sunday sermons which the Poles are addicted to." (=Spiritual rules by the high command and order of the Lord Czar and Great Sovereign Peter the First, Emperor of all the Russias, given by God and adorned with wisdom " . . . Danzig 1724, p. 56.

10. Die Schriften der Kirchenväter in der frühesten russischen Literatur. Petersburg 1888; p. 54-55, from: Palmieri, S. Giov. Crisostomo nella antica letteratura russa = Bessarione 12 (1907-1908) 44.

11. Only in manuscript in: Jerusalem, Cod. Sab. 451 (fourteenth century) f. 41: Inc. 'Ω τυφλὲ πρὸς φῶς (Papadopoulos Kerameus, Ἱεροσολυμιτικὴ βιβλιοθήκη, Petersburg 1894, Vol. 2, 531). Lastly, Dr. St. Skimina, with the angelic patience of a modern philologist, has completed a research: De Johannis Chrysostomi Rhythmo Oratoria with 26 tables. (Archiwum Filologiczne Polskiej Akademij Umiej No. 6) Cracow 1927, in which he examines the rhetorical rhythm of Chrysostom in a very penetrating way, and represents it on the basis of every tenth piece.

The knowledge of this study will in the future do good service in deciding questions of authenticity.

12. «'Ο χρυσορρήμων»=Anonymous, Vita Ch. 1. (Savile 8, 294[26]); Mychael Glykas (end of the twelfth century) Annales 4. (158, 485 A and C). «'Ο χρυσορρόας» = Johannes Euchaitensis, Encomium in tres Hierarchas, ed. Lagarde = Abhandlungen der Göttinger Gesellschaft der Wissenschaften 28 (1882) 113.

According to Moses of Khorene, History of Armenia, the name Chrysostom was already a standing epithet under Atticus (406-425). (P. E. Le Vaillant de Florival. Venice, 1841. 2, 155). Unfortunately the letter in question can scarcely lay any claim to authenticity.

'Ο χρυσόστομος appears to have been used as a permanent title from the beginning of the fifth century: Proclus ep., Or. 20; O nomen non negans acta, O *cognomen*, reddens speciem anteactae vitae (65, 832 A). Cf. De traditione div. Missae (65, 852 B). Ephrem Antiochenus: (died 545) according to Photius, Bibl. 229 (103, 993 A.). Chronicon Eddesenum (end of the sixth century) (ed. Hallier = T.u.U. 9 [1893] 105). Zacharias of Melitene (sixth century) (ed. Ahrens-Krüger) p. 42. Johannes Moschus, Pratum spirituale 157 (87, 2855). In Latin, the name Chrysostom occurs first (Primasius of Hadrumetum?) in Hebr. 4 (= ML 68, 709 D) and in Cassiodorus, in Ps. 6, 7 (= ML 70, 63 C); Institutiones divinarum litterarum, Praef. (= ML 70, 1108 A, 1121 C); K. Künstle, Eine Bibliothek der Symbole (Mainz 1900) p, 172-173. Cf. Dobschütz, Das Decretum Gelasianum = T.u.U. 38, 4 (1912) 265. Baur, S. Jean Chrysostome p. 58. Eutychius Alex., Annales (111, 1030) offers a quite uninspired explanation of the origin of the name Chrysostom, and a more than grisly legend concerning it, the Jacobite Life of Nestorius, is published by E. Goeller in Oriens Christianus 1 (1901) 283. Euthymius Zigabenus, Contra Phundagiatas (131, 53 B) finally says, that this heretic had given St. Chrysostom the nickname of φυρσοστομος. Naturally, there exists always the possibility that the surname " Chrysostom " in the individual case, goes back, not to the author but to a later copyist.

13. Mansi 4, 1037 C-D. Concerning the surname Chrysostom in Latin manuscripts, see Ad. Jülicher, in: Histor. Ztschr. 72 (1894) 485.

14. Pro defensione trium capitulorum 6, 5; "sanctum Ioannem, clarissimum doctorem Ecclesiae" (ML 67, 678).

15. Histoire de S. Jean Chrysostome 1, 1.

16. Life and times of Chrysostom 1, p. 145.

16a. Concerning the celebration in honor of the 1500th year after Chrysostom's death, i. J. 1907, see Rassegna Gregoriana 7 (1908) 185-190.

17. Acta S. Sediss 41 (1908) 594-595. Unfortunately there are no pictorial representations of Chrysostom which can make any pretension to historical truth. The oldest known representation, a wall fresco from the seventh century, is in the ruins of S. Maria Antiqua in Rome. Unfortunately the face of the Saint is badly disfigured by crumbling of the plaster of the wall. (See Grüneisen, Sancta Maria Antiqua. Roma 1911. Table XXX, Note 4). In Greek manuscripts of the tenth and later centuries one often meets with representations of Chrysostom in the typical form and attitude of a Byzantine Bishop, the Gospel in the covered left hand, the right hand raised in blessing. For example Oxford, Bodleian, Thom. Roe 6 (eleventh century) f. 1; *ibid*. Merton 28 (eleventh century) f. 3; Sinai, Cod. 364 (eleventh century) f. 1; Rom. Ottob. gr. 10 (twelfth century) f. 1; Jerusalem, Patriarchalbibliothek, in the Index of the Catalog. Cf. N. P. de Likatcheff, Materiaux pour l'Histoire de l'Iconographie Russe. Paris-Petersburg 1906-1908, vol. 1, no. 126. Wuescher-Becchi, Saggio d'Iconografia di S. Giov. Crisostomo, in: Chrysostomica 1014-15.

O

SOURCES AND BIBLIOGRAPHY
FOR VOLUME II

(IN ADDITION TO THOSE FOR VOLUME 1)

I. SOURCES

1. *Greek*

Eusebius Caes. Vita Constantini = MG 20, 910 ss.

Atticus Patr. Const. Epistola 75 = MG 77, 348-352.

Cyrillus Al. Epistolae 33 and 76 = MG 77, 159-162, and 350-360.

Proclus ep. Constpl., Oratio 20 = MG 65, 827-834.

Isidor Pelusiota, Epistolae 1, 310 = MG 78, 361.

Theodoret, Hist. Religiosa = MG 82, 1284 ss.

Callinicus, Vita S. Hypatii = Acta SS. Junii III 308-349; 3a ed.
   Junii IV. 247-282; and ed. Sodales Bonn. (1895) 3-110.

Zacharias of Melitene, The so-called Church History . . . ed. K.
   Ahrens and P. Krüger. Leipzig 1899 (= Scriptores sacri et
   profani. fasc. 3).

Anonymous, Vita S. Isaaci Acta SS. Maii VII 247-258. Alia Vita,
   ibid. 258-260.

Ioannes Moschus, Pratum spirituale 128 = MG 87, 2992-93.

Synaxarium Ecclesiae Constantinopolitanae (= Propylaeum ad
   Acta Sanctorum Novembris). ed. H. Delehaye S.J., Brussels,
   1902.

Eutychius Alexandrin., Annales = MG 111, 1030.

Constantine Porphyogenitus, De Caerimoniis aulae Byzantinae =
   MG 112, 280.

Menologium Basilii = MG 117, 21 ss.

Euthymius Zigabenus, Contra Phundagiatas = MG 131, 47 ss.

Le Martyrologe de Rabban Sliba = Analecta Boll. 27 (1908) 129-
   200.

Martène et Durand, Thesaurus novorum anecdotorum. Paris,
   1717.

Jus Graeco-Romanum, III: Novellae Constitutiones, ed.
   Zachariae de Lingenthal. Leipzig 1836.

Liturgia S. Joannis Chrysostomi ed. Pl. de Meester O.S.B. 3.A.
   Rome-Paris 1925.

Anthologia Palatina, ed. E. Gougny. Paris 1890.

Analecta veterum poetarum graecorum, ed. R. F. Ph. Brunck.
   Strasbourg 1776.

Gregoire, H. Inscriptions Grècques Chrétiennes d'Asie Mineure. Paris 1922.

Die Alexandrinische Weltchronik, edited by Ad. Bauer and J. Strzygowski. Vienna 1905.

2. *Latin*

Silviae (S.), quae fertur, peregrinatio ad loca sancta. Ed. P. Geyer=Corpus Script. Eccles. Lat. 39. Vienna 1898. p. 35-101.

Itineraria Hierosolymitana, IV-VIII centuries, ed. P. Geyer= Corpus Script. Eccles Latin. vol. 39. Vienna 1898.

S. Augustinus, De opere monachorum ch. 28=ML 40, 575.

Innocentius I, Pope, Epistolae 19-24=ML 20, 540-551.

Bonifacius I, Pope, Epistola 15=ML 20, 783.

Marius Mercator, Commonitorium super nomine Caelestii=ML 48, 67 ss.

Praedestinatus=ML 53, 587, 672.

Hydatius Lemicus, Continuatio Chronicorum Heronymianorum = Mon. Germ. Auct. ant. XI. p. 1-35.

Gennadius, De Viris Illustribus=ML 58, 1059-1120. ed. C. A. Bernoulli (Freiburg-Leipzig 1895; ed. E. C. Richardson= T.u.U. 14, 1 (Leipzig 1906), p. 57-97.

Cassiodorus, in Ps. 6.=ML 70, 63 and Institutiones divinarum litterarum, Praefatio and ch. VIII=ML 70, 1108 and 1121.

Facundus Hermaniensis ep., Pro defensione trium capitulorum = ML 67, 527-854.

(Primasius of Hadrumetum [?]), In ep. Hebr., Cap. IV=ML 68, 709.

Fasti Vindobonenses priores=Mon. Germ. Auct. ant. IX, 274-336.

Ado of Vienne, Chronicon=ML 123, 23 ff.

Anonymous Mellicensis, De Scriptoribus ecclesiasticis=ML 213, 963-984.

Martyrologium Romanum. Rome 1902.

3. *Oriental*

Hallier, L., Untersuchungen über die Edessenische Chronik. With Syrian text and a translation. (=T.u.U. 9 (1893) H. 1).

Koptische Akten zum Ephesinischen Konzil von Jahre 431. Translation and researches by W. Kraatz. Leipzig 1904 (T.u.U. N.F. XI.2).

History of the Patriarchs of the Coptic Church of Alexandria. Arabic text ed. . . . by B. Evetts=Patrologia Orientalis 1 (Paris 1907) fasc. 4.

Le Synaxaire Arabe Jacobite. Texte arabe publié traduit et annotê par R. Basset=Patrologia Orientalis 1, 3, Paris 1907.

(Moses of Khorene). Historia Armeniae. ed. P. E. Le Vaillant de Florival. Venice 1841.

Histoires Monastiques Géorgiennes. Vita S. Georgii Hagioritae. Ed. P. Peeters,=Annal. Boll. 36-37 (1917-19) 77-159.

Martyrologes et Ménologes Orientaux, I-XIII. Ed. Nau=Patrologia Orientalis 10 (Paris 1915) F.1 and 2.

II. LITERATURE

Archangelsky, A., Die Schriften der Kirchenväter in der frühesten russischen Literatur. Petersburg 1888.

Benesevic, V., Die byzantinischen Ranglisten=Byzantinisch-neugriechische Jahrbücher 5 (1926) 97-167.

Bondelmontius, Chr., Liber Insularum Archipelagi. Leipzig-Berlin 1824.

Briére, M., La légende syriaque de Nestorius=Revue de l'Orient chrétien 15 (1910) 1-25.

Brockhoff, W., Studien zur Geschichte der Stadt Ephesus, vom 4. nachchristlichen Jahrhundert bis zu ihrem Untergang in den ersten Hälfte des 15. Jahrhunderts. Jena 1905.

Budge, E. A. W., Coptic Homilies. London 1910.

Cantarelli, La serie dei Prefetti di Egitto=Atti della R. Academia dei Lincei, Cl. mor. V. Ser. 14 (1909) 385-440.

Cascioli, G., Del Corpo di San Giovanni Crisostomo venerato nella Basilica Vaticana=Bessarione 33 (1917) 61-66.

Chambers, E. K., The medieval stage. 2 vols., Oxford 1903.

Delehaye, H., S.J., Les légendes grecques des Saints militaires. Paris 1909.

Delehaye, H., Sanctus=Subsidia Hagiographica 17. Brussels 1927.

Dobschütz, E. v., Das Decretum Gelasianum=T.u.U. 38, 4. Leipzig 1912.

Duchesne, L., Histoire ancienne de l'Église. 3 vols. Paris 1910.

Dörfler, P., Die Anfänge der Heiligenverehrung nach dem römischen Inschrifte und Bildwerke. Munich 1913.

Ebersolt, J., et Thiers, Les églises de Constantinople. Paris 1913.

Egli, J. J., Nomina geographica. 2nd edition, Leipzig 1893.

Fortescue, A., The orthodox Eastern Church. London, 1920.

Funk, F. X., Die Bischofswahl in christlichen Altertum und in Anfange des Mittelalters=Kirchengeschichtliche Abhandlungen und Untersuchungen 1 (Paderborn 1897) 29-32.

Gagnard, C., Les saints Pères au tribunal de M. Thierry=Études religieuses 13 (1867) 363-375.

Goeller, E., Ein nestorianisches Bruchstück zur Kirchengeschichte des 4. und 5. Jahrhunderts = Oriens Christianus 1 (1901) 80-97.

Grafton Milne, J., A history of Egypt under Roman rule. London, 1898.

Grégoire, H. and Kugener, M.A., Quand est né l'Empereur Théodose II? = Byzantion 4 (1927/28) 337-348.

Grégoire, H. and Kugener, M.A., La Vie de Porphyre, évêque de Gaza, est-elle authentique? = Revue de l'Université de Bruxelles 1929 p. 429-441.

Grottefend, Zeitrechnung. Hanover 1891.

Grüneisen, A., Sancta Maria Antiqua. Rome 1911.

Gurlitt, C., Die Baukunst Konstantinopels. Berlin 1907.

Gurlitt, C., Konstantinopel. Berlin 1908.

Hahn-Hahn, Ida von, Eudoxia die Kaiserin. Ein Zeitgemälde aus dem 5. Jahrhundert. Mainz 1866.

Heinzel, R., Beschreibung des geistlichen Schauspiels im deutschen Mittelalter. Hamburg and Leipzig, 1908.

Heiss, Rom., O.S.B., Mönchtum, Seelsorge und Mission nach dem heiligen Johannes Chrysostomus = Lumen Caecis. St. Ottilien 1928. P. 1-23.

Hergenröther, J., Photius. 3 vols. Regensburg 1869.

Hollweck, F. G., A biographical dictionary of the Saints. London, 1924.

Jugie, M., Nestorius et la controverse Nestorienne. Paris, 1912.

Kellner, K. A. H., Heortologie oder die geschichtliche Entwicklung des Kirchenjahres und der Heiligenfeste. 2nd edition, Freiburg i.B., 1906.

Koch, H., Bischofstuhl und Priesterstühle = Zeitschrift fur Kirchengesch. 44 (1925) 170-184.

Künstle, K., Eine Bibliothek der Symbole. Mainz 1900.

Kukula, R. C., Briefe des jüngeren Plinius. Einleitung und Kommentar (= Meisterwerke der Griechen und Römer in kommentierten Ausgaben IX). Leipzig (Teubner) 1904.

Lethaby, W. R., and H. Swainson, The Church of Sancta Sophia, Constantinople. A Study of Byzantine Building. London, 1894.

Likatcheff, N. P., Matériaux pour l'Histoire de l'Ikonographie Russe. Paris-Petersburg 1906/8.

Loofs, Nestoriana. Halle 1905.

Lübeck, K., Zur ältesten Verehrung des heiligen Michael in Constantinopel = Histor. Jahrbuch 26 (1905) 773-783.

Martin, E., St. Jean Chrysostome. 3 vols. Montpellier 1860.

Mercati, G., A supposed Homily of Eusebius of Caesarea = The Journal of Theological Studies 8 (1907) 114.

Montfaucon, B. de, O.S.B., Palaeographica graeca. Paris 1708.

Morin, G., O.S.B., Le nouveau traité de Saint Jérôme sur la vision d'Isaïe = Revue d'Histoire Ecclésiastique 2 (1901) 810-827, and Pour l'authenticité du traité sur la vision d'Isaïe 3 (1902) 30-35.

Netzhammer, R., O.S.B., Die altchristl. Kirchenprovinz Skythien = Strena Buliciana 1924, p. 397-412.

Osgood, S., Chrysostom and his style of pulpit eloquence = The North American Review 42 (1846).

Palmieri, A., S. Giovanni Crisostomi nella antica letteratura russa = Bessarione Jahrg. 12, Ser. III, vol. III (1907/8) 44-63.

Papadopulos Kerameus, Ἱεροσολυμιτικὴ βιβλιοθήκη, Petersburg 1894.

Pargoire, J., Les prémiers évêques de Chalcédoine = Echos d'Orient 4 (1900/1) 27-30.

Paspatis, Al. G., Τὰ θρᾳκικὰ Προάστεια τοῦ Βυζαντίου = Ἑλληνικὸς φιλολογικὸς Σύλλογος 12 (1877/8) 33-42, and Τὰ ἀνατολικὰ Προάστεια, *ibid*. 43-52.

Peter the Great, Geistliches Reglement. Danzig 1724.

Piper, F., Zur Geschichte der Kirchenväter aus epigraphischen Quellen = Zeitschr. für Kirchengeschich. 1 (1877) 203-218.

Quentin, H., O.S.B., Les martyrologes historiques du Moyen-Age. Paris 1908.

Saltet, L., Les Réordinations. Paris 1907.

Schaffer, Fr. X., Cilicia. Gotha 1902 (= Dr. Petermanns Mitteilungen aus Justus Perthes' Geographischer Anstalt, edited by A. Supan. Supplementary vol. 141).

Schwietz, St., Das morgenländische Mönchtum. 2 vols. Mainz 1904 and 1913.

Schultze, V., Geschichte des Untergangs des römisch-griechischen Heidentums. Jena 1887.

Skimina, St., De Johannis Chrysostomi Rhythmo Oratorio . Cum 36 tabulis. (Archiwum Filologiczne Polskiej Akademij Umiej No. 6.) Cracow 1927.

Thibaut, J. B., L'Hebdomon de Constantinople = Echos d'Orient 21 (1922) 31-44.

Thierry, A., St. Jean Chrysostome et l'Impératrice Eudoxie. 3 ed., Paris 1889.

Vailhe, S., Formation de l'Église de Chypre 431 = Echos d'Orient 13 (1910) 1-10.

Weber, S., Die katholische Kirche in Armenien. Freiburg 1903.

Wilpert, J., Die Papstgräber und die Caciliengruft. Freiburg 1909.

INDEX

INDEX

Abundantius, General, II, 42

Acacius of Beroea, I, 74, 141; II, 19, 100, 158 ff., 187 ff., 247, 251, 283, 293, 315, 319, 425, 437

Acacius, deacon, II, 246

Adelphius, bishop, II, 461

Aegae, bishop of, II, 322

Aemilius, bishop, II, 398, 401 f.

Aetheria, II, 53

Alaric, II, 108

Alexander, bishop of Basilinopolis, II, 444

Alexander, bishop of Corinth, II, 400

Alexander, patriarch of Antioch, II, 445 f.

Alphius, II, 390

Amantius, II, 173-183

Ambrose, St., I, 2, 364; II, 3, 133, 167, 296

Ammonius, bishop of Laodicea adusta, II, 279

Ammonius, bishop of Pelusium, II, 410

Ammonius, bishop of Thrace, II, 137

Ammonius, monk, II, 195, 197, 249, 254

Amprucla, deaconess, II, 315, 377

Anatolius, bishop of Constantinople, II, 135

Anatolius, bishop, II, 399, 412

Ancyra in Galatia, II, 9

Andragathius, I, 22, 23

Anianus of Celeda, II, 470

Anthemius, II, 101, 399

Anthusa, I, 2 ff., 22, 80, 100 f.

Antiochus, bishop of Ptolemais, II, 100, 156 ff., 186 ff., 283 ff., 294, 315, 319, 388, 425

Antoninus, bishop of Ephesus, II, 137 ff.

Antonius, bishop, II, 247, 411

Anysius, bishop of Saloniki, II, 333, 398, 400, 402

Aphraates, monk, I, 74, 92

Apollinaris, bishop, I, 64

Apollonius of Tyana, II, 8

Apollo's Temple, I, 60 f.

Apostles' Church in Constantinople, II, 52 f., 356, 357

Aquilinus, deacon, II, 248

Arabianus, bishop in Galatia, II, 137

Arabissus, II, 366, 370 ff.

Arabius, II, 341

Arbogast, II, 107

Arcadius, emperor, I, 398; II, 29, 125, 243 ff., 281 ff., 293, 403 f.; death of, II, 436

Armenia, II, 340, 387

Arsacius, II, 250

Arsacius, bishop, II, 308 ff., 360

Ascholius, bishop, I, 129, 145

Asellus, bishop, II, 399

Asia (eccl. province of), II, 142

Asketerion of Diodorus, I, 91, 109 ff.

Asterius, II, 6

Athanasius, St., I, 53, 75; II, 67, 132, 155

Atticus, bishop, II, 305 ff., 338, 343, 375 ff.

Atticus, priest, II, 250 ff., 277

Augustine, St., I, 11, 13, 360, 365, 385

Aurelian, II, 120

Aurelius, bishop of Carthage, I, 349; II, 382, 399

Aurelius, II, 118

Babylas, bishop, I, 31, 60 ff., 147, 200

Baitanos, bishop, I, 86

Bargos, II, 105

Basiliscus, martyr, II, 421, 422

Basilius, St., bishop of Caesarea, I, 4, 11, 20, 25, 108, 141, 344, 397; II, 3, 59 ff.

Bauto, I, 131, 398; II, 32 f.

Berenice and companions, Sts., I, 200

Bizeri, II, 421 f.

Boniface, pope, II, 446

Boniface, priest, II, 398

Bosporius, bishop of Colonia, II, 410

483